AMERICA'S
RASPUTIN

AMERICA'S
RASPUTIN

WALT ROSTOW and the VIETNAM WAR

David Milne

HILL AND WANG

A division of Farrar, Straus and Giroux

New York

HILL AND WANG
A division of Farrar, Straus and Giroux
18 West 18th Street, New York 10011

Distributed in Canada by Douglas & McIntyre Ltd.
Printed in the United States of America
First edition, 2008

Library of Congress Cataloging-in-Publication Data
Milne, David, 1976–
    America's Rasputin : Walt Rostow and the Vietnam War / David Milne. —
1st ed.
        p.   cm.
    Includes bibliographical references.
    ISBN-13: 978-0-374-10386-6 (hardcover : alk. paper)
    ISBN-10: 0-374-10386-0 (hardcover : alk. paper)
    1. Rostow, W. W. (Walt Whitman), 1916–   2. Rostow, W. W. (Walt Whitman),
1916—Political and social views.   3. Political consultants—United States—
Biography.   4. Economists—United States—Biography.   5. Vietnam War,
1961–1975—Diplomatic history.   6. Cold War.   7. Anticommunist
movements—United States—History—20th century.   8. Economic assistance,
American—Developing countries—History—20th century.   9. United
States—Foreign relations—1945–1989.   I. Title.

E840.8.R67M55 2008
330.092—dc22
[B]
                                                                2007019373

Designed by Cassandra J. Pappas

www.fsgbooks.com

1   3   5   7   9   10   8   6   4   2

To the memory of Dev Cropper
(1977–1998)

Contents

Acknowledgments

I have accumulated countless debts through the writing of this book and it is my pleasure to acknowledge them here.

At Cambridge University my doctoral supervisor, Tony Badger, served as my great champion. His encouragement gave me confidence in the project from its infancy and his perceptive comments helped move my argument through to the final stages. John A. Thompson was kind enough to read the manuscript in its entirety and his trenchant criticism has improved the finished product considerably. I am also indebted to my two Ph.D. examiners—David Reynolds and Odd Arne Westad—for providing such a thoughtful critique of my thesis. My thanks also go to Richard King, Andrew Preston, Joel Isaac, Chester Pach, Fredrik Logevall, Robert Brigham, Matthew Jones, Spencer Mawby, Craig N. Murphy, and Andrew Fearnley, for providing persuasive commentary and suggestions on various chapters. Any errors are, of course, strictly my own.

At Nottingham University I am fortunate to have such bright and engaging colleagues in the Schools of Politics and American Studies. For their friendship, I would particularly like to thank Matthew Jones, Richard King, Neville Wylie, Richard Aldrich, Stephanie Lewthwaite, and Spencer Mawby. In addition to being a fine place to work, Nottingham University granted me a six-month sabbatical in the fall and winter of 2006/2007 to see the project through to completion and funded a trip to the annual Society for Historians of American Foreign Relations conference to present some of my conclusions.

Academic colleagues read the book in various stages, but I'd also like to thank my friends and family for offering suggestions from a nonspecialist perspective. My younger sister, Eve Hepburn, was a particularly insightful reader and my older sister, Kerry Spark, helped transcribe my interview with Walt Rostow. I also thank Robert Reed, Nick Hermann, Daniel Crowe, Steve Sudbury, Joel Isaac, Nathaniel Millett, Andrew Preston, Austin Fido, Candace Sobers, Samuel Windham, Dominic Sandbrook, Minsoo Kim, Carlos Lozano, Andrew Trask, Miriam Dobson, and Lucy Griffin for their friendship, encouragement, and some top-notch suggestions. My parents, Margo Milne and Kent Pickles, have given me great support through the years and I thank them for everything.

My literary agent, Andrew Wylie, provided excellent advice on honing my book proposal and matched me with a publisher of the highest quality—I am lucky to have him in my corner. At Hill and Wang, I have been fortunate to work with an editor as skilled as Eric Chinski. He read the manuscript with a wonderful eye for nuance, and encouraged me not just to add color and context, but to engage more directly with Rostow's ideas. Thanks to his efforts, the book has been improved immeasurably. His assistant, Gena Hamshaw, has guided me expertly through the process of bringing this book to print, and I am also grateful to Don McConnell and Judy Kiviat for copyediting and proofreading the manuscript and galleys with such care and to Michelle Crehan for steering it through production.

Parts of this book have been published previously in *The Journal of Military History*, *The Scribner Encyclopedia of American Lives*, and *Vietnam Magazine*. I thank the editors of all three publications for allowing me to reproduce some of the material here. Two anonymous readers at the *Journal of Military History* also helped refine my arguments.

Substantial financial resources were required to research this book. I extend my appreciation to the Arts and Humanities Research Board (for funding my doctoral research), and, at Cambridge University, to the Domestic Research Studentship program, the history faculty's Sara Norton Fund, and Sidney Sussex College's Parry-Dutton Fund. Additionally, the British Academy funded an essential research trip to the Library of Congress in the summer of 2006. In the United States, I was the fortunate beneficiary of a Fox International Fellowship, based at Yale University, and a Gilder Lehrman Fellowship, based in New York City. My thanks go to the JFK and LBJ libraries for financing six weeks of fieldwork in their archives. In Austin I dealt with an accomplished team of archivists, including John Wilson, Shannon Jarrett, and Regina Greenwell. (Martha Campbell was a wonderful host in the great state of Texas and provided a comfortable home away from home.) In Boston my thanks go to Stephen Plotkin and Sharon Kelly. I was also supported skillfully and efficiently by archivists at the Seeley G. Mudd Manuscript Library, Princeton; Yale University Archives; Columbia University's Butler Library; the Library of Congress; and the Massachusetts Institute of Technology.

I could wax lyrical about my wife, Emma Griffin, for many pages. She is a hugely talented historian and a skilled reader, and offered substantive suggestions that have improved the book at every stage. Beyond her talents as a reader, Emma has given me boundless love and encouragement over the years and has made my life a very happy one.

I dedicate this book to the memory of John Devanand Cropper, who made an indelible impression on everyone fortunate enough to know him. Dev was a wonderful friend and an exceptional writer in the making. He died from inexplicable heart failure when he was twenty, and we all miss him terribly.

AMERICA'S
RASPUTIN

INTRODUCTION

O N FEBRUARY 27, 1968, President Lyndon Johnson's closest foreign-policy advisers gathered in the White House to discuss a war that had spiraled out of control. A month previously South Vietnam's major towns and cities had been overrun by communist insurgents dedicated to unifying their nation under North Vietnam's president, Ho Chi Minh. Johnson had been promised "light at the end of the tunnel" at the end of 1967, and the Tet Offensive (so called because the assault coincided with the eve of Tet, the lunar New Year) devastated his administration's credibility. Most recognized that while the campaign was a conventional military defeat for the insurgents, their psychological victory had been comprehensive. Who could now believe that the United States was winning the war? The mood in the West Wing was accordingly funereal.

The outgoing secretary of defense, Robert S. McNamara, spoke first. He reported that General William Westmoreland, America's ranking field commander, wanted the president to dispatch 206,000 additional U.S. combat troops to Vietnam—bringing total troop levels close to 700,000. To satisfy Westmoreland's request, McNamara calculated that the president would have to call up 150,000 reserves, extend the draft, and sanction a $15 billion increase in the defense budget. To pay for this, Johnson would be forced to increase taxes and make swinging cuts to his progressive domestic program—commit electoral suicide, in other words. Aside from the fiscal and political sacrifice required, McNamara wondered how Westmoreland was so certain that 206,000 more troops would do the job where half a million had failed.

McNamara's successor as defense secretary spoke next. Playing devil's advocate, Clark Clifford asked the group to consider whether Westmoreland's request was sufficient. Why not call up a further 500,000 or even a million troops? Why not err on the side of caution to get the job done without fear of further failure? "That and the status quo have the virtue of clarity," McNamara agreed matter-of-factly. "I do not understand the strategy in putting in 206,000 men. It is neither enough to do the job, nor an indication that our role must change." McNamara believed that the time was now right to declare that the South Vietnamese government was secure and viable—accomplishing the original American objective—and then swiftly locate an exit strategy.

The president's national security adviser, Walt Whitman Rostow, regarded McNamara's assessment as ill-considered and defeatist. The Tet Offensive represented a defeat for the communist insurgents and this was no time to take any backward steps. Rostow explained that captured documents proved that the enemy was "disappointed" and unable to mount heavy attacks on the cities. He wanted to reinforce Westmoreland with the soldiers he required and further recommended that the military should up the ante by intensifying the American bombing campaign. The South Vietnamese National Liberation Front (NLF) was in disarray—some forty thousand insurgents had been killed during the assault—and Rostow believed that the Tet Offensive, if exploited correctly, might represent the birth pangs of a sustainable, noncommunist South Vietnam.

The national security adviser's pugnacity was predictable, but something snapped in McNamara when Rostow finished speaking. The two men had clashed unpleasantly over the past two years, but their relationship was about to hit a new low. While Rostow was unfailingly optimistic about military prospects in Vietnam, McNamara had become disillusioned with the conflict in early 1966, and had henceforth urged LBJ to consider de-escalation. Rostow invariably prevailed in these debates, but it was McNamara's last day in office and he was not going to miss an opportunity to confront his bureaucratic nemesis. "What then?" the defense secretary demanded of Rostow's plan. "This goddamned bombing campaign, it's been worth nothing, it's done nothing, they've dropped more bombs than in all of Europe in all of World War II and it hasn't done a fucking thing." Speaking with the intensity of a tortured soul who had helped create an unnecessary war, the defense secretary finished his sentence, broke down, and wept. Rostow could only look on, stunned, as Robert McNamara— once described as an "IBM machine with legs"—melted down in a room filled with Washington's most powerful men.[1]

IN JANUARY 1961 the atmosphere in the nation's capital could not have been more different. The United States was set to inaugurate a president whose popular appeal exceeded that of any twentieth-century incumbent not born to the name Roosevelt. John F. Kennedy was a cerebral, photogenic Massachusetts liberal with a young family and a glamorous wife. He possessed an energy that contrasted sharply with the staid conservatism of his Republican predecessor. In foreign policy Kennedy's instincts compelled him to favor action over inaction and internationalism over parochialism. Courage under pressure was a trait that he had cultivated assiduously throughout his career. If Kennedy was clearly for anything, it was for taking the fight to America's enemies.

The United States faced a clear enemy in 1960 and, unlike today, schoolchildren could find it on a map. The Soviet Union existed not just as America's tactical and strategic competitor, but it also propagated a universal value system that was dedicated to replacing the liberal capitalist worldview championed by the United States. The McCarthyite era had convinced many Americans of the relentless, insidious nature of their enemy. And while the hysteria had passed—Joseph McCarthy had died in lonely ignominy in 1957—the nation still bore the scars that are inflicted when paranoiac bullying goes unchallenged by a fearful Congress. The pragmatic Nikita Khrushchev had succeeded the tyrant Josef Stalin, but the Soviet Union still instilled fear. Yet Kennedy was aware that communism's danger lay not only in its potential to damage the United States and Western Europe. The so-called Third World was the arena in which the United States and the Soviet Union would battle for ascendancy. Who would find communism's utopian promise of absolute equality most appealing? The answer: those people living in nations newly liberated from European colonialism and driven to despair by the inequities of daily life.

A day prior to his glittering inauguration, Kennedy announced that Walt Rostow would serve as his deputy assistant for national security affairs. Rostow's appointment was greeted enthusiastically by the media, academia, and the Democratic Party. As a distinguished professor of economic history at the Massachusetts Institute of Technology, Rostow had established a reputation as an articulate champion of Third World development. Through the 1950s Rostow had worked tirelessly to convince President Dwight D. Eisenhower that increasing America's foreign-aid provision was morally unavoidable in a time of economic abundance and tactically essential in an age of global cold war. While Eisenhower was unmoved by Rostow's campaign for an international New Deal, Kennedy found the young professor's rationale compelling. If the Cold War was essentially a high-stakes geopolitical chess game—as defense intellectuals opined—then the pawns were surely critical to any winning strategy. If the United States continued to ignore the world's failing nations, what was to stop them from seeking an ideological alliance with the Soviet Union? Kennedy hired Rostow to help ensure that the developing world stuck with Washington and avoided flirtation with Moscow or Beijing. Rostow's rise to a position of influence was celebrated by activist liberals and mourned by fiscal conservatives, who were concerned that saving the world from both poverty and communism would not come cheap.

All changed in the eight years that followed. Rostow's exalted reputation among liberals sank rapidly as the Vietnam War rumbled on inconclusively, polarizing American society and critically undermining the Democratic Party. Rostow was the most hawkish civilian member of the Kennedy and Johnson administrations with respect to the unfolding conflict in Vietnam. He was the first to advise Kennedy to deploy U.S. combat troops to South Vietnam, and the first to provide a rationale for the bombing campaign against North Vietnam that Johnson later implemented. Rather than serving his country as a catalyst for Third World development—as his academic background appeared to portend—Rostow recommended the brutal bombing of a developing nation and was a chief architect of America's worst-ever military defeat. In 1961 Rostow's colleagues were sad to see one of their brightest stars leave the ivory tower but delighted that the social sciences had one of its best operating at the highest echelons of government. In 1969 Rostow's notoriety was such that none of America's elite universities were willing to offer him a job. His contribution to the making of the Vietnam War made him a pariah in the very quarters that had celebrated him ten years earlier. The former undersecretary of the Air Force Townsend Hoopes described Rostow as "a fanatic in sheep's clothing."[2] W. Averell Harriman, one of America's most celebrated diplomats, castigated him as "America's Rasputin."[3]

What had happened in the intervening years to effect this shift in reputation from liberal, cerebral development theorist to belligerent aficionado of tactical bombing? From Rostow's perspective the answer was nothing at all—one can champion foreign aid and the bombing of communist-infected nations at the same time. Through the 1960s Rostow had surely satisfied the liberals' aspirations in the field of international development. The Kennedy administration launched the Agency for International Development (USAID) in March 1961 to usher in what the president described in Rostovian terms as a "Decade of Development." Rostow provided not just Kennedy's rhetoric, but the agency's guiding rationale. Another large-scale aid program, the Alliance for Progress, was created to facilitate rapid economic growth in Latin America. Rostow provided seven of the twelve enumerated goals of the Alliance, and his economic theories were the intellectual scaffolding for the entire program. Rostow was loyal to the altruistic causes that drove his academic career. His egalitarianism was pronounced and his concern for disadvantaged nations was manifested on the grand stage of international relations.

It was what accompanied Rostow's proselytizing for an activist foreign-aid policy that irked his former friends and colleagues on the center and left. Rostow's anticommunism was more deeply held than that of any American foreign-policy adviser in the twentieth century. This intellectual revulsion at the Marxist-Leninist project led to his advocating the escalation of the Vietnam War more aggressively than any other individual through the 1960s. Rostow was an ideologue and his unerring self-confidence was evident from an early age. As a sophomore at Yale University in the 1930s, he determined that his life's calling was to "answer" Karl Marx and provide an alternative explanation of the course of world history. For the twenty-five years that followed, Rostow devoted his substantial energies to meeting this formidable intellectual challenge.

In 1960 Rostow published *The Stages of Economic Growth: A Non-Communist Manifesto* to critical and public acclaim. Just twelve months before entering the Kennedy administration, Rostow, in the minds of many, had buried Karl Marx and charted the world's true destiny—an impressive feat that discouraged modesty. In his eight years of service as a foreign-policy adviser to Kennedy and Johnson, Rostow dispensed advice that sought to crush Third World communism not just intellectually, but through the overwhelming force of America's military machine. The passion with which Rostow pursued his academic lifework made him impervious to the force of countervailing reason. He was a zealot on the Vietnam War and the story that follows is one that will be familiar to any student of the history of international relations. Individuals who hold absolute confidence in the efficacy of their ideas—who fail to account for real-world contingencies—invariably lead American foreign policy down blind alleys.

"AMERICA'S RASPUTIN" is an emotive term, and Harriman's description leads one to visualize a conniving, sinister character in possession of preternatural powers of persuasion. While Rostow was convincing in argument, it is important to note that he also inspired loyalty and respect from those who worked with him. He accumulated countless strategic adversaries throughout his career but few clear-cut enemies. Rostow's likeability was indeed a key strength that facilitated his rise through the byzantine machinations of the elite academy and Washington, D.C. Undersecretary of State George Ball and Secretary of Defense McNamara had some significant spats with Johnson's national security adviser, but both spoke warmly of "Walt" as a human being. Those who knew Rostow personally will find Harriman's "Rasputin" barb difficult to accept. He was a considerate, gregarious individual who took great care in cultivating and maintaining close personal friendships and working relationships. When it came to the Vietnam War, however, Rostow was not averse to deploying questionable tactics to achieve his aims.

Any individual's ability to influence foreign-policy decisions is of course predicated on the relationship he forms with the incumbent president. Through the 1950s Senator Kennedy was impressed by Rostow's intellectual ability, his productivity, and the originality with which he approached the then politically charged question of U.S. foreign aid. In the 1960 election campaign, Rostow coined phrases—"Let's get this country moving again" and the "New Frontier"—that deftly contrasted Kennedy's activism with Eisenhower's atavistic conservatism. The newly elected president appreciated Rostow's contribution, and rewarded him appropriately by appointing him his deputy special adviser for national security affairs. Kennedy accorded Rostow unprecedented authority and access in what was hitherto a relatively junior position. Rostow assumed White House responsibility for U.S. policy toward Southeast Asia and, indeed, for most of the world east of Suez.

Through 1961 Rostow worked hard to convince Kennedy that the communist insurgency in South Vietnam was his most pressing foreign-policy concern of the day. Given that the president faced grave crises in Cuba, Berlin, and Laos, Rostow's role in bringing Vietnam to the limelight was significant. As the historian David Kaiser observes, "Rostow's energetic pursuit of new solutions gave Vietnam a higher profile for the rest of the year."[4] In going so far as to recommend the deployment of U.S. combat troops and the bombing of North Vietnam, however, Rostow's energy and rigid belief put him at odds with a president who was skeptical about those who claimed to possess clear-cut solutions to complex problems. Kennedy's reputation as a sophisticated manager of foreign affairs had been significantly dented by the debacle at the Bay of Pigs in Cuba. Henceforth the president was more circumspect when considering options for military escalation. In arguing loudly for an American-led response to the crisis in South Vietnam, Rostow exhausted the personal capital he had accrued with Kennedy through the 1950s.

Kennedy shifted Rostow to the Policy Planning Council at the State Department but still he continued his Vietnam crusade with unchecked determination. On paper the move to the State Department was a move sideways, but in reality it was a slight. Even as new barriers were constructed to impede access to the president, however, Rostow did not lose hope. Kennedy and Rostow saw little of each other in 1962 and 1963, yet their infrequent meetings were uncomplicated and warm. Kennedy remained fond of his erstwhile mentor, but his nickname for him, "Air Marshal Rostow," explains succinctly why the relationship broke down. Ever the optimist, Rostow rationalized this shift in foreign-policy responsibilities as an opportunity. With less firefighting to do at the White House, Rostow dedicated himself to addressing the facets of U.S. foreign policy he had neglected in his crusade to wage war on Vietnamese communism. In the summer of 1962, Rostow completed the administration's clearest written expression of its diplomatic strategy with a massive blueprint paper for U.S. foreign policy. But while Rostow's productivity remained impressive, he lacked a receptive audience. This situation changed abruptly with Kennedy's assassination and Johnson's assumption of the presidency.

The closeness and mutual respect that characterized the LBJ-Rostow relationship aided Rostow's resurrection as a foreign-policy force. But the profundity of Rostow's contribution to making the Vietnam War owed as much to the force of his ideas as to the key relationship he cultivated. The "Rostow Thesis"—which claimed certainty that the United States could defeat the southern insurgency through bombing North Vietnam— brought Rostow to Johnson's attention as someone with original ideas and absolute commitment to the cause of defeating Southeast Asian commu- nism. Across the pantheon of Kennedy's "best and the brightest," Walt Rostow possessed the character traits to which Johnson was most amen- able. He was collegial, hardworking, and loyal, and he believed in the ne- cessity of America's Vietnam mission. Rostow's predecessor as national security adviser, the dry, world-weary McGeorge Bundy, had antagonized the president for reasons he could hardly avoid: his haughty, northeastern mannerisms aroused Johnson's deep-rooted sense of intellectual inferior- ity. But more than that, Bundy was willing to question a military strategy after it had been decided upon. Less emotional than both Rostow and Johnson, Bundy struck the president as coldly professorial, and insuffi- ciently instinctual.[5]

Walt Rostow's intellectual makeup, while honed at universities that or- dinarily brought out the Texan's baser prejudices, made sense to LBJ. Both Rostow and Johnson were outsiders—one a southerner and the other from a modest Jewish background. But more than anything, loyalty was a virtue that the president respected above all others—indeed, he de- manded it of all who worked with him. Johnson resented those who rocked the boat. Rostow disapproved of the fact that the president would escalate only to an insufficiently coercive point, but did not push his views to the degree that they annoyed Johnson. While the president refused to implement Rostow's more radical suggestions, such as bombing the North Vietnamese dikes, invading Laos and North Vietnam, and bombing the centers of Hanoi and Haiphong, he admired the hard-edged nature of Rostow's counsel. The Vietnam War cast the blackest shadow on Johnson's presidency, but the national security adviser's bullish advice and optimism represented a clear chink of light. It is hardly surprising that LBJ was partial to a man who compared him directly to Lincoln and claimed, like Sherman, to have an indelicate plan for victory. Rostow said what the president wanted to hear, not owing to self-regarding design, but because unflappable confidence defined his character.

As Rostow established this bond of trust and familial intimacy with the president, his views came to guide U.S. policy toward the Vietnam War. The "graduated" bombing of North Vietnam, Rostow's most significant contribution to military strategy, heightened sharply in intensity following his promotion to national security adviser in April 1966. The amount of U.S. ordnance dropped on North Vietnam increased from 33,000 tons in 1965 to 128,000 tons in 1966.[6] This sharp increase in bombing is not solely attributable to Rostow's ascension in influence vis-à-vis Secretary of State Dean Rusk and Robert McNamara, but his contribution helped allay doubts and gave a critical boost to the Joint Chiefs of Staff's case for escalation. Bundy, Rusk, and McNamara were all present at the escalatory meetings of the Vietnam War and each put forward a forceful case for Americanizing the conflict. But these men were managers, not creators. Rostow provided both a compelling rationale for escalating the Vietnam War and the most influential blueprint for "victory." The historian John Prados writes, "McNamara mostly responded to proposals brought to him by others . . . It was civilian strategists such as Rostow, or military commanders such as Westmoreland, who were the innovators and initiators . . . There is responsibility enough for Vietnam that can be shared."[7] In that spirit this book intends to share a little more responsibility, not necessarily foist it all on Rostow's shoulders.

Beyond this fateful story of military escalation, Rostow contributed to extending the conflict's duration through his hostility to peace negotiations with North Vietnam—particularly those led by third-party intermediaries. The British prime minister, Harold Wilson, held high hopes that his discussions with the Soviet premier, Alexei Kosygin, in February 1967 might produce a Vietnam breakthrough. Convinced that Wilson held little sympathy for South Vietnam's plight, however, Rostow advised the president to harden the U.S. negotiating position and hence undercut Wilson's efforts. While it is a challenge to trace precisely the degree to which Rostow's counsel proved decisive, it is surely significant that the British prime minister blamed the national security adviser wholly and directly for the diplomatic debacle that followed. In later months Rostow again cast doubts on another significant third party: Henry Kissinger. Doubtful that the "Pennsylvania" negotiating channel was ever going to amount to anything, Rostow worried that the Harvard professor of government was likely to "go a little soft when you get down to the crunch."[8] Both Wilson and Kissinger rued the fact that Rostow had the president's ear.

Averell Harriman provided the fiercest denunciation of the mesmerizing effect that Rostow exerted on Johnson's decision making. The contempt was reciprocal. While Harriman viewed Rostow as a Rasputin-like figure, Rostow thought Harriman was wholly contemptuous of South Vietnam, and hence willing to achieve peace at an inappropriate price to American credibility. Harriman's allegations contained a great deal of truth. The Harriman-led Paris peace negotiations failed to bring on board South Vietnam, and failed to convince North Vietnam of Johnson's sincerity. In both instances Rostow played a key role in ensuring the negotiations were wedded to stringent terms and worked hard to convince Johnson not to order a unilateral bombing cessation. Rostow's contribution to this fateful chapter of the conflict is hugely significant. The journalist Christopher Hitchens has alleged that Henry Kissinger, for short-term political gain, helped scupper the Paris peace negotiations in the summer of 1968.[9] It appears that Rostow carried out this task from *within* the White House. He did so not for reasons of career progression or political expediency, but because he was appalled at the prospect of any peace that failed to provide an inviolable security guarantee to South Vietnam.

ULTIMATELY, Rostow's contribution to the making and prolonging of the Vietnam War was as important as any one of that more visible foreign policy trio of Bundy, McNamara, and Rusk. And here it is possible to trace continuity between Rostow's academic work, designed to facilitate rapid economic development in the Third World, and the advice he dispensed in the ostensibly dissimilar field of strategic bombing. Rostow shaped an American response to the communist challenge in the Third World with an ideology of his own—his belief in the universal applicability of five stages of economic growth and of America's capacity to guide those developing countries toward the end point. But ironically, Rostow's "stages of economic growth" were little more than Marx's dynamic of historical materialism with a different conclusion: liberal capitalist rather than communist. Rostow's was also a model informed by economic determinism. He envisaged what would happen theoretically, but failed to appreciate the circumstances particular to those countries that his model purported to address.

This same determinism provided Rostow with a reason why bombing North Vietnam would so swiftly defeat the southern insurgency. Rostow believed that Ho Chi Minh would succumb to American bombing to protect his industrial sector—what very little there was of it. Rostow was positive that the threat of bombing was the most significant part of the equation because "Ho has an industrial complex to protect, he is no longer a guerrilla fighter with nothing to lose."[10] This rationale assumed that Ho Chi Minh's priorities were those of his own government, namely that the pursuit of economic growth was the overwhelming consideration in peace and war. But the North Vietnamese regime was more than willing to take a serious economic hit to further the overarching goal of reunification. Rostow ultimately failed to appreciate the power of an ideology not beholden to the economic sources that informed his own.

Rostow contributed profoundly to a conflict that tore gaping holes in America's societal fabric, undermined trust in government, and prematurely ended a presidency. His story is instructive not because he was foolish, or consumed by an aggression inspired by undiagnosed inner demons, but because Rostow was a standout member of what the journalist Tom Brokaw has feted as the "Greatest Generation." Rostow's rise from immigrant obscurity to the West Wing makes his story peculiarly American—

and testifies to the great strengths of the nation. His intellectual attributes were pronounced, his academic achievements were exceptional, and all were products of his own diligence and brilliance. He had no wealthy family or nepotistic network from which to claim sustenance. Rostow's life was a triumph in so many respects. Had he avoided the temptation to seek the Americanization of the Vietnam War, Rostow would have been eulogized as one of the great liberal American minds of the twentieth century. It was a great pity that his substantial intellectual strengths coalesced through the years to create an unreflective cold warrior who contributed so decisively to the making of a tragic conflict in Southeast Asia.

The EDUCATION of WALT WHITMAN ROSTOW

1916–1949

T
HE JEWISH EXPERIENCE in Tsarist Russia was one of pain and
dashed hopes. Through a series of laws that created the "Pale of Settlement," Russia's Jews were confined to living in an arc of land that
stretched from the Black Sea to the Baltic. Living conditions in the
Pale were dismal and violence was commonplace. But the accession of
Alexander II brought the promise of better things. Alexander was hailed
as the "Tsar Liberator" for his 1861 edict that freed the serfs. Jews across
the Russian Empire dared to dream that they might be next in line to receive some good news. Then two young radicals threw bombs at the tsar's
carriage in St. Petersburg. As these crude devices detonated, Jewish hopes
went up in flames.[1]

A wave of pogroms swept the Pale following the assassination of
Alexander II in 1881. Many were involved in the plot, but the ugliest vitriol was directed at a young, pregnant Jewish woman named Gesia Gelf-
man—one Jew among many gentiles. Mobs gathered to terrorize Jewish
families and ransack their properties. A few hundred Jews died in the attacks, but the legislation that followed was worse. Quota systems were imposed on Russian schools to limit Jewish enrollment to 10 percent in the
Pale and 5 percent outside it. In 1890 Moscow's police chief decreed that
all Jewish stores and workshops had to be fronted by the full Hebrew
names of their owners—providing a convenient bull's-eye for anti-Semitic

thugs. And then, in 1891, Tsar Alexander III ordered the expulsion of all Jews from Moscow. This wave of persecution devastated earlier hopes of integration and confronted Russia's Jews with difficult questions about their survival.

Some converted and others refused to be cowed, but a great many Jews rejected both of these options and escaped the Russian Empire altogether. The United States was a country where Jews did not have to make such choices, where freedom from religious persecution was a founding principle. In the decade that followed the 1881 pogroms, 135,000 Jews deserted Russia for the New World.[2] The tsar's brutality proved a boon to America's burgeoning population as some of Russia's brightest sons and daughters began new lives on the northeastern seaboard. Though America was not free of anti-Semitism, obstacles to progress for hardworking Jews did not bear comparison to those in Russia. In New York your Judaism hampered access to some dining clubs and a few private schools. In the Pale of Settlement, your Judaism disbarred you from living a meaningful Russian life.

VICTOR AARON ROSTOWSKY WAS one of many Ukrainian Jews who embarked on the long journey to the United States at the turn of the twentieth century. Born in 1886 in Orekhov, near Odessa, Rostowsky was fortunate to receive a comprehensive education in a loving family environment. His parents were devoted to Russian high culture, and they provided rigorous instruction to all five of their children. Victor read voraciously through his adolescence and was drawn to the egalitarian promise of socialism. Eschewing parochialism, he recognized that the tsarist regime repressed not just the Jewish minority, but any Russian who sought a change in the status quo. As an observant youngster in a cruel, authoritarian society, Rostowsky developed a burning social conscience.

Cocooned among sycophants he may have been, but Tsar Nicholas II (who succeeded Alexander III in 1894) was aware that acute disaffection existed across the nation. To prevent this dissent from cohering into an effective opposition, he ordered his regional police chiefs to clamp down on seditious groups who dared to challenge his rule. Such circumstances made socialism a dangerous credo to follow. It was even riskier if you chose—as Rostowsky did—to publish a socialist newspaper from the basement of your house. This noisy operation was hard to keep under wraps. A sympathetic contact at the police department alerted Rostowsky to the likelihood of his imminent arrest. There was little doubt that had Rostowsky stayed in Orekhov, his fate would have been dismal. With a lengthy jail term looming, the eighteen-year-old idealist had little choice but to run as far as his family's resources could take him.

Rostowsky plotted an elaborate escape route to the New World and embarked on a grueling voyage from Russia to New York (via Glasgow, Scotland) in steerage. Conditions were cramped, disease was rife, and he was fortunate to complete the journey without succumbing to serious illness. Exhausted after this ordeal, Rostowsky faced some significant choices when he arrived at Ellis Island. Many Jewish immigrants were resolutely wedded to Yiddish culture, having previously detached themselves from the Russian and Polish societies in which they resided. Upon arrival in New York, these same Jews re-created isolation from gentiles in Manhattan and Brooklyn. But Victor was keener on assimilation than the majority of his traveling companions.[3] Rostowsky decided to remove the final three letters of his name, becoming Victor Rostow at the stroke of a pen. Socialist he may have been in inclination, but Victor was aware that the United States offered plentiful rewards to those who were willing to work hard and play by the rules.[4]

Dedicating long, hard hours to improving his English during his first year in America, Victor quickly gained sufficient fluency to enroll in a chemistry program at the Pratt Institute in Brooklyn. Lacking sufficient funds to concentrate on full-time study, Rostow took on a number of part-time jobs waiting tables and delivering newspapers, and managed to both excel academically and subsist. Victor also improved his standard of living considerably by leaving the teeming Lower East Side—home to more people per acre than Bombay's slums—for the Flatbush district of Brooklyn.[5] Rostow's move to Brooklyn evidently suited him well, for he remained there for the next ten years. In 1907 he graduated with a certificate in applied technology and put his qualification to immediate use by gaining employment as a metallurgical chemist in Brownsville.[6] Victor Rostow grew to love American life and letters, but he remained a dedicated socialist—appalled at the inequities created by undiluted capitalism.

While worthy political causes are good for the soul, they can also often provide amorous opportunities for those with a sharp eye. It was thanks to Victor's progressive principles that he met the young Lillian Hellman (not the famous playwright) at a socialist Sunday school. Born in New York City to Russian immigrant parents, Hellman was "a star in school, and her teachers all befriended her and were enthusiastic and encouraged her to go on beyond high school and go to college."[7] Unfortunately for Hellman, her promise was never fulfilled in the form of a university education. As she was the eldest sibling, her parents expected her to get a full-time day job to help feed and clothe the family. Many years later, a family member asked if she possessed any regrets in life. Hellman replied, "Yes! I should have gone to college." The unstinting support that she would provide for her sons' education represented in part a vicarious thrill of wish fulfillment.[8]

In spite of her unrealized dreams, Hellman retained a passion for literature and penned articles for some of New York's socialist newspapers. With such a similar outlook on life—an appreciation of high culture, unerring belief in the transcendent value of education, and a shared commitment to socialism—it was unsurprising that Victor and Lillian fell in love. Hellman later recalled that it took little time for her to make a decision to marry Rostow—although he had once sounded a little arrogant in proposing to her with the justification "Think of what wonderful children we will have."[9] They married in Brooklyn on October 22, 1912, and soon after bought a small house off Flatbush Avenue.[10] Victor remained a metallurgical chemist, but Lillian gave up her job as a bookkeeper to embark upon a new life as a homemaker. Three new additions soon arrived in the Rostow household. Lillian discovered that motherhood was just as demanding, and potentially more stimulating, than the daily grind of making ends meet.

BORN IN BROOKLYN on November 7, 1916, Walt Whitman Rostow was the second of three children. His elder brother, Eugene Victor Rostow, was born in 1913. As passionate adherents of American progressivism, Victor and Lillian named their firstborn after the dogged socialist leader Eugene Victor Debs. Gene Rostow, as his friends knew him, rose to heady heights during his lifetime. He served as President Lyndon Johnson's undersecretary for political affairs, was appointed dean of Yale Law School, and played a key role in establishing the Committee on the Present Danger—a forum through which the nascent neoconservative movement criticized the Ford and Carter administrations through the 1970s. Gene Rostow concluded his public career by serving President Ronald Reagan as head of the Arms Control and Disarmament Agency. He enjoyed a varied and successful career in which he made a mark both on academia and on foreign policy. It is doubtful, however, that Eugene Debs would have approved.

Walt's younger brother, Ralph Waldo Rostow, was born in 1920 and named after the transcendentalist philosopher Ralph Waldo Emerson. Seriously wounded during the Second World War, Ralph Rostow cared little for politics, showed no aptitude for academia, and thus carved out a comfortable existence in the world of haberdashery. He managed a department store in Ann Arbor, Michigan, and retired early to Florida, where the sun apparently soothed the pain caused by his war injuries. In 2003 Walt Rostow wrote an affectionate portrait of his younger brother in his memoir *Concept and Controversy*, concluding that Ralph was "a fine man and a good brother." The three brothers were thick as thieves through their childhood and remained close as they pursued their disparate careers across the United States.[11]

Victor Rostow was determined to secure a comfortable income for his family, and he worked tirelessly to achieve this goal. It was a time of economic abundance for America, and with little fuss Victor found an excellent job as the head of the laboratory at Federated Metals. Taking the job required a household relocation, and so the Rostows moved to Irvington, New Jersey, soon after Walt's birth. In a small town on the outskirts of Newark, the family settled comfortably into what the middle son later described as a "pleasantly rural period." Showing clear precociousness— having been home educated to a high standard by their mother—Gene and Walt both skipped two grades in elementary school.[12] Walt's childhood was safe and predictable, although anti-Semitism intervened sporadically to darken the occasional day.

While America was more welcoming to Jewish immigrants than other countries, it was not free of bigotry. One memory that stayed with Walt was the day that his brother Gene responded violently to one of his classmates describing him as a "dirty Jew." Bloodied but victorious in battle,

Gene returned home, and his mother patched him up. Aware that these kinds of taunts were not always worth fighting for, his father told his eldest son, "If anyone calls you a 'dirty Jew' that's his problem not yours. I'm glad that you can look after yourself. But you would be wiser to ignore that kind of talk." Gene's bravery nevertheless impressed Walt, who recalled that he was "memorably chivalrous." A conscientious older brother, Gene Rostow looked out for his siblings, taught them games, and introduced them to his friends.[13] The relationship between the two brothers remained close as they plotted their paths through academia and government.

A formative experience in the early 1920s made an indelible mark on young Walt. Political discussion was ever-present at the Rostow home, and they often invited fellow Russian émigrés to join them for dinner parties. One evening some friends arrived with a purchasing agent from the Soviet Union who was visiting briefly. In Walt's recollection he was a "nice, ruddy-faced fellow," who appeared to make a good impression on all who spoke to him. After he left, Lillian asked her husband what he thought of him. Victor replied, "In politics you can never separate your objectives from the methods used to achieve them. These communists took over the Tsarist police and made them worse. The Tsarist police persecuted the political opposition but never touched the families. These people touch the families too. Nothing good will come of it." Walt later referred to this moment as an epiphany: "It made one hell of an impression on my brother and myself. It really transmitted." Whether this story was embellished or not—and we should remember that Victor *and* his family fled tsarist persecution—Walt later ascribed the roots of his own anticommunism to the principles instilled by his father.[14]

The Rostows' attachment to Irvington was severed in 1926, when the Guggenheim conglomerate took over Federated Metals and a new chemist was brought in to replace Victor. Not short of job options as a skilled chemical engineer, he rejected the option of relocating to Detroit, Michigan, on an equivalent salary. Instead of pursuing the safe choice, Victor resolved to take his family to New Haven, Connecticut, where he proposed to establish his own business and take his destiny into his own hands. Much of the extended Rostowsky family had fled Russia for Milford, Connecticut, making southern New England a particularly tempting destination. Another factor, however, swayed Victor's decision to move the family north. The public high school in New Haven offered its top eight graduating students a scholarship to Yale University. Victor and Lillian guessed that their sons' intellectual potential made them likely candidates to secure these awards.

The decision to move to Connecticut paid off handsomely in subsequent years. The Rostow family settled easily into New Haven and bought a series of increasingly spacious houses in pleasant parts of town. As the Great Depression ruined countless lives through the 1930s, Victor Rostow's income—made from smelting metals and selling them on to manufacturers—allowed the family to thrive. Comfortable in a settled home life, Gene and Walt continued to impress their schoolteachers with their aptitude. Entering seventh grade at just ten years old, Walt was offered a scholarship to attend Hopkins Grammar School, a prestigious private school with an excellent record of placing its students with Ivy League colleges. It was a gilt-edged opportunity for Rostow's intellectual development.

Surprisingly, perhaps, in light of his views on the inestimable value of a sound education, Victor was opposed to Walt taking up this scholarship. He explained carefully to his son, "It's not a good idea for you to go to Hopkins. These are very nice people and a very good school, but they're all from rich families. We're not poor, but we're not rich. More important than that, if you go to the public school you're going to meet everybody. Everybody in our society will be there and you will feel comfortable for the rest of your life with people no matter how poor or how rich or children of professors or businessmen."[15] Rostow later believed that his father's preference had been correct, and that his public school education played a significant part in shaping both his personality and his career: "I think that my experience at Hillhouse led to an abiding view of the American people as 'we' and not 'they.' "[16]

There was certainly something courageous and farsighted about the decision that Victor made on behalf of his son. Walt thrived at Hillhouse High School and possessed a circle of friends from all socioeconomic backgrounds. He was bright and self-confident but never haughty. He was no child of privilege and his social conscience was formed in part by his education at a public school. This common touch was certainly appreciated by President Johnson in later years. It helped Rostow's relationship with the earthy Texan immeasurably that he lacked the hauteur that someone like

McGeorge Bundy, a product of Groton Academy, possessed in abundance. Walt was an intellectual prodigy but he carried it extremely well.

From the ages of ten to fifteen, Walt was a compulsive reader of novels—a characteristic encouraged by his mother. He devoured Thomas Hardy, Somerset Maugham, Leo Tolstoy, Anton Chekhov, Thomas Mann, Mark Twain, and the early works of James Joyce. While Rostow later recalled that his reading encompassed a "fairly conventional list," some of those authors developed ideas that were far from conventional. Beyond this love of literature, he was fascinated by the tumultuous political issues of the era, and was particularly curious about the world beyond America's shores. Developing an early interest in aviation, he followed assiduously the dashing exploits of Charles Lindbergh and his successful flight to Paris on the *Spirit of St. Louis* in 1927.[17] Walt had mixed feelings when he met the notorious anti-Semite in the White House many years later. "Despite all that lowered the Colonel in my eyes," he confessed, "I could still feel echoes of a young boy's hero worship."[18]

Of his early family life, Walt recalled that "we were shaped by a particular tradition of Tolstoyan idealism," and that he was fortunate to have lived in a "socialist home." Victor and Lillian Rostow's passion for literature, philosophy, and activist politics came to shape their sons' characters in significant ways. Walt was discomfited by the stark inequality evident within American society, and followed his father in adhering to egalitarian politics. Of the novels he loved, Walt recalled that "they taught me something of the human condition; and what it was like to live in another society, in another time, in another skin."[19] This interest in other societies stayed with him through his peripatetic early years. As he grew older, however, he spent more time dwelling upon commonalities across races and nationalities than appreciating their differences. A failure to visualize life in another person's skin was a common complaint directed at Walt's rigid views toward communism in the postcolonial world. Yet from the early example set by his parents, he remained dedicated to altruistic principles throughout his lifetime.

THE ROSTOW BROTHERS PROVED their parents' confidence in their ability to be well placed when both Gene and Walt secured four-year tuition fellowships to attend Yale University. Because of his outstanding progress at school, Walt was just fifteen when he entered Yale as a freshman in 1932. Fortunately, his older brother was an old hand at the university and introduced him to friends such as Richard Bissell—who later served as director of the CIA's Office of National Estimates—and Alistair Cooke, who became a distinguished radio journalist with the BBC. Gene recalled that these contacts were important to his kid brother "in the sense that it gave him an immediate circle of friends" when he arrived at the university.[20] What might have been an overwhelming experience for some was a simple and exciting transition for Walt. He mixed with a fascinating cast of characters and had a wonderful guide to the university's many intricacies in Gene.

Yale had experienced significant physical changes through the 1920s and 1930s. In 1918 a wealthy lawyer named John W. Sterling left the university a $15 million bequest to be spent on new buildings, professorships, and improved facilities for students. Between 1922 and 1932, Yale embarked on a massive building program in which the university was remodeled on the Oxbridge model of small residential colleges in which students and academics eat together and intermingle on a more intimate basis. The academic quadrangles of these ancient English colleges were re-created in New Haven with an exacting attention to detail. To make the brickwork look more authentic, chemicals were applied to give the new buildings a tarnished, older effect. As Walt later recalled, "I saw traditions created day-by-day . . . and shared in other small ways in the adventure of transposing the British college system onto the college scene."[21] He joined Yale as one of the first residents of Pierson College.

Yale also witnessed significant cultural changes in the decade prior to Walt's arrival. Old habits died hard at Yale University, an ascetic university established by orthodox Congregationalists. Nevertheless, the passage of time was catching up with some of its more arcane traditions. The strict requirement that students attend college chapel every day was scrapped in the late 1920s. And the academic prerequisite that all incoming students show proficiency in Latin was also removed, opening the door to hundreds of public school students who knew little of that ancient language beyond *et cetera*.[22] A finishing school for the elite Waspocracy for so long, Yale was becoming a more welcoming place for young men like Walt Rostow: a secular Jew from a family of modest means. In his two volumes of memoirs, and voluminous writings for magazines and periodicals, Rostow has not a single bad word to say about his alma mater.

Settling into university life with ease, Walt achieved an academic record at Yale as impressive as that of his brother. And sibling rivalry played a part in ensuring their common success. As a freshman, Walt won the second McLaughlin Prize for history—following his brother, who had won the first prize three years before. Young Rostow's four-year grade average at Yale was 86 percent, placing him comfortably in the top 10 percent of his class. Walt engaged in a plethora of extracurricular activities, such as football, baseball, and basketball, and belonged to Phi Beta Kappa, the Yale Political Union, and the Elizabethan Club. He served as the editor of *The Harkness Hoot* in his senior year and wrote a regular column for the *Yale Daily News*. Yale University was home to many high achievers, but Walt Rostow's achievements were outstanding in light of his humble background and schooling.[23]

Thanks to his excellent exam results, Walt roused the admiration of his academic advisers, who were much impressed by his energy and ability. Yet the most significant influence on him at Yale was not a member of the faculty, but a graduate student and friend of his brother. Richard Bissell had graduated from Yale in 1932, and then moved to England to study at the London School of Economics under the tutelage of the socialist intellectual Harold Laski and the father of free-market economics, Friedrich von Hayek. Returning to Yale as a graduate student, Bissell established an unofficial seminar series in economics based around the then-revolutionary theories of the Cambridge University economist John Maynard Keynes. Through his brother's prompting, Walt began attending what became known as Bissell's "black market" seminar. Joining him in this meeting of earnest economists were two other individuals who made considerable marks on their respective fields: the future Princeton astrophysicist Lyman Spitzer and Max Franklin Millikan, who later became an economic historian at the Massachusetts Institute of Technology.[24] Rostow's friendship with Bissell and Millikan proved highly significant in later years as both men served as Walt's confidant and champion.

Rostow later wrote, "My academic work runs in a straight line from the black market seminar to the present."[25] Learning Keynesian theory in the early 1930s could not have been timelier, given that the Roosevelt administration was then wrestling with the nationwide deprivations of the Great Depression. During Rostow's first two years at Yale, he believed that the New Deal was "sloppy and inefficient" and that the National Industrial Recovery Act "was a damn fool thing to do."[26] These condemnatory opinions changed significantly following the young student's exposure to Keynes. The celebrated English economist believed that in times of high unemployment it was vital for the government to stimulate demand through increased spending on public works. Finding this argument compelling, Walt came to accept that it was often necessary to unbalance the nation's budget to create jobs. The U.S. government, in other words, had an activist role to play in ensuring the nation's well-being.

Rostow's political and economic ideology was shaped in other ways through attending Bissell's seminar. While Rostow was a devotee of Keynes, he came to abhor the theories of Karl Marx. Through his close reading of Marx's key texts, he had been "much impressed" by the "gross inadequacy of Marxist or any other single cause explanations of the ways societies develop." Rostow respected Marx's ambition, but was not impressed with his conclusions. And so as a seventeen-year-old student at Yale, Walt arrived at a momentous decision. He determined the cause to which he would henceforth dedicate his intellectual endeavors. "I would work on two problems," Rostow recalled. "One was economic history and the other was Karl Marx. Marx raised some interesting questions but gave some bloody bad answers. I would do an answer one day to Marx's theory of history."[27]

Rostow had become enamored of Keynesian economics, but could not escape the gloomy import of Marx's injunction that communism's victory was historically assured. Marx's "interesting" question was: Is it possible to identify socioeconomic conflicts through history that allow us to predict the future? His "bad" answer was that the tensions inherent in capitalism will pave the way for communism as the proletariat comes to assume control of the means of production. As Marx wrote in the introduction to *The Communist Manifesto*, "The history of all hitherto existing society is the history of class struggle."[28] The German philosopher believed that all societies pass through four transitory stages in their history—state-of-nature communism, slavery, feudalism, and capitalism—that conclude with the victory of communism, the triumph of the proletariat, and the end of class exploitation.

Rostow decided to meet the challenge head-on and provide an alternative explanation of the course of world development, one in which communism was not history's end point but an ephemeral aberration. He believed that Marxism stifled individual liberty, starved the soul of intellectual nourishment, and made for bad economics, creating an impoverished society in which meritocracy had no place. Rostow's father, a socialist, had fled autocratic Russia and flourished in the United States through hard work and ambition. Recognizing that Marx extinguished that noble individual drive, Rostow wanted to humanize capitalism: to save it from itself and the false prophet that was Karl Marx.

Seeking to provide a definitive answer to the question "What drives history?" was ambitious to say the least. Rostow's intellectual achievements at Yale were weighty and his decision to "answer" Marx was impressive and narcissistic in equal measure. Such determination and focus in one so young might suggest that what Rostow possessed in diligence he may have lacked in joie de vivre, but the bookish young student was also partial to a drink and the occasional prank, and was particularly fond of composing music. Rostow was no pale-skinned, library-bound academic machine, but possessed a fully rounded personality and the instincts of a Dionysian. Thanks to his excellent academic record, and his bevy of extracurricular activities, Rostow was awarded a prestigious Rhodes Scholarship to attend Balliol College, Oxford, from 1936 to 1938. Winning the award was a feather in Rostow's cap, as the scholarships were highly competitive. The two years in Oxford provided another significant boost to his highly promising career.

IN THE 1930S Oxford University was globally recognized as one of the two most prestigious universities in the world. As Rostow observed in his memoir, "It is hard to recall in the year 2002 what it meant in the 1930s to have a member of the family in a British college."[29] In the United States in particular, Oxford possessed the aura of an institution that represented all that was special in higher education. Most ambitious intellectuals aspired to spend some time studying or teaching in the shadow of its "dreaming spires," and the young Yalie was no exception. Rostow departed New York aboard the Cunard liner *Laconia*, and spent a mere ten days crossing the Atlantic before arriving on England's southern coast. Rostow's first experience of a foreign country was quite a thrill: "It was all new: the double-decker buses, the cars driving on the left side of the street, the distinctive trains—and still more distinctive vowel sounds."[30] Upon his arrival in Oxford, it took Rostow little time to adapt to this strange new environment. He was flexible and gregarious, and counted himself fortunate to have secured his scholarship. A fellow Rhodes Scholar, Philip Kaiser, recalled that Rostow "was full of intellectual beans" and that he held "enormous confidence in his own ideas and views."[31] It was virtually foreordained that Rostow would get on at England's oldest university.

Intellectually driven, as well as culturally inquisitive, Rostow was in a hurry to start his doctoral thesis. His tutor at Balliol College, however, thought that Rostow should hold fire for a while. A well-regarded historian of Russia, Humphrey Sumner found Rostow's energy impressive, but believed that he should take tutorials in other fields to broaden his education. Sumner told Rostow that his Ph.D. research would be improved if he gained some expertise in economic theory and history. Responding positively to this advice, Rostow set about extending the boundaries of his knowledge. This new scholarly focus reconfigured his research and drove his academic career in an original direction. Rostow shifted focus from narrowly analyzing the relative decline of the British economy in the late nineteenth century to examining the predictive potential of the British industrial revolution. From that point onward, Rostow concerned himself not just with shedding light on particular phenomena—as most academics are content to do—but with seeking to impose order on the course of world economic history. Like Marx, Rostow came to believe that it was possible to trace through the ages a number of inevitable stages through which all nations passed. The British industrial revolution was the linchpin of modern history: the event that all nations had to emulate in order to expand and mature.

Showing the same zest for life that was evident at Yale, Rostow also threw himself into a range of activities that took him far from the Bodleian Library. He developed a passion for rugby—a sport that takes no prisoners—and gained a reputation as a tenacious player on the field. Rostow also established a songwriting partnership with Gordon Craig, a Princetonian who later became a historian of modern Germany at Stanford. Rostow and Craig enlivened a number of parties at Oxford with their ribald tunes—such as "Sherry Party Girl" and "A Drinking Song"—which they belted out with gusto. Even more remarkably, Rostow established a drinking and songwriting partnership with the future British prime minister Edward Heath—a man not remembered for his bonhomie.[32]

Rostow's Oxford experience stretched beyond the pursuit of sport, drinking, and study, as it gave him the perfect opportunity to launch vacationing assaults on the European continent. In the spring of 1937, Rostow and a group of friends traveled south to imbibe Parisian culture, and "the smell of Gallois [sic] cigarettes in the Metro," before spending a couple of days relaxing on the Côte d'Azur. Rostow then traveled to Monte Carlo, only to suffer embarrassment upon being refused admittance to Monaco's glitzy casinos. The door attendant told Rostow that as he was not yet twenty-one, he was only permitted to play on the slot machines outside the main hall. "The only recompense for this humiliation," Rostow later recalled, "was that I made a small profit while the rest of our group uniformly lost money."[33]

A few months later, Rostow returned to Europe to visit Geneva and attend a seminar run by the International Union of Students based in New York. Rostow met with the other delegates in Paris and it was there that Rostow first set eyes on an attractive young Barnard College student named Elspeth Davies. Rostow later wrote romantically of their meeting in the fiftieth-anniversary album of his class at Yale: "I met Elspeth at 12.30 pm, July 13, 1937 at the Cercle Interallié, Rue St. Honoré. From that day, the round of life has been suffused with magic."[34] Davies was as sharp as a whip and keen to fashion a career in academia upon completing her studies. She was a wealthy gentile from an established family in the northeast and Rostow was a relatively impecunious child of first-generation Russian Jewish emigrants. Nevertheless, both shared views on life, society, and politics that were entirely complementary. Like Victor and Lillian before them, Elspeth and Walt constituted a near-perfect match. They courted whenever they got the chance and resolved to marry when circumstances allowed.

While Rostow traveled extensively across the continent, he was also fortunate in that Oxford attracted an impressive array of guest speakers from Europe and Britain. In 1938 Rostow and his fellow Rhodes Scholars were called to Rhodes House to hear the U.S. ambassador to the United Kingdom hold court. A strong supporter of Prime Minister Neville Chamberlain's policy of appeasing Hitler, Joseph Kennedy warned that Britain should not fight Germany under any circumstance except that of direct invasion. Kennedy was concerned that a global war would destroy capitalism and allow communism to fill the vacuum. Responding angrily to an anodyne question that made a passing reference to Keynes's *General Theory of Employment*, Kennedy denounced the Cambridge economist as a communist. Taking umbrage at this unflattering description of his intellectual hero, Rostow stood up to make clear that "Keynes was not a Communist but was simply trying to produce a policy that would cut unemployment in Britain and save capitalism." Appalled by the effrontery of young Rostow, Kennedy strode out of the lecture hall without a word. Years later Rostow told John F. Kennedy about this story. Amused and not at all surprised, Kennedy deadpanned, "It sounds like the old man."[35]

VICTOR ROSTOW DIED from a heart attack in March 1938 at just fifty-two years of age. His bereft middle son made immediate plans to return to the United States, but soon realized that rushing home might harm his career at a delicate time. Worried for his favorite student, Humphrey Sumner advised Rostow to take some time to grieve and then complete his studies. He invited Rostow to submit to the *Economic History Review* a couple of articles drawn from his B.Litt. thesis. Sumner thought that a second world war was inevitable, and believed that Rostow should get some publications out before his likely call to service. Working hard to hit the deadlines, Rostow published one article with the *Economic History Review* and the other in *Economic History*.[36] Having enjoyed two fulfilling years at Oxford, Rostow now had two articles to show for his scholarly efforts. He left England for New England in the summer of 1938.

Rostow entered Yale graduate school in 1938 with a clear head of steam behind him. He took up a position as a teaching assistant in economic history as soon as he arrived, leading seminars on Bissell's now officially sanctioned course on Keynesian economics. Among his students were William and McGeorge Bundy, who later served alongside Rostow in the Johnson administration.[37] Rostow enjoyed the teaching, and was fortunate in that he could devote significant time to preparing his classes. Having completed a comprehensive B.Litt. thesis at Oxford, Rostow found drafting and submitting his Ph.D. dissertation was a breeze. In 1940 Yale University approved Rostow's dissertation, "British Trade Fluctuations, 1868–1896." His thesis combined history and economic theory to examine the performance of the British economy in the late nineteenth century. Rostow argued that "neither British growth nor fluctuations could be explained without introducing the forces at work in the world economy, including the interaction of British growth with growth in other countries."[38] Using his study of Britain as a springboard, he planned to extend his project to identify the varied forces that drove liberal capitalism forward across the world. With this weighty project in mind, Dr. Walt Whitman Rostow was now ready to make his mark on the academic world.

Rostow's intellectual accomplishments had caught the attention of the eminent Columbia University historian Arthur Gayer. At Gayer's request Columbia granted Rostow a research fellowship to assist him in drafting his massive history of Britain from 1790 to 1850. Rostow moved to Morningside Heights in 1939 and began laying the groundwork for Gayer's magnum opus.[39] Rostow was delighted that the Barnard College–based Elspeth Davies was also teaching some courses in the immediate vicinity. As Rostow impishly recalled, "Elspeth was starting the first course of American Studies in the country and was just down the hall in a large and rather grand room. It was not a wholly professional time."[40] Having seen each other intermittently following their first meeting in Geneva, the young couple evidently had a lot of catching up to do.

Amorous distractions aside, Rostow impressed Columbia's faculty with his drive and productivity. Rostow was appointed an instructor in economics at the university in the fall of 1940. As the year progressed, however, it became increasingly apparent that America was inching toward active participation in a global conflict. As a patriotic young American, Rostow was keen to serve his country in whatever capacity the government saw fit. At the close of the spring term of 1941, he received his call to service. Rostow promptly resigned his position at Columbia University and joined what would become the Office of Strategic Services, the predecessor to the Central Intelligence Agency.[41] It was a glamorous assignment and some wags offered an alternative reading of the acronym OSS as "oh so social."[42] Secret agent fantasies aside, Rostow's government duty during the Second World War shaped his personality and career in significant ways.

THROUGH THE MID-1930S, Franklin Delano Roosevelt's government refused to engage seriously with the crises that were afflicting Europe and East Asia. Many Americans were disillusioned with European affairs following President Woodrow Wilson's failure to impose American terms on the Paris Peace Conference of 1919. The American people had no appetite for an internationalist foreign policy through the 1920s and 1930s, and FDR recognized that declaring strategic fidelity to France and Britain was political dynamite. America thus turned its back on the world. With no cohesive counterforce to repulse its acquisitive intentions, Hitler's Germany tore up the Versailles Treaty through its military reoccupation of the Rhineland in 1936, the Anschluss with Austria in 1938, and its invasion of Czechoslovakia (virtually invited by Neville Chamberlain) through 1939. In East Asia a militaristic Japan invaded and occupied Manchuria and then moved south, precipitating a brutal war with China.

It soon became clear that appeasement was a shameful failure. Following the Nazi assault on Poland in 1939, Great Britain and France were left with few credible options but to fulfill their treaty obligations and declare war on Germany. Though the American people took a great interest in these tumultuous events, the prospect of U.S. intervention remained a divisive issue. As France fell to the German onslaught in June 1940, only Britain remained standing, throwing some pretty weak punches. Many Americans, like Joseph Kennedy, were sure that Britain would lose against such a ruthless war machine. Defying the odds, however, the Royal Air Force dramatically defeated the Luftwaffe in the Battle of Britain, and England was spared invasion. Winston Churchill, who became prime minister in May 1940, had his luckiest break on December 7, 1941, when Japan launched an assault on the U.S. Navy at Pearl Harbor. Roosevelt declared war on Japan and Hitler in turn declared war on the United States. Churchill and Roosevelt met promptly and agreed that defeating Hitler's Germany should be the top priority for the Anglo-American alliance. America's most talented sons flooded to England to set upon this task.

Rostow left Washington, D.C., for England in September 1942 in "an elegant but underpowered and uncertain Sikorsky flying boat." At this stage transatlantic flights were in their infancy and accidents were commonplace. Weather conditions across the Atlantic could shift on a dime and one of his colleagues escaped death only narrowly when his Sikorsky fell apart soon after takeoff.[43] Having completed what must have been a nerve-racking journey to Ireland, Rostow flew to the outskirts of London on a plywood de Havilland plane. Undoubtedly relieved to complete the final leg of his journey by car, Rostow was escorted to London's Grosvenor Square to await orders. His superiors recognized that Rostow's intellectual gifts should be put to immediate practical use and placed him with the Enemy Objectives Unit subdivision of the OSS. Rostow's new job was to identify which German military targets were most vulnerable to Anglo-American bombing. He remained in London for two and a half years and contributed incisively to the making of Allied military strategy.

Following the Casablanca conference of January 1943, the primary objective of the air war against Germany was formulated as "the progressive destruction and dislocation of the German military, industrial and economic system, and the undermining of the morale of the German people to a point where their capacity for armed resistance is fatally weakened."[44] After examining the merits of a number of targeting options, Rostow concluded that destroying Germany's oil-storage facilities would wreak the most havoc on its war-making ability. The principle was a simple one: without oil, the Luftwaffe was impotent. Rostow's first practical lesson of war was that if you destroy an enemy's energy resources, you critically impair its capacity for effective action. It was a principle to which Rostow turned in later years when confronted with a conflict in Vietnam.[45]

While Rostow had identified oil supplies as the key German target, others believed that Germany's transport infrastructure should remain the top priority.[46] It was only through sheer luck that a single German oil-storage facility was destroyed, and its impact was so pronounced that oil immediately leapt to the top of the target list.[47] Rostow's reasoning had been vindicated by events and he was angry that it had taken so long for Britain and the United States to see the light. As head of the Allied forces, General Dwight Eisenhower was particularly culpable in that his preference for ponderous escalatory steps needlessly extended the war's duration. According to Rostow, the costs of the delay in bombing Germany's oil "may have been high not only in human life foregone but also in terms of postwar diplomacy, for in the end, the location of the Soviet and Western armies on VE-Day certainly played a role . . . in leading Stalin to conceive as realistic the creation of a Soviet empire in Eastern Europe."[48] Rostow thus believed that Europe and the Cold War would have taken a very different shape had his advice been followed sooner. This was a damning indictment of Eisenhower's decision making: that his lackadaisical approach to crushing his enemy through targeted strategic bombing had given the Soviet Union more time to penetrate Eastern Europe and take Berlin. Rostow's affinity for grand counterfactual posturing would crop up repeatedly throughout his academic and government career.[49]

Rostow's employment as an OSS bombing analyst ended promptly when President Harry S. Truman sanctioned the use of the atomic bomb against Hiroshima and Nagasaki. Confronted with piles of rubble where Dresden, Tokyo, and Berlin once were, the U.S. government launched a series of intelligence-gathering ventures to ascertain what military lessons might be gleaned from the conflict. Rostow chose not to participate in the United States Strategic Bombing Survey (USSBS)—a project designed to evaluate the effectiveness of American bombing in the Pacific and European theaters. Rostow reasoned that those who picked the bombs' targets should not analyze their impact. However, it is significant that later critics of the North Vietnam bombing campaign—George Ball, John Kenneth Galbraith, and Arthur Schlesinger Jr.—all took part in the survey. In his 1982 memoir, Ball, who served as director of the USSBS, criticized Rostow for not appreciating "the limited effect of bombing against a fanatical enemy."[50] While the USSBS's conclusions were generally supportive of the thesis that air power was a decisive component of Allied victory, it also added as a significant qualification that "continuous heavy bombing of the same communities did not produce decreases in morale proportional to the amount of bombing."[51] The survey declined to take a definitive position as to whether bombing reduced morale to the extent that it contributed to the outcome of the war, although Ball, Schlesinger, and Galbraith have little doubt that it did not. The lessons that others learned through participation in the bombing survey went unheeded by Rostow.

Rostow's wartime service brought him prestigious decorations to add to his Yale and Oxford degrees. For his work with the British Air Ministry and the OSS, Rostow was awarded the Legion of Merit and was made an honorary member of the Order of the British Empire. Rostow had enjoyed a good war, and his recommendations played a small part in ensuring the defeat of Nazi Germany. A confident young man had come of age in wartime and no strategy he championed had been contradicted by events. Yet Rostow's self-belief was worryingly absolute. Having never confronted failure, his capacity for self-criticism was significantly impaired. Confidence comes with youth, but Rostow now had the experience to back it up.

AS THE SECOND WORLD WAR ENDED and the Cold War began, the United States had attained a position of overwhelming dominance vis-à-vis its exhausted prewar industrial competitors: Germany, Britain, and Japan. Rich and powerful, the country was soon to embark on a historically unprecedented foray into the making of postwar international relations. An institutional infrastructure providing sustenance to the hitherto malnourished American social sciences was expanded through the establishment of government granting agencies, private foundations, and modern research "multiversities."[52] The American government had necessarily involved itself more directly in the welfare of its citizens in response to the Great Depression and the coming of global war. Under such conditions the social sciences—psychology, economics, law, anthropology, sociology, economic history, and political science—gained a great deal in luster.

Franklin Delano Roosevelt's New Deal agencies were packed with men (and a few prominent women) solidly grounded in those fields. Washington policymakers came to believe that the social sciences held the potential to solve intricate problems in arduous times. With the advent of total war with Japan and Germany, and the coming of the Cold War with the Soviet Union, Auguste Comte's mantra "to know in order to predict, to predict in order to control" became both a leitmotif for American government and a call to arms for positivist social science. Gorged with an unprecedented funding bonanza, the social science departments of major American universities had all of their birthdays at once. As one observer remarked, "Anthropologists who study South Pacific cargo cults had come to expect and receive research grants as much as Melanesians expect to receive cargo."[53] On this wave of government and private sector largesse, it was hardly surprising that the well-connected Walt Rostow soared rapidly through the ranks. He was in the midst of answering Karl Marx and identifying the preconditions that allowed nations to experience rapid economic growth. These intellectual interests and attributes made Rostow a valuable commodity in Cold War America.

In early 1946 Harvard University invited Rostow to take up a professorship in economic history. Twenty-nine years old at the time, he was the youngest man ever to be offered a full professorship at that august institution. Rostow initially accepted this offer to begin teaching in September 1946 but then backtracked and requested that Harvard postpone his start date by a year. Impressed by his late-1930s articles on the British industrial revolution, Oxford University had offered Rostow a one-year appointment as the Harmsworth Visiting Professor of American History. Rostow was much in demand in America and in Britain, vindicating the sagacity of Humphrey Sumner's earlier advice that he get published quickly. Consumed by wanderlust and determined to avoid any further lengthy separation from his soul mate, Rostow asked Elspeth Davies to join him for what he later described as "a full and satisfying year in Oxford."[54] Rostow knew Oxford's pleasures well from his two years there as a Rhodes Scholar. Walt proposed to Elspeth soon after their arrival and they married in that most elegant of college towns. But the England to which Rostow returned looked very different from that of the 1930s.

Rationing was still in place in Britain and many of its cities remained strewn with rubble—ghosts of their former selves. The Rostows were fortunate in that Oxford University's ivory tower provided some protection from the deprivations of life in austere postwar Britain. But the situation across the Channel was bleaker. The winter of 1947 was the harshest on record: ice floes jostled with barges on the Thames, the Rhine, and the Seine. In Paris the freezing conditions and atrophy of civic life led Isaiah Berlin to confess memorably that he was "terrified" by the city's coldness: "empty and hollow and dead like an exquisite corpse."[55] The most basic amenities across Europe—water services, sewage disposal, and the rudiments of heat and power—were in chaos. A continent was in disarray and, as interwar Germany had witnessed, hard times often lead people to seek solace from those offering extreme solutions. Marxism-Leninism held the potential to cut a political swath across a demoralized continent.

Appalled at the prospect of communism taking root in Western Europe, and invigorated by the challenges that lay ahead, Rostow extended his one-year sojourn to Europe. In late June 1947, Gunnar Myrdal, the Swedish secretary of the Economic Commission for Europe, asked Rostow to serve as his executive secretary in Geneva. After playing a part in destroying the Nazi war machine that had left Europe in ruins, Rostow now moved to help the continent rebuild itself. And thus with little hesitation Rostow resigned from the position at Harvard to which he had failed to turn up, and plunged into the gargantuan task of postwar European reconstruction. Turning down Harvard was a bold stroke from a young newlywed with no monograph to his name. Such self-belief testifies to the breadth of Rostow's interests, his desire to involve himself in the most pressing practical issues of the day, and a disregard for convention and even stability. Nevertheless, as Rostow later remarked, it was also true that turning down Harvard was not such a terrible wrench for a dyed-in-the-wool Yale man.[56]

THERE WAS a certain irony in the fact that Walt Rostow had been charged with the task of formulating a strategy to help rebuild Germany. "We took the wry view that there was a certain rude justice in all of this," Rostow recalled. "Having helped knock the place down, it was fair enough to ask us to rebuild it."[57] He set to his task promptly and produced a report that made a characteristic impact. As Rostow's OSS colleague Charles Kindleberger later wrote, "In early 1946, Walt Rostow had a revelation that the unity of Germany could not be achieved without the unity of Europe, and that the unity of Europe could best be approached crabwise through technical cooperation in economic matters, rather than bluntly in diplomatic negotiations."[58] Kindleberger believed that Rostow had provided the rationale behind the eventual creation of the European Economic Community.

Complimentary as Kindleberger's comment was, the idea that technical cooperation was the key to creating a cohesive Europe was not exclusively Rostow's. Prior to 1947 a number of United Nations agencies had helped foster European integration through regional planning, and the success and significance of this was not entirely lost on the State Department.[59] Nevertheless, repackaging an idea that had gained nebulous authority and disseminating the plan to the right people allowed Rostow to display all of his strengths of networking and self-assurance. Rostow's plan as championed by Kindleberger soon gained the support of Undersecretary of State Dean Acheson and Assistant Secretary of State for Economic Affairs Will Clayton, and finally found its way to that impassioned advocate of European unity, Jean Monnet, through Walt's brother Gene.

Rostow's plan for European unity was not as anticommunist as many in Washington would have liked. He had proposed that the various agencies established by the Allies after the war should be combined to form a binding economic community of the type that would be established in 1957 with the Treaty of Rome.[60] The benefits that would accrue through affiliation with this new family of nations, however, would also be made available to the nations of Eastern Europe. Rostow was not convinced, even at the beginning of 1947, that the division of Europe was an established fact. He believed that some sort of accommodation with those nations east of the Oder-Neisse line was entirely possible and that if Truman acted wisely, he could do some productive business with Stalin. But Secretary of State James Byrnes opposed any policy that treated the Soviet despot as a rational actor. As Rostow recalled, "It did not fit in his pattern of treaty-by-treaty piecemeal negotiation—and probably also because Byrnes at that time already planned to test Soviet intentions with his proposal for a long demilitarization pact in Germany."[61]

The upshot of this bureaucratic spat was that Rostow's recommendation for dialogue with the Soviet bloc was dismissed and he gained a reputation as a bleeding heart liberal. Rostow was more than willing to stick his head above the parapet, and his conciliatory ideas made him the subject of ridicule. To the tune of "My Gal Sal," his State Department employees composed the following lyrics to describe their woolly-minded colleague:

> They call him wistful Walt,
> Hardly worth his salt,
> A sad sort of fellow,
> He thinks the reds will mellow,
> That's our guy, Walt.[62]

This reputation for softness was reinforced by Rostow's optimism that Germany should and would soon reunify. As John Kenneth Galbraith recalls in his memoir *A Life in Our Times*, although Rostow was "one of the most effective young officers in the Department," some thought him "too favorably disposed to trying to work things out with the Soviets."[63] Rostow had an innate tendency to look on the bright side when analyzing foreign-policy issues. He underestimated both Stalin's bellicosity and his absolute desire to run Eastern Europe on his own terms. Rostow was not advocating appeasement through irresolution; he was simply displaying undue confidence in his power of reason. At this stage he thought it entirely possible to engage diplomatically with a Marxist-Leninist enemy. Like George Kennan, director of the policy planning staff at the State Department, Rostow believed that containing communism did not preclude interaction with its leaders. Nevertheless, this flexible, restrained view of superpower relations set off warning lights in later years. When security vetting brought Rostow's alleged softness on communism to President Kennedy's attention, he exclaimed, "Why are they always picking on Walt as soft-headed? He's the biggest Cold Warrior I've got."[64]

Rostow spent two years working with Gunnar Myrdal in Geneva, never viewing his position as a long-term concern. By the summer of 1949, the Rostows were pining for a return to academia. Walt later recounted, "Elspeth and I were quite well known in that generation and we were unarguably very hot academic properties."[65] He had completed his Ph.D. in 1940, and his hectic schedule thereafter meant that Rostow had been unable to devote significant time to examining the forces that drove history toward liberal capitalism. This lack of time meant that intellectual frustration was mounting. Dealing with the practical issues of European reconstruction was compelling only up to a point. Rostow wanted to complete his academic lifework—to answer Marx and chart the world's true path—before turning again to active government service. But rather than returning to the United States, Rostow chose to accept a position at another British university: Oxford's ancient rival.

Cambridge University had decided to offer Rostow a yearlong post as the Pitt Professor of American History and Institutions. He accepted immediately and enjoyed a productive year at Cambridge where, protected from a heavy teaching load, he again devoted substantial time to providing an alternative model of historical development to Karl Marx's. Elspeth also accepted a position as a lecturer at Cambridge and established a reputation on campus as an excellent teacher. Initially told by the history faculty that her proposed course on American social history was unlikely to attract more than twenty students, she (and her subject) was vindicated entirely when her lectures attracted an audience of over a hundred. Rostow recalled this period as another "delightful" year in Europe, and many of their friends and colleagues in the United States despaired of the Rostows ever returning home. Walt and Elspeth were very much at home in England and had shown no overwhelming desire to return to the rigors of American academic life. Their cosmopolitanism was pronounced.

The Rostows' marriage was strong and their overlapping careers served as a source of support to each other, creating little friction. Rostow was fortunate to have found a willing, inquisitive partner in Elspeth, who enjoyed her experience at Oxbridge and evidently shared her husband's love of travel. Walt and Elspeth were also a perfect academic team in that they read each other's work and provided criticisms when required. Elspeth's skills as a proofreader were so impressive that she was later brought on board to vet Johnson's presidential speeches, applying her "sharp pencil" to the White House's speechwriters' best efforts with little concern for hurt feelings. Rostow had found his perfect match in Elspeth—they enjoyed a settled home life and shared a high-flying professional life. The peripatetic lifestyle was no problem for the couple, as they were having so much fun globe-trotting.

This rootless existence was challenged, however, when Rostow, taking a vacation in Cornwall in 1950, received a highly attractive offer to join the economics faculty at the Massachusetts Institute of Technology. The

now MIT-based duo of Charles Kindleberger and Max Millikan had lobbied vigorously to hire their friend from Yale as a matter of priority. Given
the opportunity to teach and research in his exact subject area, Rostow
could not justifiably defer again. He accepted the position promptly *and*
turned up for work when requested. His appointment shaped MIT's reputation in the field of economics, but was also portentous in other ways.
Rostow's ten years in Cambridge, Massachusetts, marked the culmination
of his academic career, and served as a launchpad for his move into foreign policymaking.

TWO

The MAKING of an ANTICOMMUNIST ZEALOT

1950–1960

T HE COLD WAR TOOK an ominous turn through the final years of
Harry Truman's presidency. Having enjoyed a monopoly on nuclear
weapons for just four years, Washington received word in August
1949 that the Soviet Union had tested its first atomic device. The
stakes involved in U.S.-Soviet brinkmanship shifted to an entirely new
level. Any false move in the diplomatic sphere now held the potential to
unleash a war unlike anything the world had known. The shock wave that
this news created had scarcely subsided when an equally disturbing development confronted America. In October 1949 Mao Zedong emerged tri-
umphant from the Chinese civil war to unify the mainland under his iron
rule. The news that the world's most populous nation had embraced communism was profoundly unsettling. The optimism that had characterized
American society in the postwar period was replaced by trepidation and
paranoia.[1]

A feverish atmosphere took root in Washington in the wake of these
two events. Republicans criticized Truman for "losing" China when he
scarcely possessed it to begin with. Then on February 9, 1950, Senator
Joseph McCarthy of Wisconsin delivered a speech that spread panic
across the nation. McCarthy produced a piece of paper from his jacket
pocket and claimed that he possessed the names of 205 known communists who were working in the State Department. The piece of paper

might as well have been a takeout menu, for all the truth it contained. Nevertheless, McCarthy produced a barnstorming performance of which any of history's demagogues would have been proud. What followed was a paranoiac feeding frenzy of the type not seen for generations. The intrigues that gripped America over the next five years were redolent of the witch craze that had so blighted Europe and the United States in earlier centuries.

Unlike the witch hunts, McCarthy's scattergun approach was guaranteed to hit a few genuine targets. Soviet espionage was more pervasive than had hitherto been suspected. A few State Department employees were indeed guilty of possessing suspect intentions. In the minds of many, McCarthy had unearthed the most compelling explanation as to why the Soviet Union had produced a functioning nuclear weapon and China had fallen to Mao Zedong. Reds everywhere were undermining U.S. policy at home and abroad. They had to be weeded out and brought to justice. Then a conflict emerged that appeared to confirm all of McCarthy's intemperate warnings about the communist threat.

North Korea invaded South Korea in June 1950 in an audacious attempt to reunify the country. In giving Kim Il-Sung his blessing to launch the assault, Stalin made some critical miscalculations. While Secretary of State Dean Acheson lost little sleep over Korea's strategic significance, Truman could not allow such aggression to go unchecked. Allowing Syngman Rhee's repressive regime to fall to communism would have undermined America's credibility as a military guarantor, and critically harmed the Democratic Party's political prospects. To lose one Asian nation to communism was unfortunate; to lose two was a dereliction of duty. And while concerns about a Republican backlash were ever-present, considerations about the international economy also influenced Truman's decision making: a prosperous, noncommunist South Korea was vital for Japan's economic recovery. But, blind to these issues, Stalin was genuinely surprised when the U.S. response proved steadfast.

Marching into battle under the righteous banner of a UN resolution, and joined in arms by Britain, Turkey, and even Ethiopia, General Douglas MacArthur repulsed the communist advance with some deft battlefield maneuvering. Driven by an ego that was larger than most, however, MacArthur then bit off more than he could chew. Having liberated South

Korea from the communist onslaught, the redoubtable general concluded that he could wipe Korean communism off the map if he moved north of the thirty-eighth parallel. Mao's China begged to differ. In October 1950, 200,000 battle-hardened soldiers from the People's Liberation Army attacked MacArthur's forces, and sent them southward in disarray. The Korean War degenerated into a brutal war of attrition that dragged on painfully for the next two and a half years.

Observing these events from his academic perch at MIT, Rostow identified the Korean War as a turning point in the Cold War—the moment when battlefield engagements superseded ideological posturing and the nature of the conflict changed irrevocably. While Rostow had previously thought that the United States might reach an accommodation with Stalin, Kim Il-Sung's clear-cut aggression had shaken him from this complacency. A few months after arriving at MIT, Rostow delivered a public lecture that called for a significant increase in defense spending. The U.S. military needed additional resources, Rostow argued, so that a "larger full mobilization could be carried out quickly." To pay for this increase in military expenditure, Rostow made the case that Americans would have to face up to a "very high level of taxation apportioned equally."[2] It is clear from these words that Rostow was an academic and not a politician, for this call for sacrifice was unlikely to be met enthusiastically by the wider electorate. Nevertheless, Rostow made a strong call for fundamentally altering the way that the public viewed their own security. Significant material sacrifices were vital to repulse what was a monolithic communist threat to American values.

Rostow was not alone in making the case that the military needed substantially more resources at its disposal. But he had moved significantly from his earlier position that diplomacy alone might take the sting out of the Cold War. His affinity for superpower rapprochement was gradually overwhelmed by an anticommunist fervor that surpassed that of just about anyone. Rostow felt duped and embarrassed by the Korean onslaught, after being so hopeful in earlier years. As it turned out, the sneering ditties that were written about him were true—Rostow had indeed been wistful in believing that the reds would mellow. He would not make the same mistake again. As Rostow devoted substantial time to burying Marx's socioeconomic philosophy, the mere existence of communist nation-states became an affront to his academic vision. Rostow determined that it was nigh on impossible to negotiate with declared Marxist-Leninist regimes.

CAMBRIDGE, MASSACHUSETTS, was the preeminent center of excellence in America's mighty university system. Students across the nation clamored to gain acceptance to Harvard and MIT, where they received instruction from higher education's best and brightest. The U.S. government was also showing keen interest in those institutions, but from quite a different angle. In the summer of 1950, the State Department recruited a team of Cambridge-based academics to help them overcome the high-tech defenses that the Soviet Union had deployed to jam the Voice of America radio broadcasts. The code name for their mission was Project Troy, a classical reference to one of history's first covert operations. The team worked beyond their narrow remit and argued that to wage "political warfare" successfully, the U.S. government should pay much more attention to social and economic strategies, and place far less emphasis on military hardware. Yet in spite of their intensive work, the scholars achieved no significant breakthrough. They failed to penetrate the sonic wall that the Soviets had constructed.

Many in government were nevertheless impressed by the way in which America's most celebrated professors were willing to volunteer so quickly for government service. Rostow's Yale contemporary Max Millikan was one of the individuals involved in the program. He came to believe that the establishment of a permanent research center, charged with solving the most pressing problems of international relations, would represent the worthiest endeavor. Millikan believed that America's elite universities should have a significant role to play in winning the Cold War, and he lobbied MIT vigorously to create such an enterprise.

His campaign was rewarded within a year when MIT established the Center for International Studies in 1951. CENIS was an interdisciplinary think tank based in Cambridge that attracted high-caliber scholars from the many universities in the area.[3] Millikan immediately requested that Walt Rostow become a staff member and help him secure the resources to finance their work. Thanks to their joint efforts, the center soon attracted some influential backers. The Ford and Rockefeller foundations provided substantial donations, while the CIA surreptitiously funded research that spoke to its own concerns. In the 1960s the CIA's role in funding the center was made public, to the horror of academics the nation over. To what extent was intellectual freedom compromised by the acceptance of government funding to address Cold War policy questions? The center presented itself as a rigorously objective observer of the world scene, yet it depended, to a compromising degree, on clandestine federal support. And so the answer, therefore, was "rather a lot." The reality of CIA funding was an ethical dilemma over which MIT's president James R. Killian Jr. agonized, before finally admitting, some thirty-three years later, that he "came to regret it."[4]

CENIS supported individual and collaborative research on a number of different subjects—identifying socioeconomic trends in Asia, peering beyond the iron curtain to appraise communism's future prospects in Eastern Europe—but its operational purpose was to convince the U.S. government that a substantial increase in foreign aid was essential. Rostow describes its modus operandi as "a considerable propaganda activity conducted by political and academic figures: [constituting] books, articles and letters to assorted editors; speeches and symposia; appearances before congressional committees, etc."[5] Among the CENIS staff, Rostow's productivity was unmatched. Over the next nine years, Rostow wrote or collaborated in the production of eight books and a glut of scholarly articles championing a revolution in the provision of foreign aid. This remarkable drive was evident in earlier years, but the 1950s was the decade in which Rostow made his name as a foreign-policy intellectual. He wrote fast, networked skillfully, and established a list of influential contacts that spanned the political spectrum.

Moving seamlessly from economic history to international relations, Rostow focused his scholarly gaze on areas that had previously been considered peripheral to U.S. security. Shocked by the outbreak of the Korean War—by the sheer audacity of the Sino-Soviet front—Rostow believed that communism was likely to pose the most immediate threat to U.S. interests not in Europe, but in the Third World. In 1952 the Soviet Union cast a long shadow over those nations emerging from their colonial experience. At its nineteenth party conference, communist leaders announced that the Soviet Union would henceforth extend its influence through Asia, Africa, and Latin America through trade, loans, and technical assistance—that is, by utilizing the rudiments of what Joseph S. Nye would now term "soft power."[6] Decolonization presented the communist movement with significant opportunities to extend its reach and influence. Little was happening in Europe, so why not carry the battle to the developing world?

The timing of this offensive coincided with the launch of a significant development effort in the People's Republic of China. Mao Zedong had launched a five-year plan in 1953 that was a carbon copy of the Russian version of 1928. Not only was the Soviet Union aiming to buy the Third World's affections, but its development experience was to be aped by the world's most populous nation. Such events were highly disturbing to Washington policymakers, and indeed to CIA-funded academics. As Rostow retrospectively observed, this bold move represented a new and disturbing phase in the "protracted test between communist and non-communist methods of modernization in the developing world."[7] There was little doubt in Rostow's mind that this exertion of Soviet-aid muscle had to be countered by a swift American response. But the Republicans had retaken the White House after twenty years of Democratic occupation. And Truman's successor as president evinced little interest in U.S. foreign aid as a Cold War weapon. President Dwight D. Eisenhower's approach to international diplomacy seemed to involve little more than cutting costs and increasing America's reliance on the deterrent provided by nuclear weapons. Ad hoc decision making and short-term planning characterized the approach of an administration that Rostow believed was dangerously parochial.

While development theorists were unimpressed by his narrow diplomatic vision, Eisenhower was hugely popular across America. Genuinely likable, with his heroic military record and easy smile, "Ike" commanded consistently high approval ratings through his eight years in office. Some critics alleged that the president engaged in a hands-off style of leadership that was ill-suited to the new age of international flashpoints and ideological struggle. But many more believed that Eisenhower was perfectly equipped to manage foreign policy in that most perilous time. In earlier years Eisenhower had commanded the Allied liberation of France and worked effectively with the two giants of that era: Franklin Delano Roosevelt and Winston Churchill.

As president, Eisenhower chose to surround himself with tough-minded foreign-policy advisers. His secretary of state, John Foster Dulles, was implacably belligerent toward the Soviet Union, while Vice President Richard Nixon built his formidable reputation by intemperately attacking enemies both at home and abroad. In comparison to these two men, Eisenhower appeared above the fray—both dignified and wise. While Dulles had professed a willingness to rely entirely on the deterrent effect of nuclear weapons—the so-called strategy of massive retaliation—the public was willing to live with the existential threats that this strategy created. Dulles and Nixon might have been worryingly pugnacious, but most Americans recognized that it was the wily military general—a man who had seen war—who ultimately called the shots. A willingness to use nuclear weapons was the centerpiece of Eisenhower's "New Look" in foreign affairs, but it appeared virtually inconceivable that this warm, ever-smiling hero of the Second World War would take it upon himself to launch a third.

An instinctive Atlanticist, Eisenhower was keenly interested in security issues related to Western Europe, but less enamored of suggestions that America should devote significant resources to assisting Third World development. During Eisenhower's first term, the administration refused to throw money at nations mired in poverty but instead minimized America's financial burden through arranging a series of bilateral and regional security pacts—a practice that his critics derided as "pactomania." John Kenneth Galbraith criticized Eisenhower's approach to the developing world with characteristic eloquence. "Foreign policy in recent years has been dominated by a remarkable tendency to make the maximum use of our weakest weapons," Galbraith wrote. "Of personal diplomacy we have had a plethora. We have also gone in for military pacts at a time when there are grounds for debate whether they can possibly do as much harm as good. All the while economic aid for which our capacity is inherently vast has been parceled out with great and seemingly increasing reluctance."[8] Eisenhower's hostility to doling out American cash to the developing world allowed the Soviet Union to present itself as a modern-day Robin Hood—selflessly assisting the poor while the West tended to its own abundant resources. And while the United States lost credibility across the developing world, the rising force of anticolonial nationalism threatened to make a significant breakthrough in Southeast Asia.

FRANCE HAD ESTABLISHED missionary and trade organizations in Vietnam in 1664 and from this modest beginning grew a massive imperial venture. Through the eighteenth and nineteenth centuries, the French assumed control of all trade in rice, opium, and alcohol and forced countless Vietnamese peasants to work on its rubber plantations and in its mines. By the turn of the twentieth century, France governed much of Indochina: modern-day Laos, Cambodia, and Vietnam. The Vietnamese response was to ask: "Our country has been known as the land of deities: shall we now permit a horde of dogs and goats to stain it?"[9] Provoked into action by French oppression, armed Vietnamese resistance against colonial rule erupted in the 1930s.

Momentous events in Europe were felt thousands of miles away in Southeast Asia. Paris surrendered to Nazi Germany in 1940 and Japan displaced France as Vietnam's colonial overlord. Unfazed by this change in enemy, the Vietnamese fought its new Asian oppressor with equal ferocity. After Japan's surrender in 1945, the Marxist-inclined Ho Chi Minh (meaning "he who enlightens") declared Vietnam's independence, quoting approvingly from Thomas Jefferson's eloquent vision of 1776. Ho was pulling out all the stops to gain crucial American recognition. Yet Truman was unmoved by the Vietnamese nationalist leader's flattery, and permitted the French to return to Vietnam and retake their colony. As the battle resumed, Ho chose to effectively disband the communist movement and focused his energy on presenting the movement as anti-imperialist in purpose. The Viet Minh was nationalist and anti-imperialist, to be sure, but most of its leaders were clear that the teachings of Marx and Lenin would guide an independent Vietnam. The Viet Minh's strategy to secure victory was to avoid direct military engagements in the hope that the French army would make the first false move.

The Viet Minh's patience was rewarded in 1953, when the French military commander Henri Navarre marched fifteen thousand French troops to Dien Bien Phu, a small camp in a remote valley in northwestern Vietnam. Navarre reasoned that its geographical isolation rendered the position virtually impervious to nationalist attack, making it the ideal strongpoint from which to assault Viet Minh bases. This bold strategic move was to prove the beginning of the end for French imperialism in Indochina. Reacting swiftly to this blunder, fifty-five thousand Viet Minh soldiers surrounded the painfully isolated French garrison. Tens of thousands of peasants assisted the Viet Minh troops by dragging heavy artillery guns through the most unsympathetic terrain. This arduous task completed, the howitzers began pounding the French in the valley below. The assault lasted for some fifty-five days and decimated both the garrison and the morale of those who remained.

The inevitable occurred on May 7, 1954, when the Viet Minh routed their colonial tormentors. For the second time in fifteen years, the French military experienced defeat and humiliation in battle. France's presence in the northern part of Vietnam was reduced to a small enclave around Hanoi, and Paris had little option but to order its forces to return southward and retain what it could south of the seventeenth parallel. But even this aspiration was unattainable. As the French foreign minister George Bidault forlornly recalled, the French delegation at Geneva held only the "two of clubs and a three of diamonds."[10] France had lost its hold on Vietnam and the only remaining option was dignified retreat. The United States had refused to support France in its imperial struggle and Eisenhower's nonintervention effectively sealed its fate. Just one question remained: Would the whole of Vietnam be united under the communist leadership of Ho Chi Minh or would the seventeenth parallel divide the nation—as the thirty-eighth did in Korea—between a communist north and a Western-inclined south?

BACK IN BOSTON, Rostow's reaction to the French defeat combined frustration and bellicosity. He was highly critical of France's inability to provide a political framework that could "effectively rally" the Vietnamese against the "communists." In this regard Rostow, as he would do in later years, failed to appreciate that "Vietnamese" and "communist" were not necessarily two distinct species: that the Viet Minh, while Marxist in origin and leadership, attracted many supporters who simply wanted to remove the French from Vietnam—and would later feel the same way about the Americans. But Rostow also strongly criticized Eisenhower's timidity in "refusing to involve American units in combat" in Vietnam.[11] Rostow was aware that to save the entire region from a communist fate would require immediate American intervention, and he was disappointed that such actions were not forthcoming. The Pentagon had prepared a contingency study examining "the feasibility of successfully employing atomic weapons in Indochina," but Eisenhower concluded that he lacked the congressional and international support to wage a war that would be fought indirectly for French colonial *gloire*.

There was little desire for war in Congress. The usually hawkish Massachusetts senator John F. Kennedy observed that "no amount of American military assistance in Indochina can conquer an enemy which is everywhere, and at the same time nowhere, [and which] has the sympathy and covert support of the people."[12] In the wake of the enervating Korean War, Democrats and Republicans alike were horrified at the prospect of waging another war in Asia. And so the Geneva Conference of 1954 split Vietnam in two at the seventeenth parallel—a compromise that gave the French army a more orderly and dignified exit from the region. The treaty stipulated that the division was temporary and that it should not be "interpreted as constituting a political or a territorial boundary."[13] Nevertheless, South Vietnam gained a noncommunist leadership in Emperor Bao Dai and his prime minister, Ngo Dinh Diem, while North Vietnam was governed by the Marxist Ho Chi Minh. Elections were scheduled for 1956, to be supervised by an international control commission composed of Canada, Poland, and India. John Foster Dulles refused to sign the Geneva Accords, but did pledge America to honor its terms. As co-chairs of the conference, Great Britain and the Soviet Union were satisfied that they had fashioned a compromise that was amenable to most. While Ho Chi Minh was the biggest loser on the face of things, he was justifiably confident that he would win nationwide reunification elections in 1956.

Rostow, however, was appalled by this failure of will. At a speech at the Naval War College in August 1954, he argued that France had accepted "terms of limited defeat from communist China"—again ignoring the fact that Vietnamese anti-imperialists had won the key battles—before concluding that the French defeat had exposed "for infiltration or worse a major strategic area embracing India, Burma and Indonesia." Rostow's view of communist China was informed by both aggression and trepidation. At the time he remarked that "we can't drop everything and just have fun plastering the bastards [the Chinese], much as we'd like to."[14] With regard to the Indochina question, however, Rostow did appreciate that America faced problems in allying itself with France: "We had every reason to know from ample post-war experience that colonialism is an impossible base from which to fight communism." But the United States had no reason to fear being tarred with the colonial brush, Rostow contended, if it acknowledged that backing France's shaky political base in Indochina was misguided and if it pursued a policy consonant "with our own interests and those of the free world."[15]

For Rostow the Geneva Accords constituted not a compromise that stipulated future reunification based on free, democratic elections, but a binding agreement that hacked Vietnam into two separate countries at the seventeenth parallel, honor-bound to respect each other's frontiers. This belief would later sustain Rostow's moral cause in Vietnam, but this interpretation jarred with the reality of what happened. Geneva was a temporary settlement designed to be superseded by Vietnam's decisions at the polling stations. Had nationwide elections taken place in 1956—as the Geneva Accords promised—then America's Vietnam War need not have occurred. Ho Chi Minh would surely have won this election, as the CIA predicted at the time, but such an outcome had the dual merits of simplicity and democratic legitimacy. Rostow did not consider a ballot box solution then, and did not deem it an error in subsequent years. Consumed by fears of monolithic communism, Rostow felt that free elections had lost their appeal. To paraphrase Henry Kissinger, Rostow did not want to see Vietnam turn communist due to the irresponsibility of its own people. With Washington's encouragement the effective leader of South Vietnam, Ngo Dinh Diem, retracted his support for the nationwide elections that would have likely voted him out of office. Civil war was henceforth virtually foreordained.

Rostow viewed the Vietnamese insurgency in simplistic terms as one part of a grander offensive conceived and directed by the puppeteer, Josef Stalin. As Rostow wrote in 1960, "Stalin, exploiting the disruption and weakness of the post-war world, pressed out from the expanded base he had won during the Second World War . . . turning to the East, to back Mao and to enflame the North Korean and Indochinese communists."[16] This appraisal was inaccurate for a number of reasons. The Soviet Union and China certainly would have liked to exert significant control over Southeast Asia's insurgencies, but were hamstrung in their ability to do so by, first, a lack of serious military and naval power, and, second, the potency of indigenous nationalism. Ho Chi Minh was a proud leader who had not the slightest inclination to subordinate Vietnam's independence of action to its larger allies.[17] Vietnam's historic fear of China was a vital consideration not appreciated by U.S. observers of the time, and is best expressed in Ho's coarse aphorism: "It is better to sniff French shit for a while than to eat China's all our life."[18]

Finally, Ho Chi Minh had the greatest claim to carry the mantle of Vietnamese nationalism. Ho was not particularly doctrinaire and, as the historian Robert Buzzanco observes, America's failure to understand this represented its "greatest blunder." The Vietnamese leader paid lip service to Marxian class analysis but this was also combined with an eminently practical "program for land redistribution (the key issue in Vietnamese society) . . . popular front politics and an appeal to all anti-French elements to join the cause."[19] In attaching itself to the French cause, the United States had effectively taken sides with reactionary European imperialism against what was the rising force of Southeast Asian nationalism. By characterizing the Vietnamese insurgency as directed from the Kremlin alone, Rostow displayed myopia toward the aspirations and cohesive nationalism of a proud yet historically repressed people. One problem that afflicted Rostow's academic work was that he underestimated the appeal of communism to the developing world. Looking only at the big picture meant that Rostow was blind to the varied forces that made many people amenable to an ideology unsullied by association with European imperialism. In Vietnam communism was more an ideology of national liberation than of economic warfare—and so was more indigenously rooted than Rostow and others could appreciate.

THE FRENCH DEFEAT at Dien Bien Phu led the Eisenhower administration to grudgingly explore the efficacy of foreign aid as a Cold War weapon. Appalled by the prospect of communism dominating East Asia and beyond, Secretary of State Dulles sought the advice of Eisenhower's outgoing assistant for psychological warfare, Charles Douglas (C.D.) Jackson. Having worked at the Psychological Strategy Board during the Second World War, Jackson was aware that resolving serious conflicts often necessitated recourse to unconventional means. In 1954 he moved promptly to enlist Rostow's assistance in combating the communist offensive. Jackson had known Rostow since 1952, when he invited Rostow to speak at Princeton to the National Committee for a Free Europe, an organization of which he was president.[20] A strong believer that intellectuals had a crucial role to play in shaping U.S. diplomacy, Jackson hoped to smooth the route through which good ideas entered the stream of policymaking. He once remarked perceptively that "great ideas need landing gear as well as wings."[21] Through Jackson, Rostow moved toward the center of power in Washington.

Jackson charged Rostow with the task of providing a radical alternative to Eisenhower's pre–Dien Bien Phu propagation of a limited foreign-aid policy. The president's four key points had earlier been presented in the following poetic quartet:

Aid—which we wish to curtail
Investment—which we wish to encourage
Convertibility—which we wish to facilitate
Trade—which we wish to expand.[22]

Such an arrangement of priorities was grist to Rostow's mill. He abhorred the rigid manner in which Eisenhower, Dulles, Joseph M. Dodge (chairman of the Council of Foreign Economic Relations), George M. Humphrey (secretary of the treasury), and Herbert Hoover Jr. (undersecretary of state) believed that private investment in the developing world was some kind of panacea. The group assembled by Jackson set out to generate the first draft of an ambitious "world economic plan" unimpeded by any organizational commitments or intrusive media publicity.

The conference took place May 15–16, 1954, in the salubrious environs of Princeton, New Jersey. Millikan and Rostow took the responsibility of drafting a proposal based on the conference's findings. The final draft was forwarded to the president on July 23, 1954. Rostow optimistically attached a draft speech, coauthored with John K. Jessop of *Life* magazine, to which the president could turn if he launched the program.[23]

Rostow's actions were wildly hopeful, but very much in keeping with his tendency to think positively in the face of daunting odds. He had worked very hard in drafting his pitch to Eisenhower and believed that his logic would prove compelling.

Rostow's proposal called for a vastly expanded "long-term program of American participation in the economic development of the underdeveloped areas." For Rostow and Millikan, development aid "can and should be one of the most important means for furthering the purposes of American foreign policy."[24] But Eisenhower remained unmoved by this entreaty. Concerned primarily with budgetary costs, the president stuck rigidly to what Rostow called "short-run military and political alliances designed to frustrate direct communist aggression."[25] For men like Humphrey, Hoover, and Dodge, Rostow's draft also smacked of what the University of Chicago's realist scholar Hans Morgenthau mocked as "sentimentalism": that "discourse which excites moral principles without attention to the pragmatic course which successful action pursues."[26] Many in the Eisenhower administration considered expansive foreign aid frivolous and unnecessary. America was in the business of making the Western world safe for democracy, of counteracting the territorially voracious Soviet Union, but altruism for its own sake was an unnecessary luxury that circumstances precluded. In the 1955 fiscal year, the bulk of American overseas aid went to Korea and Taiwan, with relatively minor outlays allocated to Pakistan and the Philippines, traditional American spheres of interest. As Rostow points out in his 1972 memoir *Diffusion of Power*, only 15 percent of total aid was made available to countries outside of Eisenhower and Dulles's intricately crafted web of military alliances, "including such strategically important nations as Egypt, India and Indonesia."[27]

Eisenhower's priorities, in Rostow's opinion, were muddled and inexplicable. Angered by this rejection and positive that his cause remained compelling, he resolved to prepare his arguments for public consumption. In 1957 Rostow and Millikan's Princeton Inn proposal was published in book form as *A Proposal: Key to an Effective Foreign Policy*. Rostow charged opponents of his foreign-aid proposals with "isolationistic tendencies" that were "un-American and would allow the pressures imposed by the garrison state of the Soviet Union to threaten our most cherished values."[28] These were harsh words indeed. And his anti-Eisenhower slant was further bluntly expressed with this assertion: "We have put already too much emphasis in recent years on pacts, treaties, negotiation, and international diplomacy, and too little on measures to promote the evolution of stable, effective, and democratic societies abroad which can be relied upon not to generate conflict because their own national interests parallel ours and because they are politically healthy and mature."[29] Rostow ended his book with a quote from his namesake Walt Whitman that spoke to his optimistic belief that the world was heading toward a liberal capitalist end point:

> *One thought ever at the fore—*
> *That in the Divine Ship, the World, breasting Time and Space,*
> *All peoples of the globe together sail, sail the same voyage,*
> *Are bound to the same destination.*[30]

To reach that destination, however, Rostow believed that America had to take the developing world much more seriously. Disillusioned by what he took to be Eisenhower's foreign-policy myopia, Rostow looked elsewhere to identify a more receptive source. He was soon flattered by the interest of a young Irish American senator from Massachusetts.

GIVEN HIS BACKGROUND on the left of the political spectrum, it should come as no surprise that Rostow was an active supporter of Adlai Stevenson's ill-fated presidential campaign of 1956. A bookish, considered politician, Stevenson had an academic style and progressive politics that spoke directly to Rostow's basic values. Through the good offices of Chester Bowles, who represented the most liberal wing of the Democratic Party, Rostow passed a draft speech to Stevenson on foreign policy that was duly presented to the two-time presidential aspirant. Bowles wrote back to Rostow that his ideas—touting foreign aid as an essential and criminally neglected part of the U.S. diplomatic armory—were "exactly what he wanted," assuring Rostow that Stevenson would "appreciate them."[31] Rostow replied to Bowles, "I can't tell you how satisfying the convention was to this TV viewer," before admitting that a Stevenson victory would be a "minor miracle," albeit a "thoroughly possible miracle."[32] But this rather touching exchange between Bowles and Rostow—whom JFK later nicknamed "Chester Bowles with machine guns"—resulted in neither a Rostovian Stevenson speech nor a Stevenson election victory.[33]

Kennedy, meanwhile, campaigned for the vice presidential slot on the Stevenson ticket and failed. This was more a stroke of good luck than a hurdle clattered, however, for 1956 was a good election for any ambitious Democrat to miss—Eisenhower's bipartisan appeal made him virtually unassailable. It was during the Democratic convention that Rostow and Kennedy first established contact. Kennedy wrote to Rostow's brother Gene that he had "enjoyed and profited from Walt's advice" on how to best exploit the weaknesses of Eisenhower's policy toward the developing world.[34] A year later their distant flirting solidified into a working relationship. The catalyst for this shift was the Soviet launch of *Sputnik*—the world's first space satellite—in 1957. Kennedy realized that he could gain political capital through exploiting the public perception that the Soviets had stolen a technological march on the United States. While this stratagem was brilliantly realized in 1960 through the creation and exploitation of a phantom "missile gap," Kennedy, newly ensconced in an influential seat on the Senate Foreign Relations Committee in 1957, attacked the Eisenhower administration on a broad front: for not adequately sustaining either America's military advantage or its internationally preeminent position of influence, and for failing to meet the Soviet challenge in the developing world. On the final two points, Kennedy again sought Rostow's counsel.

Rostow remained in contact with Kennedy through 1957, but it was not until February 1958 that the two men met in person. As Rostow recalled, "Our dialogue expanded out over the whole field of foreign and military policy and to the domestic scene. He requested my regular support as he sought the Democratic nomination and the presidency."[35] Rostow later remarked on the two men's similar backgrounds: "We were too young to have been rooted deeply in the adventures of the New Deal; we had seen America in trouble and then in triumph as junior officers during the Second World War . . . We sensed that the domestic agenda was shifting beyond the familiar categories of conventional liberalism."[36] On the final point, Rostow was ascribing to himself a more centrist proclivity than he actually possessed in 1957, but the first two points are true generally of many of the Kennedy team later identified as the "best and the brightest."

World War II was their formative experience and Munich—to wilt in the face of aggression—was the historical analogy most commonly evoked during the Vietnam policy debates of later years. Rostow and Kennedy were erudite, ambitious, and possessed of a martial spirit. As Rostow recalled, "We communicated tersely and easily. Ties of confidence and mutual regard developed. I concluded in early 1958 that he would be a first-rate president."[37]

It was unsurprising, therefore, that the two men found much common ground at their first meeting. Both were socially graceful and Rostow was particularly adept at cultivating those with power. In turn, as the journalist and historian David Halberstam writes, "Kennedy particularly liked Rostow, liked his openness, his boundless energy, liked the fact that Rostow, unlike most academics, was realistic, seemed to understand something about how Washington really worked, liked the fact that Rostow mixed well, got on well with professional politicians."[38] When discussing their respective career trajectories, Kennedy flattered the young academic by observing that "you came along much faster than I did." Rostow recalled, "What he meant was that each of us was going forward hard in a chosen field: his, politics; mine, academic life. I had come along towards the top of my profession and he still had to make it to the top of his. It was done without affectation."[39] That Rostow considered himself an academic at the top of his profession in 1958, swallowing Kennedy's charming line that a professor at MIT was higher up the respective food chain than a U.S. senator from Massachusetts, suggests that, first, he did not want in confidence, and, second, that his critical filter was not switched on to gratuitous praise. At that stage Rostow had yet to publish a monograph worthy of a world-class academic, and his magnum opus, *The Stages of Economic Growth*, was a full year away from publication. Nevertheless, Kennedy and Rostow established a warm relationship as they set about addressing the young senator's pet issue of the moment: U.S. aid to Jawaharlal Nehru's India.

On February 27, 1958, a day after their first successful meeting, Rostow and Kennedy sat face-to-face before the Senate Foreign Relations Committee. The subject was India and as Rostow candidly recalled, "It obviously has something of the character of a put-up job, designed to build materials into the record he could, and did, later use."[40] The following exchange suggests as much:

> KENNEDY: Do you think that the proposed economic assistance which the administration has decided to give to India is sufficient to meet the minimum requirements for successful Indian development and American policy in that area?

> ROSTOW: I believe the present aid program, which amounts to about $290 million this year, is grossly inadequate.[41]

A month later, in tandem with John Sherman Cooper, the Republican senator from Kentucky, Kennedy proposed the Kennedy-Cooper Resolution to the Senate. Rostow and his CENIS colleagues had studied in some depth the economic problems afflicting India. Nehru's second five-year plan was faltering badly and sorely required an injection of revivifying capital. Rostow was particularly attuned to the dangers inherent in the creation and exacerbation of what he termed an "economic gap" between rich and poor nations. The existence of gulfs in wealth across the world's nations offended his egalitarian ethos, but he also felt that allowing India to degenerate into rack and ruin would give the Soviet Union a perfect opportunity to play the good guy.[42] And so Rostow drafted two speeches for Kennedy in which he lambasted Eisenhower's failure to demonstrate to the developing world the transformative potential and fiscal potency of liberal democratic capitalism.[43] The Kennedy-Cooper Resolution was eventually passed, and India received $150 million in exchange credits from the Export-Import Bank and $75 million from the brand-new Development Loan Fund.[44] The young senator had achieved a significant legislative triumph and, with Rostow's assistance, had carved a niche as a passionate advocate of Third World development. On domestic policy Kennedy was an unknown quantity, but in the sphere of foreign policy he forged a reputation for originality and moral fortitude.

Kennedy and Rostow grew close through their collaboration on foreign policy but their conversations often revolved around domestic politics. The hottest political issue of the day was undoubtedly the 1960 presidential election. Which Democrat was going to step up to the plate and prevent Richard Nixon from succeeding Eisenhower in 1960? One day in August 1958, Kennedy gave Rostow a lift to the State Department in his ostentatious, top-down convertible. They shot the breeze about potential nominees for the 1960 primaries and Kennedy casually mentioned that he was planning to run: "You may wish to know why I think I've got a right to go for the nomination?" Before Rostow had a chance to reply that such explanations were unnecessary, Kennedy answered that Stevenson had had two chances, "which is as much as a party owed its leader," and that while he liked the Missouri senator Stuart Symington, he thought he was "lazy" and hence unsuitable for the job. Lyndon Johnson received Kennedy's warmest praise. He described the Senate majority leader as "the man who has the most legitimate claim on the party for the nomination" but cautioned that "I do not believe a man with his accent from that part of the country can be nominated." For all of these reasons, Kennedy told Rostow, "I feel free to make a try." As Kennedy pulled into the State Department parking lot, he joked that Rostow might like to keep his head down, lest he be seen "by his Republican friends" with a potential Democratic candidate for the presidential nomination. Rostow replied that he was pleased to be seen with the senator because "they know that I'm a Democrat."[45] Rostow was beginning to realize that it made sense for him to turn his back on Eisenhower and declare exclusive allegiance to the ambitious young senator. If Kennedy defeated Nixon in 1960, an attractive job was in the offing.

WHILE ROSTOW'S HEAD WAS TURNED by politics and the prospect of power, he continued to work hard on repudiating Karl Marx. On September 13, 1958, Rostow, Elspeth, and their two young children, Peter and Ann, set off for England yet again. Rostow had been awarded a "Reflective Year Grant" from the Carnegie Corporation, and Cambridge University had offered to serve as his academic host for the year. Awaiting him aboard his ship was a farewell letter from an appreciative Kennedy. "As you begin your voyage to Europe and into the beguiling mysteries of a 'reflective year,'" joshed Kennedy, "I just want to send you a word of thanks for all the help, advice and stimulus which you have both directly and indirectly given us during these past few months."[46] Rostow remained in regular contact with Kennedy throughout his sabbatical year and American domestic politics continued to command his attention. But his focus in England returned to wholly academic pursuits: to formulating his definitive take on the course of world history.

As Rostow wrote to C.D. Jackson, his main objective while at Cambridge was to "uproot the bad works of that angry, passionate old man, Karl Marx" and replace them with those of his own.[47] In a letter to Adlai Stevenson, Rostow elaborated that "as an eighteen-year-old Yale undergraduate, much disliking the pretentious nineteenth century Germans, I promised to produce an alternative to Marxism as a theory of modern history; and I have used my sabbatical to make my bid. It's been fun."[48] And so in a series of lectures, delivered on eight consecutive Friday mornings in Michaelmas term, Rostow presented his own theory of economic growth and dismissed that of Marx. As Rostow wrote to Jackson in December 1958, "What [my lectures do] is to put communism quite technically in its place for what it is: not the wave of the future, but a disease of the transitional process from a traditional to a modern society; and I believe it illuminates where we are and what we ought to be doing."[49] This research process crystallized in the form of *The Stages of Economic Growth: A Non-Communist Manifesto*, published by Cambridge University Press in 1960. It became a clarion call for U.S. aid to the developing world and a celebrated riposte to communist aspirations in that area. As Rostow wrote in a 1958 article for *Daedalus*, "With all respect to James and Dewey, it takes more than a common sense instinct . . . to deal with the age of guided missiles, the age of revolution in Asia, the Middle East and Africa; and with the exciting but dangerous passage of history in which communism as we have known it discovers that it is not historically viable."[50]

The key question that Rostow sought to answer in *The Stages of Economic Growth* was whether global economic progress led to a communist or a capitalist end point. "Is it taking us to Communism," Rostow wondered, "or to the affluent suburbs, nicely rounded out with social overhead capital; to destruction; to the moon; or where?"[51] In his *Communist Manifesto*, Marx had famously written that capitalism "left no other nexus between man and man than naked self-interest, than callous 'cash payment.'"[52] Rostow believed that the German philosopher was wrong to impugn capitalism and its adherents in this simplistic fashion. Instead, Rostow argued that all men seek "not merely economic advantage, but also, power, leisure, continuity of experience and security; he is concerned with his family, the familiar values of regional and national culture, and a bit of fun down at the local. And beyond these diverse homely advantages, man is also capable of being moved by a sense of connection with human beings everywhere, who, he recognizes, share his essentially paradoxical condition."[53]

While Marx believed that society's decisions were governed by who owned property and the means of production, Rostow held greater faith in the capacity of liberal capitalists to shun the pursuit of selfish, private advantage and to subsume their interests within those of the larger society. Thus, "nothing in Marx's analysis can explain how and why the landed interests in the end accepted the [British] Reform Bill of 1832, or why the capitalists accepted the progressive income tax or the welfare state; for it is absolutely essential to Marxism that it is over property that men fight and die." Rostow believed that because Marx was a "lonely man, profoundly isolated from his fellows," he had failed to appreciate the infinite complexities of capitalism and of human nature.[54] For all of these reasons, Marx was wrong to assert that all nations were moving inexorably toward a communist utopia. Liberal capitalism was infinitely preferable to communism as an economic system, producing superior economic growth and material benefits to all. But the laissez-faire model that Marx disparaged could also be made more humane: its harvest could be distributed to all strata of society.

Rostow is most effective when tracing the unedifying consequences of Marx's theories as they were misapplied through the twentieth century. The Soviet Union's first leader, Vladimir Lenin, did the most to refashion "modern communism" into a system of political repression. Recognizing that Russian workers were unprepared "to fulfill their historic Marxist destiny," Lenin formed an elite political party that would compel them to do so through coercion. In modern communist states, Rostow concludes that the "ownership of the means of production" does not decide anything. Rather, "it is the control of the army, the police, the courts, and the means of communication" that was central to the continued survival of Marxist-Leninist regimes. Rostow's critique of the intellectual and moral poverty of Marx's disciples is compelling:

> Economic determinism did not work well for them; but power determinism has, quite well, filled the gap. They have operated on the perception that, under certain circumstances, a purposeful, well-disciplined minority can seize political power in a confused ill-organized society; once power is seized, it can be held with economy of force, if the Communist elite maintains its unity; and with power held, the resources of a society may be organized in such a way as to make the economy grow along lines which consolidate and enlarge the power of the Communist elite.[55]

Rostow then traces the way in which Russian communism mutated into an even greater menace as Josef Stalin and then Nikita Khrushchev succeeded Lenin at the helm. Stalin "cheerfully" accepted the police-state dictatorship as the basis for his iron rule, and then supplemented communist ideology "with strong elements of Great Russian nationalism, yielding revisions in everything from soldier's uniforms to the content of history books, primary education, and the approved pattern of family life." Following Stalin's death in 1953, Khrushchev denounced his predecessor's brutal domestic methods, which was all well and good. Rather than improving the lot of the average Soviet citizen, however, Khrushchev chose to direct the Soviet Union's energies toward fomenting revolution in the "underdeveloped areas."[56] Marxism-Leninism was inhumane, economically inefficient, and held together by a brutal police state. Nevertheless, Rostow feared that it still held the potential to convince desperate, poorer nations that it was better placed than liberal capitalism to solve the twin problems of pervasive poverty and colonial oppression.

In *Stages* Rostow identifies five stages of growth through which all nations pass in the course of their historical development: "traditional society," the "preconditions for take-off," "take-off," "the drive to maturity," and finally the "age of high mass consumption."[57] Rostow believed that it was incumbent upon the United States to push those nations languishing in the first two stages toward greater material progress—blunting the appeal of Marxism-Leninism along the way. Thus, "the underdeveloped nations [must] move successfully through the preconditions into a well established take-off within the orbit of the democratic world, resisting the blandishments and temptations of Communism. This is the most important task [of the West]."[58] The United States stood at the zenith of historical development—it luxuriated in the "age of high mass consumption"—and thus represented the model to which other nations should aspire. It best represented modernity as it stood at the cutting edge of scientific and technological research, and was militarily and economically preeminent. America was a free, meritocratic society that encapsulated all of the strengths of liberal capitalism. Capitalism *worked* best as an economic system, and it was morally superior too. With a little help from America and her Western European allies, Third World nations could avoid the grim fate of the citizens of Russia, China, Yugoslavia, and other communist regimes across Eastern Europe and the Far East—who had been seduced, manipulated, and then coerced into accepting a system that stifled liberty and brought scant material benefits.

In many respects Rostow's rationale was similar to that of missionary imperialists of the eighteenth and nineteenth centuries who justified the export of British values such as private enterprise, free trade, and an advanced legal system not solely in terms of benefits to the mother country, but because they represented an unalloyed good for those nations that had not quite made it. Rostow's work was infused with an overwhelming optimism: that America had resolved its domestic problems and could now help solve those of the world. As he wrote in 1957, "The United States is now within sight of solutions to the issues which have dominated life since 1865 . . . If we continue to devote our attention [to them] we run the danger of becoming a bore to ourselves and the world."[59] Rostow extolled liberal capitalism's merits enthusiastically in *The Stages of Economic Growth* and argued that all nations held the potential to enjoy the benefits that accrued through the pursuit of "mass production." The underdeveloped world might need substantial American assistance to arrive at that final destination, but get there it assuredly would.

Rostow's British publisher prefaced the first edition of *The Stages of Economic Growth* with the informative assertion that it "provides the significant links between economic and non-economic behavior which Karl Marx failed to discern."[60] But there are many similarities between the analytical structures employed by Marx and by Rostow. Both men postulate the same evolutionist take on history in assuming an inevitable teleological movement from tradition to modernity. The Swiss scholar Gilbert Rist describes this process sardonically as "Rostow's marvelous fresco of humanity marching towards greater happiness," and describes his theories as "Marxism without Marx."[61] Rist is correct to an extent. What are Rostow's stages of growth if not Marxist historical materialism with a happier ending? It is a faith-based system predicated on the premises that mass consumption is the end point, that the model is universal, and that it can be readily applied to the developing world. Neither Rostow nor Marx countenanced deviation from their respective analyses. Both shunned pluralist explanatory models.

Rostow's illustrious European progenitors in the field of social development were Georg Hegel, Marx, Max Weber, Ferdinand Tönnies, and Émile Durkheim. One can even trace Rostow's intellectual inspiration to the luminaries of the Scottish Enlightenment: to Adam Smith, in particular, who also split history into various stages of economic development. It is in the specific universalistic tradition of *histoire raisonée*, however, that Rostow's analysis can be most accurately placed. The *histoire raisonée* movement of the nineteenth century aimed to discern a universal process of development through which humankind and history proceeded. The historian D. Michael Shafer describes the tradition as "a logical construct, deduced from a set of universal axioms abstracted from the realm of human and temporal contingencies."[62] In other words, the movement sought to impose a linear order on the course of human history. The basic problem, however, was that such an approach—and Rostow's later model in particular—explained what ought to happen, and did not consider what might happen because of unforeseen circumstances. Human agency plays little part in Rostow's story of nations being driven through history by the unquenchable drive to consume and to provide for their families, and thus to industrialize.

And central to Rostow's thesis was the presupposition that the leaders of nations hold the health of their economy, and the strength of their industrial base, as the overwhelming consideration in peace and war; without such reasoning, the engine of growth would inevitably stall. Economic determinism, therefore, is the sine qua non of Rostow's study. The driving force behind history is the aspiration of poorer countries to attain the levels enjoyed by those in the West. It follows that to threaten a nation's economy constitutes coercion of the highest order. As a modernization theorist, Rostow believed that to attack the nascent trappings of modernity, and the infrastructural means through which modernity could be achieved, would constitute an unbearable burden on any nation. As Rostow would explain to Dean Rusk when justifying the use of U.S. airpower against North Vietnam, "Ho [Chi Minh] has an industrial complex to protect: he is no longer a guerrilla fighter with nothing to lose."[63] Rostow's model necessarily involved generalization. Specific case studies, beyond the central emulative example of the British industrial revolution, were dismissed as irrelevant. But Rostow's faith in social-scientific objectivity was misplaced. His overarching theory—and the assumption that valueless, rigorous scholarship sustained it—was, to quote the French sociologist Émile Durkheim, "like a veil drawn between the thing and ourselves, concealing from us more successfully as we think it more transparent."[64]

Critical reaction to Rostow's *Stages of Economic Growth* was largely positive among the mainstream media. *The New York Times* purred that Rostow's was an "impressive achievement" that held the potential to become "one of the most influential economic books of the twentieth century." *Stages*, wrote Harry Schwartz, amounted to "a shaft of lightning through the murky mass of events which is the stuff of history."[65] *The Christian Science Monitor* observed, "There is a sharp intelligence at work, producing paragraphs and pages which seem to distill events to an almost unbearable simplicity. This is the special quality of the writer and the book."[66] In a private letter to Rostow, Adlai Stevenson wrote, "Is the future Rostowism vs. Marxism? If so, I am ready to vote now."[67]

But Rostow's peers in the field of economics came to adopt a harsher view in subsequent years. Kenneth Boulding, in his scathingly titled "The Intellectual Framework of Bad Advice," inveighed that the stages were simply "empty taxonomical boxes." Instead of engaging in thorough, systematic analysis, Rostow "merely introduced quantitative material as a means of illustrating his preconceived points."[68] *The Stages of Economic Growth* did indeed offer an ambitious synthesis shaped by Rostow's ideological prejudices. The grandiosity of Rostow's theory necessitated a broad-brush approach to the history of societal progress that did not stand up to rigorous analysis. As the economic historian Barry Supple observed, the dynamics of the stages of growth were underspecified. Some of Rostow's critical variables did not have quantities attached to them and others that did—the "investment ratio," the extent of discontinuity, and the importance of leading economic sectors—turned out to be miscalculated. As Supple rightly concludes, *Stages* was "less a theory than a language that gained its power to invade [the] discourse of development as it lost precision and specificity."[69]

The impact of *Stages* can in part be attributed to its broad sweep and ambition. It was punchy, easy to follow, and gracefully drafted. One need not be an economist to comprehend that all nations could be situated on a spectrum of progress that began with "traditional society" and ended with the "age of high mass consumption." One need not be well versed in development theory to comprehend that to save the Third World from poverty and communist infiltration required the benevolent attention and deep pockets of the United States. In categorizing developing societies according to their place on an evolutionary scale, furthermore, Rostow's work went some way toward appeasing the demands of conservative legislators who insisted that foreign aid be dispensed according to stringent criteria and not be open-ended.[70]

And so although *Stages* was Rostow's academic magnum opus—his most significant achievement in a notable scholarly career—his work was not so much a rigorous theory of economic development as a vigorous expression of political advocacy. It would be wrong, however, to simply characterize Rostow's work as exuberant but facile, the musings of a Pollyanna. He was well aware that the injection of Western capital was not sufficient in itself; land reform, tax reform, more voluntary civic organizations, and greater political participation were accorded weight as vital determinants of economic growth. But these issues, while important, could be dealt with later, after American aid began to be dispensed with true purpose. Rostow's was a simple theory. And it was its simplicity that made *Stages* a blueprint for foreign-aid policy in the 1960s.

Why did the plight of developing nations so vex the young professor? This point requires elaboration, as it cuts to a central issue: Rostow's egalitarian instincts. Throughout Rostow's career in college, in the army, and as a policy adviser, he rose to positions of prominence not through bootlicking, although he was deft at cultivating the right people, but through the force of his intellect, personal integrity, and the appealing nature of his own personality. Rostow was self-confident but was in no way abrasive. This gentleness in debate arose in part from his self-belief—he was right, and thus did not need to shout very loud—but his character traits were genuinely appealing. As progressive socialists, Rostow's parents instilled a compassion and benevolence in Walt that never left him. He was fervent in his anticommunism but wholly sincere in his desire to fashion a new kind of liberal capitalism that ridded the world of poverty and allowed the potential of all the world's citizens to be realized, irrespective of their geographical location.

Robert Johnson later served as a member of Rostow's National Security Council staff and he opposed his boss's Vietnam recommendations. Nevertheless, he enjoyed working for Walt because he was "a very different guy from Bundy . . . He is a warm human being . . . He was a great guy to work for and he gave you the feeling that he really cared about what you were doing."[71] The "modernization theory" that Rostow expressed in his academic work in some ways was an extension of his personality—generous and unshakably optimistic. Increasing foreign aid for underdeveloped nations was a thoroughly laudable goal, irrespective of the numerous problems regarding implementation. Rostow's model might have been culturally presumptuous and excessively hopeful, but it was driven by noble intentions.

On one occasion Rostow's worthy instincts provoked southern segregationists into paroxysms of rage. In 1957 Washington recruited Rostow and his CENIS colleagues to design the American pavilion for the 1958 Brussels World Exposition. Rather than crow about America's material achievements, Rostow instead ran with the theme of "America's Unfinished Business," and devoted substantial time to the issue of race, arguing that "the desegregation problem cannot be evaded. It will be underlined rather than evaded by omission." Unsparing in his criticism but optimistic in his conclusion, Rostow presented America as a flawed society, but one in which hope sprang eternal, where economic advancement would soon be available to all. Many parts of the world were "underdeveloped," Rostow recognized, but they should not worry unduly because the American south was somewhat backward too. This "warts and all" strategy was one that failed to endear southern conservatives. One journalist described the

exhibit as "the weird spawn of Rostow's brainstorm . . . It's a sure bet that
Soviet Russia will not have any exhibits at Brussels showing the slave workers in the mines of Vorkuta, or the miserable peasants on their cooperative
farms." As the historian Nils Gilman observes, "Southern congressmen
had no intention of letting some secularizing Yankee Jew tell them that
they were backward or underdeveloped." This amusing episode serves as
a fine example of Rostow's progressive political principles in action.[72]

WHILE ROSTOW WAS in England writing *The Stages of Economic Growth*, he
still found time to correspond with his link to the Eisenhower administration, C.D. Jackson. In November 1958, Khrushchev announced that he
intended to return control of Berlin access routes to East Germany. From
that point on, the United States would have to negotiate directly with East
Germany over the explosive issue of access to West Berlin—an outcome
that was anathema to all in foreign-policy circles. Whereas the Rostow of
1947 advocated an emollient policy toward the Soviet Union and its satellites, the 1959 vintage was considerably more belligerent. Rostow urged
that CIA Director Allen Dulles "must think of a way of hotting up all the
[Soviet] satellites at once, if the Berlin thing gets rough." Rostow rationalized that while the Soviets could deal with one uprising at a time, like Hungary or later Czechoslovakia, they would have their hands full with five:
"What I am saying, in short, is that we ought to design a limited war for
central Europe, if the Russians really take us down to the barrier, and see
it through."[73]

But how does one possibly "design a limited war for central Europe" in
the nuclear age? With little consideration for the possibility that a U.S.-
Soviet war in the heart of Europe held the potential to precipitate nuclear
war, the ostensibly mild-mannered development theorist championed a policy unconscionable to all but the most extreme anti-Soviet. At exactly the
same time, Rostow was supplying Senator Kennedy with "useful bulletins,
suggestions and delicate hints" on the issue of foreign-development aid.[74]
One wonders if Rostow's subsequent career trajectory would have been
quite so stellar had he advised Kennedy on access rights to Berlin as opposed
to Third World development. In 1962 Kennedy famously remarked that he

considered himself a citizen of Berlin; but he displayed considerably more caution as president than Rostow's advice would have allowed.

All that said, Rostow's theory of economic growth had a profound impact on presidential candidate Kennedy's foreign-aid strategy. In a speech of March 1959, Kennedy discussed the Rostovian "economic gap" between the rich and poor nations of the world that posed innumerable problems to U.S. containment policy. "Unlike the missile gap," Kennedy stressed, "the gap to which I refer now [the economic gap] gives rise to no speculation as to whether the Russians will exploit it to their advantage and to our detriment . . . They are exploiting it now." Of all the foreign-policy issues that Kennedy confronted, he considered the plight of the developing world to be vitally important. The economic gap identified by Rostow "is altering the face of the world, our strategy, our security and our alliances, more than any current military challenge."[75] And so upon Rostow's return from England, on Labor Day 1959, Kennedy dispatched his aide Fred Holborn to enlist Rostow's support for his presidential campaign. As Rostow appreciatively recalled, "This fellow wanted the assets I could bring to the show, and he took great pains to do it nicely."[76]

Rostow's contribution to Kennedy's whistle-stop presidential campaign was substantial. While he provided Kennedy with many of his speeches on the need to bridge the economic gap between rich and poor nations, he also pushed the young candidate to focus on the "missile gap" during his campaign. Rostow guessed correctly that the issue was potentially "decisive," as nothing was "more likely to swing voters than the conviction that the Republicans have endangered the nation's safety." In a colorful metaphor, likening Republican lapses on national security to the quiz-show scandals of the 1950s, Rostow contended that "the missile gap can be used as the Charles Van Doren of the Republican administration."[77] In reality the "missile gap" was the Van Doren of the Democratic campaign: an impressive illusion. Following Kennedy's election his defense secretary, Robert McNamara, put the claim to the sword. Even then Rostow found a way to reassure the president that his accusation was sound, writing disingenuously on February 13, 1961, that "in your major campaign statements you defined the gap essentially as the period when our retaliatory capacity might be vulnerable to a Soviet missile salvo. This is quite a different matter than the question of the relative number of missiles on both sides. I find it hard to believe that your campaign positions and the Pentagon review will be inconsistent."[78] Inconsistent they were, but Rostow's loyalty would occasionally get the better of the actuality.

Beyond stressing the importance of the economic and missile gaps, Rostow's main contribution to Kennedy's campaign came most memorably in the form of catchy sound bites. In mid-June 1960, at the Beacon Hill apartment of one of Kennedy's campaign workers, Rostow told Kennedy that he had come up with a great first line for his acceptance speech at the Democratic convention. The sentence read, "This country is ready to start moving again and I am prepared to lead it," the exact line delivered by Kennedy on the night.[79] During that same speech, Kennedy also delivered a soon-to-be-famous phrase, the "New Frontier," first penned by Rostow in *The Stages of Economic Growth*.[80] As Kennedy exclaimed: "We stand today on the edge of a New Frontier—the frontier of the 1960s . . . Are we equal to the challenge?" According to the *Boston Globe* journalist David Wise, Kennedy considered the slogan "the single most important idea of the campaign."[81]

Following Kennedy's nerve-fraying election victory over Richard Nixon on November 8, 1960, it became clear that the president-elect wanted to place Rostow in a key foreign-policy position. *The Economist* even went so far as to tout Rostow as a plausible candidate for secretary of state, although it observed that it was "unlikely" that Kennedy would select an out-and-out academic for the job.[82] Rostow for his part felt that J. William Fulbright would make a decent secretary of state—an ironic preference in light of the Arkansas senator's dim view of subsequent events in Vietnam—because of his formidable intelligence and vast experience in the Senate. Rostow downplayed Fulbright's Arab sympathies during a meeting on December 8, 1960, telling the president-elect that he "had no need to worry about the Jews in New York," since he was "plenty strong enough" there. Kennedy next mentioned Dean Rusk as a potential candidate, but Rostow was less enthusiastic. "He would be a superb Undersecretary," Rostow reasoned. "I just didn't know whether he would be a good Secretary of State."[83] Kennedy concluded the meeting by putting Rostow out of his misery, telling him that he planned to appoint him as chairman of the State Department's policy planning staff, but, as Rostow recalled, "he couldn't make it definite until he had appointed his Secretary of State and I had talked with him."[84]

Having rejected Fulbright and a number of other possibilities, Kennedy ignored Rostow's reservations and appointed Rusk to serve as his secretary of state. It was now Rusk's turn to cast aspersions on Rostow's suitability for a post.[85] Rusk met Rostow on December 19, 1960, having previously requested that he draft an ideas paper on how America could defend its interests without resorting to nuclear war. Rusk wanted Rostow to analyze Eisenhower's strategy of "massive retaliation" and form a blueprint for what would become Kennedy's policy of "flexible response": the strategy of dealing with crises with recourse to all diplomatic and military means. Rostow completed his task diligently and stressed the vital importance of waging "limited war" if required.[86] But he did envision one scenario where "limited war might be consistent with the use of nuclear weapons," and that was "a possible breakout by Chinese communist forces on a large scale over the southern and especially the southeastern boundaries of the country."[87] This was an extreme contingency to adopt, but Rostow feared that Southeast Asia was a region that had few positive associations with the West, and was thus particularly susceptible to Marxist seduction. If Mao's China moved troops into Vietnam, Rostow recommended that America use the atomic bomb for a third time in Asia.

Following a strained meeting, Rusk decided to veto Rostow's appointment, although it is impossible to gauge how far Rostow's nuclear belligerence contributed to this fall from grace. Rostow himself felt that Rusk did not take him seriously as a mover and shaker in government: "[Rusk] had a picture of me as a professor who wrote books, who could perhaps contribute to speeches; but he had no sense that I had operated seriously in government."[88] A more likely explanation is that Rusk simply resented being forced into accepting an out-and-out Kennedy man for a key position within *his* orbit. In his memoir, *As I Saw It*, Rusk is critical of the influence that Robert Kennedy exerted over the appointments process. But within his State Department fiefdom, Rusk held sway. "On key appointments," Rusk recalled, "I managed to prevail."[89] Whatever the exact reason for his own rejection, Rostow was furious that Rusk had given the job to George McGhee, telling Rusk bluntly that "[McGhee] is a fine man . . . but he is the last man in the world to do a planning job. Planning is not his cup of tea."[90] Sour grapes may well have informed this appraisal, but the key question remained: Where was Rostow to go?

Kennedy first attempted to answer this question on January 9, 1961.[91] According to Rostow, the president-elect strutted out of the bathroom into the hotel suite "without affectation and stark naked. This was a man comfortable with human beings and human situations." Having located a robe, Kennedy attempted to sell the merits of working as McGhee's deputy at the Policy Planning Council. His sales job was virtually impossible, however, as Rostow was not interested in serving in a position of limited significance under a man he did not consider up to the job. Kennedy accepted that the young academic could well interpret the new offer as a slight and so promised that he would get back to him with something better. Rostow was undoubtedly impressed with the personal attention that Kennedy was according his predicament: "This truly minor matter was on his mind—getting the lost sheep into the fold. He really stayed with it."[92]

As inauguration day grew closer, Rostow's plight became more acute. Having worked so hard to establish a bond with Kennedy, it was beginning to look as if he would have nothing to show for his efforts. Then finally a solution came to Kennedy's mind. On January 19, 1961, just one day before his inauguration, Kennedy announced that he was appointing Rostow to serve as his deputy special assistant for national security affairs. He would serve directly under the national security adviser, McGeorge Bundy, whose achievements at Harvard ensured that he commanded Rostow's respect. Not everyone was pleased, however, by Rostow's move to the White House. The MIT political scientist Lucian Pye could not hide his concern at his colleague's rise to prominence. "You know," Pye confessed to his students, "you don't quite sleep so well any more when you know some of the people going to Washington."[93]

THREE

RATTLING SABERS

1961

F ROM TODAY'S VANTAGE POINT, the Soviet Union's collapse is no mystery. As the Warsaw Pact disintegrated in the late 1980s and early 1990s, documentary evidence emerged which proved that communism's economic performance had been dismal. What is evident now, however, was not so obvious fifty years ago. We know now that in 1961 the Soviet Union's imposing veneer masked the reality of internal decay—but it was a convincing façade all the same. The Soviet economy had responded resolutely to the hellish destruction inflicted by Nazi Germany during the Second World War and, according to American statistical measures, had expanded its industrial production six times faster than the United States up to 1960.[1] In 1957 an incredulous world learned that the Soviet Union had placed in orbit the world's first space satellite, *Sputnik*. As the historian Diane Kunz observes, "Short of actually attacking the United States, there could hardly have been a more frightening revelation."[2] The Soviet Union's apparent technological lead over the United States was brought into even sharper focus when the cosmonaut Yuri Gagarin was launched into the stratosphere on April 12, 1961. As the first man in space, Gagarin even had the temerity to taunt the West's inefficiency from orbit. "Let the capitalist countries [now] catch up with our country," Gagarin crowed.[3] From an American perspective, the Soviet

Union loomed large as a technologically innovative, militarized behemoth with a growing appetite for expansion.

This sense of being left behind by the vigor of the communist challenge was exacerbated by the fact that communist China's economic growth was surpassing that of democratic India—at least prior to the self-inflicted wound that was the Great Leap Forward. Yet other events had shaken American self-confidence. Vice President Richard Nixon was fortunate to escape serious injury during riots provoked by his 1958 tour of Latin America. Vociferous anti-American demonstrations in Japan forced President Eisenhower to cancel his 1960 visit to Tokyo. Moreover, when one adds to that mix the seismic shock of the 1959 Cuban revolution that brought Fidel Castro to power, it is no challenge to discern an increasing global aversion to U.S. development and political models. Into this volatile international environment arrived a plethora of new states finally free from colonial rule: in 1960 alone eighteen new states gained their independence.[4] As Kennedy's deliberative undersecretary of state George Ball aptly put it, foreign policy through the early 1960s necessarily "focused on the bits and pieces of disintegrating empires."[5] But an additional problem with disturbing ramifications confronted U.S. diplomacy. The Soviet Union had decided to embark upon a serious charm offensive in the postcolonial world.

Exuding the confidence that comes with presiding over a theoretically infallible political system, Khrushchev on January 6, 1961, declared ebulliently that "since the death of Stalin, the end of the Korean War and the relaxation of the western drive, one event after another has strengthened the conviction of inevitable victory . . . There is no longer any force in the world capable of barring the road to socialism."[6] With reference to the Soviet Union offering assistance to those nations in the developing world fighting for colonial liberation, Khrushchev boldly asserted, "The communists support just wars of this kind wholeheartedly and without reservation."[7] The chairman of the Soviet Politburo was invigorated by the likelihood that the Third World would look to Moscow, not Washington, for tutelage. Khrushchev later addressed this message to America in blunter terms: "We will bury you!"[8]

The Russian historians Vladimir Zubok and Constantine Pleshakov identify Khrushchev's braggadocio as part of an attempt to use a "blend of disinformation, nuclear bluffing, and the utilization of the 'movements of national liberation' around the globe, including in the United States' backyard, Latin America, to create a preponderance of power for the USSR."[9] This belligerent speech, however, primarily served to heighten American paranoia, precipitating a rapid military expansion and a sharpened willingness to intervene militarily in what George Kennan, the erudite architect of America's containment strategy, categorized as "peripheral" theaters. In his memoir *In Retrospect* Robert McNamara, Kennedy's secretary of defense, depicts the impact of Khrushchev's speech as seminal: "We felt beset and at risk. This fear underlay our involvement in Vietnam."[10] Kennedy himself did not doubt the significance of Khrushchev's avowed intent, remarking to an aide, "You've got to understand it, this is our clue to the Soviet Union."[11] However, while the Soviet leader's speech was pugnacious, the president-elect failed to appreciate the extent to which it was directed toward Beijing—where Mao had recently accused the Soviet Union of failing to adequately support Third World liberation movements—as much as toward Washington. Kennedy was wrong to interpret Khrushchev's words as an attack on U.S. interests alone. The Soviet leader was trying to prove that his revolutionary credentials were more impressive and durable than those of the upstart Chinese communists.

The new president made copies of Khrushchev's speech and distributed them to the key members of his new foreign-policy team. He even read excerpts of the speech at the first meeting of the National Security Council on Saturday, January 28, 1961. As Roger Hilsman, director of the State Department's Bureau of Intelligence and Research, recalled, "He wanted all members of his new administration [to] read the speech and consider what it portended."[12] In threatening to take the ideological fight to the postcolonial world, Khrushchev had struck a nerve with a young president who had long worried that the communist nations alone possessed the single-minded dedication to export their political and economic model to nations whose main experience of the civilized West had been that of colonial exploitation. While the United States stood idly by, Kennedy warned in a campaign speech of November 2, 1960, "out of Moscow and Peiping and Czechoslovakia and Eastern Germany are hundreds of men and women, scientists, physicists, teachers, engineers, doctors, nurses . . . prepared to spend their lives abroad in the service of world communism."[13] Like Rostow, Kennedy viewed Marxism-Leninism as a fatally flawed political ideology, but he could not help but be impressed by the vigor with which dedicated communists went about their task of painting the world red.

Kennedy's inaugural address was in part a riposte to Khrushchev's speech extolling wars of national liberation: "Let every nation know that we shall pay any price, bear any burden, meet any hardship, support any friend, oppose any foe to assure the survival and success of liberty."[14] While Eisenhower had relied on the nuclear deterrent of "massive retaliation" to ensure that the iron curtain remained fixed in Europe, the celebrated general possessed neither the will nor the counterinsurgency resources to move beyond the traditional American policy of protecting Western Europe and Japan from communism. Bearing any burden and meeting any hardship to assure liberty was the central purpose of the Kennedy foreign-policy strategy known as "flexible response"—a willingness to combat communism on a global scale, from sub-Saharan Africa to Southeast Asia, with recourse to both military and nonmilitary means. Khrushchev had upped the ante with his none-too-subtle beating of the war drum. The stage was set for heightened superpower tensions and the expansion of the Cold War into a conflict that touched all nations that chose to tie their flag to a superpower mast. The periphery was soon to become the center.

TO ENSURE THAT his administration was as good as his inaugural word, Kennedy assembled in Washington a glittering array of intellectual talent from military academies, the business world, and elite universities. Their job was to combat this expected Soviet offensive and convince the Third World that the West was best. One of the brightest stars from the business world, the highly driven, coldly analytical Robert McNamara, was drafted in from the lucrative presidency of Ford Motor Company to serve as secretary of defense. The dean of Harvard College, McGeorge Bundy, became the president's national security adviser. And Walt Rostow arrived from MIT to serve as Bundy's deputy. Kennedy was the most intellectually gifted president since Woodrow Wilson, and it showed in the faith he placed in the "Harvards" and the "Yales." As a clever, if errant, student at the London School of Economics and at Harvard, Kennedy was fascinated by the transformational power of good ideas. He was sure that the intellectual prowess of his new appointments was sufficient to deftly guide American diplomacy, remarking that "there's nothing like brains. You can't beat brains."[15] Rostow in turn was impressed by Kennedy's intellect and utilitarian ethos: "Ideas were tools. He picked them up easily like statistics or the names of local politicians. He wanted to know how ideas could be put to work."[16] Adlai Stevenson—spurned by Kennedy as secretary of state and offered the consolation prize of U.S. ambassador to the United Nations—took a dimmer view of Kennedy's creative appointments, complaining that "they've got the damndest [*sic*] bunch of boy commandos running around you ever saw."[17]

Rostow's *The Stages of Economic Growth* deftly explained why capitalism would eclipse communism in the battle for economic supremacy. Was Walt Rostow, therefore, the one man in the new administration truly capable of seeing through Khrushchev's bluster? He had devoted an academic career to proving why communism would fail and capitalism prevail. Surely, showpiece Soviet achievements in the space race and Khrushchev's hollow posturing would be seen for what they were: shiny gloss applied liberally to a crumbling superstructure. By disposition Rostow was not a worrier, and he fully expected his predictions about communism's flaws as a viable economic system to be borne out. This confidence is best reflected in an August 1961 memorandum that Rostow sent to the president. "Remarkable Soviet achievements in space . . . have been accompanied by relatively slow increase in the standard of living," Rostow observed. "I don't know what the Soviet Union will do with 250 million tons of steel in 1980 and I doubt Mr. Khrushchev knows either." Rostow also provided Kennedy with a thoughtful explanation as to why the Soviets would fail in their attempt to woo the developing world: "Most of these nations are agricultural nations; and one of the great facts of our times . . . is the record of agriculture under Communism. Whatever virtues communism may claim, it cannot claim it is an efficient system for feeding people."[18] As these observations suggest, Rostow was a perceptive analyst of the Soviet Union's many failings. But he did not feel that the United States could simply hold back and wait patiently for the Soviet Union to implode. Marxism-Leninism for Rostow represented a parasitic threat—with no appeal in and of itself—

but it was a profoundly damaging one. Communist attempts to manipulate the hearts and minds of those impressionable people in the developing world—whether located in the foothills of the Andes or the lush rain forests of the Mekong Delta—required vigorous U.S. resistance. Rostow was in a hurry to see the world's nations pass through his stages of economic growth. America's duty was to help immature societies resist the temptations of Marxism along the way.

To defeat communism comprehensively—to prove that Khrushchev's "conviction of inevitable victory" was misguided—Rostow believed that U.S. foreign policy had to move beyond Eisenhower's limited horizons, and take the fight to America's enemies more directly. In 1959 the authoritarian Cuban leader, Fulgencio Batista, had been ousted by a communist insurgency led by two young idealists: Ernesto "Che" Guevara and Fidel Castro. While Batista was no friend of democracy, his pro-American credentials were impeccable, and the regime that replaced his was dedicated to nationalization and a closer relationship with the Soviet Union. Rostow argued that the United States should act promptly to oust Castro's corrosive dictatorship. The existence of a communist Cuba—situated some ninety miles from Florida—was profoundly damaging to America's credibility, and "Fidel" served as a dangerous example for his Latin American neighbors to emulate. Rostow urged that Kennedy should first depose the insidious communist regime by "covert means" and, second, immunize Latin America from further communist infection by embarking on a massive development project akin to the Marshall Plan—the recovery program that had served so effectively as an anticommunist prophylactic in Western Europe.

Latin America had to be nudged toward Rostovian "take-off," for communists claimed that their creed alone could solve the obdurate socioeconomic problems afflicting the former Spanish colonies. The United States had to prove that Castroism was not the only viable model for poor Latinos struggling to feed their families, without land or power of their own. Over the course of 1961, this requirement was met with the launch of the Alliance for Progress: a massive aid program designed to furnish Latin American nations with $20 billion over the course of the 1960s to facilitate an economic growth rate of 2.5 percent—a figure chosen by Rostow himself.[19]

Beyond Latin America Kennedy increased aid for international development from $2.5 billion per annum (1956–1960) to $4 billion per annum, an increase of 62.5 percent on the funds provided by his Republican pre-decessor.[20] Kennedy took the significant step of setting up the Agency for International Development with the positive Rostovian insistence that "many of the less-developed nations are on the threshold of achieving sufficient economic, social and political strength and self-sustained growth to stand permanently on their own feet." Kennedy followed that up with an appeal that encapsulates his rhetorical reliance on Rostow:

> The 1960s can be—and must be—the crucial "Decade of Develop-ment"—the period when many less developed nations make the transi-tion into self-sustained growth . . . Such a unified effort will help launch the economies of the newly developing countries "into orbit"—bringing them to a stage of self-sustained growth where extraordinary outside as-sistance is not required . . . If this can be done then this decade will be a significant one indeed in the history of free men.[21]

The significance of this speech lies in the fact that Rostow was the au-thor.[22] And we can again trace Rostow's influence on the young president's rhetoric in a speech that he delivered to the American Society of Newspa-per Editors. Kennedy chose to talk expansively and philosophically about the way in which the United States should approach relations with the rest of the world:

> The message of Cuba, of Laos, of the rising din of Communist voices in Asia and Latin America—these messages are all the same. The compla-cent, the self-indulgent, the soft societies are to be swept aside with the de-bris of history. Only the strong . . . the visionary . . . can possibly survive.[23]

In addition to covert action and expanded foreign aid, the third thread of Rostow's vision for U.S. foreign policy involved the use of direct armed force, and it was driven by the same fears of Third World susceptibility to Marxism-Leninism that consumed Kennedy. Communism had made seri-ous inroads in the former French Indochina since General Vo Nguyen Giap's famous victory at Dien Bien Phu. North Vietnam had been offi-cially established as a communist state under the leadership of Ho Chi Minh as part of the Geneva Accords of 1954. Laos and South Vietnam seemed to be on the brink of befalling a similar fate. Faced with a rapidly deteriorating situation in Southeast Asia, Rostow believed that the United States had to repel the communism contagion at virtually all costs. To shirk from the task would be tantamount to throwing the rest of Asia to the dogs. Like most of his colleagues in the Kennedy administration, Rostow believed wholeheartedly in the domino theory: that if one nation fell to communism, its neighbor would soon follow. It was thus imperative that South Vietnam and Laos retain their independence from communism. Were these small, fragile nations to fall, the knock-over effect might later affect Thailand and eventually India. Rostow believed that flexible response should truly prove its elasticity through taking on communist insurgents in arduous terrain some ten thousand miles from Washington, D.C.

Here a number of inconsistencies in Rostow's strategy become apparent. If it was inevitable that communism would fail in the long term, why was it necessary to use military means to defeat a movement that was dying on its feet? Rostow believed that once communism's economic inefficiencies were exposed, popular resentments would become unappeasable, and the movement would cease to exist. He further argued that the repression required to sustain communism would produce a nationalist reaction that could not be extinguished: "While power can be held with economy of force, nationalism in Eastern Europe cannot be defeated; and within Russia, Stalin's tactical evocation of nationalism in the 1930's and 1940's, steadily gathering force, has set up important cross-strains."[24] So how did the potential spread of communism, promised by the domino theory, tally with its inevitable defeat outlined in *The Stages of Economic Growth*? All "stage" theories of group or individual development imply a form of determinism. This leads nonbelievers to wonder why, if history is foreordained, anything need be done at all. Marxism itself is caught in this contradiction. Reading *Das Kapital*, poring over the *Grundrisse*, and waiting expectantly for a new world to emerge was not getting Marx's followers anywhere fast. Communist movements quickly realized that some intervention was required to hurry history along—for example, organizing, consciousness-raising, and, latterly, the funding of insurgent movements. Rostow may well have found a way around this contradiction by claiming that his "stages of growth" were inevitable in the long term, but that short-term indeterminacy necessitated a series of timely interventions. Dispensing foreign aid to ensure that the developing world followed the virtuous path to "high mass consumption" was understandable enough. It dovetailed with Rostow's altruistic belief that U.S. aid should be vastly increased to facilitate Third World economic development. Sending American troops to Southeast Asia, however, was quite another thing. Why were South Vietnam and Laos so important if communism was ephemeral for the reasons that Rostow outlined so incisively in *The Stages of Economic Growth*? This unanswered question runs like a fault line through Rostow's foreign-policy career.

ROSTOW'S NEW JOB TITLE, deputy special assistant for national security affairs, placed him at the very center of executive power in the White House. While Rostow had previously operated in the lecture theaters and seminar rooms of England's and America's elite universities—where scholarly musing, not rapid decision making, was the order of the day—he adapted quickly to his new job coordinating the nation's foreign policy. Clashes of ego are a common occurrence at the highest echelons of government, and McGeorge Bundy and Walt Rostow were no shrinking violets. Nevertheless, the two men negotiated the parameters of their national security brief with little fuss and bother. With overwhelming belief in their own abilities, and little specific knowledge of the areas to which they directed their energies, Bundy and Rostow split the world between them in January 1961. Of the major problem areas, Bundy assumed responsibility for Cuba, the Congo, and Berlin while Rostow "took" Laos, Vietnam, Indonesia, and "the developing world generally."[25] Broadly speaking, Bundy dealt with crises affecting those nations west of Suez and Rostow those to the east. Rostow was clearly the junior partner in this team—Bundy's *deputy* for national security affairs—but the working relationship between the two men was one of rough equality, particularly with regard to access to the president. It was unprecedented for a deputy national security adviser to assume such responsibility and it spoke volumes about Rostow's exalted reputation in January 1961.

Like Rostow, Bundy had enjoyed a glittering career at Yale and in the military, before being appointed dean of Harvard College at just thirty-four years of age.[26] "Mac" was a master of the tart memorandum, a consummate manager with impressive acuity of mind. In many respects the two men were intellectual opposites. While Bundy was direct, pragmatic, and hence suspicious of ideological constructs, Rostow was prolix, dogmatic, and seemingly wedded to theories he had himself created. In later years, after their relationship soured following disputes over Vietnam, Bundy described Rostow acidly as a man who had to decide on an issue "before he thought about it."[27] At the beginning of 1961, however, each man profoundly respected the other's achievements and strengths. According to Rostow, "Mac understood that the president would want me to report through him . . . [and so we] found a common law split which roughly matched our respective talents . . . We would both have been uncomfortable, I think, if we had tried to make it work in a more conventional way."[28] Amid a broad brief, Rostow assumed primary White House responsibility for U.S. policy toward Vietnam. When they divided their areas of geographical responsibility, Bundy and Rostow could hardly have foreseen how significant that distant peninsula would become to the United States.

Kennedy had given Vietnam considerable thought prior to his assumption of the presidency. In the fall of 1951, accompanied by his brother Bobby, Kennedy embarked upon a seven-week tour of Israel, Iran, Pakistan, India, Singapore, Thailand, French Indochina, Korea, and Japan. Kennedy had long believed that it was an urgent priority for the United States to establish a more coherent policy toward the developing world. The young congressman argued that the best way to achieve this was to celebrate the virtues of liberal capitalism and distance American aims from those of the European powers still clinging to their fading imperial *gloire*. In Indochina, Kennedy remarked, the United States had mistakenly

allied ourselves to the desperate effort of a French regime to hang on to the remnants of empire . . . To check the southern drive of communism makes sense but not through reliance on the force of arms. The task is rather to build strong native non-Communist sentiment within these areas and rely on that as a spearhead of defense rather than upon the [French] legions . . . And to do this apart from and in defiance of innately nationalistic aims spells foredoomed failure.[29]

Kennedy's critique of U.S. policy was well founded in the sense that he recognized that noncommunist Vietnam needed a leader of impeccable nationalist credentials—and clear distance from the French colonial regime—to impose any order across a fractious nation. The pony that the U.S. chose to back was Ngo Dinh Diem, a puritanical Catholic who appeared to possess the kind of "Third Force" credentials that State Department analysts had long been striving to locate.[30]

Prior to the Second World War, Diem had resigned from a prominent position under the puppet emperor Bao Dai, whom he castigated not unjustly as a "tool" of the French. In 1945 Diem was imprisoned and exiled to China following clashes with French communists over the best way to remove the Japanese from Indochina. Following release from prison, Diem refused to serve in the short-lived government of Ho Chi Minh—a popularly feted leader whom Diem despised for his Marxist leanings. The fact that Diem antagonized virtually everybody with whom he established contact would serve as his unique selling point in later years. In spite of communist claims to the contrary, Ngo Dinh Diem—while pro-American—was nobody's puppet.

Rather than suffer the ignominy of eking out a living in Ho Chi Minh's Vietnam, Diem sought exile in the United States, where he remained until June 18, 1954, when Bao Dai—South Vietnam's first president—swallowed his pride and summoned Diem to serve as his prime minister. This invitation came back to haunt him. On October 26, 1955, following an election that most observers took to be fraudulent, Diem was elected president of South Vietnam at Bao Dai's expense. Having backed Diem to the hilt, the United States now had little option but to support South Vietnam's new president even when his rule proved repressive and polarizing. This haughty Catholic leader failed to endear himself to the majority Buddhist population. His appointments were invariably nepotistic, and Buddhists held few positions of genuine influence within the government. Diem pursued policies that accorded with his and his wife's religion—such as outlawing divorce and abortion, and banning gambling and opium dens—but his unwillingness to press ahead with progressive political and social reform provoked nationwide antipathy toward his regime. Secretary of State John Foster Dulles conceded that Diem was far from perfect, but "that there is no one to take his place who would serve American interests better." As one perceptive French journalist observed at the time, Diem has that "one rare quality, so precious in Asia. He is pro-American."[31]

Kennedy was a key member of the American Friends of Vietnam (AFV), a pressure group constituting distinguished individuals—including the archbishop of New York, Cardinal Francis Spellman; Senator Mike Mansfield of Montana; the California Republican William Knowland; and the Supreme Court justice William O. Douglas—whose common purpose was to advance the standing of South Vietnamese president Ngo Dinh Diem within the United States. In its statement of purpose, the AFV declared that "a free Vietnam means a greater guarantee of freedom in the world," and that "there is a little bit of all of us in that far-away country."[32] While this lobby group was a potent force in the nation's capital, the Eisenhower administration needed little encouragement to maintain its support for Diem. Through the late 1950s, the U.S. embassy helped foil coup attempts made against Diem, and Washington provided significant financial aid to South Vietnam. From 1955 to 1961, the United States supplied Diem's despotic regime with $1 billion in economic and military assistance. By 1961 South Vietnam ranked fifth among all recipients of American foreign aid and the U.S. diplomatic mission in Saigon was the largest in the world.[33]

Kennedy backed this increased American support for Diem at every point. In a speech to the AFV in 1956, Senator Kennedy declared, "The fundamental tenets of this nation's foreign policy . . . depend in considerable measure upon a strong and free Vietnamese nation . . . Vietnam represents the cornerstone of the Free World in Southeast Asia, the keystone in the arch, the finger in the dike . . . It is our offspring, we cannot abandon it, we cannot ignore its needs."[34] Such sentiments were designed to pack maximum political punch, but they totally undermined Kennedy's diplomatic flexibility as president. Kennedy's rhetoric could not help but tie the United States to a potentially unsustainable proxy that the president would find difficult, if not impossible, to disown. Referring to South Vietnam as "our offspring" compelled the United States to act as the good father. Kennedy said a lot of things while pursuing the presidency that would return to haunt him. He did not live to see the consequences of America's declaration of unconditional support for South Vietnam's independence.

IN DECEMBER 1960 the Democratic Republic of Vietnam (North Vietnam, or DRV) approved the establishment of the National Liberation Front (NLF) in the south. Its avowed aim was "to overthrow the dictatorial . . . Diem clique, lackey of the U.S. imperialists, to form a . . . coalition government in South Vietnam, to win national independence and . . . to achieve national reunification."[35] Edward Lansdale, a well-regarded expert in the field of counterinsurgency methods, had toured Vietnam that same month the NLF was formed. In spite of his close relationship with Diem, he was deeply troubled by what he witnessed. Outside of the cities, the central government evoked neither warmth nor respect and exerted little control. Diem seemed blissfully unaware of his unpopularity and steadfastly refused to implement U.S. demands for military, social, and political reform. While Lansdale was loath to criticize Diem directly, he spelled out the nature of the communist threat unambiguously. He produced a bleak assessment of the situation on the ground, "an extremely vivid and well-written account of a place that was going to hell in a hack," as Rostow recalled. On a crisp Washington morning on January 26, 1961, Rostow "came in to see the president with this [report] in my hand."[36] He had identified the crisis area that was to consume American foreign policy for the next twelve years and destroy a presidency.

Kennedy at first had little time for the report; he was a busy man and field analyses were low on his list of priority reading. Never one to give up easily, Rostow persisted and Kennedy eventually "read every word" before looking up and remarking, "This is the worst one we've got, isn't it?"[37] Lansdale's warnings had struck a chord with an untested president keenly aware of the vitriol heaped on the Truman administration following its "loss" of China. Indeed, Kennedy had joined the bandwagon himself by criticizing Truman's complacency directly. In 1949 Kennedy had declared, "The failure of our foreign policy in the Far East rests squarely with the White House and the Department of State . . . What our young men had saved [in World War II], our diplomats and our president have frittered away."[38] Kennedy's anticommunism now had to be steadfast lest he be deemed an opportunistic hypocrite—an allegation that would carry all the more resonance in light of his previous designation of South Vietnam as the "cornerstone" of the free world. Concerned that Diem might go the same way as the Chinese nationalist leader Chiang Kai-shek, Kennedy ordered Rostow to "go deeply into the problem of Vietnam," an instruction that was eagerly acted upon.[39] Over the course of the year, Rostow unleashed a succession of increasingly bellicose memoranda advocating a vigorous military response to communist violations of the 1954 Geneva Accords in Laos and South Vietnam. For Rostow this initial meeting with JFK was key, a critical juncture in the history of the Vietnam conflict: "From that moment, the president's work on Vietnam, guerrilla warfare and all the rest can be dated."[40]

Rostow was the first adviser to alert Kennedy to the scale of the task ahead in Vietnam, but Eisenhower had identified Laos as the most critical pending challenge to American interests in the region. The historian Ernest May has eloquently criticized the skewed rationale of those cold warriors in 1961 who "*believed* that the fate of at least Southeast Asia and perhaps of the civilized world hinged on what happened in Laos, a landlocked country of mountain hamlets, with three million people who, according to their own king, devoted themselves primarily to singing songs, making love and smoking opium."[41] At the time, however, Laos's survival as a noncommunist state appeared absolutely vital. At the turn of 1961, the communist Pathet Lao group was on the ascendancy, while the U.S.-backed rightist leader, Phoumi Nosavan, was in all kinds of trouble. On January 19, 1961, President Eisenhower advised Kennedy that the fall of Phoumi's Laos to communism would pose a "falling dominoes" threat to Thailand, Cambodia, and South Vietnam. The departing president advised that Kennedy first attempt to deal with the communist insurgency in Laos by deploying a multilateral force sanctioned by the Southeast Asian Treaty Organization (SEATO). But Eisenhower deemed the threat so profound that if allies were not forthcoming, the United States might have to go it alone. Vietnam was not even mentioned during the conversation, having been dismissed as a "back-burner" problem by the outgoing administration.[42] While Vietnam was a curious omission on Eisenhower's part, the two crises were inextricably linked in the minds of some. Rostow helped push Vietnam to the top of the list of U.S. foreign-policy crises—its size, location, and natural resources made it the paramount American concern in Southeast Asia—but he maintained that a resolute American response to the communist insurgency in Laos was an essential corollary to securing South Vietnam's independence.

Two weeks prior to Kennedy's inauguration, Rostow met with Robert Komer, a bright, abrasive member of Bundy's national security team, to discuss potential U.S. responses to a number of flash points overseas. As Komer reported to Bundy, "Walt was most anxious that we bring to the president's attention [four words deleted] on how current Chicom (Chinese communist) economic difficulties are affecting their military . . . Walt, of course, is primarily interested in Laos/Vietnam angle. He regards this as further bolstering unlikelihood of Chicom intervention in SEA, unless we push them very far."[43] Throughout much of 1961, Rostow would regularly make the case that economic disarray in the People's Republic of China gave the United States carte blanche to intervene aggressively in Laos and in South Vietnam.[44] There would be no repeat, in other words, of the Korean War.

Rostow's reading of the situation paid little heed to any influence that ideology might have exerted upon Chinese decision making. The vast nation had suffered terrible economic degradation primarily owing to the failure of the Great Leap Forward, an insanely dogmatic attempt to reconfigure China's agrarian economy that had led to catastrophic famine. But while economic weakness might halt military adventurism in more stable nations, Mao Zedong's China of 1961 was some way from fitting that description. If one adds to the mix the sheer proximity to China of any American troops stationed in Vietnam, Rostow's appraisal looks risky indeed. Two factors did suggest that a Chinese military intervention on the lines of Korea was unlikely: Sino-Vietnamese historical antagonism and the steadily worsening Sino-Soviet split. The former, however, did not figure in Rostow's rationale, while the latter often led to each communist donor trying to outdo the other in terms of equipment supplied to North Vietnam. Economic determinism informed Rostow's contention that China was no serious threat—its economy was laughable, and so its military threat was minimal—but it ignored the significance of *belief*.

Rostow was at first partial to the modish theories of counterinsurgency espoused by Lansdale. Attentive to new developments in military theory—

an interest stimulated by his wartime service with the OSS—Rostow told Rusk on January 6, 1961, that countering communist guerrilla warfare "depended . . . on a mixture of attractive political and economic programs in the underdeveloped areas and a ruthless projection to the peasantry that the central government intends to be the wave of the future."[45] This "ruthless projection" was expressed more evocatively a few months later when Rostow advised the president, "We must somehow bring to bear our unexploited counter-guerrilla assets on the Vietnam problem . . . In Knute Rockne's phrase, we are not saving them for the junior prom."[46] Rostow wanted Vietnam to be taken more seriously than it had been. He strongly believed that the United States had the capacity to deal with the insurgency effectively. But the will of the U.S. government had to be emboldened to match its boundless resources.

Kennedy permitted Rostow to "get the Pentagon and the whole town to take guerrilla warfare seriously," yet overcoming inertia made it a challenging task. Even with the president leading the way, Rostow recalled, "it was like turning the Queen Mary around in the Hudson with a tug . . . to get this business taken seriously."[47] Kennedy ultimately created a new military resource—the Green Berets—to wage counterinsurgency warfare of the type advocated by Lansdale and Rostow. *Newsweek* identified Rostow as the "man behind the plan to increase U.S. guerrilla warfare capabilities," who had given the president "two books by one of the world's recognized authorities on the subject—Red China boss Mao Tse-Tung."[48] But Rostow soon lost faith in the ability of low-intensity warfare to neutralize the NLF. Even the most sophisticated strategy of counterinsurgency in the south, Rostow reasoned, would be circumscribed by northern infiltration through Laos. He believed "that the outcome of a guerrilla war hinged mightily on the degree of external margin—on whether the frontier was open."[49] To win "hearts and minds" in the south, its internal security had to be first guaranteed. Counterinsurgency warfare with an open frontier was an exercise in futility.

Turning first to the crisis in Laos, Rostow criticized the State Department's predilection for "pure diplomacy" and lack of interest in what the coercive force provided by the "CIA and military" might bring "until an acute crisis occurs." Rostow believed that diplomacy and force should be coordinated on the American side, and was aware that "Communist policy" was adept at "orchestrating force and diplomacy intimately at every stage."[50] Later in the month, Rostow advised that the United States might wish to implement the diplomacy/force combination by dispatching a small military unit to Thailand. While "the Seventh Fleet is a marvelous instrument," Rostow observed, it is not "nearly as persuasive as a small unit on the ground."[51] This escalating advice reached its logical conclusion in the spring of 1961, when Rostow first advocated increasing military pressure on Laos to repel communists within its borders and protect South Vietnam from infiltration. Rostow clashed with his immediate boss on this issue.

"When I supported putting troops into the Mekong valley in the spring of 1961," Rostow recalled, "I believe Mac thought I was slightly mad." Rostow ascribed this extreme reaction on Bundy's part to "a slightly Lippmannesque quality in Mac's thought that this part of the world isn't all that serious."[52] Rostow's analysis is interesting as he later used the same argument when confronted with the critiques of the Vietnam War made by George Kennan, the heavyweight journalist Walter Lippmann, and George Ball. Rostow's counterparry was one that contained a great deal of truth—that these men were simply not interested in the fate of the non-European world beyond Japan. But Bundy was no Atlanticist in the mold of Lippmann and Kennan. His later dedication to escalating the Vietnam War—albeit never to the extent urged by Rostow—suggests that Bundy was far from parochial when it came to estimating the communist threat. In ascribing such a rationale to Bundy, Rostow showed early signs of the intellectual rigidity he would display when confronted with doubts on Vietnam. Opponents of the war were either communist sympathizers or uncaring Atlanticists. Dismissing Vietnam critics required little thought on Rostow's part.

ONE ISSUE THAT TENDED to unite those who took an expansive view of the Cold War and those who held a European-centered conception of its legitimate parameters was the Monroe Doctrine of 1823, which warned European powers against interfering in the affairs of the western hemisphere. The continued survival of Fidel Castro's Cuba—in the minds of many, a Soviet Trojan horse—was an affront to principles that had been enunciated over a hundred years ago, and Kennedy felt compelled to do something about it. On the early morning of April 7, some 1,400 Cuban exiles boarded landing craft and moved toward Playa Girón, the Bay of Pigs, with the intention of forcibly removing Castro's regime and liberating the island. "Project Zapata" was planned during the Eisenhower administration, but Kennedy felt obliged to implement it. During his presidential campaign, the young senator had criticized Republicans for being soft on Cuban communism. In one particular televised debate, a simmering Richard Nixon was forced to bite his tongue as Kennedy pilloried Eisenhower's administration for sitting on its hands as Castro augmented his power base. Nixon knew that plans were afoot to topple Fidel but could say nothing lest he give the game away.

Senator Kennedy's macho posturing left him little choice but to greenlight the CIA's optimistic plan to land Cuban exiles on the mainland. The exiles' primary objective was to establish a bridgehead on the island, and then await popular insurrection. But everything that could go wrong did go wrong. The engines of the landing craft failed and the working boats careered into a coral reef that the CIA had mistakenly designated as seaweed. As the bedraggled insurgents finally made their way to shore, Castro's regular army methodically cut them to pieces. It was a disaster of significant dimensions and Kennedy took full responsibility. While he dispensed this task with humility, however, it was CIA Director Allen Dulles, Deputy CIA Director Charles Cabell, and Deputy Director of Operations (and Rostow mentor) Richard Bissell who lost their jobs.

In the aftermath of the debacle, Rostow advised Kennedy to shift the emphasis back toward Southeast Asia: "Viet-Nam is the place where—in the Attorney General's phrase—we must prove that we are not a paper tiger." But Rostow also struck a note of caution, criticizing the rationale that informed the Cuban invasion. "It was mounted on simple ideological grounds," Rostow complained, "and these grounds cannot be generally acceptable. If accepted they would justify any nation which has the military capability and logistical advantage, marching into the territory of a government it does not like." A casus belli had to be more concrete, Rostow reasoned, than simply disliking the leader in question. "We must either do what we do covertly," Rostow continued, "or find a new overt basis for dealing with communist strategy . . . The crucial element may be forms of international action on the question of Communist arms shipments." The deputy national security adviser well understood that appearances were vital, and that the Bay of Pigs invasion *looked* terrible: both flawed in conception and botched in implementation. He concluded his memorandum by cautioning that "when you are in a fight and knocked off your feet, the most dangerous thing to do is to come out swinging wildly."[53] This caution would elude him over the course of the year as Rostow aimed all kinds of punches at the NLF, Laotian communists, and North Vietnam.

On the issue of dispatching a U.S. military force to Laos and its environs, Rostow's recommendations were not heeded at the highest levels of government. Along with the intelligence community and the Joint Chiefs of Staff, Rostow presented various proposals to dispatch U.S. troops to Laos to support the U.S.-sponsored government there. Kennedy, however, refused to bite at every point. The Bay of Pigs disaster had diminished the president's faith in the CIA and the military and he was concerned—in spite of Rostow's sanguinity—that any aggressive U.S. action in Southeast Asia held the potential to provoke a response from the People's Republic of China. Laos was landlocked, furthermore, and presented a logistical nightmare from the military standpoint. John Kenneth Galbraith's advice to Kennedy that as "a military ally the entire Laos nation is clearly inferior to a battalion of conscientious objectors from World War One" may also have struck a chord—its clarity reinforced by a dry wit the president undoubtedly appreciated.[54] Whatever the main reason, Kennedy in late April decided that Laos was not the place to take a military stand, and so he agreed to seek accommodation at a peace conference in Geneva. The president chose Averell Harriman to lead the U.S. negotiation, a man of huge experience in the field of foreign affairs. His influence can indeed be traced through the U.S. rise to internationalism catalyzed by Franklin Delano Roosevelt's presidency. A dedicated public servant with a proud record as a diplomat, Harriman grew to dislike Rostow intensely.[55]

Rostow profoundly disagreed with the president's move to the conference table with respect to the possible neutralization of Laos. But once this fact was established, Rostow's focus moved away from Laos and back toward North Vietnam. On June 28, 1961, Rostow made a speech titled "Guerrilla Warfare in the Underdeveloped Areas" to graduates of the counterinsurgency program at Fort Bragg, North Carolina. "The sending of men across international boundaries . . . is aggression," Rostow observed, and without some form of international action, "those against whom aggression is mounted will be driven to seek out and engage the ultimate source of aggression they confront."[56] Rostow, therefore, became the first man in the Kennedy administration to publicly threaten that the United States might strike North Vietnam: the perceived "source" of aggression in Indochina. In his oral history interview of April 11, 1964, Rostow proudly recalled that his was "the first suggestion that we might have to go north."[57] Yet Rostow's rationale was predicated on a misplaced premise. In June 1961 northern infiltration in aid of the overwhelmingly indigenous insurgency was but a trickle. Even by August 1967, Hanoi would have a maximum of 55,000 North Vietnamese army troops in the south; the remaining 245,000 soldiers were indigenous.[58] The concept of coercing the north to desist through a direct American attack was laid on erroneous foundations.

Two days after his Fort Bragg speech, Rostow proposed to Kennedy three possible means through which the frontier with Laos, the infiltration hot spot, could be closed. The first was diplomacy (of which Rostow was skeptical), the second was to patrol the border through the deployment of ground forces and air attacks, but the third was a "direct attack on North Vietnam sufficiently costly to induce Hanoi to end its war against South Vietnam. I had in mind not only the possibility of air action but, after a suitable program of diplomatic warning, moving forces into North Vietnam itself."[59] It is worthwhile pausing here to appreciate the unsurpassed bellicosity that informed this recommendation. Nobody came close to advocating options as controversial as the bombing and invasion of North Vietnam in the summer of 1961. Indeed, it would be some years before such options were even discussed at the highest levels. Yet Rostow persisted in pushing a policy well out of step with prevailing orthodoxy.

While his views on resolving the Vietnamese insurgency were unique with regard to their martial intent, Rostow again touted the panacea of military coercion—again, with little support—as a possible solution to the Berlin crisis. In 1961 Khrushchev had cranked up the heat on Kennedy by threatening to withdraw Soviet forces from Berlin and cede control of access routes to the city to East Germany. Such an action would have substantially increased the likelihood that the German Democratic Republic would unilaterally remove the anomaly of having a Western enclave within its communist borders. Rostow on this issue was as partial to nuclear brinkmanship as he was in earlier years as a consultant to Eisenhower: "We must find ways of putting pressure on Khrushchev's side of the line with conventional forces or by other means." Rostow advised Kennedy that "we must be prepared to increase the risk of war on his side of the line as well as facing it on ours." The United States should wait, in other words, for the other side to blink.

As Rostow's memorandum unfolds, its intensity increases; the tone becomes more strident. "We must begin now to present Khrushchev with the risk that if he heightens the Berlin crisis, we and the West Germans may take action that will cause East Germany to come unstuck." For Rostow this meant not simply sending a "divisional probe down the Autobahn," which he considered an insufficiently stern signal, "but to take and hold a piece of territory in East Germany that Khrushchev may not wish to lose (for example, Magdeburg)." Rostow's speculative conclusion is hardly surprising given the aggression of what had come before: "the crisis raises the question of whether we may not wish to place some tactical nuclear weapons in Berlin at an appropriate tense moment."[60] Rostow guessed that the threat of such actions would "reduce" the Soviet leader's appetite "for a Berlin crisis."[61]

There is little doubt that Rostow's recommendations constitute an interesting strategy: a precursor to Richard Nixon's "madman theory," which aimed to convince the Soviet Union that the president was an uncontrollable anticommunist who was capable of anything. There can be little doubt, furthermore, that implementation of Rostow's strategy would have shaken Nikita Khrushchev to his very core. What is surprising is that Rostow reveals no fear that nuclear saber-rattling and the U.S. invasion of East Germany might lead not to a Soviet climb-down, but to a full-scale military retaliation—World War III, in other words. This was an outcome that appeared not to faze him.

For Rostow, a resolute American response to communist troublemaking in Germany and Vietnam required immediate, and possibly concurrent, action. The use of air power in Vietnam, Rostow wrote Kennedy again on June 30, "puts pressure on the point that is not merely the source of aggression but a point of true anxiety and vulnerability on the communist side—Hanoi." Conceding that such actions "put a very serious issue to both Moscow and Peiping," he points out that "it does so at a moment when Soviet missile capabilities are incomplete; before Peiping has nuclear weapons [and] at a time of great hunger and relative weakness in China." Rostow advised that the United States provide ample warning before implementing any bombing campaign or invasion strategy as it "offers the Communists ample opportunity to draw back if they are not prepared to press their offensive all the way to nuclear war." If nuclear hostilities commence, however, "we had better face it now [rather] than two years from now, in Southeast Asia as well as in Central Europe."[62] And so five months into his first job in government, Walt Rostow—an economic historian and theorist of Third World development, lest we forget—advised the president that he consider waging nuclear war in two separate theaters. Rostow later recalled that nuclear war was Kennedy's "greatest nightmare."[63] In this respect, the deputy national security adviser's belligerency could not help but lead the president to question the otherworldly quality of his counsel.

Rostow's fixation on North Vietnam was further manifested on July 13, 1961, when he proposed to Dean Rusk that the United States should aim to "impose" on Hanoi "about the same level of damage and inconvenience that the Viet Cong are imposing on the South . . . using American Air and Naval strength." If in response the North Vietnamese were to "cross their border substantially," Rostow suggested the United States should implement "a limited military operation in the north, e.g. [the] capture and holding of the port of Haiphong."[64] Like the "capture Magdeburg" gambit, it would seem that the word "limited" does some injustice to the sheer scope and complexity of attempting to capture a city in enemy territory. Rostow was temperamentally inclined to ignore the most imposing of odds. He was also disinclined to contemplate the death and destruction that his recommendations held the potential to wreak. His approach to problems was conceptual, and often brutal. As Nicholas Katzenbach—who served as attorney general and undersecretary of state—remarked despairingly to a colleague in later years, "I finally understand the difference between Walt and me. I was the navigator who was shot down and spent two years in a German prison camp, and Walt was the guy picking my targets."[65]

On the subject of military escalation in Berlin, Rostow's was a lonely voice. On Vietnam, however, his views on crushing the NLF by attacking its perceived "source" in North Vietnam were gaining respectability. And all the while Rostow worked diligently at the task to which he had devoted the bulk of his academic career: creating institutional machinery through which the United States could disburse foreign aid to the developing world. One day Rostow would advocate military steps that held the potential to precipitate nuclear war, the next he worked on establishing an expansive U.S. aid policy to combat world poverty. Jack and Bobby Kennedy, Maxwell Taylor, and Robert McNamara all fit the description of the liberal cold warrior. These men combined toughness toward communism with an appreciation that the sources of global poverty required keen attention. Disadvantaged peoples mired in poverty tended to see communism simply as a route to escape. The liberal cold warrior reasoned that to provide hope to these people would be to diminish communism's appeal. Walt Rostow took these two priorities to their polar extremes. He was the ultraliberal, über–cold warrior.

DURING THE SUMMER and autumn of 1961, Rostow proselytized on the issue of attacking North Vietnam, while the president and his foreign-policy principals—McGeorge Bundy, McNamara, and Rusk—dithered as to what constituted the best way forward. As Rostow wrote Kennedy on August 17, "We must produce quickly a course of action which convinces the other side that we are dead serious."[66] In September the NLF significantly stepped up their offensive operations, and had even seized control of a provincial capital just fifty-five miles from Saigon. While Kennedy was not convinced that South Vietnam's position was so parlous that it merited the extreme response advocated by Rostow, he did want further information at hand before any military decision was made. To this end, Kennedy informed Rostow that he wanted him to travel to Saigon to assess the situation firsthand and propose remedies to any problems encountered. On October 13, 1961, the president announced that General Maxwell Taylor would head up this fact-finding mission and that their departure was imminent.

Taylor possessed a glittering military record, having served with distinction during the Italian campaign and parachuted with his troops into Normandy on D-Day. Taylor later served as the superintendent of West

Point (1945–1949) and as the U.S. commander in Berlin (1949–1951) before returning to the field during the Korean War (1950–1953). From 1955 to 1959, Taylor served as Eisenhower's army chief of staff but, contemptuous of "massive retaliation" as a credible strategy of deterrence, he resigned his position to complete a book project. In 1959 the intellectually gifted general published *The Uncertain Trumpet,* a critically well-received tome that outlined a new approach to U.S. diplomacy that was strikingly similar to Kennedy's "flexible response." Recognizing Taylor as a kindred spirit, Kennedy appointed him to serve as his military representative and opted to send him to South Vietnam with another young, creative defense intellectual. Maxwell Taylor was enthusiastic about his traveling companion: "Walt Rostow was of great help partly because of his broad historical approach to events taking place in Southeast Asia."[67] Taylor does not elaborate on what this might mean; Rostow presumably infused the mission with the spirit of historical optimism that underscored *The Stages of Economic Growth.* But in choosing Rostow to accompany Maxwell Taylor, Kennedy had made a rather surprising choice.

On October 9, 1961, the Joint Chiefs of Staff had summarily rejected a Rostow proposal that a SEATO army of 25,000 men be dispatched between the demilitarized zone (DMZ) and Cambodia to prevent infiltration along the Vietnam-Laos border. The Joint Chiefs were scathing in their assessment of Rostow's military rationale: a force deployment of this kind was susceptible to North Vietnamese or Chinese assault, the supply difficulties were horrendous, and its thin spread meant the troops were vulnerable to being "attacked piecemeal or by-passed at the Viet Cong's own choice."[68] Rostow's military recommendations were being disparaged for their lack of battlefield realism by the people that mattered most. And so while the military held serious reservations about Rostow's ability to formulate a tenable military strategy, was it the case that the president had fewer qualms? The most likely explanation for the president's decision to send Rostow to South Vietnam is that Kennedy wanted an aggressive report and knew that Rostow and Taylor would provide it, but desired latitude with regard to implementation. By choosing a maverick such as Rostow, Kennedy could easily reject the report's conclusions if they were not to his liking. "Well, Rostow would say that . . ." was an excellent get-out clause.

THE TAYLOR-ROSTOW MISSION marked a break of sorts with the theory, championed by Edward Lansdale, that pacification in the south was the key to successful resolution of the conflict. Maxwell Taylor evinced no interest in the complex questions for which Lansdale sought answers—such as how to make the South Vietnamese government more appealing to its citizens— and Rostow readily acquiesced.[69] Instead, Rostow sought to discover for himself why communism held appeal in the south, and in little time formed a theory. Rostow interviewed a series of captive NLF insurgents and described them as "young men in a developing region who had been caught up for the first time—and found various degrees of satisfaction and disappointment—in a modern organizational structure reaching beyond the family, hamlet and village."[70] Rostow had thus concluded that the NLF's appeal lay not in its espousal of nationalism or communism, but because it represented a large modern institution.

Discounting the possibility that the South Vietnamese insurgents sought national reunification on grounds of patriotic cohesion, or a belief in the necessity of the redistribution of wealth, Rostow instead discerned a desire on the part of the NLF to be "modern." Denigrating the ideological foundations of the southern insurgency followed logically from the economic determinism implicit in his academic work. He slotted the NLF neatly into the value system outlined in his academic work, with "modernization" driving people and societies toward a capitalist end point through the ages. Rostow viewed the Vietnamese condescendingly as confused, naïve, and hence restive rather than angry, economically disadvantaged, and hence inclined toward not just nationalism but Marxism-Leninism. *The Stages of Economic Growth* skillfully showed why communism would fail as a political and economic system. Yet Rostow's prior certainties about Marxism's flaws blinded him to the reality that poor people find the promise of radical equality appealing. His disregard for the sources that motivated South Vietnamese insurgents to fight for national reunification encouraged Rostow to offer a familiar solution to what was a problem of some complexity. He concluded that NLF insurgents were misguided and that North Vietnam was the real villain of the piece, instigating most of the troubles that afflicted Diem's regime.

Today the Taylor-Rostow report is remembered for its recommendation that six to eight thousand American combat troops in the guise of "flood-relief workers" be dispatched to South Vietnam.[71] Less well remembered is the Taylor-Rostow suggestion that the United States should consider liberating the north if they maintained their aggression: that they "not only had something to gain—the South—but a base to risk—the North—if war should come."[72] This startling proposal was supplemented by Rostow's idée fixe: bombing the north. As Taylor and Rostow cabled Kennedy on October 23, 1961, "NVN is extremely vulnerable to conventional bombing, a weakness which should be exploited diplomatically in convincing Hanoi to lay off SVN."[73] The report concluded by urging that all options be kept open with regard to coercing the north. "In our view, nothing is more calculated to sober the enemy and to discourage escalation in the face of limited initiatives proposed here than the knowledge that the United States has prepared itself soundly to deal with aggression at any level."[74] "At any level" was the operative phrase in this instance. This belief that the threat of impending force would constitute a sufficient deterrent formed the crux of what would become known as the "Rostow Thesis." Ho Chi Minh had a base to lose. Ideological considerations were secondary to those of economic growth. Bombing, even the threat of bombing, would prove sufficient to curb a southern insurgency primarily instigated by the north. And China would not dare intervene because "I do not see how a country which is depending on Australia and Canada for a critical margin for feeding its cities . . . would go to war except as a suicidal act."[75] Rostow believed that the timing could not be more propitious for the United States to launch a military assault against North Vietnam.

Kennedy, however, was not wholly receptive to such reasoning. He confided to Special Assistant Arthur Schlesinger Jr. that sending U.S. combat troops to Vietnam "will be just like Berlin. The troops will march in; the bands will play; the crowds will cheer; and in four days everyone will have forgotten. Then we will be told we have to send in more troops. It's like taking a drink. The effect wears off, and you have to take another."[76] The president rejected the troop option out of hand, yet concurred with the report's conviction that the situation was critical, that action was required. As Rostow recalled, "The advisory structure the Taylor mission outlined was, essentially, approved; the number of American advisers expanded rapidly;

and the support for the South Vietnamese in military hardware and other resources was substantially increased." This appraisal is essentially correct. The Taylor-Rostow report substantially expanded the American commitment to South Vietnam both in aid and "advisers." Significantly, the concept of bombing the north had also been rationalized, for use at a later time. Chester Bowles later referred to the report as "the beginning of the end."[77] George Ball warned with remarkable foresight that "within five years we'll have three hundred thousand men in the paddies and jungles and we'll never find them again. That was the French experience. Vietnam is the worst possible terrain from both a physical and political point of view." On November 7 Ball told an aide, "We're heading hell-bent into a mess and there's not a Goddamn thing I can do about it. Either everybody else is crazy or I am."[78] As it turned out, everyone else was crazy.

At the conclusion of the cabinet meeting called to discuss the report, Kennedy opined that "if this doesn't work perhaps we'll have to try Walt's Plan Six."[79] This remark was made in jest—"Walt's Plan Six," attacking North Vietnam, was simply a pun on SEATO Plan Five, the military contingency for protecting Laos—but was to prove prescient in the sense that Walt's Plan Six was indeed implemented in later years. Doubts were forming in the president's mind, however, about the equanimity with which Rostow contemplated war. Speaking to the National Security Council staff member Michael Forrestal, Kennedy remarked, "Walt is a fountain of ideas; perhaps one in ten of them is absolutely brilliant. Unfortunately six or seven are not merely unsound, but dangerously so. I admire his creativity, but it will be more comfortable to have him creating at some remove from the White House."[80] Rostow had simply overwhelmed the president with his output, a great deal of which was considered suspect. Kennedy once remarked, "Walt can write faster than I can read," and this was not meant as a compliment.[81] Such prolixity was useful in certain environments—such as in the academy—but not so useful in the White House with a president who "put a premium . . . on laconic, decided peoples."[82] And so, as part of what became known as the "Thanksgiving Day Massacre," Rostow was moved on November 29, 1961, to serve as chairman and counselor of the newly named Policy Planning Council at the State Department.

THE POLICY PLANNING STAFF was originally established in 1947 to perform four main functions: to "formulate long-term programs for the achievement of U.S. foreign policy objectives . . . anticipate problems for the Department of State . . . study and report on broad politico-military problems . . . [and] evaluate and advise on the adequacy of current programs."[83] Secretary of State George Marshall selected George Kennan to serve as the planning staff's first, most illustrious chairman. Kennan was charged with a specific task: to rebuild Western Europe and save it from a communist fate. As Kennan recalled in his memoir, his only instruction was "to avoid trivia."[84] As the Cold War developed, however, momentum for the planning of foreign-policy initiatives came increasingly from the National Security Council and far less from State. As the policy planning staff's influence waned vis-à-vis the NSC, so did the quality of the incumbents and the power afforded them. Rostow was appointed to a position occupied not just by the brilliant Kennan, but by Robert Bowie, Gerard Smith, and George McGhee—three names that do not loom particularly large in the history of twentieth-century U.S. foreign policy. While the chairmanship of the policy planning staff was a great opportunity in the right hands, it also held the unnerving potential to represent a graveyard for ambition.

Prior to Rostow's departure to the State Department, Kennedy told him, "Over here at the White House . . . we are pretty much restricted to what comes out of the bureaucracy. I want you to go over [there] to State and catch hold of the process where it counts."[85] Kennedy's parting words were, in all likelihood, motivated by a desire to provide Rostow with some restorative cheer. The former deputy national security adviser had referred to his shift ambivalently as leaving "his comfortable and cheerful parish church in Rome to become a bishop or something—in the provinces."[86] It would be wrong, however, to characterize Rostow's move to the State Department as a simple demotion. Chairman of the policy planning staff was the job that Rostow was originally slated for—it was his preferred position in January 1961. What he lost in terms of proximity to the president was made up, to some degree, by the acquisition of a serious staff. Rostow now exerted far more control over what issues he could focus on. James Reston in *The New York Times* wrote that if the president were to make foreign policy more effective "he had to do it, not by relying so much

on his White House Staff, but by strengthening the State Department . . .
Accordingly Mr. Rostow was moved to . . . State."[87]

Yet while planning had its intellectual rewards, there is little doubt that
Kennedy had positioned Rostow at a significant distance from his inner circle—both literally and figuratively. Adamant that he would retain a serious
channel to Kennedy, Rostow "took steps to keep the lines to the president
open through three channels: Bundy's shop, the sending of planning papers to the president for weekend reading, and direct personal communications."[88] Rostow later recalled that "because of his voracious reading habits
[Kennedy] was able to follow the evolution of a major planning paper all
the way through."[89] It does seem unlikely that a president who continued
to place a premium on getting to the point digested Rostow's often voluminous reports diligently. His prolixity did not abate with time and distance.

At the State Department, Rostow was soon given an important job: the
creation of a policy planning document designed to serve as a blueprint for
the administration's foreign policy. The task was truly significant, but the
degree to which the proposed document carried a guiding sanction remained undecided. On December 6, 1961, the NSC staffer Robert Komer
advised Rostow that he should aim to inject some forceful clarity into the
workings of the Policy Planning Council: "State has an in-built tendency to
emphasize the risks of doing something as opposed to the costs of doing
nothing. Seldom do I see the latter indicated as explicitly as it should be.
This is a perspective that S/P [State/Planning] could help [encourage]."[90]
Rostow was certainly not shy about stressing the costs of "doing nothing" in
Southeast Asia. While he had been removed from the core group charged
with Vietnam planning, he soon recovered from the blow and put his mind
to how U.S. foreign policy should tackle other areas of the world utilizing
nonmilitary means. He redirected some of his energies, for example, toward
creating new initiatives to spur Latin American economic development.

But Rostow would not let Vietnam go. His final memorandum of the
year to Kennedy was characteristically forthright: "I do not believe that all
the choppers and other gadgetry we can supply South Viet-Nam will buy
time and render their resources effective if we do not get a first-class man
out there to replace [General Lionel] McGarr."[91] Rostow believed that
General McGarr—the highest-ranking U.S. military general in the region
as head of the Military Assistance Advisory Group, Vietnam (MAAG)—

was overconcerned with pacifying the south and improving its government at the expense of transforming the South Vietnamese Army (ARVN) into a battle-ready machine, ready to take on the NLF in conventional engagements. Rostow's was not a lone critical voice, but he brutally expressed the rationale for removing McGarr better than anyone else. On December 23 the chairman of the Joint Chiefs of Staff, General Lyman Lemnitzer, informed McGarr that he was on the way out. McGarr was upset by the decision "professionally and personally" but his main concern was that Washington policymakers were misguidedly trying to solve "a very unconventional situation in a basically conventional manner."[92]

The MAAG group was downgraded following McGarr's departure and the Military Assistance Command, Vietnam (MACV)—activated on February 8, 1962—assumed primary responsibility for the direction of U.S. military units and aid. This change was not simply one of acronym, but represented a fundamental shift in the way that the United States approached the war. Bruce Palmer, who later served as army chief of staff, charged that the downgrading of MAAG was a critical mistake, that it signaled a shift in emphasis from the development and training of native forces to the provision of U.S. military aid and muscle, hard and simple.[93] It was a move that Rostow had advocated throughout the year, and would continue to do so throughout the conflict. The U.S. military in this view had the undoubted capacity to deal with the southern insurgency promptly and efficiently. Rostow was confident that the armed forces, having helped America defeat the potent military power that was Nazi Germany, could achieve rapid success in undertaking the less daunting task of safeguarding South Vietnam's independence. To win this battle decisively, however, meant supplying the army with the right resources, and charging it with the power to use them. In his report with Maxwell Taylor, Rostow had helped draft a military blueprint for the Americanization of the Vietnam War. It was now up to the president to decide whether he wanted to follow their advice by taking the fight northward to Ho Chi Minh's North Vietnam.

FOUR

A DISTANT VOICE

1962–1963

FOR ROSTOW'S SABER-RATTLING on Vietnam, Kennedy had moved him to a more contemplative environment in which he could do less immediate damage. Yet in line with what the Taylor-Rostow report had urged in November 1961, the U.S. commitment to South Vietnam intensified steadily over the next two years. Over the course of 1962, the number of American "advisers" sent to help train the South Vietnamese army increased from 3,205 to over 9,000, while the overall provision of U.S.-supplied hardware doubled.[1] Nineteen sixty-two was also the year that Kennedy first authorized the use of what was to become a controversial military device: chemical defoliants were deployed to spoil NLF food supplies and strip the forests of their protective foliage.[2] Through an increasingly incendiary series of means, the United States increased its stake in a successful resolution of the conflict. With each American who reached South Vietnam, the possibility of a plausible exit strategy receded even more.

But this increase in America's military presence appeared to be making its mark on the conflict. Local intelligence suggested that the NLF's momentum had been stymied in the face of what was now a well-supplied, professionally drilled opponent.[3] Pentagon officials were optimistic that the communist insurgents were retreating in the face of superior military hardware and a revitalized South Vietnamese army. The use of U.S.-supplied helicopters, for example, gave the ARVN an undeniable, if ephemeral, edge during direct military engagements. As Roger Hilsman recalled, "Roaring in over the tree-tops, they were a terrifying sight to the superstitious Viet Cong peasant. In those first few months, the Viet Cong simply turned and ran—and flushed from their foxholes and hiding places, and running in the open, they were easy targets."[4] Yet those insurgents would not remain intimidated by the American helicopters for long.

One person, at least, was not impressed with this escalation of America's commitment. Walt Rostow feared that Kennedy was simply not serious about defeating communism in South Vietnam. If he was, Rostow reasoned, then the president would have ordered a direct attack on North Vietnam when he had suggested it, in the summer of 1961. Years later, in his memoir, Rostow revealed the true extent of his disappointment. He judged Kennedy's failure to move promptly and decisively against North Vietnam during the first year of his presidency "as the greatest single error in American foreign policy in the 1960s."[5] The president certainly did not have the excuse of not having warnings and solutions available to him at the time. Rostow had unleashed a series of belligerent memoranda arguing a similar point each time—hit the north—and each was met with deafening silence. Robert McNamara, McGeorge Bundy, and Dean Rusk were all unwilling to accept that bombing the north, and dispatching U.S. troops in serious numbers, was necessary to protect South Vietnam's independence. It was not until the close of 1963 that Rostow's plans for attacking North Vietnam were taken seriously again at the highest levels.

Rostow failed to convince Kennedy of the severity of the situation. While Rostow was unrelenting in his advice that North Vietnam be bombed, Kennedy had become convinced that the key to building a credible South Vietnamese nation was winning the "hearts and minds" of the populace. Rostow's theories on "modernization" were ironically and inadvertently to help shape what became the Kennedy administration's central strategy for defeating communism in South Vietnam: the strategic hamlet program.

IN SOUTHEAST ASIA the driving force behind revolutionary change came not from the proletariat of the cities, as Karl Marx envisaged, but from those living in the countryside, as Mao Zedong's 1949 success exemplified. Rostow's catchy explanation for this divergence was that "Marx was a city boy."[6] Over 85 percent of South Vietnam's population of four-teen million lived in rural settlements.[7] In order to blunt the appeal of the NLF, therefore, and to regain a measure of control over the countryside, thousands of fortified strategic hamlets were forged from the existing vil-lage communities of South Vietnam. To paraphrase Mao Zedong, the goal was to drain the insurgent fish from the sea of peasantry. South Viet-nam's rural communities would be uprooted by central government and then put together again.

The director of the State Department's bureau of intelligence and re-search, Roger Hilsman, presented the program's blueprint—"A Strategic Concept for South Vietnam"—to Kennedy on February 2, 1962. Hilsman operated from the same set of guiding principles as Rostow: communist insurgencies were a global threat that fed off powerful social forces un-leashed by the drive to modernization. As the historian Douglas Blaufarb observes, "Hilsman's effort took Rostow's analysis as a starting point but opened new terrain and in the process introduced new complexities."[8] At heart, however, the plan was far from complex; it constituted a crude at-tempt at social engineering. Hilsman correctly identified that South Viet-nam's villages provided sustenance, recruits, and a safe haven for the NLF. To prevent the insurgents from requisitioning these vital commodities— often through coercion—he contended that the South Vietnamese gov-ernment had to provide villagers with a draconian form of physical security. He proposed that a series of fortified hamlets be established with bamboo-spiked ditches dug around the exterior and barbed wire attached to the hamlet itself. South Vietnam's villagers would then be removed from their traditional homes and relocated to these fortified oases of non-communist security. In the words of the influential head of the British Advisory Mission in Vietnam, Robert Thompson, "Curfews will be intro-duced on certain roads and waterways and in areas surrounding defended hamlets . . . from 7.00 pm until 6.00 am. The necessary authority will be given for the security forces to shoot on sight anyone breaking the cur-few."[9] The program was designed to cut off at the source the assistance that South Vietnam's villagers provided the NLF.

While American and British advisers like Hilsman and Thompson were significant forces behind the strategic hamlet program as implemented, President Diem and his brother Ngo Dinh Nhu also contributed greatly to its planning and realization.[10] The program had indigenous precursors. The Agroville (*khu tru mat*) program was introduced by the Diem regime in July 1959, and had sought to regroup thousands of peasants in the Mekong Delta into newly built settlements. The aim was both to provide security to the people and to stimulate regional economic development. Only twenty Agrovilles were created, however, and they soon dissolved owing to the fact that South Vietnam's peasants did not take well to forced relocation at the behest of a distant Catholic president. Yet when the U.S. government proposed swift implementation of the strategic hamlet program in 1962, Diem enthusiastically embraced a program that bore striking similarities to one that had so recently failed. The president sought to use the program to mobilize the population politically and drum up support for his unloved regime. And his brother Nhu remained hopeful that an Agroville-style program might spur significant economic development. In a speech delivered to the graduating class of the National Institute of Administration, Nhu referred directly to Rostow's *The Stages of Economic Growth* and the necessity that "traditional society" be overcome to make way for "economic take-off." Diem and Nhu sought to implement the program to assert their will over the people and to facilitate economic growth of the type predicted by Walt Rostow.[11]

In explaining why forced relocation was good for the peasants, the South Vietnamese government highlighted the dangers that the communist insurgents posed to their livelihood: the NLF could attack their villages and liberate their grain and supplies with impunity. But such justifications were perplexing to poor farmers who had little need for protection from the NLF. Rather, it was the landlords and government officials—those with the most to lose from radical land reform—who did. Furthermore, insufficient matériel was provided to the hamlets' inhabitants. They were compelled to give much of their own labor and resources to build the defense stockades and installations that fenced them in. As the officer in charge of Vietnamese affairs reported to Frederick Nolting, the U.S. ambassador in Saigon, "The burden on the local populations is heavy. I believe the villagers are generally buying their own barbed wire."[12] As David Halberstam aptly put it, "It was little wonder that the Vietcong looked like Robin Hoods when they began to hit the hamlets."[13] The strategic hamlet program was little less than an assault on the organic structure of agrarian society and it signally failed either to modernize South Vietnam or to negate the appeal of the NLF. As *The Pentagon Papers* concludes: "It may be that the [strategic hamlet] program was doomed at the outset because of measures which changed the pattern of rural life . . . The Strategic Hamlets Program was fatally flawed in its conception by the unintended consequence of alienating many of those whose loyalty it aimed to win."[14]

By the spring of 1963, only 1,500 of the 8,500 strategic hamlets remained viable. These figures contrast starkly with the fact that by June 1963 the NLF was levying taxes in forty-two of South Vietnam's forty-four provinces.[15] In his memoir *To Move a Nation*, Roger Hilsman ruefully admits that the hamlets eventually served as a well-supplied weapons dump into which the NLF could dip with little fear of reprisal.[16] The hamlets themselves came to be deployed offensively against South Vietnamese and American troops. The barbed wire was removed, cut up, and used in mines and booby traps. When the Vietcong liberated a hamlet, the peasants would gratefully leave, but not before removing the sheet-metal roofing for use in restoring their ancestral homes. In September 1963 United Press International's Neil Sheehan reported that the strategic hamlets were little more than "ghost towns along the road. From a helicopter the sense of the guerrilla's power was greater and those ghost hamlets stranger. The rows of roofless houses looked like villages of play huts that children had erected and then whimsically abandoned."[17] As Policy Planning Council staff member Robert Johnson wrote to his boss, the strategic hamlet program as early as October 1962 was "mostly pure façade."[18]

One would expect Rostow to be enthusiastic about a program that put a premium on developing village communities and attaching these "clusters" to the modernizing force represented by central government. His intellectual imprint on the program is indeed clear. The program was about modernizing South Vietnam, about combating the assault of "parasitic" communism. The assumptions that informed the plan were born of an intellectual hubris that was especially potent in the America of the 1950s and early 1960s.

The Yale anthropologist James C. Scott has written eloquently and provocatively about the unfounded self-confidence that drove U.S. foreign policy and the dream of exporting alien values to foreign cultures. Of those rational planners who imposed visionary schemes such as the strategic hamlet program, Scott writes, "The progenitors of such plans regarded themselves as far smarter and farseeing than they really were and, at the same time, regarded their subjects as far more stupid and incompetent than they really were."[19] To American policymakers in the early 1960s, South Vietnam represented a malleable construct to be pushed toward modernity. In February 1961 Kenneth Young—a Kennedy adviser and later U.S. ambassador to Thailand—sent a memorandum to Rostow that encapsulated the rationale that would inform the strategic hamlet program. Speaking generally of East Asia, Young defined America's task as tantamount to "social chemistry—putting the molecules of villages together one by one until over the years they aggregate a social band or belt across that circle of land. Our job is to pitch a hard ball into this catcher's mit [sic] of Asia."[20] These sentiments speak volumes about the surfeit of confidence that energized Kennedy's foreign-policy cohort. Such belief drove men to impose schemes with little regard to a particular situation on the ground because blind trust in the universal applicability of "modernization" rendered area studies—the study and appreciation of those local conditions—irrelevant.

The violent opposition that greeted the strategic hamlet program was for many, including Rostow, difficult to comprehend. Resistance to such an inevitable and beneficial process was anachronistic and simply a sign of what Rostow would describe as the long-run fatalism of the "traditional person."[21] Of course, North Vietnamese communists were similarly not averse to imposing top-down planning on a recalcitrant population. Indeed, the hubris of communist societal planning, and the brutality that its cadres visited upon those who failed to get with the program—in North Vietnam, and with inhuman venom in Cambodia—far exceeded anything that Nhu's men managed to achieve. Yet the appeal of communism was real: NLF fighters restored land-use rights, provided security from central government encroachment, and opposed the inequitable land tenure system that the Saigon government left virtually untouched. Catering to these basic needs, and tapping into latent nationalism, the NLF achieved remarkable success in winning the allegiance of the South Vietnamese peasantry.

Rostow was ideologically incapable of understanding this appeal, and in later years he explained the failure of the strategic hamlet program with sole reference to the unguarded open frontier that allowed North Vietnam to send soldiers southward through Laos. In this instance Rostow's explanation fails to pass muster: the North Vietnamese Army did not commence significant infiltration into South Vietnam until the autumn of 1964. Nevertheless, "while I had great sympathy for American efforts to press toward pacification and village development," Rostow recalled, "I was skeptical that Vietnam could be saved, except at prohibitive cost, if the Vietnamese frontier remained open to infiltration."[22] The development theorist gave way to the bombing advocate as South Vietnam proved immune to modernization on the Western model. The implementation of the strategic hamlet program was like watching an infant attempt to hammer a square plastic block through a triangle-shaped hole. The emergence of a communist South Vietnam did not fit into the schema of liberal capitalist progress outlined in *The Stages of Economic Growth,* and so its viability would be achieved by devastating its enemy. The problem was that this theory ignored the reality that South Vietnam was being torn apart by a civil war. Rostow believed that the communist threat to the south came overwhelmingly from the north, but the NLF had overwhelming indigenous roots.[23]

While bombing North Vietnam was not seriously considered at this stage by those in charge of U.S. foreign-policy planning, the merits of a direct attack were identified in November 1962 by an unlikely source. The French intellectual Bernard Fall wrote on November 24 that while "North Vietnam is not becoming a Japan, it is acquiring an industrial backbone stronger than that of any non-Communist country on the Southeast Asian mainland . . . While Ho's guerrillas in South Vietnam can evade American air power, his factories in North Vietnam are extremely vulnerable."[24] Fall marshaled persuasive anecdotal evidence that suggested that Pham Van Dong—the effective, if not titular, leader of North Vietnam in the 1960s—was genuinely concerned by the prospect of direct attack. "The North Vietnamese genuinely fear American retaliation," he wrote. "They fear it not only because it would wreck their country but because it would raise the specter of Communist Chinese intervention and occupation."[25]

Rostow's was not a lone voice, therefore. He had allies in the military, and his thesis was being given inadvertent support by a celebrated war correspondent and historian. Fall's appraisal was based not on flimsy conjecture, but on a direct interview that he had secured with Pham Van

Dong—detailed in his journalism and his fascinating memoir *Viet-Nam Witness*.[26] The historian Robert Brigham has recently backed up the veracity of Fall's reporting, persuasively showing in *Guerrilla Diplomacy* that the prospect of American aerial bombardment frightened the North Vietnamese leadership terribly.[27] It is thus clear that North Vietnam was concerned at the prospect of its cities being bombed by the most powerful military in the world—to be otherwise would have been irrational. But whether a U.S. bombing campaign would be coercive enough to convince North Vietnam to abandon its campaign for national reunification was another question entirely. Regardless, Rostow lacked serious support within government and so his radical strategy fell on deaf ears. His attention now turned to a weighty task that the president had allocated to him as chairman of the Policy Planning Council—the creation of a statement of Basic National Security Policy (BNSP).

IN *Strategies of Containment*, the historian John Lewis Gaddis describes Walt Rostow's 284-page BNSP statement as "the most comprehensive guide to what the [Kennedy administration] was trying to do in world affairs."[28] Completed in various draft forms from March 12 to June 22, 1962, Rostow's paper represented a bold attempt to formulate what he described as "clear statements of policy," while at the same time "frankly identifying unsolved problems." The degree to which the paper served as a "comprehensive guide" to U.S. foreign affairs, however, is less significant than Gaddis asserts. Kennedy was wary of the project from the outset, being doubtful of the utility, and fearful of the consequences, of putting his name to a "guide" to foreign policy. Rostow himself was aware that the BNSP was unlikely to serve as holy writ, writing to Dean Rusk that "it would have more status than a background task force report; but it would not, of course, be regarded as the Mosaic Law of the Kennedy administration."[29] What the paper does is provide a clear written representation of Rostow's foreign-policy philosophy. It was a confident, declarative paper that provoked a strong reaction from various quarters.

Rostow's paper is a composite of what he had advocated in government and theorized throughout the 1950s in his academic monographs. He stresses the vital importance of the developing world, delineates the nature of the current Soviet threat, and explains why Marxism-Leninism will ultimately lose the battle. Recognizing that "in the end, one conception or the other will constitute the framework for organizing the planet," Rostow explains that "the underlying aspiration of peoples for forms of political and social organization which protect the individual against the unlimited authority of the state is strong, and rooted in abiding historical, cultural, and religious commitments. If an environment of regular movement towards economic progress and social justice can be created, the long-run chances of victory for political democracy—in one form or another—are good."[30]

Presenting significant opportunities, as well as a number of threats, "the revolution of modernization in Latin America, Africa, Asia and the Middle East," the paper says, is the most pressing issue of the day, requiring sharp attention. The key battleground, in Rostow's estimation, is "the arc from Iran to Korea" where "the free community cannot afford an extension of communist influence without risking loss which would extend far beyond the area immediately affected." As a region making its first steps toward liberal capitalist modernity, Southeast Asia is highlighted as being particularly susceptible to communist infection. Rostow provides a reformulation of Eisenhower's "falling dominoes" theory as applied to the area in that "the loss of South Vietnam or Thailand would endanger the whole Southeast Asian position and place in jeopardy the independence of the Indian peninsula itself." The paper exemplifies the inconsistency at the core of Rostow's thinking in that communist threats are amplified, a stern response is advocated, and then the conclusion emerges that communism will die regardless. As Rostow puts it, "The principles of national independence and freedom shall, in time, peacefully triumph."[31] The counterpoint is instinctive. If capitalism will triumph peacefully, why bother confronting communism—a movement in terminal decline—in distant theaters using military means?

Rostow then provides a pen-portrait of his ideal world and explains why expanded American foreign aid can play a vital part in achieving its realization. The United States should take the lead in attempting to achieve higher aims such as "an environment of material progress, peaceful reconciliation of differences, increasing social justice, and movements towards the norms of political democracy." This emphasis on social justice is peculiar for a foreign-policy draft. Indeed, it would be incongruous in the realm of domestic policy, for although Rostow adhered to old-school Democratic values, Kennedy did not share his dedication to the overt redistribution of wealth. Rostow's profound liberalism and his concern for disadvantaged peoples and nations shines through the document, providing an uplifting counterweight to his gloomy warnings of communism's nefarious ways. But it was the latter that overwhelmed the former in terms of urgency.

Containment of communism, according to Rostow, is a policy that "requires of us all a sustained combination of courage and circumspection; of initiative and patience; of resolute struggle against Communism and the ability to work subtly with processes of change within the communist bloc." Sounding like George Kennan (circa 1946) at the close of the document, Rostow concludes that his version of containment "is consistent with powerful historical forces at work on the world scene; its demands fall well within the material resources available to us and to the free world as a whole . . . Time is on the side of the things that we stand for, if we use time well." The phrase "use time well" is revealing. It was a general statement that might encompass a multitude of foreign-policy initiatives. But it was this issue of how America should best use "time" that sharply distinguished Rostow from Kennan. Rostow was clear that it was the duty of the United States to "create a wider community of free nations, embracing Latin America, Africa, Asia, and the Middle East [and] . . . to defend this community against communist aggression."[32] Kennan believed that "creating" a world of free nations and then defending them all from communist aggression was hubristic, unachievable, and strategically unnecessary.

The BNSP draft was distributed widely across the administration for feedback. Based on this response, Rostow was then to make revisions and submit it to Kennedy for authorization—making his paper official government policy. It provoked a great deal of criticism but less by way of praise. McGeorge Bundy was predictably first concerned by the document's length. It was a "pudding" that had "most of the plums," Bundy observed, but they should be "pulled out and made more feasible." Something else worried Bundy, however, that was more substantive than the feasibility of Rostow's plums. He had "grave reservations" about Rostow's habitual use of the words "doctrine" and "strategy," worrying that "they imply that our attitudes are doctrinaire and our activities all bound by a single 'strategic' concept." Rostow's grandiloquence and tendency to make big statements grated with the sharp, cynical Bundy, who found adherence to any comprehensive ideology anathema.

Bundy was further concerned that Rostow's preference for promoting modernization and resisting communism "everywhere" would lead the United States to overstretch its finite resources. "We have to have a clear sense of limits and priorities," Bundy urged. These were significant criticisms that cast a harsh light on Rostow's whole enterprise. But Rostow's old boss did have one or two good things to say about the paper, describing it as the "most important forward move in . . . framing basic policy positions since we came in."[33] This endorsement is not as generous as it first appears. Rostow's was *the only* serious attempt made by the Kennedy administration to frame basic policy positions.

Next up with the brickbats was Carl Kaysen, who had replaced Rostow as Bundy's deputy in November 1961. In private Kaysen described Rostow's draft as "bean soup," "blah, blah, blah," "silly," and a "lot of nonsense."[34] In a more diplomatically worded letter to Rostow, Kaysen explained that he disliked his Manichaean view of the world in which ambiguities and tensions within the communist bloc were "not reflected in the grand scheme." While conceding that Rostow's paper "cogently states the significance of the revolution of modernization which is sweeping the underdeveloped two-thirds of the world," he qualified his remark by pointing out that Rostow had dwelled on "hopes" but had failed to mention "costs." It was in this "calculus of cost," Kaysen observed, "that the draft is deficient."[35] Kaysen's critique was one to be echoed throughout Rostow's ensuing years in government. Sunny in disposition and generous to a fault, Rostow took the most expansive possible interpretation of where U.S. interests lay. In some respects Rostow's vision for American foreign policy was a forerunner of the global vision advocated by today's neoconservatives, such as Paul Wolfowitz and Richard Perle. The main difference between Rostowism and neoconservatism is that the former placed its emphasis on global social justice, while the latter stresses the unilateral extension of political freedom and the transformative power of capitalism. Both worldviews share a common theme, necessitating U.S. military intervention anywhere at any time. And Rostow, like today's neocons, devoted less time to considering how the government might finance such an activist foreign policy. It was Rostow's expansive view of what U.S. foreign policy might achieve that stirred America's most eloquent exponent of "realism" in foreign affairs to respond to the BNSP.

George Kennan was serving as the Kennedy administration's ambassador to Yugoslavia in 1962 and his critique is remarkable in its range and vehemence. Kennan admired Rostow's draft "from a technical standpoint" and was deeply impressed by a "document of such scope" that was "so lucid, so comprehensive [and] so well written." The praise, however, ends right there. Rostow's paper, Kennan admitted, "challenges me on a plane so personal there can be no escape into the official personality." Kennan first finds fault with Rostow's dependence on nuclear weapons as the centerpiece of basic military doctrine. The contrast here with Maxwell Taylor could not have been starker. Taylor's only substantive criticisms of Rostow's BNSP paper both related to nuclear issues: first, that it did not specify what level of provocation would warrant a nuclear response, and second, that it failed to explore the battlefield potential of "small nuclear weapons."[36] George Kennan, on the other hand, disliked Rostow's overreliance on the nuclear option. He personally favored "an agreement with the Russians for the total abandonment of the cultivation, maintenance and the use of this sort of weaponry."[37] While Rostow may have viewed nuclear war as a winnable position, Kennan would "rather see my children dead" than experience such hell. This was a radical position that did not unduly concern Rostow or any other significant member of the Kennedy administration. Kennan was pretty much alone with Bertrand Russell and a few million other "peace loving pinkos" on the issue of banning the bomb.

Kennan's second critique was more substantial, was taken more seriously, and aimed at the core of Rostow's value system. With regard to helping the Third World move toward Western-style capitalist democracy, Kennan felt Rostow's efforts were simply a waste of time. He criticized Rostow's draft for being "deeply imbued with a relatively optimistic view of the sources of human behavior . . . a view which when applied to the great mass of humanity I cannot share." The ability to harmonize "various elements into the political life of a state," Kennan observed brutally, is "peculiar to peoples who have had their origins on or near to the shores of the North Sea." Economic and political success stories like Scandinavia, Great Britain, and Germany were not ones that Kennan expected "to be readily or generally imitated elsewhere."[38] Kennan was narrowing the ability to attain societal progress to an exclusive club: the Nordics and Anglo-Saxons.

Aware perhaps that his diatribe was sounding racist, Kennan then qualifies by way of balance that "some of the most hideous manifestations of modern totalitarianism have come in some of the most highly industrialized and best educated countries." This is an incisive identification of a serious shortcoming in *The Stages of Economic Growth*. Rostow does struggle to explain how European totalitarianism in the 1920s and 1930s knocked liberal capitalist progress off track. But it is Kennan's less savory views on the inability of the non-European world to achieve any credible form of political and economic success that dominate the letter. "Whether *absence of encouragement* on our part would steady these people down and temper their demand for earlier industrialization," Kennan wondered with regard to Africans, "I think it irresponsible of us to encourage them along this path." Such views were diametrically opposed to those of Rostow. In Kennan's opinion, the Third World should not receive any form of U.S. assistance, lest it further inflame the passions and desires of the natives: "Divided and weak they are no menace to us. Given strength, God knows what they will do," although Kennan does not specify "what" exactly armed Africans might do.[39] Rostow, on the other hand, believed that leaving the developing world alone would be both strategically foolhardy and morally abhorrent. First, a communist periphery would present a massive problem to U.S. diplomacy, and, second, poverty-stricken nations constituted a challenge to the West's conscience that could not be ducked. Kennan, in turn, cared little as to whether the nonwhite population of the world either lived well or looked to Karl Marx or Adam Smith for guidance. It was irrelevant as these nations, left alone or to the communists, were destined for international impotency.

This exchange between Rostow and Kennan is fascinating, as they represent the two guiding philosophies that have driven U.S. foreign policy from the Second World War to the present: Wilsonian internationalism and realism. These two schools collide perfectly with Rostow's BNSP draft and Kennan's withering response. Rostow believed in the perfectibility of man and instinctively maintained that it was a possibility available to all, regardless of race, religion, or proximity to the North Sea. This optimism was criticized by Kennan as hopeless with repeated reference to Africa, where there might exist "God knows how many independent states, all with neat borders, UN membership . . . and all thrusting happily ahead into the nirvana of an industrial civilization." Kennan saw Rostow as a Pollyanna—a kind but unrealistic dreamer.

Where Rostow identified hope and potential, Kennan could not see beyond "childishness, bewilderment, inexperience, violence, racial strife and internecine warfare of every sort . . . I cannot agree that it will always be compatible with the safety of our country to increase the industrial strength of these peoples, to put weapons in their hands, to discourage violence among them, to encourage their proliferation."[40] For all his brilliance, Kennan's views are unsettling. His critique of Rostow's unreflective anticommunism was utterly convincing. With respect to the future of the underdeveloped nations, however, Rostow's Wilsonian vision is far more palatable than Kennan's Hobbesian worldview and ethnocentric chauvinism. If Rostow's progressive views on global poverty had been married to a more reasoned appraisal of communism's threat to peripheral theaters, then Rostowism might have been an enduring force indeed.

This stark example of internationalism and realism slugging it out marks an important juncture in the intellectual history of twentieth-century U.S. foreign policy. In 1946 George Kennan formulated containment as a guiding principle designed to repel Soviet adventurism in the central European theater. But the communist threat did not remain static. One of Rostow's predecessors as head of policy planning, Paul Nitze, broadened the range of U.S. foreign-policy concerns to include East Asia and kick-started a vast expansion of the U.S. military—set out in April 1950 in the seminal foreign policy document, NSC 68—to sustain these expanded interests. Rostow carried this expansion of U.S. foreign-policy concerns to the extreme. Nowhere in the world could America afford to stand idle.

In this battle of ideas with Kennan, Rostow ultimately prevailed. The 1960s marked the apogee of internationalism and Rostow himself was the most influential of the liberal cold warriors. It was his ideas that, above all, guided U.S. foreign policy toward a dual approach in the 1960s: a combination of aggressive and altruistic interventionism. In many respects John Gaddis is right about the revelatory nature of Rostow's BNSP draft. But the president disliked the idea of having the bureaucracy tied down to an official policy blueprint. As the historian Richard Neustadt explained to Rostow in 1964, Kennedy "was never going to sign BNSP. He was temperamentally against nailing down where history was going until he could see it bit by bit—he just shrank. He was too fond of you . . . to say to you take it away and don't bring it back."[41] Rostow reluctantly agreed with Neustadt, recognizing that "[Kennedy] didn't want the bureaucracy to nail him down with promissory notes." But while the paper did not carry a guiding sanction, it does provide us with an invaluable perspective on Rostow's foreign-policy rationale. In 1962, however, Rostow was viewed by too many people at the top, including the president, as a trigger-happy maverick. This designation appeared to be borne out during October 1962, when Rostow counseled incendiary military action during the Cold War's most perilous crisis.

FOR THE THIRTEEN DAYS that followed October 16, 1962, the United States and the Soviet Union confronted each other in the Caribbean over the highest possible stakes. American surveillance technology had uncovered an audacious Soviet attempt to equalize the nuclear balance of power through the placement of ballistic missiles in Cuba. The rest of the world could do little else but look on fearfully as the two superpowers squared up. John F. Kennedy prevailed during the crisis; it was his finest hour as commander in chief. But in spite of the effusive praise heaped on the president's coolness under pressure and adept consultative management, the avoidance of World War III in the autumn of 1962 owed as much to chance as to design. Robert McNamara recently conceded that many events surrounding the Cuban Missile Crisis were simply outside the president's control, with diplomatic communication between the superpowers often resembling farce.[42] Central to the resolution of the crisis was a secret bilateral channel established between Bobby Kennedy, the attorney general, and Anatoly Dobrynin, the Soviet ambassador in Washington. While the president's public posture was one of strict resolution—the removal of the Soviet missiles was nonnegotiable—his younger brother offered as bargaining chips the removal of obsolete Jupiter missiles in Turkey and an assurance that Cuba would not be invaded again. Walt Rostow was not privy to these surreptitious moves, but his position on the undesirability of negotiation was made abundantly clear at the time.

Asked to report to McGeorge Bundy on how the Policy Planning Council was reacting to the crisis, Robert Komer explained that Rostow believed that if the "Soviets and Castro don't respond by liquidating what's left of the Cuban missile capacity once we have blockaded . . . we should move in fast to take care of it ourselves. He favors an air strike." Komer was concerned both by Rostow's bellicosity and the fact that his activism was distracting him from the job he was charged to do: policy planning, not crisis resolution. "Walt is going to be hard to hold down," Komer observed. "He wants to charge on all fronts, forward planning or no."[43] In an attempt to temper his enthusiasm, Komer explained patiently to Rostow that implicit in Kennedy's crisis diplomacy "is the idea that our target is the missile threat, not Cuba itself."[44] Rostow, however, saw the crisis as a fine opportunity to topple the Castro regime through a direct attack. Once again the threat of nuclear war was an issue that did not seem to spook Rostow.

Rostow and Bundy had a "big fight" during the crisis over whether to cut a quid pro quo deal with the Russians. While Rostow "didn't think we had to give away anything in order to get the missiles out," his former boss was willing to look at any option that might avoid nuclear war without seriously compromising U.S. credibility. Rostow prepared a policy planning report that urged a hard-line response to Khrushchev's challenge—the option of removing the Turkish missiles was not considered—but Bundy refused to pass such hawkish advice on to the president. When Bundy's veto came to Rostow's attention, he confronted him directly and demanded an explanation. Bundy snapped and scolded Rostow: "Why don't you stop trying to be the President of the United States and do staff work?" Rostow replied doggedly, "Our bargaining position in the crisis is such that we do not have to sell out the Turkish bases or take any other costs in the alliance."[45]

In his 1964 oral history, Rostow criticized Bundy for designating the Cuban imbroglio the "biggest crisis" since the Second World War and for conveying the fallacious impression that "we were in bad trouble and had to pay a price to avoid nuclear war." Rostow did not see the standoff in Cuba as a particularly vexing issue: it was inevitable that Khrushchev would fold in the face of diplomatic rigidity and America's overwhelming strength. In his retrospective appraisal of the crisis, Rostow erroneously observed that Kennedy "firmly excluded the Turkish bases for bargaining . . . [for] the use of our Allies' weapons as bargaining counters would have terribly damaged the alliance."[46] He was indignant at the mere possibility that America might cut a deal in the face of what he took to be unprompted Soviet aggression. Rostow saw the world in black and white. Bundy and Kennedy, on the other hand, were both more attuned to nuance; to appreciating, in Bundy's phrase, that gray was the color of truth, or at least of survival.[47] Calmer minds prevailed, and Rostow's distant fiefdom at Foggy Bottom fortunately played a minor role in the deliberations of the Executive Committee (Excomm).

On just one occasion during the crisis was Rostow asked to interact directly with the president and his celebrated committee. At 5:00 p.m. on October 25, Excomm members assembled to discuss the possibility of extending the naval quarantine to include certain nonmilitary items. Earlier that day the success of the quarantine strategy was becoming apparent. A total of twelve Soviet vessels had turned back at the perimeter while one, carrying oil supplies, was allowed to carry on to its final destination. Rostow was unhappy, however, that petroleum, oil supplies, and lubricants (POL) had been left off the list of prohibited items. He advised that adding POL to the list would have the most dramatic coercive effect on Cuba and the Soviets.

As was his wont, Rostow marshaled a pertinent example from the Second World War to bring to bear on a current issue: "We had this experience in the German war," Rostow recalled. "As soon as [POL] was cut, it had the most dramatic effect."[48] Robert McNamara was skeptical that cutting POL would be as decisive as Rostow maintained. During the meeting the defense secretary told Rostow that many of his own staff members were extremely doubtful of its utility. The president then interjected: "Your point, Walt, is that if we go to POL it is a very strong act?" "It's a very strong act," Rostow replied. "The clock begins to tick [while] on the other hand it still gives them time to negotiate."[49] The upshot of this meeting was that the quarantine continued unaltered—oil stayed off the list, to Rostow's dismay. But the debate over oil's merits as a target was prophetic. A few years later, Rostow and McNamara were again at loggerheads over the same issue. At that stage, the target was North Vietnam.

The resolution of the Cuban Missile Crisis was, in Rostow's opinion, a salutary example of how the United States should correctly deal with communist aggression. Not realizing that Kennedy had offered inducements behind the scenes, Rostow was delighted that Khrushchev had folded so abjectly in the face of what appeared to be rigid American pressure. Rostow decided to apply this lesson to Vietnam. On November 28 he recommended to Dean Rusk "the launching, initially at a modest level, of limited air attack on selected North Vietnamese targets." It was a shift in military strategy that Rostow had advocated before, but this time he could marshal recent powerful evidence to suggest that it would prove decisive and go unchallenged. "The whole lesson of the cold war, including the recent Cuban crisis," Rostow explained, "is that the communists do not escalate in response to our actions."[50]

Not content with simply sending Rusk this memo—titled "Mikoyan, the Laos Agreement, and Continued Infiltration into South Vietnam"— Rostow forwarded the same paper to Averell Harriman on February 2, 1963, with an endearing preface that began "Before you decide your old and respectful friend has gone off his rocker . . ."[51] Harriman was predictably unimpressed by Rostow's plan. His opinion of the man's caliber had been slipping for some time and he considered Rostow's views on how to stop infiltration through Laos to be particularly asinine. Undeterred, Rostow put the same argument to Rusk again, with the additional consideration that "if we are to have a showdown with Ho (and implicitly Mao), we should bring it about before the Chinese communists blow a nuclear device."[52] Writing on Independence Day, Rostow may well have been affected by the red, white, and blue revelry surrounding him and the fireworks erupting overhead. Whatever the reason, this advice did not sit well with those at the top.

———

MARGINALIZED, FRUSTRATED, and perceived as a joke figure in some quarters, Rostow was desperate to return to the center of policymaking. On January 2, 1963, he sent Bundy a memorandum hopefully titled "How to Assist the Role of the Planner." Rostow's first and most pressing request was that he be allowed to attend NSC meetings. Following their ugly spat during the Cuban Missile Crisis, however, more Rostow was not at the top of Bundy's agenda. Rostow closed his memo with a rather plaintive request: "When immediate decisions which cast long shadows are being taken, we ought to consider whether a conscious effort should be made to assure the voice of the planner . . . is present and heard."[53] Sensing that Bundy was not the most receptive of audiences, Rostow made a similar pitch to Rusk two days later. Going so far as to identify faults with the president's "pragmatic style in decision-making," Rostow observed that from his own personal experience "meetings with the president lacked structure . . . and some factors bearing on a decision were not fully taken into account." To remedy this unsatisfactory situation, Rostow advised that he both attend NSC meetings—something he claimed was promised to him when he "came aboard"—and have a say in setting the agenda for these deliberations. Conceding that long position papers are "not appropriate to many sessions with the president," the answer might be "a one page memorandum briefly—even cryptically—setting out the key factors before a well-balanced decision is reached."[54]

Rostow's strategy was to identify decision-making forums that cast a favorable light on what he perceived to be his own particular strengths: his drive and ability to grasp the bigger picture. And his importunacy produced some tangible results. While Rostow's attendance at NSC meetings was rare, he was invited to be present on certain issues where his regional expertise might be needed. In July 1963, for example, Bundy agreed that with regard to a forthcoming NSC meeting on "Chicom intentions all around their border . . . I guess by treaty we do accept Rostow."[55] While hardly a ringing endorsement—"I guess" reveals a distinct lack of enthusiasm—Bundy's concession did seem to augur some kind of progress. What Rostow did not know was that Robert Komer was dismembering his performance at the Policy Planning Council at Bundy's behest.

Robert Komer was later nicknamed "Blowtorch" by Henry Cabot

Lodge, who had occasion to witness his volatility firsthand in Vietnam. Komer was a veteran of the Italian campaign of World War II, had received his M.B.A. from Harvard, and had spent over ten years at the CIA. Brutal and incisive, Komer delighted in taking on the bureaucracy and had little time for those who failed to provide crisp, focused analyses. On January 12, 1963, Komer reported to Bundy that he had "spent two hours trying to convince WWR that planning doesn't consist either of dividing the world into squares or taking the whole world as one's oyster . . . His planning list had 33 (count 'em) projects, many of which logically broke down into half-a-dozen sub-topics which were major in themselves." While Komer was sympathetic to Rostow's plight of lacking a truly receptive audience, he disliked the manner in which Rostow had his staff tackle so many diverse topics with insufficient direction from above.

If Rostow were to put his ideas in a more "saleable form," then, Komer urged, Bundy could "allow him a bit more of a market in which to peddle them."[56] This ambivalent assessment hardened later in the year. Annoyed that Rostow had failed to heed his advice with regard to focusing his efforts, Komer dismissed one of Rostow's papers as "gobbledygook." He again criticized Rostow's propensity to misuse the "talent" available to him at the Policy Planning Council "at the expense of their normal roles." Losing faith in Rostow's ability to produce any report of practical significance, Komer conceded that letting him pursue his own path unmolested might not be a terrible idea—it "will keep Walt and S/P quite busy for a while."[57]

By April 1963 the president was displaying serious doubts about the efficacy of U.S. involvement in Vietnam. Speaking to the journalist Charles Bartlett, Kennedy confided, "We don't have a prayer of staying in Vietnam. Those people hate us. They are going to throw our asses out at any point." The president explained that he was tied to supporting Diem's corrupt, unpopular regime in the south primarily for domestic reasons: "I can't give up a piece of territory like that to the communists and get the people to re-elect me."[58] Such cynical sentiments were anathema to Rostow, who held reservations about the quality of Diem's leadership, but none about the U.S. commitment to Southeast Asia.

Kennedy had earlier decided that Laos was not the place to draw a line in the sand against communism. The communist Pathet Lao group in

Laos had been locked in a struggle with the American-backed forces of Phoumi Nosavan for control of the nation. Following months of protracted negotiations, Ambassador-at-Large Averell Harriman negotiated the neutralization of Laos in Geneva on July 23, 1962. To all intents and purposes, the country had been removed from the Cold War chessboard. Rostow deemed the agreement a craven sell-out and repeatedly put the case that America must respond militarily to communist violations of the agreement. "I regarded the continued use of infiltration trails [through Laos] as a fire bell in the night," Rostow wrote in later years. "I felt that the United States should move promptly and decisively to force a confrontation on the violation of the recently signed Geneva Accords, backed as they were by the unambiguous understandings achieved by Harriman with Pushkin in Geneva."[59] The "neutralization" of Laos was shown to be a sham in subsequent years. Writing to Rusk on June 7, 1963, Rostow urged that the U.S. directly repulse communist insurgents in Laos, who were paying scant attention to the agreement brokered in Geneva.

Resolute military action in Laos was, in Rostow's estimation, vital for a multitude of reasons. Displaying a hitherto dormant appreciation for the existence of the "Sino-Soviet" split, Rostow wrote that an insurgent victory in Laos's Plaine des Jarres would be interpreted as a victory for hardliners in the People's Republic of China, which would be damaging for "moderates" in both the Soviet Union and China. Following China's recent military victory against India, Rostow also argued that American inaction in Laos would be seen by both India and Japan as base irresolution. This was likely to further encourage both nations to pursue a more independent course in foreign affairs.[60]

But Rostow's far-reaching analysis of the situation yet again failed to convince a wary Rusk, who was in little doubt that the civil war in "neutralized" Laos did not merit a U.S. military response. Rostow's extreme recommendations were again at odds with the more moderate predilection of the president he served. On June 10, 1963, Kennedy made a celebrated speech at American University, in which he called for peaceful cooperation with the Soviet Union. The president was striving to downplay the intensity of the ideological conflict with communism, to retreat from the conventional Manichaean portrayals of the Cold War presented by Truman and Eisenhower. In such a dialogue-inclined atmosphere, Rostow's escalatory ideas simply could not thrive. And this was in spite of the fact that South Vietnam appeared to be collapsing under the weight of its incompetent leadership.

THE U.S. POSITION AS guarantor to a cohesive South Vietnam, united under Diem's firm, sagacious leadership, was looking increasingly disconnected from reality. In the summer of 1963, chaos engulfed South Vietnam over the issue of Buddhism's standing within society. The issue that precipitated the protest was an apparently minor one: the freedom to display flags on the anniversary of Buddha's birth. The stakes were dramatically heightened on May 8, 1963, when ARVN soldiers shot wildly into a throng of anti-Diem protestors in Hué, killing nine. Rather than offering a conciliatory response, Diem's government ratcheted up the tension with their overreaction. Buddhist bonzes responded with a series of spectacular self-immolations. The sight of fire engulfing those orange-clad figures made clear to the world the sincerity of their cause. Madame Ngo Dinh Nhu—the wife of the president's brother—added flames to the fire by offering to provide gasoline and matches to any other Buddhists who were keen on martyrdom.

On the American side, it was becoming obvious that something had to be done to rein in Diem. One Kennedy adviser remarked that while the Buddhist mind remained "*terra incognita*," the South Vietnamese government was making a bad situation much worse.[61] Recognizing the need for a change of personnel at the scene, Kennedy appointed the prominent Massachusetts Republican Henry Cabot Lodge to replace Frederick Nolting as U.S. ambassador to South Vietnam on June 27. Lodge was appalled by Diem's inability to provide resolute leadership to a nation that appeared to be falling apart at the seams. Following Lodge's August request to Washington that Diem be marginalized in the event of a coup, the writing was on the wall for the South Vietnamese president. The United States' position shifted from unstinting support for Diem to covertly communicating the message to disillusioned Vietnamese generals that while the United States would not provide support for a coup, it would be amenable to any new government dedicated to uniting the nation. As Lodge put it,

America was "launched on a course from which there is no respectable turning back."[62] Diem's days were numbered.

In retrospect Rostow characterized the "Buddhist affair" as a reflection of the "widespread unwillingness of every group that mattered to see Nhu succeed Diem," arguing this was why "things fell apart from June of 1963."[63] But Rostow's analysis fails to convey the real sense of crisis that afflicted South Vietnam during the summer. While Nhu was undoubtedly a reviled figure across the country, Diem was the focus of popular antipathy for reasons that went beyond his sibling's proximity to power. As a repressive, Catholic president, Diem failed to command sufficient loyalty across an overwhelmingly Buddhist nation. While the Kennedy administration pressed the South Vietnamese president to introduce "democratic" reforms, Diem worried that such steps might open the floodgates of criticism, undermining his leadership position. Rather than adopting a progressive stance, Diem's government turned in the other direction. On August 21, in response to antigovernment protests, Ngo Dinh Nhu's American-trained Special Forces directly attacked Buddhists in Hué, Saigon, and other cities, destroying their pagodas and arresting some 1,400 people. Roger Hilsman was furious that Diem's brother had pursued such a counterproductive action: "We could not sit still and be the puppets of Diem's anti-Buddhist policies."[64]

Roger Hilsman, Averell Harriman, and Henry Cabot Lodge were particularly active in urging a move against Diem in the summer and autumn of 1963. And when a military coup ousted Diem on November 1, 1963, the official U.S. reaction did not deviate from the CIA position that had been agreed on in early October "not to thwart a change of government."[65] South Vietnam's generals seized key military installations in the capital and neutralized Nhu's Special Forces before requesting that Nhu and Diem resign. Panicked by the unfolding crisis, President Diem called Ambassador Lodge and asked him what America intended to do about the coup. Lodge procrastinated and told him, "I do not feel well enough informed to tell you . . . It is 4:30 am in Washington and the U.S. government cannot possibly have a view."[66] Lodge's disingenuous response sealed their fate: Diem and Nhu escaped and found temporary refuge in a Catholic church in the Chinese sector of the capital. The brothers went to confession and received what was to be their last communion. Soon afterward they were captured by troops sympathetic to the military coup and stabbed to death in the back of an armored truck. The Diem regime had come to an appropriately Shakespearean end.

Reaction to the news in South Vietnam and the United States was mixed. Jubilant scenes were evident on the streets of Saigon, although Diem's removal—and his replacement by General Duoung Van Minh—was not met with universal favor, particularly among elite Catholics with much to lose from a change of leadership. In Washington Hilsman was unflustered by the news, remarking, "Revolutions are rough. People get hurt."[67] Kennedy, on the other hand, was dismayed to learn of the double killing. While many considered Diem's demise a necessary act of tyrannicide, Kennedy was visibly shaken by the brutal slaying of his fellow Catholic. Arthur Schlesinger Jr. observed that the president at that juncture was more depressed than at any time since the Bay of Pigs.[68] It was a shameful end to America's strategy of burnishing Diem's nationalist credentials, of building up his military and his nation. Over the course of the following eighteen months a total of six leaders came and went in one palace coup after another. The stability that some in Washington expected to emerge in South Vietnam through Diem's removal was shown to be illusory.[69]

Rostow was not vexed by the dramatic turn of events in Saigon, and looked upon Diem's death primarily as an opportunity to up the military ante, rather than as an obstacle to creating a viable South Vietnam. The dual problem that faced U.S. policymakers was to "find ways to close the frontier; and to solve the problem of crystallizing political life around the young modernizing generation, which Diem did not understand, trust or use effectively."[70] Rostow gave considerably more thought to the first part of the problem, however, than to the rather more complicated second. The strategic hamlet program was the one significant attempt that the Kennedy administration had made to modernize South Vietnam, and that strategy came to an inglorious end. With Diem and Nhu removed from the equation, the systemic failure of the program to reconnect central government to agrarian South Vietnam became truly apparent: skewed reporting gave way to some hard truths. Rostow was a theorist of Third World modernization, but he consistently failed to provide a credible plan for achieving genuine economic and political progress south of the seventeenth parallel. This was a pointless task, Rostow reasoned, if something was not done to kill north-south infiltration through Laos.[71]

Closing the frontier, on the other hand, was a problem with which Rostow could associate, as it could be solved by military means alone. Killing infiltrators did not necessitate a complicated dedication to nation building. And so before news of Diem and Nhu's murder had even reached Washington, Rostow wrote to the secretary of state, "Assuming the Saigon coup succeeds . . . I urge that we consider promptly bringing to a head the issue of infiltration . . . [We should] confront Hanoi with the choice of ceasing to operate the war or accepting retaliatory damage in the north." To make certain that Rusk got the point, he reattached his November 28, 1962, "Invade Laos" memorandum, and also sent it to Roger Hilsman, George Ball, and Averell Harriman (a less receptive trio could hardly be imagined).[72]

Again, Rostow's plan to invade Laos and bomb North Vietnam was ignored by Rusk; and it did not even get close to the president's line of vision. Hilsman recalled that Kennedy at the time thought that "Walt Rostow was laughable on Asia and Vietnam."[73] In terms of influence and access, November 1963 was a nadir for the chairman of the Policy Planning Council. After a glittering rise through the ranks of academe and government, it was now abundantly clear that Rostow was assuredly not one of the president's men. An influential voice in 1961, Rostow was a marginal, albeit noisy, figure in 1962 and 1963. In late 1961 Kennedy had decided that Rostow's anticommunism was simply too strident to have him in the White House. Kennedy was partial to many of Rostow's ideas, but the ones he liked related primarily to Third World modernization, not strategic bombing. It is hard to imagine that Rostow would have prospered during a second Kennedy term. That second term, however, did not come to pass. Twenty-one days after Diem's murder, John F. Kennedy was shot dead in Dallas, Texas. Lyndon Baines Johnson stepped in to fill a colossal vacuum of leadership.

PLAYING COUNTERFACTUAL HISTORY with the question of what Kennedy might have done in Vietnam had Lee Harvey Oswald missed is a game that few historians resist playing. David Kaiser believes that

Kennedy might have eventually withdrawn the U.S. commitment to South Vietnam, writing in *American Tragedy* that the president was "the most skeptical senior official of his administration regarding the war in Southeast Asia."[74] Yet Rostow had little time for those who argue that Kennedy would have acted any differently from his successor. Looking back on the Kennedy years, Rostow was clearly frustrated that his ideas did not convince the White House. But he had no doubt that Kennedy would have pursued the same escalatory path in Vietnam that President Johnson followed. Citing persuasive evidence to back up his claim—such as Kennedy making "the flattest statement of the domino theory that any-one ever made" in September 1963—Rostow was adamant that his read-ing was correct because he understood the president better than most. In his Lyndon Baines Johnson Library oral history, Rostow displayed no doubt in his reading of JFK's intentions: "I'm now telling you Kennedy's thoughts, which I know intimately because I was his man on this . . . [and] because we were old friends."[75]

Rostow even argued that Kennedy might have been more hawkish on Vietnam than his successor: "Having been an elected president he may well have been more willing than President Johnson to bite the bullet be-fore November [1964]."[76] In later years Rostow would continually reas-sure LBJ that his predecessor would have followed exactly the same course. On September 15, 1967, for example, Rostow wrote to Johnson, "I don't believe any objective person can read the record without knowing that Kennedy would have seen this [the war] through whatever the cost . . . This is the nut of the issue."[77] In a 1971 interview with CBS tele-vision, Rostow maintained that Kennedy was adamant that leaving Viet-nam would be highly destabilizing to international relations. He alleged that the president had warned him in late 1961 that "if we moved out [of Vietnam] the answer would not be peace but a larger war, quite soon, and quite possibly a nuclear war."[78]

In making his case, Rostow points to the fact that Kennedy was an un-stinting supporter of the domino theory and dedicated to preserving South Vietnam's freedom in the face of communist aggression. Much evidence exists to verify his claim, such as Kennedy's "flat" statement of the domino theory mentioned by Rostow above. Asked by the NBC reporter David Brinkley on September 9, 1963, whether he believed in the domino theory, the president's answer was unambiguous: "I believe it."[79] Yet other evidence also exists to suggest that withdrawal from Vietnam was the last thing on Kennedy's mind in November 1963. On the day he died, Kennedy was due to give a speech in Dallas which stressed the continued necessity of a truly expansive foreign policy. The president was to remark that Providence had deemed that the current generation of Americans would serve as the "watchmen on the walls of world freedom" whose assistance to nations fighting communism must be maintained even though it "can be painful, risky and costly, as it is in Southeast Asia." With regard to maintaining the U.S. commitment to South Vietnam, the president's resolution could not have been made clearer: "We dare not weary of this task."[80]

The overall balance of evidence tends to undermine the arguments of those who suggest that Kennedy would have withdrawn U.S. troops from Vietnam in a second term. This is a parlor game, however, that fails to provide definitive answers. It is perhaps sufficient to say that Rostow's claims that Kennedy would not have shirked from his commitment to Southeast Asia can be backed up with some persuasive evidence. Those who argue the other side point to Kennedy's private doubts and his decision made in October to withdraw a thousand U.S. military advisers. These tentative moves to de-escalate are interpreted by men such as Arthur Schlesinger Jr., Chester Bowles, and Robert McNamara as a potential foretaste of the farsighted diplomacy that might have followed: an issue that is central to Camelot's subsequent canonization.

What is not in doubt is the fact that Kennedy had escalated the U.S. commitment to South Vietnam both materially and rhetorically. The president's public pronouncements stressed that the defeat of the insurgency was essential, thus tying success in Indochina to America's credibility as a military guarantor in the Cold War. This could have done little else but raise the costs of withdrawal for his successor. Lyndon Johnson is surely correct to say that Kennedy would have "continued to believe that the conquest of Southeast Asia would have the most serious impact on Asia and on us."[81] It is significant that Johnson retained all of his predecessor's foreign-policy advisers. Would they not have counseled a similar escalation had Kennedy lived?

In Rostow's estimation Kennedy made a grave error in strategy by failing to sanction Rostow's invade-and-bomb strategy with regard to Laos and Vietnam. Rostow blamed this irresolution on Kennedy's tendency to pay too much deference to the liberal northeastern establishment: "He was too much a Georgetown resident. He took *The New York Times* and *The Washington Post* too seriously. He was too much concerned with what Scotty Reston said, or Joe Alsop or Phil Graham. After all, in the country as a whole, awfully few people read this stuff."[82] Rather than heeding the advice of the progressive cocoon that surrounded Washington, D.C., the president would have done better to wage the war with less restraint.

Rostow was correct that Middle America cared little for the elite liberal house journals or their readership. This was a lesson that the Republican Party would increasingly appreciate in subsequent years. But while Johnson was acutely sensitive to criticism, no one could accuse him of pandering to the chattering classes, to the journalists and readers of *The New York Times* and *The Washington Post*. Three days after assuming the presidency, Johnson made clear that he was not going to "be the president who saw Southeast Asia go the same way China went." He instructed his advisers to "tell those generals in Saigon that Lyndon Johnson intends to stand by his word." The following month Johnson ordered the implementation of Operations Plan 34A (OPLAN 34A), which increased military and political pressure on North Vietnam by providing covert military assistance to "punitive" operations carried out by the ARVN. The shift from Kennedy to Johnson may well have been one of style rather than substance. But the atmosphere with regard to taking the fight to North Vietnam became far more amenable to those counseling aggression.[83] Johnson made clear on November 24 that he believed that the United States had erred in trying to "reform every Asian into our image" and that the overwhelming priority for the U.S. was simply "to win the war."[84] This signified a strategic move away from pacifying the south toward deploying military force potentially on both sides of the seventeenth parallel. This shift toward greater belligerence meant that Walt Rostow's star would rise again.

FIVE

The ROSTOW THESIS

1964–1965

You noted that I seemed excessively cheerful in contemplating this track. That cheerfulness does not reflect either a naïve or blood-thirsty character. It reflects, simply, a deeply held conviction . . . that the maintenance of our world position requires that this confrontation with Ho takes place.

—WALT ROSTOW TO WILLIAM BUNDY, *May 19, 1964*

L YNDON JOHNSON'S ASCENSION to the presidency appeared not to bode well for Ivy League–educated development theorists. Untutored in foreign policy, and determined to make history as a progressive domestic president, Johnson took as his role model the Franklin Delano Roosevelt of the 1930s, not the internationalist incarnation of later years. Toward the issue of foreign aid, and the centrality of development policy to the broader Cold War struggle, the new president appeared apathetic. According to the historian Robert McMahon, LBJ did not see the Third World as a "towering ideological challenge" as Kennedy had done, but as an inconsequential collection of "countries that want something from us."[1] Other critics have alleged that Johnson did not share his predecessor's sureness of touch with regard to international diplomacy. Roger

Hilsman later observed that Johnson brought to foreign policy the "sophis-tication and subtlety of a Texas state legislator at a lobbyist's barbecue."[2]

While subtlety was not his forte, Lyndon Johnson was a great negotia-tor and persuader. He was arguably the nation's most effective ever Senate majority leader.[3] Johnson's consuming passion was the creation of the Great Society: a radical reshaping of America on socially progressive lines. All else was to come a distant second in terms of the president's priorities. In foreign affairs Johnson was inexperienced, and most of the world was terra incognita. Aside from a few visits to Mexico—no stretch from John-son City, Texas—and his wartime military service, the new president had not ventured beyond America's borders prior to 1961. Of course, Harry S. Truman had little knowledge and experience of international affairs prior to his assumption of the presidency. And the diminutive Missourian now possesses the grandest possible reputation in the history of U.S. foreign re-lations. Conversely, a presidential résumé packed with global travel and an expressed interest in international relations is no guarantee that the candi-date will be as good as his experience suggests. One need only think of Her-bert Hoover's ill-starred incumbency to see this point. Yet Johnson's parochialism led many domestic and international critics to underestimate the sharp intellect he possessed. Charles de Gaulle could not have been more wrong when he remarked sarcastically that he liked Johnson because "he doesn't even take the bother to pretend he's thinking."[4]

The portrayal of Johnson as a brilliant domestic president who was doltish and crude in the cauldron of international affairs has been taken too far—particularly with regard to his alleged contempt for Third World development. Johnson shared with Rostow a genuine concern for the world's poor. He hoped that U.S. foreign aid might help solve the peren-nial global problems of "ignorance, poverty, hunger and disease."[5] While Johnson was at one with George Kennan in viewing sub-Saharan Africa as an unredeemable disaster, the president believed that Latin America and Asia could achieve the sort of infrastructural development that he had wit-nessed transform central Texas in the 1930s.[6] In subsequent years, John-son focused a great deal of energy on how New Deal–style public works programs might be applied to Vietnam. During a celebrated speech at Johns Hopkins University in April 1965, Johnson explained that he wanted to build a new Tennessee Valley Authority (TVA) in the Mekong Delta. Robert Komer recalled that Johnson would drive him "up the wall" on the issue of rural electrification in Vietnam. The president once remarked that he wanted to leave the "footprints of America" in Vietnam in the form of tangible development projects: monuments to the largesse and foresight of the world's richest nation.[7]

As it turned out, America's imprint on Vietnam's topography often took the more distinguishable form of bomb craters and torched villages rather than electricity pylons and hydroelectric plants. Turning the Mekong Delta into the Tennessee Valley was laudable in theory, but successful implementation of such an ambitious proposal was predicated on South Vietnam achieving cohesion as an independent nation—an arduous task that verged on the unrealistic. Vietnam became not just a thorn in Johnson's side, but the foreign policy issue that he could neither master nor escape.

The fear that Vietnam might be reunified under communist rule was one that consumed the new president. Were Vietnam to go down on his watch, Johnson feared that a reinvigorated Republican Party would destroy his Great Society:

> I knew that Harry Truman and Dean Acheson had lost their effectiveness from the day that the Communists took over China. I believed that the loss of China had played a large role in the rise of Joe McCarthy. And I knew that all these problems, taken together, were chickenshit compared with what might happen if we lost Vietnam.[8]

With characteristically colorful language, the president further explained to the journalist Joseph Kraft, "I don't give a damn about these little pinkos on the campuses, they're just waving their diapers and bellyaching because they don't want to fight. The great black beast for us is the right wing. If we don't get this war over soon they'll put enormous pressure on us to turn it into an Armageddon and wreck all our other programs." Kraft observed that LBJ was following JFK's strategy of having "no enemies on the right."[9] This meant that Johnson had to follow his predecessor in leaving no chinks in his anticommunist armor that the Republicans might exploit.

To ensure continuity in foreign affairs, Johnson persuaded all of Kennedy's foreign-policy advisers to stay the course with their new commander in chief. Robert McNamara in particular made a significant, positive impression on the new president. In Johnson's view his crisp briefings and facility with statistical analysis made his defense secretary "the brightest star in the cabinet."[10] Yet McNamara, Bundy, and Rusk offered Johnson little with regard to resolving the unfolding crisis in Southeast Asia. In January 1964 Johnson had no plan to resolve the conflict, no proactive strategy for defeating the communist insurgency in the south. All he had was a negative objective: not to let the south fall to a communist-inflicted defeat. Those with a strategy to win the war, therefore, faced a far more accommodating audience in the Oval Office.

Walt Rostow did have a plan. He was the first of Kennedy's foreign-policy advisers to identify the insurgency in South Vietnam as a critical problem requiring prompt American counteraction. Rostow was consistent in his advice that bombing the north was the key to defeating the NLF in the south. He had been ignored and ridiculed in equal measure over the previous two years but, through force of repetition, the concept of bombing North Vietnam had burned its way into the foreign-policy establishment's consciousness. The so-called Rostow Thesis—which held that the United States must deal with externally supported insurgencies through bombing their source—was well known to Bundy, Rusk, and McNamara as early as January 1962. However, Johnson—who as vice president was some way removed from Vietnam planning—was first presented with Rostow's argument, in memorandum form, in December 1963.[11]

It is difficult to trace the president's immediate reaction to reading Rostow's advice that the United States must bomb North Vietnam to protect the south. But it is surely significant that Hanoi received due rhetorical warning in the president's first State of the Union address. Responding to Rostow's December 23 recommendation that he stress the issue of communist cross-border infiltration, the president declared:

> In 1964 we will be better prepared than ever before to defend the cause
> of freedom, whether it is threatened by outright aggression or by the in-
> filtration practiced by those in Hanoi and Havana, who ship arms and
> men across international frontiers to foment insurrection.[12]

After spending the previous two years trying and failing to persuade Kennedy that serious steps were required to save South Vietnam from communism, Rostow's warnings appeared increasingly prophetic as that threat to Saigon worsened. When launching the Alliance for Progress and USAID in 1961, Kennedy had spoken Rostow's language, using terms like "Decade of Development" and "self-sustaining growth." At the beginning of 1964, another American president was sounding distinctly Rostovian.

For three years Robert Komer had criticized Rostow's management skills and cast repeated doubts on his ability to produce a clear report of any practical applicability. On January 2, 1964, Komer wrote to Bundy that Rostow again was hammering home the necessity of "reprisal in Vietnam." This time, however, Rostow's case "seems to make more sense now than it did previously." Conceding that bombing North Vietnam was a radical step that held the potential to widen the war, Komer was now convinced that "unless we ourselves move forward here we may find ourselves playing a losing defensive game, while the Sihanouks, Sukarnos, Maos and De Gaulles nibble at our flanks."[13] Rostow's prolixity and lack of focus irritated Komer, but Rostow had convinced this earlier skeptic that direct military action against Hanoi was necessary. As the situation in South Vietnam deteriorated, Rostow was winning new adherents to his cause.

Writing to Dean Rusk on February 7, Rostow stressed that the crucial issue of cross-border infiltration "may prove to be the last major problem we have to solve in the Cold War." Rostow's solution to the problem—the apparent key to achieving world peace—was to generate "a conviction that those who are caught in this illegal game render themselves [liable] to at least equal damage at source."[14] This memorandum was little different from the plethora that had preceded it, but his audience was not now as ill-disposed toward the man who had been previously dismissed as a dangerous armchair general. According to Roger Hilsman, it was at this juncture that Johnson began to take Rostow seriously. Kennedy threw Rostow's memos "in the bin," Hilsman recalled, but when Rostow again "wrote his usual memo urging the bombing of the north," Johnson "appointed a committee to consider if the time ever came to bomb, what some of the implications might be."[15]

Hilsman later claimed that he resigned from the administration because of this shift in presidential receptivity. Rostow's gaining an audience was simply too much for Hilsman to take. As the situation on the ground deteriorated in South Vietnam, Rostow's previously laughter-inducing war planning began to look prescient. In *The Washington Post*, Joseph Alsop wrote that "more and more converts are being gained to the view that 'we can't play the game with two sets of rules, one for us and one for them.'" He added that "originally, no one took this view but . . . Walt W. Rostow." If North Vietnam continued to flout the 1962 Laos Accords regarding infiltration, Alsop observed, there was no reason for the United States to "accept rules forbidding an air and sea blockade of the North Vietnamese frontiers."[16]

In extrapolating his thesis, Rostow stressed to the new president, "By applying limited, graduated military actions reinforced by political and economic pressures on a nation providing external support for insurgency we should be able to cause that nation to decide to reduce greatly or eliminate altogether support for the insurgency . . . The threat that is implicit in initial U.S. actions would be more important than the military actions themselves."[17] On February 14 Rostow wrote to Dean Rusk that the imposition of "graduated" military pressure would cause the DRV to "call off the war principally because of its fear that it would otherwise risk loss of its politically important industrial development." With its industry in tatters, Rostow believed, North Vietnam would reject the option of falling into the "arms of Communist China."[18]

Rostow expanded this argument the following day with yet another substantial memorandum dispatched to the under-siege secretary of state. "For centuries all Vietnamese have had as an objective of policy to keep an arms-length relation to China," Rostow correctly explained, "and I do not for one moment believe . . . that the North Vietnamese are prepared to forego that kind of independence, whatever their present relations with Peking." North Vietnam would rather be defeated, Rostow argued, than seek help from its historical adversary. And in the unlikely event that Ho Chi Minh did accept China's gold, the consequence would be "the permanent reduction of [North Vietnam's] status from junior partner to Chinese province." Rostow was adamant that Sino-Vietnamese hostility would be "one among other constraints on their conduct in the face of the policy we have been discussing."[19]

The director of the Policy Planning Council was thus one of the few U.S. foreign-policy officials to appreciate that Vietnam's antagonistic relationship with China was a crucial consideration for U.S. policymakers. Yet while the bad blood between these nations was important to recognize, Rostow did not believe that it made South Vietnam any less important to America. George Ball later argued that this schism in the communist bloc decreased South Vietnam's importance to the United States. Ball believed that a unified Vietnam under Ho Chi Minh might come to resemble Marshal Josip Tito's Yugoslavia: a communist nation certainly, but one whose independent-mindedness irritated its giant communist neighbor. Rostow, however, was immovable in his belief that saving South Vietnam from its communist insurgency was vital for the United States, and the liberal capitalist world. He was not interested in losing any Southeast Asian nation to communism, whether it was Titoist or not.

IT IS IMPORTANT to consider—particularly in light of Rostow's later assertion that the U.S. military "fought with an arm tied behind its back"—that the Joint Chiefs of Staff opposed Rostow's plan for a "graduated" attack on North Vietnam's infrastructure.[20] The Joint Chiefs' position, maintained with customary rigor by the pugnacious Curtis LeMay, Air Force chief of staff, was some way removed from the idea that the threat was more important than the execution. What was required were "damaging actions, designed to affect Hanoi's will by destroying a significant portion of their capability."[21] By August 1964 LeMay, as head of a Pentagon planning study, concluded that bombing North Vietnam's supply, ammunition, and POL storage facilities in one fell swoop would compel Hanoi to cease infiltration. LeMay's planning team formed a list of ninety-four targets that constituted "the essential components of the North's war-making capability." Through a "severe" application of air power, the group determined that all targets could be destroyed in sixteen days.[22] As LeMay wistfully recalled, had all targets been attacked "we would have bombed [the North Vietnamese] back into the Stone Age."[23] LeMay was keen for the United States to "stop swatting flies and go after the manure pile."[24] This was a principle with which Rostow only partly agreed.

Pursuing such an extreme military course was, in Rostow's opinion, unnecessary. This was not so much out of ethical concerns, but because the essence of applying force—as he stressed to McNamara in September 1964—lay not "in the damage we do, but the character of our military disposition and our diplomatic communications."[25] Paraphrasing LeMay's earthy analogy, Rostow wanted to threaten the "manure pile" first, swat it if threats went unheeded, and destroy it if all else failed. Rostow was simply elaborating on his theory that in times of war, threatening a nation's economy would prove decisive in itself. But this argument ran counter to the received orthodoxy, expressed most powerfully by the Prussian military strategist Carl von Clausewitz, which holds that in times of war "because each side is driven to outdo the other, states tend to escalate their efforts."[26]

In March 1964 Robert Johnson completed an appraisal of his boss's plan for bombing North Vietnam. His report was highly critical of the assumptions on which Rostow's rationale was based. The U.S. bombing plan would fail, Johnson contended, because North Vietnam "was motivated by factors which were not affected by physical change and physical damage." In an observation that was clearly designed to cast doubt on the universality of Rostow's *Stages* theory—and point out the dangers of applying it to the Vietnamese civil war—Johnson concluded that "the North Vietnamese were not hooked on the idea of economic growth determination . . . but were determined to extend their regime's control to the entire country rather than maintain their industrialization."[27] It was apparent to Johnson that the majority of northern communists believed that reunifying Vietnam was more important than protecting infrastructural development in a part of it.

Johnson's critique was not simply a one-sided assault on Rostow's thesis. Titled "Alternatives for Imposition of Measured Pressures Against North Vietnam," the report conceded that bombing might well provide a psychological boost to Saigon while amply demonstrating the degree to which the United States was dedicated to South Vietnam. These two considerations provided some satisfaction to Rostow, as they partially reinforced his belief that taking the fight to the north would build South Vietnam's confidence both in itself and in the United States as a military guarantor. But the crux of the report was critical. As Johnson later recalled, it "recognized that the United States would have serious problems both in convincing the American public and others that escalation was justified and prudent."[28]

Rostow was unmoved by this perceptive critique. According to David Halberstam, he attempted to suppress widespread dissemination of a document that so significantly detracted from his own bombing thesis. Later in the year, sections of Johnson's analysis did find their way to other members of the administration. The reservations expressed in the report helped cement George Ball's doubts about bombing, and, according to Halberstam, provided him with some of the intellectual ammunition for his "dissenting papers."[29]

Roger Hilsman also formulated a compelling counterargument to the Rostow Thesis: if the United States were to bomb North Vietnam "before we [have] demonstrated success in our counterinsurgency program" it would be "interpreted by the communists as an act of desperation and will, therefore, not be effective in persuading the North Vietnamese to cease and desist."[30] Bombing North Vietnam without establishing cohesion in the south did smack of desperation. Resorting to such means signaled a defeat of sorts for the liberal strain of U.S. postwar social science that Rostow represented. Surely the "modernization" of South Vietnam was not beyond America's Olympian capabilities both in terms of resources and strategy? In 1963 the social scientist Seymour Martin Lipset wrote, "The fundamental political problems of the industrial revolution have been solved . . . This very triumph of democratic social revolution in the West ends domestic politics for those intellectuals who must have . . . utopias to motivate them to social action."[31] If this was the case, could not America's domestically sated intellectuals have turned their attention elsewhere? Was building a functioning South Vietnam really beyond a nation that had recently solved its own fundamental political issues? While Rostow would attribute any failure in protecting South Vietnam to America's reluctance to stem north-south infiltration, the Rostow Thesis and the credibility of Third World development theory were being subjected to some searching questions.

Other significant figures were skeptical that this gradual escalation in bombing would prove as decisive as Rostow envisioned. Many of these criticisms were leveled from a purely strategic standpoint. On February 25, 1964, the U.S. ambassador to Laos, William H. Sullivan, wrote that he was sure that "Mr. Rostow agrees that action against North Vietnam can never be a substitute for the hard, grubby job of routing out the Viet Cong in the areas where they have established themselves in the south." Rather than viewing bombing North Vietnam as a panacea, Sullivan stressed that this plan was seriously compromised by the fact that "the Viet Cong have a sustaining strength of their own."[32] Rostow disagreed. He replied to Sullivan's paper the following day in a memorandum predictably titled "The External Element in Viet-Nam." He rebutted Sullivan's analysis by contending that "the best chance of lifting morale in the south" is to target this "external but critical margin of intrusion."[33]

The idea that the NLF insurgency had internal roots—that a civil war had engulfed South Vietnam—was one that Rostow declined to countenance. To accept this reading implied that communism held genuine appeal to the people of South Vietnam. Writing to Dean Rusk on May 6, Rostow complained that skewed reporting of the war "tends to portray it as a vicious, indigenous civil war in which the United States has somehow got involved in ambiguous ways."[34] This appraisal of the conflict, however, conformed to the reality on the ground more than that provided by Rostow. In a nation where land reform was neglected, and where successive South Vietnamese regimes were popularly perceived to be American puppets, the NLF held distinct appeal to many people south of the seventeenth parallel. In the autumn of 1964, Lieutenant General Andrew J. Goodpaster complained to Robert McNamara, "You are trying to program the enemy and that is one thing that we must never try to do. We can't do his thinking for him."[35] This criticism could easily be directed at Rostow, his thesis of graduated, coercive pressure, and the priorities he ascribed to North Vietnam's leaders and to South Vietnamese insurgents.

Rostow's plan was assailed by other critics who felt that American resources should be devoted to a massive air campaign from the get-go, not watered down through a dedication to escalation on "gradualist" lines. Maxwell Taylor, a former ally, commented that "a surprise attack from the air could be very effective, but thereafter attacks would be less effective and losses would go up."[36] The military was overwhelmingly opposed to the idea that a bombing campaign was a suitable channel through which to send coercive messages. If North Vietnam was the designated target, then it should be bombed without constraint. The point was not to threaten a nation's industry, but to destroy it with as many sorties as necessary as quickly as possible.

Gradualism, however, still appealed to one man, and fortunately for Rostow it was the one who mattered. In the run-up to the November 1964 presidential election, the Democratic Party's strategy was to lampoon the Republican candidate Barry Goldwater as an uncaring fiscal conservative and a potential threat to world peace, a hard-line anticommunist who countenanced nuclear war a little too readily. During his acceptance speech at the Republican national convention, Goldwater had famously declared, "Extremism in the defense of liberty is no vice. And let me also remind you that moderation in the pursuit of justice is no virtue." Provided with some great ammunition, LBJ's supporters replaced Goldwater's campaign slogan, "In your heart you know he's right," with "In your guts you know he's nuts."[37]

On Vietnam Goldwater charged that Johnson's failure to prosecute the conflict aggressively was devoid of "goal, course, or purpose." These barbs had very little effect on the course of the campaign. LBJ recognized that plotting a moderate escalatory path in Vietnam was sufficient to defeat his opponent's shrill warnings of impending defeat and would also allow him to focus the bulk of his energies—and America's financial resources—on his Great Society program of domestic reform. In these circumstances Johnson found solace in Rostow's contention that an extreme, costly Americanization was unnecessary to secure South Vietnam's independence. Bombing was cheap and, if Rostow was right, it promised much in terms of cost-benefit calculations. It was on those grounds that on March 17, 1964, Johnson approved planning for "graduated, overt military pressure" on North Vietnam in National Security Action Memorandum (NSAM) 288.[38] This plan set in motion a series of recommendations that culminated less than a year later in the Rolling Thunder bombing campaign against North Vietnam.[39]

TWO WEEKS PRIOR to the president's approval of NSAM 288, an incident occurred that brought Rostow to Johnson's attention for all the wrong reasons. In late February 1964, Johnson had referred to North Vietnam's support for the southern insurgency as a "deeply dangerous game." The president was annoyed that the press had characterized his comments as a rhetorical shift toward inevitable escalation. *The Washington Post* journalist Chalmers Roberts had apparently sought clarification on this issue from Rostow, who had obliged by criticizing North Vietnam and asserting—not without reason—that the president was seriously concerned about the issue of infiltration. Speaking to Robert McNamara on March 2, the president explained, "I blew my top here for a whole damn week." Johnson told his defense secretary that he got it from "people in Saigon" that "Rostow had a propaganda move on to really invade North Vietnam . . . Now they want to hang it on a higher person and say that I indicated that we're going to invade North Vietnam."[40] LBJ was incensed that Rostow might have discussed such a sensitive issue with the press. Rostow was taking a well-deserved holiday at the time, but such minor details were not to stand in the way of a presidential dressing down.

Having finished a day's skiing on the slopes of Aspen, Rostow was enjoying a bath when he received a phone call from one irate Lyndon Johnson. The president angrily informed him that the press had been using his name to define the bombing policy that they alleged the administration was planning to pursue. Johnson complained that "they're quoting you as advocating Plan 6, or plan something else that I don't know anything about," before finally snapping "the president doesn't know the position of the administration so you can't know it."[41] A chastened Rostow mumbled that he had not deliberately leaked any information, but responded to Johnson's tirade more comprehensively five days later. "Since my Fort Bragg speech," Rostow explained carefully, "my name has been associated with the proposition that the war in South Vietnam could not be won unless infiltration from the north was stopped; and that this could only be done if Ho Chi Minh were made to pay a price greater than his venture into Laos and South Vietnam was worth . . . My connection with this line of thought goes back a long way; and . . . public references to me arise from that fact, not from any current activity."[42] Fortunately for Rostow's career, this explanation mollified the president. As Johnson warmly remarked in late 1964, "The only place in the State Department where I get any new ideas is the policy planning staff."[43]

Johnson's good opinion of Rostow's creativity may also have been enhanced in contradistinction to some of the truly dreadful ideas that were presented by his other advisers. On a June 1964 trip to Honolulu, Johnson's foreign-policy principals met to discuss ways to make President Nguyen Khan's short-lived government "*look* inspiring." This in itself was a goal that spoke volumes about the scale of America's task. Henry Cabot Lodge suggested that the United States "try to write a nice song for SVN," arguing that the "Reds use guitar-playing, story-telling types to good effect." When Ambassador Lodge suggested that "we could use [a] U.S. singer who memorized bits," Army Chief of Staff Earle Wheeler, aghast perhaps at the prospect of his army devoting time to communal sing-alongs, replied that the ARVN already "does a good job of this."[44] Rostow's bombing plan had at least the merit of simplicity, putting the U.S. military to its intended use.

On August 3, 1964, McNamara's Defense Department joined "with the State Department in a thorough analysis of and report on the Rostow thesis" and arrived at an ambivalent conclusion.[45] Of prime concern was the fact that the "economy of North Vietnam is 88% agricultural. It is not an island and there is no great dependence on maritime trade." Furthermore, the "kind of action envisaged by the Rostow thesis will in general not be sufficient to deal with the problems of insurgency. Successful action against insurgency requires, above all, an effective counterinsurgency program in the country under attack." These reservations would prove prescient, yet despairingly the report concludes that the "counterinsurgency picture is not encouraging. The alternatives are not bright . . . the Rostow thesis may be the only viable, albeit risky, alternative."[46] This far from ringing endorsement was complemented by McNamara's office directly, whose analysts warned that the "likelihood and political costs of failure of the approach and the pressures for U.S. escalation if the early moves should fail require serious examination."[47] Both State and Defense had cast significant doubts on the viability of a graduated bombing campaign. These reservations were cast aside the following day, however, when a portentous event occurred that lent the Rostow Thesis decisive momentum as "the only viable" military alternative.

DURING A STORMY NIGHT in the Gulf of Tonkin, on August 4, 1964, the captains of two American destroyers, the *Maddox* and the *C. Turner Joy*, reported that North Vietnamese torpedo boats were attacking them. Both ships were engaged in electronic espionage to support South Vietnamese gunboat assaults on the North Vietnamese mainland, previously authorized by the president in December 1963 under OPLAN 34A. While the *Maddox* had been incontrovertibly involved in a naval engagement with torpedo boats just three days previously, North Vietnam's culpability with regard to the second attack was murkier. Years later Johnson confided, "For all I know, our navy was shooting at whales out there."[48] The absence of definitive proof, however, was an irrelevant detail to the president's foreign-policy principals at the time. The Gulf of Tonkin incidents provided exactly the pretext that hawks like Walt Rostow had been looking for. According to James Thomson Jr., a liberal member of McGeorge Bundy's NSC staff, Rostow was invigorated by the news: "You know the wonderful thing is we don't even know if this thing happened at all. Boy, it gives us the chance to really go for broke on the bombing. The evidence is unclear, but our golden opportunity is at hand."[49] According to David Halberstam, Rostow told his allies at the State Department, "Things could not have gone better had they planned them this way."[50] Exasperated by Rostow's ebullience, Bundy told his former deputy to "button his lip" lest his indiscreet language reach the press.[51]

Sensing a rare opportunity to press home the advantage, Rostow wrote to Dean Rusk the following day, "The Tonkin Gulf incidents, taken as a whole, are likely to have a momentum of their own which we should seek to direct for our own purposes." Rostow was pleased that the incident would necessarily "shift the vision of the problem" among the American public from "the U.S. as marginal defenders of the area, to one of direct confrontation with the Asian communists." Following on from such a grave incident, the "fundamental issue" was whether or not the Johnson administration should utilize this "transient unity" among the American public to "force Hanoi to cease its aggression and to return, essentially, to compliance with the 1954 and 1962 Accords." Rostow had no doubt that the time was right for a more forceful approach: "We should seek to guide the forces set in motion by the communist attacks to the maximum extent possible."[52]

Rostow himself was given the opportunity to "guide" public opinion toward a resolute military stance when the president requested that he help draft his first public response to events in the Gulf of Tonkin. Johnson's peroration at Syracuse University was once again provided by Rostow's busy pen: "There can be no peace by aggression and no immunity from reply."[53] In his 1972 memoir Rostow recalls that Johnson's Syracuse speech was truly significant in that he "fully elaborated the reasons for his commitment to the defense of Southeast Asia."[54] While LBJ did not come close to disclosing all the facts—what the U.S. destroyers were really doing off the coast of North Vietnam, for example—Rostow's contribution was undoubtedly significant. Rostow provided the administration's rhetorical response to the Gulf of Tonkin incident, while the military strategy that was eventually employed also bore his signature. Congress approved the Tonkin Gulf Resolution against the wishes of only two dissenting senators: Wayne Morse from Oregon and Ernest Gruening from Alaska. Joint Resolution 1145 was signed into law on August 10, 1964. It stipulated that "the United States regards as vital to its national interest and to world peace the maintenance of international peace and security in southeast Asia . . . The United States is, therefore, prepared, as the president determines, to take all necessary steps, including the use of armed force, to assist any member or protocol state of the Southeast Asia Collective Defense Treaty requesting assistance in defense of its freedom."[55] The president now possessed carte blanche to wage war in Vietnam as he saw fit. As it turned out, the main strategy that the United States pursued was one of graduated bombing.

To put the Rostow Thesis through its final paces, the Joint Chiefs of Staff set up the SIGMA II war-game simulation to assess how an escalatory bombing campaign might affect Hanoi's behavior. A virtual affair designed and umpired by the RAND Corporation, SIGMA allocated to opposing teams of high-ranking officials strategic priorities and military resources, and requested that the participants move their pieces to achieve victory as they would in a game of chess. The SIGMA I simulation of April 1964 had challenged the assumption that bombing North Vietnam would hinder its ability to support the southern insurgency. SIGMA I predicted a clear victory for North Vietnam in spite of the "virtual" deployment of 500,000 U.S. troops and the launching of a sustained bombing campaign. As the second war game progressed, it became apparent that the same principle was holding true: North Vietnam's overwhelmingly agrarian society rendered it less vulnerable to the use of air power. As the historian H. R. McMaster writes, "The [virtual] bombing . . . had minimal effect and actually stiffened North Vietnamese determination, as the Viet Cong used existing stockpiles and civilian support to sustain the insurgency in the South."[56] As bombing failed to do the job, each side escalated their actions steadily until the "blue" American team opted to deploy ground troops. At that point, the leaders of the "red" communist team observed that once these virtual soldiers began to take casualties, "You're there, you're committed. Your honor is at stake, now you've got to do something."[57]

The conclusion of the war game was sobering, and indeed it closely corresponded to what unfolded in subsequent years. Graduated pressure did not compel Hanoi to cease infiltration but provoked an intensification of effort that led to the deployment of American ground troops on a large scale. As the simulation progressed, American casualties mounted and the players guessed that domestic criticism of the war would become more widespread. From the starting point of graduated bombing pressure, SIGMA II predicted that the ultimate outcome would be a bloody, divisive, protracted war.[58] Yet according to William Bundy, the assistant secretary of state for Far Eastern affairs (and McGeorge Bundy's brother), the influence of SIGMA II's doom-laden conclusions on those charged with Vietnam planning "was not great."[59] All of the illustrious members who participated, including McGeorge Bundy, John McNaughton, and Earle Wheeler, ignored the war game. Even Maxwell Taylor, who led the red team to victory, was unfazed by this crushing virtual defeat for the U.S. military. (He may have attributed the communist victory to his own strategic brilliance.) A weight of criticism had assailed Rostow's bombing thesis and yet it had retained its position as the best of all possible options. It was a significant juncture in the history of America's involvement in the second Indochina War. As George Kennan wrote perceptively on October 5, 1964, "Once on the tiger's back, we cannot be sure of picking the place to dismount."[60]

That Rostow's strategically compromised idea staggered on regardless owed much to the fact that by the autumn of 1964 the political and military situation in South Vietnam had reached a crisis point. The central government exerted little authority across the nation and conditions in the cities were anarchic. General William Westmoreland later recalled that in Saigon "the atmosphere fairly smelled of discontent [with] workers on strike, students demonstrating [and] the local press pursuing a persistent campaign of criticism of the new government."[61] The strategic hamlet program had dissolved away quietly, and the NLF insurgents were becoming increasingly emboldened as North Vietnamese support for their cause increased. Something had to happen to improve South Vietnam's prospects, and little else was on the table. Johnson's coterie of foreign-policy advisers opted for the Rostow Thesis not with enthusiasm but resignation. On September 7, 1964, Johnson finally sanctioned retaliatory raids, but not on the Rostow criteria: "We should . . . respond on a tit-for-tat basis against the DRV in any event of any attack on United States units."[62] Unconvinced by such half-measures, and fearful that the Gulf of Tonkin momentum was ebbing away, Rostow immediately shot back, "I question whether a tit-for-tat approach is wise . . . What is required in Hanoi and Peiping is the conviction that we have decided to [escalate] on a scale sufficient to raise the question in Hanoi as to whether the war in the South is worth pursuing."[63] Rostow further urged that the United States "make lucid" to the leaders of the People's Republic of China that if they opted to intervene militarily in Vietnam then "the mainland of China will be subject to attack."[64] Once again Rostow countenanced the widening of the war to include China.

On November 1, 1964, NLF forces attacked an American air base at Bien Hoa, killing four American servicemen and destroying seventeen of the thirty-six B-57 aircraft that had been sent to South Vietnam following the Tonkin Gulf Resolution. The president did not want to rush into ordering a swift military counterstrike, and so he directed an NSC working group, headed by William Bundy, to examine alternatives for bombing on the Rostow criteria—options that went well beyond tit-for-tat. With "A" the status quo, "B" a LeMay-style heavy air assault, and "C" a graduated air campaign on the Rostow model, the last option was, unsurprisingly, adopted by the Johnson administration with alacrity.[65] And so Bundy's "Option C" was authorized in January and implemented in March 1965 in the form of the Rolling Thunder campaign against North Vietnam. Conscious that direct Chinese intervention was a distinct problem with LeMay's plan, Lyndon Johnson had opted for the Rostow Thesis.[66]

IT SHOULD BE made clear that while Rostow's ideas were present at the crucial escalatory meetings of the Vietnam War, his person was not. His impact on the decision-making process prior to the launch of Rolling Thunder was significant, although he should not be placed alongside Bundy and McNamara as a direct participatory force for escalation. The defense secretary had become convinced that the United States could defeat the South Vietnamese insurgency through the application of its superior military force. The national security adviser was equally convinced that America could not duck this battle. But the foundations on which these men made their recommendations were not formed in a vacuum; they were shaped by many influences, one of which was the man who fashioned a Vietnam bombing strategy before anyone else. Both State and Defense referred to the option of bombing North Vietnam as the Rostow Thesis. The usage of such terminology suggests that Rostow's influence—even from the distant remove of the Policy Planning Council—was profound.

Robert McNamara was a brilliant manager of facts and data, but no innovator. He took his ideas from others, subjected them to a searching, usually quantitative critique, and if the numbers worked, his decision was made. Dean Rusk was deferential and unwilling to impose himself on the big foreign-policy questions, seeking constant approval and encouragement from his president but refusing to champion a distinctive line. McGeorge Bundy had a fine mind. He could prioritize information, write pithy memoranda, and terrify subordinates with his rationalism and impatience with flabby arguments. Yet Bundy also lacked creativity. He was leery of ideology and happiest managing crises, not formulating broad strategies. Rostow was different. He was the prophet of American victory in the Vietnam War. He felt that he intuitively understood the nature of communist insurgency—as the "disease of the transition to capitalism"— and was confident that he knew how to win the war. Unlike McNamara, Bundy, and Rusk, Rostow had a number of plans to defeat communism in Vietnam. He was unfailingly optimistic that the conflict would be resolved to America's satisfaction. Lyndon Johnson needed new ideas to protect South Vietnam and constant reassurance that the war was winnable. Walt Rostow provided both with a smile.

During the wilderness years that followed his removal from the National Security Council in November 1961, Rostow had argued, in the face of overwhelming apathy, that striking North Vietnam was vital. Although by late 1964 this recommendation had found belated favor, and was planned for future implementation, Rostow was frustrated that it proved not to be the year for bombing: "I had failed to persuade Kennedy in 1962; and I failed to persuade Johnson in 1964."[67] This frustration with regard to Kennedy is comprehensible, but Johnson by the fall of 1964 had essentially been convinced of the merits of bombing. Nevertheless, as Rostow recalls in his memoir, "my nightmare since 1961 had come true; that is, the United States acted to save Southeast Asia late in the day, in the waning situation."[68] He chose to address this waning situation, however, not with a policy of all-out attack, but with one of limited bombing with the threat of more to come. Rolling Thunder was the Rostow Thesis writ large. He was for gradualism, and opposed to the aggressive targeting advocated by the Joint Chiefs of Staff. Rostow criticized Johnson's military timidity on many occasions in his later career, yet it was partly of his own making.[69] If the U.S. military did indeed fight with an arm tied behind its back, it was Rostow who helped secure the knot.

Beyond the enthusiasm of one man, it is striking that the bombing campaign was accepted in government circles with such absence of hope. In December 1964 Johnson cabled Maxwell Taylor with disturbing candor, "I have never felt that this war will be won in the air."[70] In a particularly blunt discussion with McNamara, the president further despaired that "now we're off to bombing these people. We're over that hurdle. I don't think anything is going to be as bad as losing, and I don't see any way of winning."[71] McGeorge Bundy was visiting South Vietnam on February 7 when the NLF attacked the Pleiku airfield, killing nine Americans and injuring a further five hundred more. Upon visiting the site and witnessing the carnage, William Westmoreland recalls that Bundy fell under a spell of "field marshal psychosis." He recommended that Johnson implement the bombing contingency not as a one-off, but in "sustained reprisal."[72]

Yet once the psychosis subsided—and it took little time for the rationalist to return—Bundy's belief in the potency of bombing was short-lived indeed: "It may fail, and we cannot estimate the odds of success with any accuracy—they may be somewhere between 25% and 75% . . . [but] even if it fails, the policy will be worth it. At a minimum it will damp down the charge that we did not do all we could have done."[73] It is a challenge to conceive—particularly in the current climate—that America would embark on war with such negative objectives, but such was the reality of Rolling Thunder. By June 21, 1965, Lyndon Johnson's frustration at the somewhat limited effects of bombing, and the fear that his earlier prediction would be proved correct, was expressed again to McNamara: "I'm very depressed . . . I see no program from either Defense or State that gives us much hope of doing anything, except just praying . . . they'll quit. I don't believe they're ever going to quit. And I don't see any plan for victory—militarily or diplomatically."[74]

Such gloomy musings were in accord with the fact that early signs indicated that Rolling Thunder was not making a significant dent on either northern morale, southern infiltration, or what Rostow took to be Ho Chi Minh's overwhelming consideration: he "has an industrial complex to protect."[75] Gallup opinion polls showed that 67 percent of the public supported the American bombing campaign against North Vietnam, but the actual impact on northern resolve was less impressive.[76] Johnson would not go as far as the Joint Chiefs desired in extending the bombing, as he feared direct Chinese intervention—an outcome that did not bother Rostow, as he believed that economic disarray in Mao's China would ensure that it would not intervene or lend significant military support to Hanoi. And so an uneasy compromise was struck between the president's relative reserve and the Joint Chiefs' bellicosity, which would continue through most of the bombing campaign.

While Rostow was immersed in the minutiae of targeting priorities, he did find time to compose a number of memoranda that played to his supposed academic strengths: Third World economic development. With Rolling Thunder authorized, and the debate over military strategy resolved to his apparent satisfaction, Rostow turned to the softer side of U.S. foreign policy (and his own personality). Writing to Dean Rusk on February 17, 1965, Rostow advised that "if the President is to make a major policy statement on Vietnam, he might usefully place our current efforts there in a longer term context which would emphasize our interest in promoting the welfare of the peoples of Asia." North Vietnam was to suffer the worst of its military might, but the United States, as a benevolent nation, was also to devote time and resources to economically invigorating the region. Rostow urged that "if Asian countries wish to set up an Asian Development Bank, the U.S. would be prepared to join other developed nations in contributing." Rostow also recommended that the United States contribute to the "multipurpose development of the Lower Mekong Delta." While Rostow recognized that "nothing useful can be done on this until the war is settled," he was keen for the president to stress the "long term possibility" of a plan such as this coming to fruition.[77] Of course this is exactly what the president did during his celebrated speech at Johns Hopkins University on April 7, 1965, in which he promised Vietnam a Mekong River development program that would "provide food and water and power on a scale to dwarf even our own TVA."[78]

Rostow's ideas, farsighted and altruistic as they were, did verge on the Panglossian. The president himself was perhaps less confident than Rostow that building a TVA on the Mekong Delta was likely to happen, joking with his advisers the previous day that his speech was primarily designed to throw a bone to the "sob sisters and peace societies" across the United States.[79] The creation of a credible South Vietnamese nation was well-nigh impossible given its social divisions and lack of historical legitimacy. Having completed a comprehensive survey on how the South Vietnamese viewed their government, the U.S. Information Agency had concluded that "the population is largely apathetic and is primarily interested in ending the twenty years of war; they care less as to which side will win, although there appears to be a substantial degree of support for the Viet Cong."[80] Victory in the war was a distant prospect given that "in the eyes of the average rural South Vietnamese, Saigon neither knows nor cares about his needs and desires."[81] The very fact that Rostow was devoting intellectual attention to U.S. economic policy toward postbellum Southeast Asia suggests that he possessed great faith in the critical impact that the Rolling Thunder bombing campaign was likely to have on the conflict.

In April 1965 Rostow informed McNamara, "I'm an old pro in the field . . . This is how we should use air power properly," before advising that attacks be ordered on North Vietnam's electric power station—a target amenable to the Joint Chiefs but not to the president. Attacking those skeptics who argued that Hanoi "will accept the destruction of its industrial establishment in the north for the right to continue infiltration and the continued guidance of war in the south," Rostow replied confidently, "I am personally skeptical of such skepticism." He reiterated that "our optimum bombing strategy should not be the destruction of their industrial capital." Bombing North Vietnam's electric power facilities was coercive, but it "would leave their industrial capacity idle, but in being, still to be saved."[82]

This final stricture fell away gradually as it became increasingly clear that the U.S. strategy of threatening North Vietnam with airborne destruction was not scaring its leaders as intended. On July 26 Rostow wrote to Dean Rusk that "we must soon bite the bullet on hitting serious (but non-sanguinary) targets in the Hanoi-Haiphong area." Whereas in April Rostow had stressed that a comprehensive bombing strategy was unwise, he now believed that "in Hanoi the critical measure of whether the U.S. is totally committed to achieving our limited, legal objective is whether we hit those targets. They regard their success in deterring us thus far as a major achievement and a measure of the limits of our will to see it through."[83] If Hanoi looked upon America's self-imposed bombing limits as some kind of a "major achievement," then Rostow deserved the credit. It was the Rostow Thesis that imposed limits and that stressed warnings and intimidation, not destruction.

By September 1965 Rostow had entirely jettisoned the concept of threatening the north with attack in favor of simple attack. As he confidently wrote to Rusk—with no blushes at his volte-face on "gradualism"—there "is little doubt that the most effective use of airpower against North Vietnam would be systematically to attack certain target systems which are critical to the military supply and production capabilities of that country. The two best candidates are: oil storage and electric power." Surprisingly, in light of his earlier stricture that what was left untouched by bombing was as important as what was destroyed, Rostow complained that "there is evidence that the lack of system and follow through in attack . . . is denying us their full potentialities." As a sop to his earlier thesis, Rostow maintained that Hanoi would retain "its hard-won industrial and urban infrastructure."[84]

But after bombing North Vietnam's transport system, POL storage facilities, and electric power stations, what exactly was left for American bombers to threaten? As Rostow's desperation increased in later years, he would call for bombing targets as peripheral to the infiltration effort as Hanoi's three radio stations. He rationalized that "the military case is not strong; although they are a source of vicious propaganda throughout Southeast Asia . . . Radio Hanoi is a symbol of the regime's power and regional pretensions."[85] The Rostow Thesis, as the early stages of Rolling Thunder proved, was an inadequate response to the gargantuan task that America faced in South Vietnam. Rostow paused little to consider how wrong his original assumptions had proved to be, however, but shifted his attention elsewhere to more aggressive options. His U-turn on gradualism went apparently unnoticed by his colleagues and superiors. While the president was not yet keen on hitting the expanding range of targets that Rostow now advocated, he did admire the optimism and dedication with which he made his case. As National Security Adviser McGeorge Bundy fell out of favor, so Rostow looked increasingly like a potential replacement.

THE MEDIA HAD CRITICIZED Bundy heavily for canceling his attendance at a May 1965 Vietnam teach-in. It was a decision that Bundy had been compelled to make by Johnson, and was one that greatly irritated the former dean of Harvard College—a man who did not duck an intellectual challenge. A month later Bundy agreed to debate the celebrated exponent of realism in international affairs, Professor Hans Morgenthau of the University of Chicago. The president was again angered at Bundy's failure to consult. Johnson barked at his press secretary Bill Moyers, "I want you to go to Bundy and tell him that the president would be pleased, mighty pleased, to accept his resignation." Rendered mute by the ferocity of the outburst, and the unlikelihood that LBJ actually wanted his request to be carried out, Moyers said nothing. "That's the problem with all you fellows," Johnson erupted. "You're all in bed with the Kennedys."[86]

Rostow attended the May teach-in that Bundy was prevented from attending, but he had been granted the president's blessing in making the administration's case for the war. Following the event Rostow reported to Dean Rusk that the antiwar academics "represent in American academic life a minority of no great distinction" and that "the only truly objectionable feature of the occasion was the sanctimonious assumption of higher virtue among the academic critics—an attitude as inappropriate to the spirit of academic life as it would be within government."[87] While not exactly sanctimonious, Rostow himself was not averse to making claims of higher virtue—particularly with regard to the anticommunist crusade—but this partisan report was one that would have pleased Rusk and the president. Following the teach-in imbroglio, Bundy had lost the president's trust. By November Johnson was expressing a clear preference that Rostow succeed Bundy.

In a conversation with Rusk about a possible vacancy at the NSC, the president rationalized that "Rostow would give us more protection from the intellectual and college crowd." On this count Johnson could not have been more wrong, and it is hard to accept this justification at face value. But the president's second reason for picking Rostow was more significant, less disingenuous, and speaks volumes about his influence with regard to the use of air power: "He had a little idea about bombing that we didn't have." The president recognized that Rostow had led the way with regard to the bombing strategy. Rusk was less enamored with the prospect of Rostow as national security adviser, cautioning that "McNamara thinks he is a little verbose" (read: "From personal experience, I know he is verbose"), and stated that Deputy Undersecretary for Political Affairs U. Alexis Johnson was his preferred option.[88] Johnson, however, was clear that Rostow impressed him and that he viewed his potential appointment favorably.

Johnson's good opinion of Rostow as an ideas man was enhanced by an increased bellicosity that mirrored his own. On December 8 the president informed his defense secretary, "I'm inclined to believe it's about time to give them a little crack through bombing," specifying that he was keen to take out "a power plant" in Hanoi.[89] McNamara, Rusk, and Bundy were all doubtful that destroying Hanoi's and Haiphong's power plants and POL storage facilities was the right thing to do, strategically and morally, but the chairman of the Policy Planning Council had no doubts at all. On December 23 Rostow advised that the president should "systematically bomb the oil refining and storage capacity and the electrical power facilities in North Vietnam," a plan that LeMay had earlier championed as an alternative to "gradualism." Rostow explained that he had "long felt" that the U.S. should pursue a "systematic but surgical" use of air power to take out the POL storage facilities and "electric power systems in the Hanoi-Haiphong area." Of course Rostow had not "long felt" that bombing these supplies was necessary, but had retracted his idea that threatening them was sufficient. Nevertheless, Rostow closed his memorandum by citing his experience during World War II as a significant lesson from which to learn. "It is difficult for those who did not live through the application of systemic, precision bombing against [Germany]," Rostow explained, "to understand how vastly more effective this kind of bombing is than generalized air strikes."[90]

IN *The Diffusion of Power*, Rostow identifies July 28, 1965, as the critical date in the history of America's intervention in the Vietnam War. Robert McNamara visited South Vietnam in July and recommended that the president "expand promptly and substantially the U.S. military pressure against the Viet Cong in the South," including an increase in U.S. ground forces.[91] Responding to his defense secretary's recommendation on July 28, Johnson announced the prompt dispatch of 50,000 U.S. ground troops and added that more would follow if requested. Johnson's decision increased the total number of American troops in Vietnam to 125,000—a truly significant step that placed the overwhelming burden on America, not South Vietnam, to win the war. But not all in the hawk column were pleased. Maxwell Taylor in particular was perplexed as to why Johnson would dispatch U.S. troops so readily when air power had not yet been deployed systematically. Like Rostow, Taylor believed that bombing could be the decisive weapon.

In 1972 Rostow wrote, "On that day—July 28, 1965—the die was cast. It was cast, however, in a particular form at a particular time." Rostow was critical of the fact that the ground troop decision was made "a full year after Hanoi's decision to commit regular North Vietnamese troops to the battle . . . As in 1917 and 1941, 1947 and 1950, the American weight was thrown into the scales late, long after the aggressors had committed themselves to the venture."[92] Rostow, however, had said very little on the issue of deploying U.S. combat forces to Vietnam, believing instead that the threat of aerial bombardment would alone be sufficient to curtail infiltration through Laos and compel Hanoi to cease its support for the southern insurgency. His retrospective criticism of Johnson's timidity with regard to deploying ground troops therefore seems unfair.

Rostow was critical of the primarily "defensive" application of military force that Johnson implemented, explaining that "his diplomatic advisers urged strongly that this was the route best calculated to minimize the likelihood of Soviet or Chinese Communist military intervention." In Rostow's estimation such an approach risked ushering in the grim reality of a protracted war that was "a difficult course to undertake" given the "strains it would impose on American life."[93] While less bothered than others by the prospect that either the Soviet Union or the People's Republic of China would intervene militarily, Rostow's criticism that Johnson failed to wage war vigorously is compromised by his own mixed record. More than anyone else, Rostow designed the Rolling Thunder bombing campaign, and provided the most compelling rationale for gradualism. Rostow disavowed and then castigated America's limited bombing strategy. But that should not detract from the fact that he helped build it.

That is not to say that North Vietnam was stoically immune to the devastation wreaked by American bombs. At the close of 1965, the North Vietnamese premier Pham Van Dong lamented that bombing "is costing us terribly dear. I'm not acting when I say that. I am obliged to cry— literally cry—at the suffering and the losses."[94] Yet while American bombs hurt the leadership, infrastructure, and populace of North Vietnam, it did not decisively undermine the fortitude of the nation. On December 17 George Ball lamented that "we are not breaking the will of North Vietnam. They are digging in a hardened line. I was in charge of bombing surveys in World War II and bombing never wins a war . . . The only hope we have is to stop bombing and seize every opportunity not to resume."[95] Ball's case against bombing was no surprise given his repeatedly avowed skepticism about the efficacy of air power as a whole. Yet less predictable quarters were also casting doubts.

On December 21 a special intelligence estimate concluded, "The US/GVN air strikes to date fall short of crippling the North Vietnamese economy." While the northern economy had developed a "noticeable limp," there was no "indication of any significant decline in North Vietnamese morale."[96] To the eyes of many, the richest nation in the world was devastating a Third World nation with little credible justification. Yet in an administration that lacked imagination with regard to the conflict in Southeast Asia, Rostow's plan held sway. His return to the center of U.S. foreign policymaking reflected a victory for Rostow's long-held conviction that America's boundless resources should overwhelmingly focus on crushing North Vietnam's will. Over the course of 1966, as Rostow gained closer proximity to the president, Johnson escalated the war to include targets opposed by both his secretary of state and his secretary of defense. The intensification of the American bombing campaign is not solely attributable to Rostow's rise in influence, but his absolute belief helped tilt the outcome of many arguments away from an increasingly doubtful and marginalized Robert McNamara. Having backed to the hilt the Americanization of the war through 1964 and 1965, the secretary of defense, in time, would turn against the military and diplomatic debacle that he had helped create. As others lost faith, Rostow dispensed the elixir of inevitable victory in Vietnam, and it soothed and emboldened Lyndon Johnson.

SIX

The PROPHET RETURNS

1966

WORLDLY, OBSTINATE, and a champion of diplomacy above all, Averell Harriman was contemptuous of Rostow's belief that air power alone would force North Vietnam to cease infiltration and negotiate. Aerial bombardment was "applying the stick without the carrot," and Harriman's time in England during World War II convinced him that bombing simply hardened resolve.[1] Whereas Rostow arrived in London in the autumn of 1942, some time after the worst of the Blitz, Harriman, as a trusted envoy of President Roosevelt, had been in England during the heaviest bombing. He was full of admiration for the doughtiness displayed by Londoners and this experience informed his perspective of the conflict in Vietnam. Harriman doubted that the U.S. bombing campaign would decisively dent either North Vietnam's morale or its ability to furnish its southern comrades with critical sustenance. Rather than cowing a nation, bombing solidified popular resolve like little else.

Responding to Harriman's doubts in a forceful letter, Rostow restated his recently modified case for bombing. Posing the question, "What should we hit?" Rostow replied, "The line of supply, but more systematically than we have thus far done . . . the way we kept out the Seine-Loire bridges in 1944." He placed oil storage at the very top of the target list and confessed, "As for electric power and mining the harbor at Haiphong, I do not share your reservations . . . I would accept no asymmetry in our freedom of action in the North so long as Hanoi supplies men, supplies and direction to the south."[2] Having shed the last vestiges of his earlier gradualist thesis, Rostow called for a serious escalation in bombing indeed. As he stood alone in advocating the bombing of North Vietnam from 1961 to 1963, so he would begin in 1966 urging the destruction of targets that would not be considered by McGeorge Bundy, Dean Rusk, and Robert McNamara. His letter to Harriman concluded with a striking analogy: "I would use our air power as the equivalent of guerrilla warfare."[3]

Not everyone was so belligerent. After nine months of steadily increased bombing, many within the Johnson administration felt that North Vietnam might now be willing to negotiate an end to the conflict. To test the ground, these optimists argued that the United States had to prove its peaceful intent by making a unilateral, emollient gesture. At the close of 1965, McNamara advised that the president cease bombing North Vietnam over the Christmas period to facilitate a possible move to negotiations. It was around that time that the first stirring of doubt had begun to chip away at McNamara's veneer of absolute certitude. The president was skeptical that the pause would amount to anything, but his faith in his secretary of defense's clarity of reason was still strong. On December 24 Johnson ordered a temporary cessation of bombing. For the thirty-seven days that followed, North Vietnam's skies were clear of the U.S. Air Force's vapor trails.

To McNamara's embarrassment the pause came to nothing. North Vietnam's leaders were not willing to compromise on the essential goal of reunification, and were not going to be manipulated into making concessions. Northern-directed infiltration of men and matériel heightened in intensity, as its leaders took advantage of the military respite that the pause afforded. By early January Johnson felt duped—humiliated. With renewed determination he sought to prove his mettle to both his domestic enemies and those in North Vietnam. Barry Goldwater had criticized LBJ's timidity in the November 1964 presidential election, and Johnson did not want to present Republican hawks with any more opportunities to question his credentials as a war leader. The president was adamant that bombing should resume with increased ferocity. The debate within the administration revolved simply around a matter of degree. Just how hard should the U.S. military strike?

McNamara had slipped in the president's high estimation following his advocacy of a pause that failed. Rather than angrily swing back in favor of unrestricted bombing, however, he was opposed to the plan, pushed by Rostow and the Joint Chiefs of Staff, that the United States should destroy Hanoi's and Haiphong's POL and power plants.[4] While the defense secretary recognized that an attack on POL supplies held the advantage of "surprise and [that] antiaircraft will be less alert," he recommended against pursuing such a radical course—one that was likely to result in significant civilian casualties and provoke international condemnation. McNamara instead advised that U.S. bombers drop their payload on "perishable targets" (of a definably military nature), although he was at pains to specify that this did not mean anything "north of Hanoi." Maxwell Taylor, then serving as a special White House consultant, was unimpressed with McNamara's hesitancy, stating, "I hope we'll get back to hitting the key rail and bridges. POL will help stop the trucks too."[5] Taylor wanted the U.S. Air Force to drop many more bombs on North Vietnam's industry and oil storage supplies. He felt that such a course would preclude the necessity of sending more American ground troops. The United States had the technical ability, Taylor reasoned, to defeat a nation from the sky alone.

The chairman of the Joint Chiefs of Staff, Earle Wheeler, was scathing in his dismissal of North Vietnamese industry as a potential target: "You hear a lot about industrial targets. There are no worthy industrial targets except for one: steel and iron works. But even that is [a] low return item."[6] On this count one might surmise that the Rostow Thesis was Wheeler's intended target. Wheeler opposed gradualism and obviously had doubts about Rostow's theory that Ho Chi Minh had an industrial complex to protect. But the two men were at one on the decisively coercive nature of destroying a nation's oil-storage supplies. Wheeler urged Johnson to sanction the destruction of North Vietnam's "POL system," which he deemed "vital."[7] The administration was decisively split over the extent to which bombing should escalate. McNamara, Bundy, and Rusk all opposed POL bombing on predominantly moral grounds—fearful of an international outcry—while Taylor, Wheeler, and Rostow were unhesitatingly in favor. The upshot of these often-heated debates was that POL stayed out of the military's sights for the moment. Yet the balance of contending opinion was finely poised. If one of the key foreign-policy trinity (McNamara, Bundy, and Rusk) were to change tack, a shift toward escalation was almost inevitable. The departure of Johnson's national security adviser soon opened up this possibility. Johnson's choice to replace McGeorge Bundy would provide significant clues as to how fiercely the president planned to wage the Vietnam War.

ON DECEMBER 4, 1965, an out-of-favor McGeorge Bundy tendered his resignation and informed the president that he planned to accept the presidency of that philanthropic behemoth, the Ford Foundation. To give the president sufficient time to locate a suitable replacement, Bundy agreed to remain in the post until February 28, 1966. Robert Komer stepped in to assume the role on a temporary basis—he was Bundy's choice to succeed him permanently. This blessing, however, may have proved a kiss of death for Komer's ambitions. Bundy's relationship with the president was at that stage strictly formal.

For whatever immediate reason, Lyndon Johnson did not view Komer as a viable long-term option for the national security adviser post. The president called Komer into the office midway through his brief tenure and informed him, "You are going to be my special assistant for the Other War in Vietnam. It's a full-time job and I'm going to pay you top dollar." The "other war" was in many ways more vexing than America's military campaign: it was the battle to help build a viable, secure South Vietnam, and to convince its people to support the Saigon government. Komer was dispatched to Saigon with full ambassadorial rank to head up Civil Operations and Revolutionary Development Support (CORDS). The newly established organization brought together experts from the military, USAID, the CIA, and the United States Information Agency (USIA) to develop strategies to win the loyalty of South Vietnam's peasantry. The position was not as glamorous or influential as that of national security adviser, and after digesting this disagreeable turn of events, Komer was understandably curious as to who "would mind the store" after his departure. The president refused to answer, parrying that "we will worry about that." In fact Johnson was increasingly inclined to believe that Rostow was the best long-term replacement for Bundy and Komer.[8] It was a choice that the president's special assistant, Jack Valenti, urged upon him enthusiastically. Komer was about to be beaten to the job he wanted by Walt Whitman Rostow—a man he had ridiculed mercilessly for the past few years.

A close intimate of the president, Jack Valenti held Rostow in the highest possible regard, admiring his intelligence, confidence, and ability to get along with mostly everyone. Responding to Johnson's request to consider how the United States might help build a cohesive South Vietnamese polity, Valenti advised that the president should "have Walt Rostow gather a group of political scientists like James McGregor Burns, Dick Neustadt, and others to develop a party system in Vietnam."[9] This was quite a vote of confidence. Valenti made it sound as though Rostow and his academic peers could formulate a winning plan for South Vietnam, with minimal trouble and fuss—in a wood-lined common room over a glass of sherry. Reflecting on his appointment in later years, Rostow recalled, "Jack Valenti was my great advocate."[10] This much seems clear.

Interestingly, South Vietnam was enduring one of its familiar political crises at the time of Valenti's hopeful suggestion. In June 1965 a military coup, with American backing, had brought to power the repressive government of two military strongmen, Nguyen Cao Ky and Nguyen Van Thieu. Over the course of the previous year, South Vietnam's most decorated general, Nguyen Chanh Thi, had risen to virtual warlord status within the nation. From the time of Diem's assassination, Thi had a hand in most of the coups that had toppled successive Saigon governments. Recognizing that Thi's Machiavellian proclivities might eventually prove a problem for his own leadership, Ky, in March 1966, attempted to relieve him of his command.

Thi refused to depart with a whimper, however, and in combination with the Buddhist leader Tri Quang led a combined Buddhist and student revolt against the Catholic-dominated Saigon regime. Not for the first time, internal divisions threatened to tear South Vietnam asunder. Yet amid the chaos, Johnson's pick for national security adviser instead discerned hope. In Rostow's estimation Ky and Thieu represented "the kind of second generation figures I had hoped in 1961 Diem would bring forward—young, intensely nationalistic, inexperienced, energetic." Rather than witnessing a bloody throwback to the summer and autumn of 1963, Rostow instead concluded that South Vietnam was experiencing "the pangs of a nation being born." According to Rostow, "an old friend almost shouted across the Cabinet table: 'Walt, are you mad!' "[11]

The old friend in question was McGeorge Bundy, who had long felt that Rostow's deep-set optimism led him to view foreign-policy crises, from the Berlin and Cuban confrontations to the Vietnam War, in dangerously simplistic terms.[12] Robert Komer had helped bolster Bundy's low opinion of Rostow. Komer certainly doubted that Rostow possessed the ability to achieve the daunting task of remaking South Vietnam's political structure to America's satisfaction. The president, however, believed that Rostow possessed the skills and loyalty to prosper in the job that he had planned for him. Lyndon Johnson viewed Rostow as a man with original ideas, someone who recognized, before anyone else did, that the U.S. must confront North Vietnam directly. Rostow's foresight, dedication, and self-belief were traits that recommended him to the president. Before making a final decision, Johnson decided to gauge his staff's reaction toward Rostow's potential appointment.

During a conversation with Robert McNamara on February 27, the president remarked, "I like Rostow but I don't want to get started off here and get everybody thinking that we're going back to war and hardliner [*sic*]." Johnson may have felt that Rostow's appointment might project an escalatory signal, but surely that was unavoidable and in line with his intention. The president was increasingly convinced that a harder military approach was necessary. By appointing Rostow as national security adviser, Johnson was sending an unambiguous message, both domestically and internationally, that the United States was going to win the Vietnam War. And for these reasons, McNamara was unenthused by the prospect of Rostow returning to the White House, pleading, "I'd still like [Bill] Moyers for that."[13] The defense secretary believed that LBJ's urbane, moderate press secretary would provide more restrained advice on military matters than the hard-line chairman of the Policy Planning Council. Rostow's bellicosity unnerved McNamara as his doubts about the necessity of American involvement in Vietnam became more pervasive. Scrabbling around for plausible alternatives to Rostow the following day, McNamara advised that "[Paul] Nitze could do it all right," although he was forced to concede, "I don't know if you'd find it pleasant to work with him; he's an abrasive character."[14]

Johnson was unconvinced by Rusk's earlier suggestion that he appoint Alexis Johnson to replace Bundy and did not even pass comment on McNamara's offbeat idea that Paul Nitze—serving at that point as secretary of the navy—might be the man for the job. Having made his decision, the president called Jack Valenti into his office and told him, "I think Walt's the man to take Bundy's job, but I want you to talk with him about his prolixity, his verbosity. I want you to tell him how I like to be handled." As Valenti recalled, Johnson "liked the crispness, the dispatch with which, say, a Bundy or a McNamara presented his case." He now faced the unenviable task of communicating this requirement to Rostow. He opted for the direct route, telling Rostow face-to-face that "if he were opening the meeting to state the issue and briefly, very briefly, state the pros and cons and then shut up." When writing memoranda Rostow was told to be "very spare, very lucid, and whenever there was one redundant word it ought to come out." Rostow accepted this advice with "amazing good grace and great humility" and apparently made a genuine attempt to cut down his memoranda to a more digestible size.[15] While Rostow undoubtedly tried very hard, however, he never quite achieved the clarity that was Bundy's hallmark in memoranda form. Anyone with time to spare in the Lyndon Baines Johnson Library archives will form a clear opinion on this issue. As Dean Rusk pointedly recalled, "McGeorge Bundy was a somewhat more skilled draftsman than Walt Rostow."[16]

PRESIDENT JOHNSON APPOINTED Walt Rostow to be McGeorge Bundy's long-term successor on April 1. According to his biographer Kai Bird, Bundy was "dumbfounded" upon hearing the news that the president had appointed Rostow to replace him. He had significant concerns about the new assistant's intellectual integrity. Johnson's reasoning, however, is simple enough to discern. If Bundy displayed, at his occasional best, some willingness to question the edifice of dogma on which America's Vietnam policy was based, Rostow adhered to the essential verities of the extended Cold War. He would see the conflict through to any denouement and was, in Johnsonian parlance, as loyal as a beagle. The president knew exactly what appointing Rostow signified. Securing South Vietnam's independence was essential to the president, and Rostow was one of the

few men to claim to know how to achieve this goal. His optimism and ex-
uberance endeared him to a president who was tiring of bad news, a disenchanted press, and an increasingly glum secretary of defense.

The New York Times greeted news of Rostow's promotion more enthusiastically than most of Johnson's cabinet, observing that "the appointment
places beside the President an independent and cultivated mind, that, as
in the Bundy era, should assure comprehension both of the intricacies of
world problems, and of the options among which the White House must
choose. No President could ask for more."[17] This glowing appraisal was off
the mark in one important respect. While Bundy's working practice was to
identify a foreign-policy crisis, gather and analyze the pertinent information, and present options to the president, he was careful not to inject his
own views. According to one political scientist, "Bundy remained basically
a facilitator, more oriented towards making the system work than towards
monopolizing the action himself and excluding others."[18] Rostow, on the
other hand, was less inclined to gather and synthesize the views of others
when they conflicted with his own deeply held beliefs. He did not just
pluck proposals from the lower levels of the bureaucracy and present them
to the president; Rostow adopted a position at an early stage and *then* located the evidence that supported his particular viewpoint. Nowhere was
this truer than with regard to the war in Vietnam.

The office of national security adviser affords both power and close
proximity to the president he or she serves. While the secretary of state is
encumbered by bureaucratic, institutional, and geographic impediments,
the national security adviser serves the president personally, immediately,
and flexibly. Rostow's key functions were to coordinate the various agencies, synthesize information, and present these reports to the president.
With such a broad remit, a strong-minded policy advocate such as Rostow
assumed a position of considerable influence. The relatively circumspect
Bundy once observed that 80 percent of all initiatives in foreign policy
came from the White House. Asked whether Bundy was correct to cite
such a high figure, Rostow responded, "Yes. The bureaucracies are labor-
ing to carry out current policy. This is hard arduous labor. They're trying
to keep their nose above water."[19] While serving as chairman of the Policy
Planning Council, Rostow recalled that he had a number of ideas as to
how to overcome the "fragmentation of the political system" in South

Vietnam. Realizing that bringing the bureaucracy with him was likely to be time-consuming, Rostow simply communicated with the U.S. ambassador to South Vietnam, Henry Cabot Lodge, directly, managing to get his ideas "into the stream of policy without bothering the Secretary of State or the President. I knew it was right, and so on."[20] This proclivity for taking action without consulting his superiors was technically an irregular extension of his limited powers. Questionable or not, circumventing the State Department was a process familiar to Rostow. And as national security adviser, he was in an even better position to press his own views without bothering the likes of Rusk and McNamara.

In his 1971 oral history deposited at the Lyndon Baines Johnson Library, Arthur Schlesinger Jr. observed that "there was a marked difference between Bundy and Rostow. Bundy made more of an effort to try to get both views presented. Intelligent people in the State Department have told me that Walt would funnel in the stuff which sustained his own thesis."[21] The accusation that Rostow sold his own arguments with partial vigor, and would even bury CIA reports that questioned the degree of military progress being made in Vietnam, has also been made recently by McNamara, who argued that his reading of the conflict was hindered by the fact that Rostow hid skeptical reporting from his view.[22] The director of the CIA, Richard Helms, responded to this accusation as early as 1969: "Whatever Rostow might have done to help the President to reinforce his impressions with facts, figures, statistics and so forth, they weren't necessarily mine, and mine were not kept from the President."[23] While Helms is adamant that his reports reached their intended recipient, his qualified response suggests that the allegations made by Schlesinger and McNamara—two men not noted for their retrospective fondness for Rostow or the Vietnam War—have some basis in fact.

One example serves to reinforce this case. In early 1967 Rostow requested that the CIA deputy director for intelligence, Russell Jack Smith, prepare a list of Vietnam-related accomplishments for the president to use in a speech. Many in the CIA thought that the war was going badly, and hence there was great resistance to providing such a partial picture. Under pressure from his political masters, however, Smith had little choice but to agree to Rostow's request. Smith formulated a plan that could both maintain his reputation for veracity and satisfy the president's need for good news. Smith produced a report that listed the "achievements" requested by Rostow but that also included a weightier hard truths section headed "Setbacks and Losses." According to CIA sources, Rostow, unperturbed, simply cut out the bad news and forwarded the paper to the president. According to the historian John Prados, Rostow's partisan use of CIA evidence left a "sour taste at Langley."[24]

Rostow's new job placed him in a strong position to dictate what material reached the president. He also enjoyed a proximity to the Oval Office that became increasingly significant as Johnson became more sullen and isolated as political attacks intensified. Undersecretary of State George Ball later recalled that Rostow was a "terrible influence" on the president. He did not just put a distorting gloss on bad news, and amplify the good, but Rostow also created "an image of Johnson standing against the forces of evil. He used to tell him how Lincoln was abused by everybody during a certain stage in the Civil War, and 'this is the position you are in, Mr. President.' "[25] The relationship between the two men became closer as domestic criticism intensified and American combat troops died in ever-greater numbers. On December 31, 1965, there were 184,300 U.S. troops in Vietnam and, at that point, just 636 soldiers had lost their lives. Over the next two years, Johnson increased troop levels in Vietnam to 485,600, as 19,562 Americans were killed in the field.[26] This escalation impacted negatively on Johnson's popularity and laid bare his unedifying tendency toward making quiet deceptions as to the scale of the task ahead. Having been reassured in 1964 that the situation in Vietnam did not require the extreme military measures counseled by Barry Goldwater, many Americans were disappointed when Vietnam became an unambiguous "war." A political colossus in 1964 and 1965, Lyndon Johnson's approval ratings slumped below the psychologically significant 50 percent mark in 1966.[27] In an increasingly hostile national environment, Rostow's good cheer and loyalty were very much appreciated.

The president claimed his proprietary rights to Rostow early. To one "Kennedy intimate," he boasted that "he's not Galbraith's intellectual. He's not Schlesinger's intellectual. He's going to be my goddamn intellectual and I'm going to have him by his short hairs."[28] While Johnson had the physicality and force of personality to place him in that unfortunate position, Rostow held his own in this bilateral balance of power. The pres-

ident had initially decided to downgrade the operational significance of
Rostow's new position. Bundy's reputation as the president's foreign-
policy brain rankled with Johnson, and he wanted to reassert himself as a
leader who exerted deft and pervasive control over foreign affairs. While
McGeorge Bundy had held the title that Kennedy originally assigned him,
"special assistant to the president for national security affairs," Rostow was
given the reduced title of "special assistant to the president." Johnson also
requested that his press secretary Bill Moyers assist Rostow in carrying out
his duties—to help apply a media-friendly gloss on some of the foreign-
policy decisions being made. This uneasy arrangement did not last long,
however, for Moyers resigned over the escalation in Vietnam some nine
months later. Moyers, in comparison with Rostow, had little influence over
foreign policy in 1966.

In removing "for national security affairs" from Rostow's job title,
Johnson may well have been conveying the message that he did not need
another Bundy. Yet Rostow soon assumed control of all the tasks that
Bundy had discharged, and went on to forge a much closer personal bond
with the president. According to both men, their working relationship was
smooth and genuinely warm. Rostow held his new boss in high regard, re-
calling, "He was about the most considerate man I've ever worked for."[29]
It is likely, though, that this warm appraisal says more about Rostow's gen-
erosity of spirit than about Johnson's management skills. Rostow's comment certainly jars with the portrayal of LBJ presented by his biographers
Robert Caro and Robert Dallek, who both highlight the shoddy way that
Johnson invariably handled his staff.[30] It also conflicts with the way that
Johnson actually dealt with Rostow just prior to his taking up his new job.

A press leak in late March about Rostow's impending appointment infuriated Johnson, who deemed Rostow the culprit, berated him furiously for
his loose tongue, and then slammed down the phone in a fit of pique. According to Robert Dallek, it was "more likely that Johnson himself was the
source of the leak on Rostow's selection."[31] The president's performance
was familiar to all of Johnson's staff; it formed an initiation ritual of some
kind. According to presidential aide Joseph Califano, Johnson, when dealing with subordinates, "always seemed to have to break him in some way or
get him to do something, or even in the worse sense he'd humiliate him in

some way to make him totally his man . . . to make sure he was totally loyal."[32] "Considerate" hardly seems the right word for Johnson's behavior.

Genuine or not with regard to the consideration accorded him as part of the working relationship, Rostow was clear that he "saw a great deal of the President. He took me into his house as well as to his staff, into his family; took my family in as well as me. It was an openhearted human relationship. I came to hold the greatest possible affection for him, love for him, as well as respect for the job."[33] Rostow was hardworking, good-natured, and unswervingly positive. While originally an intimate of John F. Kennedy, he was now viewed by the Kennedy set as an unreflective hawk. All these personal qualities—and especially Robert Kennedy's dim view—endeared Rostow ever more to Johnson.

This closeness was aided by the siege mentality that had taken root in the White House. The president, who often lapsed into debilitating bouts of self-pity, considered himself unjustly under fire from a Kennedyite press that simply did not understand the complexities of the Vietnam War. Rostow provided the strongest possible reassurance that Johnson was fighting a just war in Southeast Asia, and that the press could not be more wrong. Warming ever more to Rostow, the president in turn advised him to "generate a series of initiatives in every part of the world. Despite the burdens of Vietnam, I want to have a total foreign policy, and I want, in addition to what Mac did, for you to be the catalyst in generating a new set of initiatives." Impressed by Rostow's creativity, Johnson wanted his new national security adviser to serve as an "ideas generator."[34] Rostow thrived in this role, offering suggestions on all manner of problems, stressing, in particular, the continued relevance of increased development aid. But most of his creative capital was exerted concocting military strategies to defeat the communist insurgency in South Vietnam. Johnson once described Rostow as "a man of conviction who doesn't try to play President."[35] Rostow was not shy, though, about expressing strong views on the Vietnam conflict, displaying bellicosity well beyond the president's. Where Rostow stood on the issue of escalation was obvious to all. As the former undersecretary of the Air Force Townsend Hoopes recalled, Rostow "proved to be the closest thing we had near the top of the U.S. government to a genuine, all-wool, anti-communist ideologue and true believer."[36]

ROSTOW'S APPOINTMENT PROVED a boon to strategic bombing enthu-
siasts the administration over. When McNamara lost faith, Rostow found
himself alone—Dean Rusk was flapping in either direction—with the
Joint Chiefs in pressing Johnson to further extend the bombing. Rostow's
first recommendation following his appointment was to apply the lesson
he had learned during World War II: bombing a nation's POL storage facilities constituted a potentially critical blow in wartime. McNamara's influence within the administration had waned following his strong push for
the December 1965 bombing pause—it had failed, as Johnson predicted
it would. But while McNamara, Rusk, and Bundy had all opposed attacking POL in late 1965, McNamara had begun to feel that Rostow's bombing strategy should be given a final chance to prove its worth. Sensing
receptivity to his ideas, Rostow first reasoned to the president that "oil hits
the over-all military logistical capacity in the North, as well as industrial
and civil operations . . . We should lean harder on Hanoi, on a precision
bombing basis." "It is not," explained Rostow with a familiar refrain, "that
I am bloody minded or a hawk. But the strain of trying to do the job principally by attrition of main force units places almost intolerable burdens on
the political life of our country and on the war weary South Vietnamese.
We've got to try to shorten the war without doing unwise or desperate
things."[37] Aware that domestic discontent was harming the Democratic
Party's political prospects, as midterm congressional elections loomed,
Rostow believed that attacking North Vietnam's oil facilities would win
the war quickly and allow the president to return promptly to achieving
the domestic promises made in 1964.

On May 6, 1966, Rostow wrote to Johnson, Rusk, and McNamara that
while "simple analogies are dangerous . . . I feel it quite possible the military
effects of bombing POL . . . may be more prompt and direct than conventional intelligence analysis would suggest."[38] Rostow's analogy was that
bombing oil would do to North Vietnam's vehicles of infiltration what it had
done to the Luftwaffe in World War II. This belief led Rostow to question
directly the findings of America's intelligence services. It would become a familiar exchange: the rational versus the visceral. For the next two and a half
years, Rostow poured scorn on a vast array of CIA reports that failed to ap-

preciate what he took to be air power's significant impact: that it sapped morale and curbed infiltration. He had no evidence upon which to make a case beyond simple hope, reinforced by his experience in a war that held few plausible parallels to that in Vietnam: the defeat of Nazi Germany.

Not all were convinced that Rostow was right about the impact of bombing. The secretary of state continued to worry that the POL campaign would have the most harmful effect on America's world standing. Rostow dismissed Rusk's response that bombing POL would "greatly heighten international tensions" as "debatable."[39] A fortnight earlier he had advised Johnson to order the U.S. military to "hurt them badly around Hanoi-Haiphong," a course that Rusk opposed. Paying lip service to the secretary of state's doubts, Rostow conceded that he was "conscious of the international issues these [targets] raise, and there can only be one target officer in this government." Nevertheless, Rostow deemed it sensible that the president order a "fresh look" at adopting such a potentially decisive military course.[40] In his first month as national security adviser, Rostow had vigorously sold the merits of a strategy earlier rejected out of hand, and directly opposed the secretary of state's diplomatic objections. His energetic sales pitch proved successful.

As Robert McNamara remarked in the June NSC meeting called to debate the attacks, "Strikes on POL have been opposed by me for months. The situation is now changing . . . Military infiltration is up sharply . . . Such attacks will limit infiltration."[41] One may attribute McNamara's renewed belief in bombing to a whole host of reasons, but it is surely significant that he presented his rationale in Rostovian terms. Rusk again voiced his concerns about the shift in strategy: "It is difficult to separate in the minds of the people attacks on POL supplies from attacks on the civilian economy . . . A go decision will produce sharp reactions across the world."[42] But with the mood shifting in favor of a sharp escalation in bombing, Rusk moved with the current and gave his assent. This time it was not simply Rostow's ideas that were present at the meetings, it was his person. As Robert Komer recalled, "Walt was more of an enthusiast and less of a cold, hard calculator of odds than Bundy and he would be more inclined to press his own views than Bundy had been."[43] On POL, as on many issues in previous and subsequent years, Komer's description is pitch-perfect.

Even prior to the commencement of the POL bombing campaign, Rostow was positive that America was winning the war. On June 25, 1966, Rostow wrote, "Mr. President, you can smell it all over. Hanoi's operation, backed by the Chicoms, is no longer being regarded as the wave of the future out there. U.S. power is beginning to be felt."[44] This may well have been the kind of cheering observations that Johnson expected from Rostow when he appointed him, but it had little basis in reality. It was Rostow's impression from the distant remove of the White House, based on a partial reading of the available evidence. Mao's China continued to supply significant material support to Hanoi while the bombing campaign had an emboldening effect on Vietnamese resolve to defeat the alien, imperialist force that was the United States. Under interrogation, one captured North Vietnamese soldier told his captors after the air raids "the people got very mad and cursed the Americans . . . To them the Americans were the cruel enemy who had bombed the civilian population."[45]

The U.S. Air Force commenced its attacks on North Vietnam's POL storage facilities on June 29, 1966. Rostow wrote to the president in gushing terms, "I believe the POL bombing . . . has caught the nation's attention. Our people sense new determination; new ideas; new hope."[46] The American public was indeed impressed by Johnson's escalation of the bombing campaign. Support for Johnson's war policy increased from 42 percent to 54 percent, and a massive 80 percent of the public thought that the bombing would lead to straight military victory.[47] The international reaction, however, was broadly condemnatory, even among America's closest diplomatic allies. On June 29, 1966, the British government publicly disassociated itself from the U.S. attacks on North Vietnam's oil and petroleum supplies. Prime Minister Harold Wilson was appalled that Johnson had authorized a bombing campaign that destroyed targets so close to the civilian centers of Hanoi and Haiphong.[48] This was the first occasion that the British prime minister would rue Rostow's influence on Johnson's decision making, but it would not be the last.

The impact of bombing POL on the war itself failed to live up to expectations. In August 1966 a joint CIA-DIA (Defense Intelligence Agency) report concluded that "there is no evidence that the air strikes have significantly weakened popular morale." While it was "certain that economic growth had stagnated . . . there have been no sustained and critical hardships among the bulk of the people."[49] On September 12 a special national intelligence estimate (SNIE) observed that the POL bombing did not create "insurmountable transportation difficulties, economic dislocations or weakening of popular morale."[50] The reasons were simple. Both China and the Soviet Union had supplied North Vietnam with additional oil supplies to the extent that its limited POL supply requirements were essentially unhindered by the massive U.S. bombing. And once the nature of the American strategy became clear, North Vietnam dispersed the new supplies of oil flooding in from its two generous donors. In World War II, following the loss of Romania in August 1944 and Hungary in February 1945, Germany had no source to which it could turn, and no route through which to receive supplies. North Vietnam, in contrast, had no such logistical problem—it could be supplied by sea and through its land border with China. It is estimated that Rolling Thunder caused North Vietnam approximately $600 million worth of damage from direct destruction and lost productive capacity. Between 1965 and 1968, however, North Vietnam received over $2 billion in foreign aid, more than enough to replenish losses and fuel the relatively limited supply needs of waging guerrilla war.[51] North Vietnam was actually turning a net profit.

Confronted with a number of reports that cast significant doubts on the POL strategy he had championed, Rostow looked elsewhere to provide cheer for the president. A report completed on August 2 by Leon Gourré of the RAND Corporation served this purpose. Based on a series of interviews with captured NLF insurgents, Gourré's team found that only 20 percent believed that the VC (Vietcong) would win, 60 percent believed the GVN (South Vietnam) would win, and 20 percent were unsure. This contrasted starkly with an earlier survey in which 65 percent of the interviewees claimed that an NLF victory was inevitable. For Rostow the report showed "a progressive decline in the morale and the fighting capacity of the VC." While not directly attributable to American bombing, the signs, Rostow explained, were overwhelmingly positive in that "all the interrogators are convinced that if the VC fails this time in the South they—and the whole country—will be swept by a mood of wanting no further violence and killing. They are close to having had enough." Rostow did add a cautionary note, lest the president lose himself in a reverie of self-congratulation. "It is of course, extremely important that we not overestimate these trends and develop excessive optimism," Rostow conceded, "but it is equally important that we look at them soberly and, especially, mount the kind of political as well as military operations that will accelerate them."[52] The CIA and DIA were skeptical that U.S. military strategy in Vietnam was making any kind of significant progress—and even the Joint Chiefs were expressing concern that bombing was failing to achieve the desired results—but at least RAND was on hand with some kernels of comfort. In the wake of some very bad news, Rostow instinctively stuck to the positive, wherever that might be found, and on whatever often-flimsy foundation it rested.

REACTING SOMEWHAT TO the fact that the POL campaign had failed, and much more to its public relations value, Johnson in August 1966 appointed Averell Harriman to serve as his "Ambassador for Peace." The president doubted that anything would come of this move—he did not give Harriman a specific mandate, putting nothing in writing—but the basic idea was that this distinguished elder statesman would serve as a conduit through which to promote negotiations with North Vietnam. Harriman had a track record of success with regard to waging peace. And as Rostow was the president's champion of war, it was inevitable that the two men would clash directly over the escalation of the conflict. In late May Harriman warned the Soviet ambassador to the United States, Anatoly Dobrynin, that Rostow "was the administration's most dangerous hawk" who enjoyed the "unqualified support of the Joint Chiefs of Staff."[53]

A few days later, Harriman met with Rostow and the president to discuss the military rationale for expanding the air campaign. In what Harriman described as "an almost maniacal tone," Rostow informed him, "The President is going to stick it out. The bombing will escalate." Harriman cautioned the national security adviser to be careful not to push the military campaign too hard lest it lead to a nuclear confrontation as dangerous as the Cuban Missile Crisis. Rostow replied that President Kennedy had "looked down the barrel of nuclear war" and Khrushchev had backed down. Harriman retorted that such a nuclear confrontation was best avoided in the future for the better interests of life on the planet. Rostow disagreed because "it is only in extreme crises that such settlements will come." In a memorandum for his personal file, Harriman recorded that "the above confirmed my worst fears of Rostow's reckless and mistaken attitude on bombing escalation."[54] His brinkmanship frightened Harriman and he was not alone. The secretary of defense was also airing serious doubts about the merits of following Rostow's escalatory course.

The POL bombing campaign was the last act of military escalation to which Robert McNamara gave his unqualified assent. On August 30 the "Jason Sumner" study group—consisting of forty-seven top scientists briefed on the war by the administration—found that only 5 percent of North Vietnam's POL infrastructure was necessary to support truck-led infiltration and that the Soviet Union could supply additional oil supplies via easily dispersed barrels. The report concluded that "North Vietnam has basically a subsistence agricultural economy that presents a difficult and unrewarding system for air attack."[55] According to the military historian Mark Clodfelter, reading the report was a moment of epiphany for McNamara. On October 14 he advised the president "at a proper time we should consider terminating all bombing in North Vietnam."[56] Johnson's defense secretary was advocating the untrammeled search for diplomatic solutions, while his national security adviser believed quite the opposite. McNamara had embarked on a painful course of revisiting the prominent role he had played in Americanizing the Vietnam War. His vigor and self-confidence waned as his regrets became more pronounced.

Walt Rostow remained unshaken in his certainty that bombing was having its desired effect. Pessimistic intelligence estimates would not stand in the way of this conviction. "Clearly bombing the North has not . . . by itself brought Hanoi to the conference table," Rostow conceded, but "nor has anything else we have done by way of military, civil or diplomatic action." This "Has anyone got any better ideas?" defense was desperate. Later in the memorandum, Rostow again conceded, "Bombing as we have conducted it is not a decisive instrument," but nor are "guerrilla operations in the south a decisive instrument." This observation is problematic for two reasons. First, according to Rostow just a few months earlier, bombing POL was supposed to prove decisive—and he claimed to have the experience from World War II to prove it. Second, the NLF did not view its insurgency as likely to win "decisively" in the short term but believed that it would sap America's will and South Vietnam's viability to the point that both were exhausted, at which point reunification under the communist regime would become inevitable. Rostow's analogy, again repeated, that "bombing in the North is our equivalent of Viet Cong guerrilla operations in the South" does not stand up to serious analysis.[57]

For Rostow the equivalence of bombing and guerrilla warfare lay in the fact that bombing tied up the North Vietnamese workforce in repairing the damage wreaked. In countering the U.S. bombing campaign, North Vietnam displayed a great deal of ingenuity in avoiding its most devastating consequences. In a similar fashion to what happened to working-class Londoners during the Second World War, the most vulnerable inhabitants of North Vietnam's cities were dispersed across the countryside. Industries and storage facilities were buried deep under the ground and the government claimed to have built some thirty thousand miles of tunnels. In eking out a harsh, often subterranean existence for much of the war, the North Vietnamese spared the lives of many of their soldiers.[58]

The McNamara-Rostow feud began in earnest in October 1966. "The Rolling Thunder program [has not] either significantly affected infiltration or cracked the morale of Hanoi," stressed McNamara. "There is agreement in the intelligence community on these facts."[59] Rostow's familiar riposte came ten days later, and eloquently testifies to his remarkable capacity for positive thinking: "I am convinced that bombing the North is a greater asset than our intelligence people realize . . . Our first duty is to mop up more oil because there is now evidence that they are hurting."[60] While Rostow strove to locate evidence that supported the claim that the North Vietnamese were "hurting," the CIA provided yet more reports that cast doubts on bombing's efficacy. Noting that the intensity of the Rolling Thunder campaign in 1966 was far greater than in 1965—the U.S. dropped 2.6 times the level of ordnance on the north in 1966 than in 1965—the CIA could detect no decrease in north-south infiltration. In fact quite the opposite was holding true. "North Vietnam continues to increase its support to the insurgency in South Vietnam," a CIA report in November observed. "The Rolling Thunder campaign has not been able to prevent about a threefold increase in the level of personal infiltration in 1966 . . . In particular, despite the neutralization of the major petroleum storage facilities in the North, petroleum supplies have continued to be imported in needed amounts."[61]

Rostow's plan was not working. McNamara had turned against him, Rusk was ambivalent, and while the president was sympathetic to the plans proposed by Rostow and the Joint Chiefs, he was both exasperated at America's inability to put down the insurgency and emotionally drained by the bloodshed that the conflict necessitated. Johnson's old mentor, Senator Richard Russell, stopped visiting the White House at the end of 1966. The president would invariably begin to sob when the topic of Vietnam was broached, and Russell was simply unable to deal with that level of raw emotion.[62] The president's internal anguish was not something to which Rostow paid serious attention. More of the same was what Johnson's national security adviser recommended to break North Vietnam's spirit.

Rostow's positive reporting instilled an air of unreality into internal appraisals of the war's progress. Intelligence did exist which suggested that North Vietnam was suffering in the face of American military pressure. Usually, however, this good news was placed in the context of a broader conclusion that an end was assuredly not in sight. On December 5, for example, Rostow sent a fifteen-page CIA report to the president with a one-page covering memorandum in which he quotes one paragraph that begins, "There is a growing conviction among Vietnamese that they have no possibility of winning."[63] Rostow failed to mention that the report also observed that "the North Vietnamese can point to some significant achievements: their main forces are larger today than a year ago and the flow of men and matériel is at least adequate to maintain this level. The intervention of the U.S. has not yet shaken morale importantly. And an entire area—the Delta—has been relatively unaffected by the U.S. action."[64] Rostow's method was simple: he filtered out bad news and amplified the good.

ROSTOW CONCLUDED his year by advocating a shift to those targets he had previously been careful to avoid: North Vietnamese industry, of which there was little, and electric power. "We must now begin to move more heavily against the North," he wrote on November 9, concurring with the Joint Chiefs' position that bombing be radically expanded in 1967.[65] The Joint Chiefs called for the bombing of power plants, industry, port facilities, locks, and dams. Registering his and Rusk's reservations about this extension, McNamara protested, "We recommend that we do more than we are presently doing but not nearly as much as they recommend."[66] Responding to this equivocation, Johnson made inimitably clear where his sympathies now lay: "I think if we're causing 'em damage and they're hurtin' but we haven't got their children's hospital afire and so forth, I think Moscow can say to Hanoi, 'Godammit, this thing is getting awfully costly on you and on us and on everybody else. Let's try and find an answer here.' "[67] Johnson and his cabinet now found themselves split over policy. Moreover, across the wider ideological spectrum, politicians were expressing increased doubts about the merits of deploying more troops, and dropping more bombs.

Rostow reported some uncharacteristically bad news to the president on November 28. The previous evening, the Democratic Missouri senator Stuart Symington had bluntly informed Rostow, "You and I have been hawks since 1961. I am thinking of getting off the train soon." Highlighting an issue with which Rostow sympathized, Symington observed, "It looks to me that with the restraints on the use of airpower, we can't win. We are getting in deeper and deeper with no end in sight. In 1968, Nixon will murder us. He will become the biggest dove of all time. There has never been a man in American public life that could turn so fast on a dime." Symington was displaying a prescience that was beyond his interlocutor's ken. While Rostow was also annoyed that Johnson imposed significant constraints on the bombing campaign, he was certain that North Vietnam would succumb during a Democratic administration—if not this one, then certainly the next.

Rostow responded to Symington's gloom by recommending that when he did visit Vietnam he should spend enough time there "to get a feel for the situation and understand why the mood of our people out there is more hopeful than his."[68] To further this end, Rostow cabled the U.S. ambassador in Saigon, Henry Cabot Lodge, in advance urging him to "let [the visiting U.S. senators] see the good side of things. These men are sophisticated and not vulnerable to a hard obvious sell, but they are also good Americans and like to see a serious job done well and with conviction. It is important that they come home with that conviction."[69] Unfortunately for Rostow and Lyndon Johnson, Lodge's upbeat demeanor—and whistle-stop tour of

South Vietnam's safer parts—left the touring party unmoved. Symington's visit did not allay the well-founded doubts that he was experiencing. With a keen sense of political realism, the senator later remarked, "We should express less interest in South Asia and more in South St. Louis."[70] Symington's loss of belief was a foretaste of what was to come from other quarters.

In a memorandum titled "A Strategy for Viet Nam, 1967," Rostow reported to the president on November 28, 1966, that "there is no doubt that the bombing in the North constitutes a heavy burden on Hanoi." What Rostow could not be sure about was whether "the effects of the bombing are judged in Hanoi as a major degenerative factor, with a time limit on what is endurable, or a stabilized factor, given the level of external assistance." This was a critical question. Harking back to his earlier analogy, Rostow observed that "at its present level" bombing involved the same kind of "painful but endurable pressure on the North as small-scale guerrilla warfare in the South." This was quite a move away from the idea that threatening North Vietnam's industry would compel Ho Chi Minh to desist from supporting his southern comrades. Unless there was a significant escalation in the bombing campaign, Rostow urged that U.S. policy redirect some of its energy to putting pressure on the NLF in the south. Unless Johnson gave free rein to the U.S. Air Force, Rostow now recommended that the president had to engage seriously with a challenge neglected since the demise of the strategic hamlet program: the building of a credible South Vietnam.[71]

Was this too little too late? Was Rostow serious? His reasoning was informed to a large degree by the hope that the president would simply agree to bomb the targets that he wanted to see destroyed. Expanding a target list was certainly a simpler plan to execute than winning "hearts and minds" in the south. Yet it does seem clear that Rostow wanted the United States to do more to defeat communism south of the seventeenth parallel, and this meant the deployment of more ground troops. As Rostow wrote to the president on November 30, "Westmoreland must allocate more of his own military resources to pacification as well as press the ARVN forward into this task; and he should work up a plan for the military side of pacification for 1967."[72] As bombing alone had proved incapable of defeating North Vietnam, so would Rostow follow General William Westmoreland's lead in requesting more troops. The Vietnam War was taking on significant dimensions and cracks within the Johnson administration were becoming increasingly difficult to paper over.

At the close of 1966, Walt Rostow was Lyndon Johnson's most trusted adviser on foreign affairs. Throughout the year, the president had escalated the war based largely on the optimistic advice of the administration's preeminent hawk. The problem from the American perspective was that the other side was escalating in a fashion that mirrored America's considerable efforts. North Vietnam had mobilized the entire nation to "foil the war of aggression of the U.S. imperialists." North-south infiltration increased rapidly along the six-hundred-mile Ho Chi Minh Trail. In what was a remarkable logistical operation, North Vietnam managed to move an estimated four hundred tons of supplies and as many as five thousand men a month down the trail. America found strategic solace in the hope that its war of attrition would sap the will of NLF insurgents and North Vietnamese regulars. The main problem was that the NLF and the North Vietnamese Army (PAVN) did not sit still and take their airborne medicine. They were a highly elusive enemy. And when the bombs reached their intended targets, an estimated 200,000 North Vietnamese reached draft age each year to fill the depleted ranks.[73] Rostow's "war-winning" strategy had quite a fight on its hands.

SEVEN

POSTPONING the INEVITABLE

1967

THE PEOPLE'S REPUBLIC OF CHINA was an ever-present consideration for American policymakers during the Vietnam War. A fast-growing but impoverished nation of some 700 million inhabitants, Mao Zedong's China supplied North Vietnam with large quantities of military equipment and manpower through the 1960s. In 1964 China sent fifteen MIG-15 and MIG-17 jets to Hanoi and began training North Vietnamese pilots. In April 1965 China signed agreements with North Vietnam concerning the dispatch of combat troops and commenced the supply of ground-to-air missiles, anti-aircraft artillery, minesweepers, and logistical units. From 1965 to 1968, 320,000 Chinese troops performed invaluable service in North Vietnam—the peak year was 1967, when 170,000 Chinese troops were present in the north. As the historian Quiang Zhai writes, "They operated antiaircraft guns, built and repaired roads, bridges, and rail lines, and constructed factories. They enabled [North Vietnam] to send large numbers of troops to South Vietnam for the fighting. When the last Chinese troops withdrew from Vietnam in August 1973, 1,100 soldiers had lost their lives and 4,200 had been wounded."[1] As China and Vietnam were bitter historical adversaries, it is important to understand why Mao made the costly decisions he did. Through the Kennedy years, Rostow had claimed that China would not get involved in the Vietnam War due to the economic crises that were afflicting the Middle Kingdom. China was evidently not behaving in the restrained manner that Rostow had prophesied.

Why did Mao divert invaluable resources to North Vietnam and risk war with the United States? The answer is that ideological belief and the vagaries of Chinese domestic politics compelled Mao to support North Vietnam generously. Mao believed that his violent path to power was a viable blueprint for his communist brethren across the developing world. China supported Vietnamese communism to assert its identity and to prove the potency of its development model. But there was an equally compelling political rationale that led Mao to intervene in the conflict. As Zhai writes, "Mao had become increasingly unhappy with the course that [his political rivals] Liu Shaoqi and Deng Xiaoping were following in the wake of the Great Leap Forward. Convinced that his successors had lost interest in continuing the revolution, Mao felt the need to rekindle class struggle in order to maintain revolutionary momentum."[2] This campaign of extremism and ideological purification—the Great Proletarian Cultural Revolution—led Mao to adopt a more belligerent course in foreign policy. Millions died across China from 1966 to 1969 in the name of communist "purity." Placed in such a brutal context, providing comradely support to Ho Chi Minh's North Vietnam was entirely unremarkable. A desire to solidify communism and eliminate revisionism within China enhanced Mao's support for Marxist revolution across Southeast Asia.

Rostow disagreed with this explanation even though it happened to tally with reality. In July 1966 the national security adviser informed the president that "the internal crisis [in China] serves to reduce the chance of Chinese intervention in Vietnam."[3] As Mao's grip on power appeared more tenuous, as the bloodletting of the Cultural Revolution continued and elite political fault lines were exacerbated, Rostow believed that it was unlikely that China's appetite for overseas adventurism would continue as before. On September 20 Rostow opined, "I cannot help thinking that this wild trouble in China may make it easier for Hanoi to get out of the war."[4] Mao's aggressive supplying of North Vietnam flatly contradicted this optimistic rationale. But as China's actions made little sense from Rostow's perspective, he simply could not fathom what was going on. It made no logical sense for Mao to continue to support North Vietnam when his nation was in disarray and threats to his leadership were mounting. But Mao believed that radicalizing the Marxist revolution—both at home and abroad—actually solidified his position, and undermined his enemies.

As the Cultural Revolution gathered pace from 1967, Rostow reported in January that "Mao's regime is in serious difficulty, to a degree that civil war has become a distinct possibility."[5] Hopeful that Mao was on the way out, and that a more moderate leader might take his place, Rostow wrote on January 13 that "Mao's own prestige has been seriously, perhaps irretrievably, tarnished in this as yet unavailing fracas."[6] While the Cultural Revolution was a horrific spectacle, it was not making things any easier for the United States in Vietnam. Rostow was not facing facts when he wrote that "on the economic side, the Vietnamese don't really want more Chinese around."[7] North Vietnam did not want to subordinate its freedom of action to China. But its leaders were delighted to accept any material support that was offered their way, so long as no binding strings were attached. For the remainder of Johnson's presidency, Rostow had little to say on the reality of large-scale Chinese support for North Vietnam. Mao Zedong's support for North Vietnam was difficult for Rostow to comprehend as it conflicted with a universal principle expressed in *The Stages of Economic Growth*: all nations pursue economic growth single-mindedly.

MOVING AWAY from the intellectually bothersome Chinese, Rostow had identified the most "important task in 1967" as the creation of "a setting in which the VC appears to be disintegrating. This would make the rationale for continuing to accept the costs of bombing the north less persuasive." Rostow believed that this might be achieved by making "a dramatic and sustained psychological appeal to the VC to join in the making of a new South Vietnamese nation." Rostow does not elaborate on how this might possibly work in practice, beyond an underspecified "enlarged and sustained effort to defect VC leaders." His plan is difficult to fathom. Once again Rostow was impervious to the most significant force that drove the NLF insurgency: nationalism. Their purpose was to destroy the artificial construct that was South Vietnam and reunite the nation. It was unlikely, to put it mildly, that the NLF would join America in constructing what they viewed as an illegitimate regime. And this position was unlikely to change, no matter how "dramatic" and "sustained" the American psychological appeal might be.[8]

For Rostow this was a rare foray into the southern theater of the Vietnam War, and this interest was not sustained. The intensified bombing of North Vietnam was the course that Rostow repeatedly urged; nation building in the south continued to receive short shrift. Nineteen sixty-seven was to be a year of sharp escalation, and Rostow's views were ascendant. Rostow's rise was aided by the fact that other talented members of the cabinet and the NSC staff either jumped ship voluntarily or were given a nudge by the captain. The strong-minded Vietnam skeptic George Ball left the administration on September 30, 1966. Over the course of 1966 and 1967, Carl Kaysen moved to Princeton, NSC staff member Francis Bator took up a professorship at Harvard, Michael Forrestal returned to practice law, Robert Komer departed for field duty in Vietnam, James Thomson went to Harvard, and senior NSC analyst Chester Cooper joined Averell Harriman's office.[9] Critical voices were on their way out and those that remained were frozen out of the debate as the escalation intensified. Rostow and those who opposed the escalatory path he favored were at loggerheads over the course of 1967. The secretary of defense came out of the fight as the biggest loser.

Rolling Thunder 52 was presented to the defense secretary on November 8, 1966, and it represented a shift in strategy from targeting North Vietnam's war-making capability to aiming to destroy its will to fight. The Joint Chiefs had opted to target eight major power plants in order "to affect to a major degree both military and civilian support to the war effort."[10] In the wake of a midterm election that had produced significant Republican gains, Johnson was amenable to this shift in approach. Through a Polish intermediary, Janusz Lewandowski, however, North Vietnam had in December displayed a willingness to commence negotiations (referred to in the U.S. government by the code name Marigold), and so the plan for more extended bombing was put on ice.[11]

This peace feeler fizzled out into nothing. The Marigold channel collapsed following intense American bombing raids against North Vietnam on December 13 and 14, 1966.[12] In Rostow's opinion the collapse of these talks was both unsurprising and not something to mourn. While Rostow identified on Hanoi's side an "impulse to get out of the war," he doubted at this stage that the communists held any inclination to make the necessary concessions to facilitate negotiations. North Vietnam was "unlikely to negotiate an end to the terror in the south" as it would "cause the Viet Cong rapidly to collapse and North Vietnam thus to lose its international bargaining position."[13] Rostow also insisted that if serious negotiations were to emerge, they should be direct, and with no intermediary.[14]

With this consideration in mind, Rostow came up with an exceedingly hopeful suggestion on January 5, 1967. Sensing, despite intelligence reports suggesting otherwise, that Hanoi actually wanted to "get out of the war but [didn't] know how," Rostow drafted a letter from Lyndon Johnson to Ho Chi Minh that he urged the president to approve and dispatch. Rostow had decided that intermediaries were unnecessary and that a simple appeal to the spiritual leader of North Vietnam might clear the path for an honorable retreat on North Vietnam's part. In the letter Rostow had the president call on Ho Chi Minh to consider entering direct talks at a neutral and secure site, preferably Burma. While Rostow did not give the plan "very high odds," he did have "the nagging feeling that they could be well in a position of wanting to get out and not knowing it." As an additional consideration, Rostow added that he could "even reconstruct the reasons for [Ho's] view"—that he wanted to spare his industrial sector from further destruction.[15] We will never know whether this direct approach might have passed muster. Rostow's letter was never sent. When Johnson did write to Ho Chi Minh suggesting a move to negotiations, the terms presented were unacceptable to North Vietnam and the offer was spurned.[16]

Rostow was implacably opposed to the president authorizing any third-party negotiation with Hanoi. When a significant intermediary did dip its oar in—even in the case of the United States' closest diplomatic ally—he made sure that discussions were wedded to the most stringent possible terms. Prime Minister Harold Wilson had long thought of himself as a potential peacemaker. Owing to Britain's role as joint chair of the Geneva Conference, the clout that came with the historic "special relationship" (usually more apparent than real) with the United States, and what he mistakenly believed to be some measure of genuine influence in Moscow, Wilson believed that he could engineer a negotiated settlement to close the Vietnam War. In pursuing this most challenging task, Wilson displayed an inflated sense of his own importance and was painfully oblivious to the fact that Lyndon Johnson disliked him. Yet his efforts were sincere. Wilson was optimistic that something significant might come from his efforts; that his unique combination of negotiating talent and Britain's diplomatic prestige could be effectively brought to bear in resolving the conflict. When the Soviet premier Alexei Kosygin visited London from February 6 to 13, Wilson grabbed his opportunity to act as peacemaker.[17]

Rostow and Johnson were uneasy about Wilson's initiative. Rostow in particular felt that the British prime minister was untrustworthy (Johnson, Rusk, and Rostow were highly disappointed that Wilson had refused to send British combat troops to South Vietnam) and that his eagerness to secure a breakthrough might trap the United States into negotiations on unacceptable terms.[18] At the same time, Johnson was sensitive to the fact that if the United States backed away from an initiative launched by its closest diplomatic ally, then its global reputation as a nation dedicated to peace would be tarnished. Johnson had little option but to give Wilson his reluctant permission to proceed. To assist communication between Washington and London, the president dispatched Chester Cooper to Britain to assist Wilson on any issue that required swift clarification.

Wilson's peacemaking initiative was based on an earlier American formulation known as "Phase A–Phase B," whereby the United States would appear to stop bombing unconditionally, but this cessation would actually be based on a previously arranged understanding that the two sides take concurrent steps to de-escalate the conflict. Such an agreement allowed both sides to save face. Hanoi could claim that the United States had agreed to an unconditional bombing halt and Washington would secure the mutual de-escalation that had long been a policy goal.[19] Just prior to Kosygin's arrival, however, the U.S. shifted its stance on Phase A–Phase B. The Johnson administration now insisted that it would only terminate the bombing after infiltration "had stopped."[20]

The U.S. government initially failed to communicate this shift in stance to Harold Wilson with sufficient lucidity. And when clarity was forthcoming, it became clear that Walt Rostow was the driving force behind the hardening of Johnson's position. On February 7 the American president sent a cable to Wilson informing him that he "should not suggest a stoppage of the bombing in exchange merely for talks."[21] Michael Palliser of the British Foreign Office described the message as "pure Rostow" and advised that while the viewpoint presented was harsh, the U.S. State Department did not share the appraisal.[22]

Wilson chose to ignore the president's Rostow-penned admonitions and plowed on regardless with the Phase A–Phase B criteria. In his discussions with Kosygin, Wilson even alluded to divisions within American government that did not need to be taken entirely seriously (although he did not refer to Rostow and McNamara by name). Wilson thus advised by way of persuasion that "these American leaders who deeply desire a military settlement must be able to convince those who are urging that the military activities must be maintained, that by stopping the fighting the other side would not be placed in a position of military advantage."[23] Wilson held excessive faith in the ability of latter-day doves like McNamara to prevail over hawks like Rostow. The prime minister's confidence was shown to be misplaced just a few days later.

Washington communicated its definitive position to London on February 10, the fifth day of Kosygin's visit to London. As Rostow phrased it, "The United States will order a cessation of bombing of North Vietnam as soon as they are assured that infiltration from North Vietnam has stopped."[24] Chester Cooper was furious that Rostow had reversed America's earlier adherence to Phase A–Phase B, and told him so directly. In response Rostow said that he did not "give a Goddamn" about how he and Wilson felt, and that Cooper had "to damn well change the text."[25] Harold Wilson went incandescent with rage when he heard the news that evening. Reflecting on this diplomatic debacle in later years, Cooper recalled that "he had never seen anyone so angry."[26] The British prime minister's dreams of facilitating U.S.–North Vietnamese rapprochement lay in tatters. In spite of Wilson's desperate final efforts to keep the negotiations on track, Hanoi firmly rejected Rostow's amended version of the Phase A–Phase B formula.

Looking back on the debacle decades later, Robert McNamara wrote that the Wilson-Kosygin talks were "very, very close to a breakthrough" until Washington shifted tack by "requiring Hanoi to cease infiltration *before* Washington instituted a bombing halt."[27] Assistant Secretary of State Joseph Sisco later identified "that occasion in London" as being the brightest opportunity for peace in the late 1960s.[28] Harold Wilson blamed Rostow entirely for the failure of "Kosygin Week." In March Wilson wrote to his foreign secretary, George Brown, "I suspect that Rostow himself was largely responsible for the misunderstandings during the Kosygin visit and may well have reported to the President in the light of responsibility." Harold Wilson was thus accusing Rostow of manipulating the president through a series of outright deceptions. Surprised by the severity of Wilson's tone, Brown advised the prime minister against raising this incendiary allegation with Lyndon Johnson: "Better not run the risk of unnecessarily irritating L.B.J."[29]

WITH THE POLISH CHANNEL GONE and Wilson's initiative scuppered, the bombing debate could now recommence in earnest. On January 23 Rostow wrote to Johnson, "Before we go into any new target systems . . . you should hear systematic argument on alternative 'northern strategies' so that we may decide something more fundamental than merely adding a few targets to the existing list."[30] What Rostow meant became clear on February 15, 1967, when he recommended that the United States mine Haiphong Harbor. "We ought to lay a few of them and see what happens," Rostow urged flippantly. Johnson was intrigued, but was not keen on direct American involvement: "Can't the South Vietnamese do it [with boats]?" inquired the president hopefully. "Well, it's kind of far to get up in a little boat," replied Rostow patiently.[31]

Mining Haiphong Harbor was one Rostow recommendation too far for Lyndon Johnson. But he was most receptive to Rostow's call for more bombing. On February 20 Rostow wrote to the president, "As you know, I am for applying more weight [on the north] . . . They should feel that the sheriff is coming slowly down the road for them, not that we are in a spasm of anxiety or desperation."[32] Keenly aware that McNamara now viewed his ideas with deep suspicion, Rostow fired a broadside at the defense secretary's March 9 recommendation that the U.S. curtail its bombing around Hanoi. "He honestly believes," wrote Rostow incredulously, "that our bombing around Hanoi stiffens the resistance of the people in authority there and makes it harder for them to negotiate an end to the war . . . I am not so sure that his picture of the mind of the men in Hanoi is correct."[33] Owing to McNamara's moral concerns about the brutality of the war, and his dawning realization that the United States was not in any position to "win" in the conventional sense, Johnson's previously exalted opinion of his defense secretary was in freefall by this stage. And so the president ignored McNamara and approved attacks on Haiphong's two thermal power plants on March 22 and authorized hitting those Rolling Thunder 52 targets postponed from November. Brooking no lily-livered opposition to the extension of bombing, Johnson had, on February 8, 1967, informed the NSC that the bombing would continue "until we get something from the North Vietnamese."[34] Given that his defense secretary and, intermittently, his secretary of state were both doubtful as to what extended bombing would achieve, it is very likely that the one senior civilian adviser who believed in bombing had an influence in convincing Johnson, against his earlier skepticism, that it could win the war.

On the issue of ground force escalation, if not on the air war, Rostow and the Joint Chiefs were frustrated in their April 27 call to deploy 200,000 additional combat troops to South Vietnam and across the Ho Chi Minh Trail into Laos. General William Westmoreland reasoned that "killing guerrillas is like killing termites with a screwdriver, where you have to kill them one by one and they're inclined to multiply as rapidly as you kill them."[35] There is much in Westmoreland's metaphor to criticize. As the historian Robert Buzzanco astutely observes in *Masters of War*, "The record does not indicate whether anyone asked if 200,000 more screwdrivers could kill an indeterminate number of termites."[36]

Rostow in fact wanted to go a step further than Westmoreland—to eschew half-measures and simply invade North Vietnam. He described Westmoreland's recommendation as "ladling some water out of the bath tub while the tap is still turned on." The national security adviser had a grander vision for U.S. military strategy. He believed that the American public would rather that the president "do something big and hopefully decisive rather than something small."[37] With this in mind, Rostow later recalled, "I indicated to Johnson my preference. It was to invade the southern part of North Vietnam in order to block infiltration routes and to hold the area hostage against North Vietnamese withdrawal from Laos and Cambodia as well as from South Vietnam." Rostow was adamant, furthermore, that counterintervention was highly unlikely, that the People's Republic of China would not "march the length of Vietnam, risking long supply lines, vulnerable to air and sea harassment if American forces moved [north.]"[38] Of course General Douglas MacArthur had taken a similar gamble in October 1950—one that he was called on. That Chinese intervention in the Korean War might be paralleled seventeen years later in Vietnam was a dark possibility that consumed the president.

In his memoir *Concept and Controversy*, Rostow recalls that a potent triumvirate decisively rejected his bold plan: "The military and I were turned down by the President, Rusk and McNamara."[39] On April 27 Rostow made an impassioned case in favor of Westmoreland's troop request, and presented his strategic masterstroke that was invading the north. During the meeting Rostow paced the room, propped up a map of Vietnam on an easel, and then, gesticulating with a pointer, explained in minute detail why his invasion strategy would work. Yet this remarkable display left the other participants only bemused and unmoved. As Westmoreland recalled, "No one around the table, to include the President, expressed any great enthusiasm for the operation, and the discussion died with only Rostow and me participating."[40]

The Rusk-McNamara axis coalesced to oppose not just Rostow's bombing strategy, but his call to increase America's troop presence and take the fight northward. Their rejection was a source of some frustration for Rostow. He contemplated so radical a course as resigning from the Johnson administration in protest. After enjoying a period of significant influence over the president for the year that followed his appointment as national security adviser, his advice on escalating the Vietnam War appeared once again to be slipping outside the mainstream. Ultimately, Rostow opted to stay "with Johnson until the last day, while steadily but quietly opposed to the way the war was being fought."[41]

Rostow was aghast at Johnson's rejection of additional ground troop deployments—it was a mistake of some magnitude. For Rostow the "last word" with regard to Johnson's failure to wage the war effectively belongs to General William Westmoreland, who remarked in later years that "one of [the President's] main strategic objectives was to confine the war. He did not want it to spread . . . Having said that, that's not the way I felt at the time. I felt that our hands were tied."[42] Despite these efforts to "confine the war," the pace of bombing escalation increased ever more. On April 8 U.S. bombers attacked Hanoi's central electric power station, and on April 20 Haiphong's thermal power plant was destroyed.[43] Even Earle

Wheeler realized that the air campaign was reaching its natural limits, observing that bombing "is reaching the point where we will have struck all worthwhile fixed targets except the ports."[44] Johnson had given Rostow and the Joint Chiefs the free rein they desired in one field, if not the other, and it further exacerbated his administration's fault lines.

In May 1967 Robert McNamara made a concerted effort to convince the president of the merits of neutralizing South Vietnam, just as John F. Kennedy had earlier accepted the creation of a "neutral" Laos. Having subjected every available escalatory option to exacting statistical analysis, the defense secretary had concluded that South Vietnam could not be protected indefinitely by the application of American military force, and that the least bad option was to secure its Cold War neutrality in collaboration with the Soviet Union. As McNamara recalled in his 1995 memoir, *In Retrospect*, "Walt Rostow . . . strongly disagreed and reported to the President that my memorandum 'aroused strong feelings' within the government. The memo unleashed a storm of controversy, the result of which being that the possibility of a neutral government in South Vietnam was not properly debated in the upper levels of our argument."[45] McNamara blames Rostow directly for convincing Johnson to reject his proposal. Rancor between the two men was evident then as it was in later years. McNamara later recalled that Rostow believed "we were justified in doing what we were doing and that I am wrong to think otherwise because I don't understand Asia and I don't understand where we'd be in Asia had we not intervened."[46] In the summer and autumn of 1967, Rostow and McNamara were implacably opposed to each other's position—that of rapid military escalation and of sincere moves toward peacemaking and neutralization, respectively. Undersecretary of the Air Force Townsend Hoopes observed in his memoirs that "Rostow's insensitivity to the opinion of others was legendary."[47] This insensitivity riled McNamara intensely.

On May 19 Rostow shifted his attention from McNamara's neutrality gambit to Dean Rusk's reservations on bombing. "Secretary Rusk feels the diplomatic cost of bombing Hanoi-Haiphong overwhelms whatever the military advantage might be," Rostow informed his president, "but he has not devised—nor can he guarantee—a diplomatic pay-off for moving the bombing pattern to the south."[48] By this stage Rostow's bellicosity was such that even Maxwell Taylor—former chairman of the Joint Chiefs of Staff, ambassador to Saigon, and now part of the distinguished coterie of foreign-policy advisers known as the "Wise Men"—complained to the president, "I would be cautious in extending the target system much farther." Normally rock-solid in his support for aerial bombardment, Taylor now concluded pointedly that "some of our bombing advocates still think in terms of World War II and forget . . . there is really no industrial target system in Vietnam worthy of its name."[49] Other sources were homing in on Rostow's damaging influence. During one of his regularly scheduled briefings with the national security adviser, the *New York Herald-Tribune* journalist Rowland Evans asked what Rostow was "going to do now that [his] policy has failed." "What policy?" Rostow inquired, taken aback by Evans's directness. "The policy of forcing Hanoi to negotiate by bombing," replied Evans. "It's worse than the Bay of Pigs." Rostow later reported to LBJ that he "explained to him that in the 14 months I have been over here, I have never heard anyone put the proposition to the President that bombing alone would end the war."[50] This defense was disingenuous, to say the least. Rostow had consistently maintained that bombing North Vietnam was a panacea.

Robert McNamara was becoming increasingly vocal in his criticism of the U.S. bombing campaign. In a May 18 memorandum to the president, the defense secretary observed that "the picture of the world's greatest superpower killing or seriously injuring 1,000 non-combatants a week, while trying to pound a tiny, backward nation into submission on an issue whose merits are hotly disputed, is not a pretty one."[51] The manner in which the administration was critically split—with McNamara favoring diplomacy, the Joint Chiefs and Rostow escalation, and Dean Rusk expressing few concrete opinions on what to do next—required some bridge building. "The question is," Rostow asked the president, "what kind of scenario can hold our family together in ways that look after the nation's interests and make military sense?" Rostow's answer was first to bomb Hanoi's thermal power plants, as he and Earle Wheeler had long advocated, and then "cut back radically on attacks in the Haiphong area for several weeks," to placate Rusk and McNamara. If diplomacy should fail in this interlude, as Rostow expected it would, then the president should reconsider "the mining of the ports (and attacks on the import routes)" and the maintenance of pressure to ensure Hanoi did not "rebuild the power grid."[52] And so on May 9, 1967, in what was to be an intensity high point of Johnson's bombing campaign, Hanoi's thermal power plant was destroyed by American bombing.

A coalition of William Bundy, John McNaughton, Robert McNamara, and McGeorge Bundy (who still wielded some influence as one of the Wise Men) registered their opposition to any extension of the air war in the summer of 1967.[53] On the same day that Hanoi's thermal power plant was destroyed, McNamara made clear his opposition to escalation in the starkest terms: "The war in Vietnam is acquiring a momentum of its own that must be stopped. Dramatic increases in attacks on the north . . . [are] not the answer."[54] Just a few weeks later, Rostow advised that the president pursue the opposite course, that "during July we might have to up the ante in Vietnam: with respect to troops and even with respect to bombing."[55]

Johnson held far more respect for Rostow's dedication, loyalty, and bellicosity than for McNamara's recent conversion to hand-wringing liberal angst. Yet he did not follow Rostow's counsel by systematically escalating the war. Yielding partly to McNamara's advice that he restrain bombing, and perhaps worried that his "family" was becoming irreparably dysfunctional, Johnson prohibited further air attacks within ten miles of Hanoi. With 500,000 American troops in Vietnam by August, and the Joint Chiefs and Rostow lobbying vigorously for the deployment of a further 200,000, Johnson had arrived at the conclusion that further escalation at this stage was likely to damage not only cabinet unity, but also his prospects for reelection. While the bombing campaign remained intense, Johnson rejected the key strategies that Rostow had championed: the dispatch of further combat troops, the invasion of North Vietnam, and the removal of the remaining constraints to the U.S. bombing campaign. Rostow took to prefacing his calls for further bombing and more troops with lines like "No matter how many call me a rosy optimist . . . ," but the combination of Rusk, McNamara, and the Bundy brothers had taken the wind out of his sails.[56]

The president was becoming increasingly disenchanted with the repetitive advice dispensed by the Joint Chiefs. "Bomb, bomb, bomb," Johnson complained to his military advisers, "that's all you seem to know."[57] LBJ could have easily directed the same criticism at his national security adviser, although Rostow somehow managed to elude blame. The Rostow

Thesis was now a dead letter—it had failed in its expressed intention of compelling North Vietnam to cease infiltration. Instead of wondering what had gone wrong, however, Rostow rationalized that Johnson had erred by not bombing harder and invading North Vietnam. As there was little chance of this happening, Rostow necessarily moved his attention elsewhere. He argued in favor of more bombing and more troop deployments until the very end, but increasingly Rostow shifted his focus to Averell Harriman's pursuit of peace negotiations, political progress in South Vietnam, and even to domestic crises within the United States.[58] If America could not win the Vietnam War, Rostow was going to make sure that any peace to follow would be based on terms entirely favorable to South Vietnam. When it came to negotiating strategy, Rostow disagreed with Harriman's argument that Johnson should reduce the intensity of the conflict to allow serious negotiations to commence. Averell Harriman soon displaced Robert McNamara as Walt Rostow's bête noire.

IN THE SUMMER OF 1967, the United States was approaching a period of pervasive domestic turmoil. Lyndon Johnson's hopes of creating his epoch-defining Great Society were unraveling due to the soaring costs of maintaining a massive military presence ten thousand miles from home.[59] In April 1967 Martin Luther King Jr. voiced his first public opposition to what he described as an "immoral war," issuing a "declaration of independence" from America's role in the Vietnam conflict.[60] In large part King's opposition grew from his pacific objections to the use of violence. But he also recognized that Johnson could not have it both ways. Without rival economically and militarily, even the United States could not bear the combined financial burden of winning a war in Southeast Asia and refashioning domestic society on the radical lines envisioned by the president. King lamented, "A few years ago there was a shining moment," when it appeared "there was a real promise of hope for the poor." Then came the Tonkin Gulf Resolution and the "build-up in Vietnam, and I watched the program broken and eviscerated as if it were some idle political plaything of a society gone mad on war."[61]

King's moral authority lent his words particular potency. His intervention came at a time when racial violence was increasingly prevalent in the

ghettoes of urban America. In July 1967, in response to rumors (later sub-
stantiated) of police brutality against inner-city blacks, urban riots erupted
in Newark and Detroit. Forty-three people died. Many Republicans and a
fair few Democrats blamed the riots on the permissiveness engendered by
Johnson's legislative program. The president was understandably keen to
pin the blame elsewhere. To further this end, Johnson directed Rostow to
coordinate an effort to collect "such evidence as there is on external involvement in the violent radical community of the Negro community in
the U.S." Responding to this request, Rostow, according to the historian
Kenneth O'Reilly, "mobilized the entire intelligence community," but to no
avail; he "came up with a blank."[62] The fact that Johnson chose his national security adviser for the task suggests the president thought highly of
Rostow's varied skills. That Rostow was now devoting substantial time
to domestic blame-deflection, however, also suggested that his fourteen-
month tenure as Johnson's most influential Vietnam adviser was approaching its end.

Johnson's escalation of the Vietnam War stabilized, with spasmodic
eruptions, through the final months of 1967. Johnson adopted this position in spite of Rostow's clearly expressed opposition. In urging the president to instead wage war with greater intensity—to invade North Vietnam
and bomb Hanoi and Haiphong—the national security adviser was heart-
ened by the fact that his fellow citizens backed a more belligerent American
strategy. In July 1967 a Harris poll reported that 72 percent of the public
favored the continued bombing of North Vietnam and that 40 percent
wanted the military to increase direct pressure on Hanoi. A mere 15 percent of the American public opposed bombing outright.[63] With such
steadfast public support, it is not surprising that Rostow continued to question McNamara's hesitancy, urge the removal of restrictions on bombing,
and confidently predict U.S. victory. On July 8 Rostow informed the president, "The Viet-Nam situation is not a stalemate. We are moving uphill
slowly but steadily. The enemy is moving downhill, paying an increasingly
heavy price for its aggression."[64] Johnson had the option of hastening
North Vietnam's "downhill" momentum through deploying more force.

A few days later, the CIA reported that Lieutenant General Van Tien
Dung, chief of staff of the North Vietnamese Army, had written a series of
published articles in which he mocked the restraints imposed on U.S. mili-

tary strategy. Because the U.S. Air Force was prevented from attacking "the north swiftly through strategic, large-scale and surprise bombing," the morale of U.S. "air pirates" was very low. Rostow hoped to use Dung's words to goad the president into some serious bombing and gratefully latched upon this intercept. On July 11 he wrote to the president that this particular "Hanoi hard-liner's view of the war is worth reading, including his mockery of our bombing limitations."[65] Dung's comments may well have rankled, but Johnson was too worried about the mercurial People's Republic of China to sanction the strategic shift that Rostow urged upon him. During a stormy meeting in July with J. William Fulbright, chairman of the Senate Foreign Relations Committee, the president had snapped, "As for stopping the bombing in North Vietnam, I am not going to tell our men in the field to put their right hands behind their backs and fight only with their left."[66] But this was precisely what Johnson was doing, in Rostow's opinion.

In August 1967 the Mississippi Democrat John C. Stennis, chairman of the Senate Armed Services Committee, presided over hearings designed to appraise the effectiveness of U.S. bombing strategy. Stennis was a conservative Democrat with a keen desire to untie the knot that restrained the military's arm. Johnson recognized that, coaxed by the committee's courtly chairman, it was highly probable that John P. McConnell (Air Force chief of staff) and Ulysses S. Grant Sharp Jr. (commander in chief, Pacific) would make clear to the committee that political controls were impeding military effectiveness. Fearing a domestic furor, Johnson thus opted to respond favorably to a request made by the Joint Chiefs that he authorize the destruction of previously restricted targets. Serving as the Joint Chiefs' wingman, Rostow poured scorn on the defense secretary's objections. On August 9 Rostow wrote to the president, "If we weren't bombing, the total level of attempted infiltration would be much, much higher than it is. With the greatest possible respect, I don't back away from the differences with Bob McNamara on this."[67] The combination of pressure from the Joint Chiefs, and Rostow's internal politicking, led to a momentary expansion of the air campaign that hit six targets within the ten-mile Hanoi circle and nine on the northeast railroad that fell close to the Chinese border.[68] On this occasion Robert McNamara was not alone in protest.

Upon scanning the options recommended by Rostow and the Joint Chiefs on August 16, Dean Rusk wrote that "there appears to be no ascertainable connection between some of these targets and winning the war. It's a question of what do you ask a man to die for. Some of these targets aren't worth the men lost."[69] On August 9 the Senate called McNamara to testify before the Stennis Committee. The secretary of defense turned in a bravura performance, resolutely defending the restrictions that the president had imposed on the bombing. McNamara further argued that no amount of bombing could decisively interdict the north-south flow of supplies or decisively break North Vietnam's will. The defense secretary added that those who argued that bombing was a potentially decisive instrument ignored the predominantly agrarian character of North Vietnam. He candidly informed the committee that "you cannot win the war on the cheap by bombing."[70]

Johnson was appalled by McNamara's performance—by this public venting of what were some serious reservations. Rusk's and McNamara's objections to bombing were increasingly ignored by a president keen to avoid Stennis-generated flak. In the autumn of 1967, Johnson authorized the destruction of 52 of the 57 targets that the Stennis Committee had criticized the government for failing to hit.[71] Rostow was pleased that some restrictions had been lifted, but his broader advice that the U.S. invade North Vietnam and bomb Hanoi and Haiphong went unheeded. The president was now plotting a compromise course between Rostow's extremism and McNamara's reserve. Emotionally, Johnson sided with Rostow, but he recognized that his administration was fundamentally split and that the middle course was the least painful one to pursue.

At the same time as McNamara was questioning the Joint Chiefs' belligerency at the Stennis Committee hearings, he was also devoting considerable attention to launching a new peace initiative known by the code name Pennsylvania. Walt Rostow, as evidenced by his earlier response to Harold Wilson's efforts, was profoundly skeptical of the merits of third-party negotiations. Writing on the limited opportunities presented by this new diplomatic channel, Rostow observed to the president, "If and when they are ready to settle, we will—in my judgment—hear much more directly and without all this ambiguity."[72] Yet there were few avenues open to U.S. diplomacy in the autumn of 1967. The president gave McNamara his approval and ordered him to proceed.

The Harvard-based professor of government Henry A. Kissinger was charged with the task of handling negotiations with the North Vietnamese through two French socialist intermediaries, Herbert Marcovich and Raymond Aubrac. Vainglorious and brilliant, Kissinger was confident that he could fashion a diplomatic breakthrough where others had failed. Some in the Johnson administration were less confident that Kissinger was up to the job. During a Tuesday lunch on September 12, the president requested that the attendees voice their opinions on Kissinger's political judgment and deftness of diplomatic touch. Dean Rusk endorsed Kissinger's "trustworthiness and character," concluding that "he is basically for us." Rostow offered qualifications that were more significant. While he appreciated that Kissinger was "a good analyst," he worried that "he may go a little soft when you get down to the crunch."[73] Rostow is thus one of the few people to have ever accused Henry Kissinger of being a soft touch at the negotiating table. In spite of these doubts, the president's foreign-policy principals endorsed the credentials of the man who would later succeed Rostow as national security adviser. With LBJ's blessing, Kissinger departed for Paris to begin talks.[74]

Robert McNamara oversaw the entire Pennsylvania negotiation in what was his last significant role as secretary of defense. He held great hopes for the mission and exerted close control over Kissinger's brief, personally dictating all of the messages that he was authorized to present to Aubrac and Marcovich.[75] Responsive to the failure of the earlier Marigold channel, McNamara was adamant that U.S. bombing would not again scupper negotiations. He stressed that destroying targets of "no real value" in the early stage of talks would place Kissinger in a precarious position. As McNamara told the president, "It would be harmful to the Paris talks if we were to intensify the bombing."[76] For Rostow, however, there was no need to restrain bombing to facilitate negotiation. "I do not see any connection between bombing and negotiations," he coolly informed McNamara during a September 26 meeting. "I do not think we are going to get negotiations by bombing," Undersecretary of State Nicholas Katzenbach snapped in response. Weighing in on Rostow's side, Johnson remarked that "they have no more intention of talking than we have of surrendering. In my judgment, everything you hit is important. It makes them hurt more."[77]

In spite of these obvious obstacles evident at the very top of government, the Pennsylvania channel stayed alive longer than any had done previously. Aubrac and Marcovich delivered messages to Kissinger sufficiently appealing to keep the Johnson administration interested. In response McNamara authorized Kissinger to offer a reformulation of the Phase A–Phase B formula: that the United States would cease bombing North Vietnam on the understanding that North Vietnam would not take military advantage of the cessation. To attach greater credibility to the compromise deal (and score points internationally as a man of peace), the president in a speech of September 29 went public with this proposal in San Antonio, Texas.

The Pennsylvania channel as a whole, however, was pursued in absolute secrecy. McNamara took great care in communicating to Hanoi that the precise details were confidential—to save face on both sides—and that North Vietnam should be similarly discreet. But in spite of McNamara's diplomatic tact, Hanoi responded familiarly and obstinately by asserting that bombing must cease without condition, directly rebuffing the offer. The Johnson administration again split over how to react. Rostow denounced Hanoi's intractability, while McNamara argued in favor of an unconditional halt. Bombing could surely resume later, McNamara reasoned, if negotiations came to nothing.[78]

At the beginning of October, Rostow became concerned that McNamara was lavishing needless attention on what was a futile negotiating exercise. He believed that McNamara and Kissinger had shown excessive zeal in seeking compromise, and that their overwhelming desire for peace would lead to their presenting South Vietnam with a fait accompli—one that might lead to Vietnamese reunification on northern terms. To prevent this from happening, Rostow sought to obtain hard evidence that Hanoi's position had hardened from the stance adhered to previously. He instructed Richard Helms to investigate whether "hardening" had actually taken place, but the CIA director found nothing. "Per your request," Helms replied, "we simply cannot discern any convincing indication that the Hanoi position [words deleted] is significantly different from or has ever been appreciably more forthcoming than the Hanoi position enunciated through other means, including public statements. We do not read the most recent [words deleted] messages as a 'hardening' of Hanoi's position."[79] Helms's response disappointed Rostow, for he wanted to persuade the president to recall Kissinger from Paris.

Rostow was relieved to discover that he was not alone in viewing Pennsylvania as a chimera. The chairman of the Joint Chiefs of Staff, Earle Wheeler, was frustrated that the president had followed McNamara's advice by toning down the U.S. bombing campaign, and was keen to resume the targeting of Hanoi's bridges and power plants. For his part Johnson instinctively tilted toward Rostow and Wheeler, and was frustrated that he had restrained bombing "just because two professors are meeting." Wanting to believe that Rostow's positive appraisal of the war *was* in tune with reality, the president expressed certainty that the bombing campaign was hurting North Vietnam—"I feel it in my bones"—and displayed a renewed desire to "pour the steel on."[80] Impatient with Kissinger's lack of success, Johnson informed his beleaguered negotiator, mafioso-style, "I'm going to give it one more try, and if it doesn't work I'm going to come up to Cambridge and cut off your balls."[81] When the Pennsylvania channel quietly expired in late 1967, Walt Rostow was in no mood for mourning. In October Kissinger pleaded with Rostow that the channel be given more time to prove its worth, that Hanoi had in fact displayed a willingness to discuss terms that could prove a starting point for decisive negotiations. Rostow responded skeptically: "I told Henry that, with the best will in the world, none of us have been able to find anything but a rather dignified flat negative in the message."[82] In later years Kissinger remarked that he considered Rostow "a fool."[83]

With the Kissinger channel gone, McNamara was despondent. Yet another Jason Study, authorized by the defense secretary, despairingly concluded that "as of October 1967, the U.S. bombing of North Vietnam has had no measurable effect on Hanoi's ability to mount and support military operations in the south."[84] Upset by the lack of attention devoted to his pursuit of peace, McNamara recalled in his 1993 oral history, "I didn't believe we did all we might have done in creative use of bombing pauses to advance [peace negotiations] . . . I didn't believe then and I don't believe now that there was any significant military cost to the U.S. resulting from such a pause."[85] In a bruising clash on October 3, 1967, Rostow told McNamara, "If we stop the bombing, it will bring them back up and permit them to increase their commitment in the South. Less bombing means less strain and less cost." McNamara was less than impressed, replying curtly, "I do not agree with that." At this time Johnson was considering ways to remove McNamara from his post, while preserving both his and his defense secretary's reputation. Arbitrating the Rostow-McNamara confrontation, Johnson told them, "I want the best case from you, Walt, for bombing all targets and I want from Secretary McNamara a position on this."[86] Johnson had asked Rostow to provide not just an argument for an unrestricted air campaign, but also a case against Robert McNamara.

Both men sat down to address the president's request. Rostow was relentless in questioning McNamara's desire to wind down the war. He dispensed this task efficiently and with what Robert Komer would have viewed as uncharacteristic clarity. The president appointed Townsend Hoopes to serve as his undersecretary of the air force in October 1967. In his colorful memoir, Hoopes recalls that Rostow "shaped the evidence and maneuvered to set at discount with the president the views (of men like McNamara and Harriman) that were at odds with his own."[87] On October 7 Rostow forwarded to the president a number of CIA-intercepted letters written by North Vietnamese citizens that expressed disillusionment with the conflict. One soldier wrote sadly, "My brothers only come home once in every two or three weeks because it is very dangerous to go from place to place. They always come and bomb the roads. Most terrible of all are their fragmentation bombs." Another wrote that "the U.S. aggressors are striking our dear capital like mad." While hardly constituting comprehensive evidence that bombing was working wonders, Rostow was delighted. He declared to the president, "This is what bombing of Hanoi and Haiphong is really like—with all due respect to intelligence analysts 10,000 miles away."[88] Rostow clearly had McNamara's Jason Study in his sights when making this pointed comparison.

On October 18 Rostow wrote a lengthy memorandum presenting what he considered his clearest possible case for bombing. He argued, "At little cost in civilian casualties and at acceptable costs in our loss rates, the bombing has severely curtailed North Vietnam's industrial and agricultural production . . . Soviet aid [is] up from $100 million to $700 million annually."[89] In this instance Rostow's reasoning had veered significantly from his original intention. When he formulated his original thesis of graduated bombing, Rostow had envisaged that this would bring Hanoi to its knees, not place an unpleasant strain on the Soviet Union's public finances.

Perhaps sensing that he might do better if he upped the rhetorical ante, Rostow dispatched another memorandum to the president two days later. This time he praised the recently published official U.S. military history of the Korean War. "I was skeptical when I began reading this," Rostow confessed, "but ended up half persuaded, namely that we finally got a Korean settlement out of the truce talks by some very tough bombing, including especially the destruction of dikes in North Korea."[90] Rostow had thus made his strongest case for unrestricted bombing. Destroying North Vietnam's dikes may well have imposed a potentially decisive strain on Hanoi. As a development theorist, Rostow may have been better able to visualize just how coercive starving a "developing" nation might be. But inducing famine was not on Lyndon Johnson's agenda then, or at any time. Even Richard Nixon balked at such a brutal measure during the heaviest bombing of the war some three years later.

Rostow's cruel recommendation shocked the defense secretary. McNamara expressed his anger and frustration at the course of the war in a memorandum delivered to the president on November 1, 1967. McNamara wrote, "There is no reason to believe that the . . . continued infliction of grievous casualties, or the heavy punishment of air bombardment, will suffice to break the will of the North Vietnamese . . . Nothing can be expected to break this will other than the conviction that they will not succeed." By this stage McNamara had abandoned all hope that the United States could force victory in Vietnam through more bombing and more combat troops. Instead, he argued in favor of a policy of "stabilization" in which "we will gradually transfer the major burden of the fighting to the South Vietnamese forces." "At a minimum," McNamara wrote carefully, "we would have to make clear that our bombing is not preventing a peaceful political settlement."[91] McNamara wanted Johnson to disengage from the conflict and leave South Vietnam's fate in the hands of its people. Dean Rusk, Maxwell Taylor, and Abe Fortas—Supreme Court justice, and the president's close confidant—all opposed McNamara's line of argument. Walt Rostow provided a truly focused critique.

Rostow was convinced there was no need to tone down the U.S. bombing campaign. Citing public opinion, Rostow wrote that "in a recent

Gallup poll, some 67% of the people want us to continue bombing the North (as I remember it). Acknowledging my limitations as a judge of domestic politics, I am extremely skeptical of any change in strategy that would take you away from your present middle position; that is, using rationally all the power available, but avoiding actions likely to engage the Soviet Union and Communist China. If we shift unilaterally towards de-escalation, the Republicans will move in and crystallize a majority around a stronger policy." Rostow was contemptuous of the middle-course strategy that the president opted to follow, but to counter McNamara's arguments effectively he recognized that he had to ground his analysis in the center, not in the extremes that came more naturally. Reining in what was a visceral reaction to McNamara's memo, Rostow's comments were measured, not shrill.[92] "If I felt Bob's strategy would measurably increase the chances of a true settlement, I believe the risk might be worth taking. But both a unilateral bombing cessation and an announced policy of 'stabilization' would, in my view, be judged in Hanoi a mark of weakness rather than increased U.S. capacity to sweat out the war . . . I believe Bob's strategy would ease their problem and permit them rationally to protract the negotiation."[93] Abe Fortas was more emotive in conveying his opposition. Were the president to follow McNamara's recommendations, it would be "an invitation to slaughter."[94]

Johnson concurred with Rostow's and Fortas's analyses. The call of McNamara's conscience—his candid November 1 memorandum—cost him his job. Johnson nominated his emotionally spent defense secretary to serve as president of the World Bank, and Clark Clifford—previously a close, if unofficial, adviser to President Johnson and a distinguished member of the Wise Men—officially replaced him in February 1968. In her Lyndon Baines Johnson Library oral history, the *Washington Post* publisher Katharine Graham observed perceptively that the president "could not tolerate anybody who disagreed with him." Ultimately, Lyndon Johnson "cut himself off from all but about four people who agreed with him . . . You know, when he got rid of McNamara in that really terrible way and then he left himself with Rusk and Rostow."[95]

While Rusk was a devoted public servant, he disagreed with Rostow on the necessity for further military escalation. On November 20 Rusk warned LBJ against destroying the targets recommended by Rostow that were "of marginal utility from a military point of view." Confronting Rostow's rationale directly, and drawing on some of the conclusions provided by the CIA, the secretary of state wrote, "I would reject the political judgment that a continuous escalation of the bombing will break the will of Hanoi."[96] Casting doubts on the veracity of U.S. intelligence, Rostow responded with scant self-awareness, "I sometimes feel that the CIA is leaning against an excessive optimism that does not exist."[97] While never going nearly as far as his national security adviser desired, the president approved the destruction of ten of the Joint Chiefs–recommended twenty-four targets on December 16. As 1968 approached, the president was waging war with an intensity that Dean Rusk thought needless and unwise, but not nearly as hard as his national security adviser would have liked.

NOW AND AGAIN Rostow was taken to task for his relentless positive thinking. On December 8, 1967, an abrasive former U.S. Army lieutenant colonel, John Paul Vann, visited Washington to present his assessment of the war in Vietnam. Vann, then working under the auspices of the Agency for International Development and charged with the task of assisting Robert Komer's CORDS in pacifying South Vietnam, presented a gloomy picture of the conflict from an ideal vantage point. Discomfited by this dose of reality, based on the firsthand experience of a decorated soldier, Rostow failed to contain his impatience. In spite of all the flaws that Vann claimed to see, Rostow interrupted, did he not think that the worst of the war would be over in six months? "Oh hell no, Mr. Rostow," Vann replied without missing a beat. "I'm a born optimist. I think we can hold out longer than that." The national security adviser was not amused. Rostow later remarked that a man with Vann's attitude should not be working for the U.S. government in Vietnam.[98]

As Johnson looked back on 1967, he could detect scant military progress in Vietnam—despite Rostow's insistent claims to the contrary—and a fair few political portents that augured ill for the future. College students were turning out against the war in ever-increasing numbers and rumblings of political discontent—led by Senator J. William Fulbright—were becoming more audible in the Senate. The insistent demonstrators' chants of "Hey, hey, LBJ, how many kids did you kill today?" were beginning to hurt a president who prided himself on his humanity and common touch. Johnson could scarcely travel across his own country without encountering vociferous demonstrations and complained that he was trapped in the White House "like a jackrabbit hunkered down in a storm."[99] By the close of 1967, the United States had nearly half a million combat troops in Vietnam. It had dropped more bombs on Vietnam than in all theaters during World War II, and the war was costing the taxpayer $2 billion per month.[100] Lady Bird Johnson confided to her diary, "A miasma of trouble hangs over everything. The temperament of our people seems to be 'you must either get excited, get passionate, fight and get it over with, or we must pull out.' It is unbearably hard to fight a limited war."[101] Lady Bird's comments were perceptive. And the situation was about to get a whole lot worse. While little had gone right in 1967, mostly everything went wrong in 1968.

EIGHT

A WORLD CRASHES DOWN

1968

NINETEEN SIXTY-EIGHT WAS an election year in the United States. Most pundits assumed that Lyndon Johnson would defeat his likely opponent, Richard Nixon, in November. A towering figure in twentieth-century progressive politics, Johnson had successfully forced through Congress the broadest civil rights program in America's history. He had smoothed the ratification of the most redistributive raft of legislation since Franklin Delano Roosevelt's heyday. The president had fought to secure these achievements with singular determination and political aplomb. Yet in spite of his considerable achievements—clustered around the rallying point that was the "Great Society"—vultures were circling above.

The United States was slowly but discernibly losing faith in its domestic institutions and hitherto crystalline foreign-policy mission. Inflation was on the march, cutting into the paychecks of the nation's blue-collar workers. New generations of younger, militant activists were restless with LBJ's inability to wage a truly effective "war" on poverty, inequality, and the pervasive racial slights of everyday life. But while these issues were hugely significant, they were not justification alone for a palace coup. Most dangerous of all from Johnson's career perspective was the fact that the Vietnam War had become a focal point for disaffection within the Democratic Party. The conflict had dragged on painfully for four expensive years to little apparent effect. The Minnesota senator Eugene McCarthy launched the first electoral challenge to Johnson's management of the conflict. A journalist later asked McCarthy what he would do if elected president. McCarthy paraphrased Dwight Eisenhower in the 1952 campaign and replied, "I shall go to the Pentagon."[1] What Johnson had to do to secure the Democratic nomination in 1968 was clear enough. He had to achieve a significant military breakthrough in Southeast Asia and silence the gripes of his many detractors.

Walt Rostow was Johnson's last best hope to achieve this goal. The systemic bombing of North Vietnam's industrial centers was the strategy that Rostow believed would guarantee American victory and the president's reelection. The Rostow Thesis of graduated bombing had convinced Johnson of its merits in 1965. Through 1966 and 1967, Rostow had advised the president to escalate sharply the intensity of the air war. A strong believer that bombing both sapped popular morale and imposed unbearable economic costs, the national security adviser drafted a blueprint for victory in the Vietnam War that placed American pilots at the vanguard of the war effort. While the Marines and Army had dominated the limelight in earlier conflicts, the Vietnam War was the arena in which the U.S. Air Force was to revolutionize warfare by imposing maximum damage at minimal loss. Basking in glories past, the managers of American air power doubtless felt well equipped to do just as Rostow demanded. The Air Force's combat record up until the Vietnam War constituted a line of unbroken domination. The Korean War, in particular, had been a gloriously one-sided experience for America's fliers.

The air war in Vietnam was more keenly contested. While U.S. pilots won their dogfights over the Korean peninsula by a ratio of fifteen to one, their winning margin in Vietnam's skies slumped to two to one.[2] Visiting airborne destruction upon North Vietnam depleted America's ranks rapidly, and greedily consumed money previously allocated to Johnson's Great Society program. It was for this reason above all that the Democratic Party had entered a period of such turmoil. Johnson had allowed the conflict to spiral out of his control, and America's poor bore the disproportionate brunt of feeding an insatiable military machine. But placing party politics to one side, the overall cost of the war was borne successfully if uncomfortably by the world's richest nation. While the conflict came to scar Americans psychologically, the everyday experience of being "at war" scarcely registered across the nation. The effects of the war on Vietnam were altogether more harrowing. Being on the receiving end of America's bombing campaign was a scenario that even a reliably evocative writer like Tom Wolfe struggled to visualize:

> American pilots in Vietnam often ran through their side of the action ahead of time as if it were a movie in their mind . . . But just try to imagine the enemy's side of it . . . Try to imagine your own aircraft (encasing your own hide) sliding onto their screens as a ghost stroke (observed by what Russian?) and the trawler signaling the coast and the cannon crews and SAM battalions cranking up in the delta and devising (saying what exactly?) their black trash for the day, which would be inexplicably varied.[3]

One can hardly fault Wolfe for failing to represent adequately the Vietnamese perspective. But the gap in U.S. journalistic accounts has been filled by recently translated Vietnamese testimonies—eyewitness accounts that disturb and affect us all the more for their brevity. The NLF insurgent Truong Nhu Tang starts where Wolfe concludes:

> Nothing the guerrillas had to endure compared with the stark terrorization of the B-52 bombardments . . . an experience of undiluted psychological terror, into which we were plunged, day in, day out, for years on end. From a kilometer away, the sonic roar of B-52 explosions tore eardrums, leaving many of the jungle dwellers permanently deaf. From a kilometer, the shock waves knocked the victims senseless. Any hit within a half kilometer would collapse the walls of an un-reinforced bunker, burying alive the people cowering inside.[4]

Such was the impact of America's Rolling Thunder campaign on the scorched land below. A North Vietnamese woman, Nam Duc Mao, recalled that 1968 ushered in a new period of hardship in the north as conscription was extended swiftly to take the weight of the losses wrought by the U.S. bombing campaign.[5] Trinh Duc, a Vietnamese nationalist who fought for both the NLF and the north Vietnamese Army, recalled that the American B-52 raids had a hellish impact: "One of the things that demoralized a lot of guerrillas were the B-52 attacks. The fear these attacks caused was terrible. People pissed and shat in their pants. You would see them come out of their bunkers shaking so badly it looked as if they had gone crazy."[6] But crushing as it was in many respects, the U.S. campaign of aerial bombardment also helped forge among the North Vietnamese a spirit of defiance in the face of adversity. As the RAND analyst Oleg Hoeffding observed, "In terms of its morale effects, the U.S. campaign may have presented the [North Vietnamese] regime with the near-ideal mix of intended restraint and gore."[7]

On January 22 Rostow forwarded to the president a "pretty well balanced" CIA cable suggesting that the "peasants just want the bombing to end," that "many lower level cadres are yearning for peace," and that "stealing food has increased."[8] The CIA's appraisal was most likely correct, but said very little about how the war was perceived across North Vietnam as a whole. General Edward Lansdale later observed, "In Churchillian style, the [Hanoi] Politburo portrayed the north as a set-upon David fighting a bullyboy Goliath, the United States, and thereby was able to rally the North Vietnamese into grimly determined war efforts."[9]

At the turn of 1968, three decorated retired generals—Matthew Ridgway, James M. Gavin, and David M. Shoup—each expressed independent opposition to the U.S. bombing strategy in Vietnam. While the generals held no official position within the administration or military hierarchy, their glorious pasts made their criticisms particularly resonant. Not only was the bombing campaign provoking deep unease across America, the world, and the Democratic Party, but some of the U.S. military's most famous sons were also casting aspersions.

General Matthew Ridgway rose to prominence as the U.S. Army chief of staff from 1953 to 1955. He commanded Army combat divisions during World War II and the Korean War, but opposed U.S. intervention in Vietnam to spare French defeat during the 1954 battle of Dien Bien Phu. He intuitively knew which battles to fight and which should be left well alone. A strong-willed man, Ridgway clashed with General Douglas MacArthur during the Korean War over what he took to be the latter's megalomania. Usually conservative in military matters and manners, Ridgway permanently had a hand grenade attached to one shoulder strap on his battle jacket, and a first aid kit dangled from the other. "Some people thought I wore the grenades as a gesture of showmanship," he remarked years later. "This was not correct. They were purely utilitarian. Many a time in Europe and Korea, men in tight spots blasted their way out with hand grenades."[10] No shrinking violet evidently, Ridgway vehemently opposed the escalation of the Vietnam War during the Kennedy and Johnson presidencies. At the start of 1968, with U.S. prospects apparently as dim as ever, Ridgway was particularly vocal in his opposition to further escalation. In Ridgway's estimation South Vietnam was simply not worth the fight.

General James M. Gavin had been commended fulsomely for his heroism in earlier conflicts. Gavin was always the first to jump from the lead aircraft, and he led his men from the front in the field of battle. During World War II, Gavin had become the youngest man to attain the rank of major general since George Armstrong Custer, some eighty years before. Yet in spite of his humble origins and adrenaline-fueled bravery on the field of battle, Gavin was not short on sophistication. He served as Kennedy's ambassador to France from 1961 to 1963. Gavin had distinctive qualities of intellect, bravery, and craft. He opposed the Vietnam War not for reasons of liberal angst, but because he visited South Vietnam in 1967 and concluded that any hope of U.S. "victory" would require massive military escalation of a scale likely to draw China into the conflict. At the start of 1968, Gavin wondered what Johnson would do now that American bombs had turned Vietnam into a "parking lot." During World War II, Walt Rostow had picked bombing targets from the comfort of London's Grosvenor Square. Gavin led in the field, flew numerous combat missions, and viewed airborne warfare favorably with respect to the rapid troop mobility it allowed, but not as an excuse for bombing targets of marginal military utility.[11] Given that Gavin was a pioneer in matters of aerial combat, his opposition to the U.S. bombing campaign in North Vietnam was particularly damaging.

Finally, General David M. Shoup was the highest-ranking military officer to oppose publicly America's commitment to the Vietnam War. Shoup commanded the Second Marines as it spearheaded its successful assault on the Tarawa atoll in November 1943—a turning point in the Pacific War. For valor in combat during that daunting engagement, Shoup was awarded the Medal of Honor and his second Purple Heart. In later years President Eisenhower named Shoup the twenty-second commandant of the Marine Corps and promoted him to the rank of four-star general. On January 21,

1964, immediately following his retirement, President Johnson awarded Shoup the Distinguished Service Medal for "exceptionally meritorious service," a fitting end to a glittering military career. Shoup was implacably opposed to the Vietnam War for a variety of reasons. During a speech in May 1966, Shoup said that none of Southeast Asia "was worth the life and limb of a single American." Leaving geostrategy to one side, Shoup later ridiculed Rostow's belief that air strikes could halt north-south infiltration, describing the main communist supply route as the "Ho Chi Minh Autobahn." On December 19 Shoup demanded a prompt end to the air war "unless we want to commit ourselves to genocidal actions."[12] Shoup opposed the war both through the prism of moral considerations and through an affinity for unvarnished Realpolitik.

In the face of some weighty opposition, Rostow resolutely stuck to his guns. Winning the Vietnam War and securing the president's reelection were the paramount concerns that consumed the national security adviser. Maintaining the intensity of the U.S. bombing campaign was the quickest way to achieve this goal. That Rostow did not amend his views was entirely predictable. Once he constructed a theory or proposed a course of action, he viewed any deviation from this now firmly established route as a personal intellectual defeat—an outcome it pained him to even countenance. A good-natured ideologue, Rostow rarely got angry with those who disagreed with him, possessing the serenity of someone who knows he is right. That a Yale-educated development theorist could so cursorily dismiss military objections levied by three of America's greatest generals suggests either that his vanity was more pronounced than that of mere ten-a-penny narcissists or that he was becoming detached from reality. In a five-page memorandum to the president, Rostow identified three reasons why bombing was critical—why Ridgway, Gavin, and Shoup were all wrong. First, "bombing has denied North Vietnam a sanctuary," second, "North Vietnam is paying a heavy penalty for continuing the war," and third, "we have substantially increased the cost of infiltration of men and matériel from North Vietnam."[13] That Rostow could maintain such optimism in the face of the failure to make identifiable military progress, and a cacophony of criticism emanating from quarters not easily dismissed, testifies to his unbreakable self-confidence.

On December 16, 1967, Rostow wrote a memorandum to the president titled "Are the Next Four Months Decisive?" Rostow's answer was affirmative, that "the war is probably entering a turning point and the outcome of the 1967–68 winter-spring campaign will in all likelihood determine the future direction of the war."[14] These words were prophetic, though not for the reasons that Rostow described. Johnson had some difficult decisions to make. Should he escalate the war to the extremes that Rostow counseled? Should he heed the warnings of Ridgway, Gavin, and Shoup and de-escalate the conflict? Was there any middle ground between these polarized opinions? On the eve of the lunar New Year, Vietnamese insurgents forced the president to make a decision.

AS DAWN BROKE on January 30, 1968, a combined force of some 84,000 NLF combat troops launched attacks on every significant town, city, and U.S. base in South Vietnam. The assault was as comprehensive as it was intense. The NLF penetrated five of South Vietnam's six main cities, thirty-six out of its forty provincial capitals, and sixty-four district capitals. In what was their greatest media coup, NLF troops infiltrated the U.S. embassy in Saigon, killed two U.S. military policemen, and then held off a furious counterreaction until mid-morning. All nineteen of the young NLF commandos were killed, but their sacrifice—in what was effectively a suicide mission—constituted a huge propaganda victory. Turning on their televisions, the American people were confronted with a bloody portrait of war, at significant odds with the official government version. As Frances FitzGerald wrote in *Fire in the Lake*, "The pictures of corpses in the American embassy cut through the haze of argument and counterargument, giving flat contradiction to the official optimism about the slow but steady progress of the war." For the first time, the major newsweeklies—*Time*, *Life*, and *Newsweek*—criticized the war, while America's favorite news anchor was flummoxed. "What the hell's going on here?" Walter Cronkite wondered. "I thought we were winning this war."[15]

Walt Rostow had a strong inkling that an NLF attack during Tet was in the offing, and he claimed to have "briefed the press in detail on a background basis of what was afoot . . . But the effort to prepare the public was inadequate, and I must assume some responsibility for not urging Johnson to speak out in January."[16] It is probably sensible not to take Rostow's self-justificatory 1972 memoir entirely at face value. But whatever his predictive prowess—and recently declassified memoranda suggest that he did in fact foresee a major conflict around the corner—Rostow failed to visualize the sheer scale of the communist offensive. In this failure of imagination, however, Rostow was not alone. The CIA had failed to predict that the communist offensive would be so pervasive and intense. Who could have guessed that so many young men could have thrown themselves into a battle in which the odds were stacked so overwhelmingly against any lasting victory?[17]

The Vietnamese fought furiously but suffered devastating losses. Forty thousand Vietnamese soldiers died during the offensive. And while the countrywide assault hit its intended target—the American people and media—its local effect was almost wholly negative. In Hué the communist insurgents executed 2,800 South Vietnamese citizens and buried them in mass graves. Such actions not only terrorized South Vietnamese patriots as intended, but also caused many who silently backed Ho Chi Minh to transfer their allegiance to the nation in which they resided.

Most of Johnson's key foreign-policy advisers recognized that while the Tet Offensive was a heavy attritional defeat for the insurgents, their psychological victory had been complete. The chief of staff for the U.S. Army, Harold K. Johnson, candidly remarked, "We suffered a loss, there can be no doubt about that."[18] Rostow and General Westmoreland had earlier identified a "light at the end of the tunnel," but some wits opined that the light was actually a train, heading full-speed in the opposite direction. Rostow's retrospective assessment was that he and the military remained calm in the face of an attack that he had predicted, and that Tet was a resounding military defeat for the communists. The incoming secretary of defense, Clark Clifford, who was present alongside Robert McNamara at all the key crisis meetings, paints a different portrait in his memoir. "Despite their retrospective claims to the contrary," Clifford observed, "at the time of the initial attacks the reaction of some of our most senior military leaders approached panic."[19]

Worried that the president might lose his nerve and sanction a comprehensive reassessment of the war, Rostow quickly mounted a campaign to convince Johnson that Tet in fact constituted a clear American military victory and that he should approve the additional dispatch of 206,000 combat troops that General Westmoreland had promptly requested. On February 5 Rostow sent Johnson a memorandum on which he drew two simple lines to express the relative strength of the two sides. Beside one curve rising steadily, Rostow scribbled "allies" and above the second curve, falling gradually, he wrote "communists." Rostow appraised the impact of the Tet Offensive with a second graph overleaf. The "allies" line sailed ever upward. The "communist" line jumped sharply, and then plummeted. Rostow concluded that "the net effect of Tet could be a shortening of the war."[20] Rostow's sunny analysis ducked an important issue. What the Tet Offensive surely illustrated was the redundancy of his belief that bombing North Vietnam would sap enemy morale and curb infiltration to the south.

With a keen sense for untimely machismo, Rostow then advised Johnson that "it is time for a war leader speech instead of a peace-seeker speech."[21] The president now had the opportunity to "slay the credibility dragon with one blow." To do that Rostow attached a speech draft that concluded, "We are going to give them the fight they want—and more than they want. We are going to mete out the measure they asked for—and more than the measure. Do not look to Iowa or New York, or Oregon, or Alabama for a reward for your acts of last week. You will not find it."[22] Paramount in Rostow's mind was the necessity that the president make sure "that Westy and our men go into the battle ahead with everything they need at hand and a united America back home."[23] Exasperated by this delusional self-belief—and that of the Vietnam War's great champion in the media, Joseph Alsop—John Kenneth Galbraith later referred acidly to the "Rostow-Aesop-Alsop thesis of military strategy that holds that there is nothing like a series of really major military defeats to bring a country to the brink of victory."[24]

Johnson ultimately decided that blood, sweat, and tears were somewhat out of step with the general mood of the country, and that Churchill's pugnacious persona of 1940 was an inappropriate model to emulate. In spite of their close personal relationship, and the fact that the president had so often sanctioned Rostow's escalatory advice, the situation had changed irrevocably, and LBJ rejected the national security adviser's recommendations. In the offensive's immediate aftermath, Johnson's per-

sonal approval ratings had plummeted to 26 percent, the lowest point of
his now hemorrhaging presidency. Rostow was the only civilian adviser
who concurred with Westmoreland's request for more troops. It was as if
the national security adviser was observing a different war than his colleagues. Following an attack that had shaken the nation's belief in the veracity of its government's pronouncements, Rostow discerned "a hawkish
balance" of public opinion and "a desire to do something about the situation."[25]

Rostow dispatched a thoughtful memorandum to the president on February 12 that crystallized all his intellectual strengths, but also testifies to his
lack of political realism. Titled "A Philosophical Note," the memorandum
observed that rather than embracing the NLF and rising in revolt, South
Vietnam's citizenry had "turned their back on the Communists . . . They
did not want to be pushed around and taken over. They want an increasing
welfare; a government increasingly honest and concerned with them; and
they want the most fundamental right which Communists deny in politics;
namely the right to change your mind about a government." As an appraisal
of human nature, and the virtues that distinguished liberal capitalism from
communism, Rostow's analysis is astute. He foresaw the collapse of communism in his academic work. The fault lines he identified from a young age
were the ones that finally brought down the Soviet house of cards.

Nevertheless, the Vietnamese War was more complicated than that.
While the communist Tet Offensive failed to bring the people of South Vietnam on board, it was not accurate to say that the citizens respected their
government, or that the nation held the potential to attain societal legitimacy and structural permanency. Had Rostow more faith in his predictive
model delineated in *The Stages of Economic Growth*—in the virtues of capitalist development and the inherent faults in communism—then Vietnam
might have been left alone to determine its own fate. The fervency of its
leaders' ideology might have mellowed in time, for Vietnam was no North
Korea. As China sought to emulate Western economic management through
the 1970s, so Vietnam might have been forced by circumstance to embrace
a more pluralistic system—indeed this is exactly what transpired in subsequent years. But even if this was a complacent dream, Rostow was unfair to
characterize those who opposed his post-Tet U.S. escalation as uncaring
"liberals." Doing nothing is not always a morally reprehensible option.

Rostow advised that the president ought to attack "those who claim to be liberals, but who, in fact, are willing to see a purposeful minority take over the majority by force and lock them up in a society which denies every objective in which liberals profess to believe."[26] The United States was a divided nation, politically and socially, but the division was not between those who were "good" and "bad" as Rostow viewed it, but between internationalists, realists, pacifists, red-baiters, conservatives, liberals, Democrats, and Republicans—with the hawks and the doves not always coming from the ostensibly obvious side. But the intractability of Rostow's ideological self-belief rendered such nuance irrelevant. There were those who believed in the Vietnam War and cared for the fate of all citizens of the world, like Walt Rostow, and those who dissented against the war and did not care about the fate of non-Western nations, like the Pulitzer prize–winning journalist Walter Lippmann and the conservative diplomat George Kennan. But many opposed the Vietnam War from a profoundly moral standpoint that was impervious to charges of ethnocentrism. It was a conflict best avoided because wading into a civil war on a side that lacked legitimacy and pervasive support was foolhardy. Expanding that conflict through dispatching U.S. troops and bombing North Vietnam and Laos to make up for South Vietnam's inadequacies was wrong. Not all antiwar activists were content to see a poor nation subjected to communist tyranny. Some just saw an awkward situation that American intervention could only make worse.

IN HIS ORAL HISTORY deposited at the Lyndon Baines Johnson Library, Clark Clifford described the post-Tet landscape: "After Tet . . . there was no suggestion that we could see any light at the end of the tunnel."[27] Clifford had omitted to mention the national security adviser. In a February 27 meeting of the president's foreign-policy principals, Rostow again supported Westmoreland's troop request. Rostow was adamant that Westmoreland should have his way, and was dismayed by the irresolution shown by others. The departing defense secretary responded emotionally to Rostow's belligerent advice. "What then?" McNamara demanded of Rostow, "this goddamned bombing campaign, it's been worth nothing, it's done nothing, they've dropped more bombs than in all of Europe in all of World War II and it hasn't done a fucking thing." Clifford later recalled that Mc-Namara's voice then disintegrated into "suppressed sobs."[28] While Rostow had baited and undermined McNamara effectively for the past two years, this was the first recorded instance in which he had made him cry.

Reporting this extraordinary scene to the president, Rostow observed with studied understatement that points of agreement among the attendees were "rare." Rostow recommended that Johnson "order a team to go to work full time to staff out the [military] alternatives and their implications" and that "perhaps Clark Clifford could chair this intensive working group."[29] Frustrated by the polarized advice offered by his defense secretary and national security adviser, the president agreed to reappraise his options. The eventual choice of Clifford to lead the inquiry was portentous and was one that Rostow came to regret. Clifford's report brought to an abrupt end Rostow's strategic vision for the Vietnam War.[30]

A major player in U.S. postwar diplomacy and a key member of the president's circle of so-called Wise Men, Clark Clifford had served as a naval aide to President Harry Truman in the latter stages of World War II. He then went on to play a key role in drafting the 1947 National Security Act, which constructed the U.S. foreign policy–making apparatus as we know it today. In 1950 Clifford returned to his lucrative law practice, but the lure of power proved irresistible again in 1961 when John F. Kennedy appointed him to serve on the Foreign Intelligence Advisory Board. Clifford was in possession of a sharp mind and a doggedly independent judgment when it came to matters of foreign policy. These were traits that Kennedy could not help but find appealing.

President Johnson formally introduced Clark Clifford to the Vietnam War in 1965, when he initiated a broad debate on the necessity of deploying U.S. combat troops to South Vietnam. Clifford was George Ball's only ally in the losing battle against American escalation. With considerable prescience Clifford appraised the military and social prospects in South Vietnam and offered a bleak assessment. The sixty-year-old lawyer examined Vietnam with a forensic eye for detail and concluded first that the conflict was probably unwinnable and second that Vietnam's strategic insignificance made it a fight from which it was best to walk away. But Clifford's advice changed entirely once American escalation became an established fact. Through 1966 and 1967, Clifford chose to accept the military's briefings at face value, and he advised strenuously against any halts in the U.S. bombing campaign. He viewed such diplomatic ploys as military irresolution, and believed that North Vietnam would view them accordingly—as a sign of military and political weakness. Clifford advised Johnson to stay the course in Vietnam right up until his appointment as defense secretary. Then, at that most sensitive juncture, Clifford shifted tack again. The Tet Offensive destroyed any belief that Clifford might have possessed in America's military prospects.

Rostow had initially applauded Johnson's decision to appoint Clifford as secretary of defense. Given that Rostow knew Clifford primarily as an ally on the issue of bombing pauses—and as a strong supporter of Johnson's resolution to win the war—this endorsement would appear entirely predictable. Yet Clifford supported Johnson's management of the war only because he was a "rally around the flag" man, not for any deep-rooted ideological attachment to the conflict. Just as Bob Dole opposed sending U.S. troops to Bosnia in 1995, before wholeheartedly supporting the military engagement as it commenced, Clifford was only reflexively supportive of America's troops in battle. Yet he possessed a more nuanced diplomatic mind than most, and his initial opposition to the Americanization of the conflict in 1965 testifies to this. Just as Rostow filtered out negative military intelligence and amplified the positive, he had located in Clifford only the martial qualities that he wanted to see, not the flexibility that evidently lurked beneath the surface.

As Clifford embarked on his appraisal of military alternatives, Rostow stepped in to recommend the execution of a military course that few had even considered. On February 29 Rostow wondered whether the time had not come to "Invade Laos, Cambodia [and] North Vietnam." This was about as complete a military response to Tet as one might imagine—surpassing even Westmoreland and Wheeler in bellicosity. Yet Rostow believed that while "we may wish to mount such operations at some time . . . Westy has his hands full for the next months inside South Viet Nam."[31] Rostow thus stopped short of suggesting that March 1968 was the time to invade two additional sovereign nations. Rostow reasoned sensibly that flushing communists out of Saigon and Hué was a necessary precondition to declaring war on all of Indochina. On March 6 Rostow again advised the president that he order the mining of Haiphong Harbor. With a skewed sense of history, he concluded, "Not since the Civil War has quite so much hinged for our country on immediate battlefield events."[32] One wonders where Midway and D-Day stand in Rostow's history of significant American battles.

By this stage the relationship between Walt Rostow and the CIA had soured to a point of undisguised reciprocal contempt. Rostow sought to supply to the president intelligence that bolstered his case for escalation, and which suggested that the Tet Offensive presented a significant opportunity for the U.S. military. On February 25 *The Denver Post* reported that Rostow had adopted "an optimistic view of the Viet Cong attacks on the cities," and that he was using CIA intercepts to prove that North Vietnam's leaders viewed Tet as a resounding strategic defeat. The CIA, "on the other hand," doubted "whether the captured documents show conclusively that the attacks were designed as a conventional military operation to gain territory, rather than a guerrilla campaign to lay the psychological groundwork for longer-range objectives."[33]

Although roundly dismissed by the administration at the time, *The Denver Post*'s identification of a CIA-Rostow spat was entirely correct. On February 13 Rostow had forwarded to the president a document written by a "ranking [NLF] cadre" that admitted "a failure of the VC to gain popular support . . . a big mistake." Accompanying the intercept was Rostow's effusive observation that "this is a summary of the captured document we have been waiting for. You will wish to read every word."[34] Rostow dismissed other, less promising CIA intelligence of the time as defeatist and ill-informed. He was manipulating evidence to hasten escalation of the war. Following the *Denver Post* story, the chastened director of the CIA, Richard Helms, was compelled to write to the president that "relations between the White House Staff, particularly Mr. Rostow, and the Agency have never been better."[35] It is clear, however, that Rostow's partial reporting infuriated the CIA, and vice versa. The cutting and pasting of CIA reports was also unlikely to win a turf battle with the incoming secretary of defense.

After five days' hard labor, Clark Clifford reported to the president on March 4 with some sobering conclusions. Casting "grave doubts" on the escalatory route urged by Rostow, Westmoreland, and Wheeler, Clifford recommended that the president only dispatch those troops necessary to meet the exigencies of the next few months—22,000 troops in total.[36] Johnson's new defense secretary followed his broken predecessor and doubted whether "we can ever find a way out if we continue to shovel men into Vietnam."[37] Clifford surmised that Westmoreland could do little else with 206,000 further combat troops but postpone communist victory for a little while longer. Through Americanizing the conflict, the Johnson administration had already done "enormous damage" to the country "it was trying to save." Clifford concluded by observing that if Johnson were to accede to Westmoreland's request, it would not be long before he was confronted with a request for "another 200,000 or 300,000 with no end in sight."[38] This was Johnson's greatest fear. Government coffers had depleted to a critical level owing to America's vast overseas military commitments. Robert McNamara had been fired for expressing a similar negativity, but his successor was harder to dismiss, because LBJ held the utmost respect for his judgment, patriotism, and clarity of reason. Clifford's blunt appraisal shook the president to his very core, and scored direct hits on its intended targets—Westmoreland and Rostow.

On March 11 *The Washington Post*'s influential columnist Drew Pearson bluntly informed the president where he thought he had gone wrong: "I fear you have been led astray by such short-sighted advisers as Rostow and the military, while some of our advisers have not spoken up."[39] In the aftermath of Tet, a cacophony of criticism assailed Johnson. The CBS news anchor Walter Cronkite's critique was particularly difficult to dismiss because of the regard and affection with which he was held across the country. "If I've lost Cronkite, I've lost middle America," the president despaired.[40] Damaging political challenges also confronted Lyndon Johnson. On March 12 the liberal Democratic senator for Minnesota, Eugene McCarthy, won 42 percent of the primary vote in New Hampshire.[41] Sensing his opportunity, Robert F. Kennedy announced his intention to stand for president on March 16. Appalled by the opportunism of Kennedy's candidacy, Rostow pandered to Johnson's loathing of Bobby by quoting Karl Marx's dictum that "history never repeats itself except as farce." Rostow cattily observed that he "suspected this would prove true of both Dienbienphu and Khe Sanh; and the Kennedy efforts of 1960 and

1968."[42] Rostow knew his audience well, for LBJ continued to detest Bobby Kennedy with undimmed passion. In a discussion with Averell Harriman, the Soviet ambassador to the United States Anatoly Dobrynin remarked that there was a "joke going around the Diplomatic Corps of President Johnson's preference for a successor: First, Hubert Humphrey; second, Nelson Rockefeller; third, McCarthy; fourth, Nixon; fifth, Ho Chi Minh; sixth, Kennedy."[43]

The so-called Wise Men had repeatedly urged Johnson to stay the course in Vietnam. While the president could just about dismiss the retired generals Ridgway, Shoup, and Gavin as mavericks, this small group of elder statesmen possessed a gravitas less easily ignored. In 1968 the Wise Men constituted ten prominent former foreign-policy officials, including the former secretary of state Dean Acheson, the former assistant secretary for war John McCloy, the former U.S. ambassador to the Soviet Union Charles E. Bohlen, and the former national security adviser McGeorge Bundy. The group was convened periodically by the president, who sought to deploy their vast reservoir of foreign-policy experience on the most vexing issues of the day. Lyndon Johnson had enjoyed his meetings with the Wise Men, as they told him exactly what he wanted to hear. These sober-minded, Ivy League–educated men would invariably counsel Johnson to hold the line in Vietnam, drawing edifying lines of continuity with Franklin Delano Roosevelt's and Harry Truman's dedication to resisting tyranny. In a meeting of the group on November 1, 1967, for example, Dean Acheson had declared that "we certainly should not get out of Vietnam" and that "we want less goddamn analysis and more fighting spirit." Most members of the group compared Vietnam to Korea, where Harry Truman's decision to repulse communism had clearly been correct.[44]

But the widespread communist offensive of January 1968 had shattered that consensus. The solace that Johnson located during his meetings with the Wise Men ended abruptly as some of its members broke away to question the war's necessity. After Tet the reputably phlegmatic Dean Acheson requested that Rostow "tell the president—and you tell him in precisely these words—that he can take Vietnam and stick it up his ass."[45] On March 14 Acheson advised Johnson in a personal meeting to stop listening to Rostow and the generals and seek advice further down the advisory hierarchy. (Interestingly, had Johnson done so on March 11, he would

have encountered the NSC staffer, and Rostow protégé, Robert Ginsburgh's recommendation to "raze Hanoi and Haiphong after giving warning to evacuate."[46]) Rostow walked in on this uncomfortable scene and, in
Acheson's recollection, "listened to me with the bored patience of a visitor
listening to a ten-year-old playing the piano."[47]

Rostow actually viewed Dean Acheson and George Kennan as one
and the same: uncaring Atlanticists whose lack of concern for communism in Asia was tantamount to racism. During a party at the *New York
Herald Tribune* journalist Joseph Alsop's house, Rostow and Acheson had
argued passionately about the Korean War. The former secretary of state
declared that he advised Truman to intervene only in order to "validate
NATO," not because East Asia held any strategic significance to the
United States. Rostow observed that Acheson had decided that another
year of war was "too much blood to spill for those little people just out of
the trees."[48] The racist card was one that Rostow often deployed when
confronted with those who argued that the United States should wash its
hands of the Vietnam conflict. Prepping the president for another dinner
party with the same Joe Alsop, Rostow stressed that he should clearly
"convey your own opinion that it would be a disaster for the U.S. and the
world if we adopt a racist security policy and let Asia go."[49]

On March 25 Rostow's world of assertive internationalism collapsed
as the Wise Men advised the president to wind down the conflict. Rostow
recalled that he "smelled a rat" and described the meeting as a "put-up
job." John McCloy, the former secretary of defense Robert Lovett, Dean
Acheson, McGeorge Bundy—each man in turn advised the president that
the "U.S. could no longer do the job we set out to do in the time we have
left and we must take steps to disengage."[50] Expecting steadfast support
from a group that had always been on hand to provide it, Johnson lost
hope entirely, lamenting on March 28 that "everyone is recommending
surrender."[51] The game was up. It was Walt Rostow against every significant foreign-policy personality in Washington, and the national security
adviser did not prevail. "I thought to myself," Rostow recalled, "that what
had begun in the spring of 1940 when Henry Stimson came to Washington ended here tonight. The American Establishment is dead."[52] Having
spent much of his life venerating the steadfast anticommunism of the

northeastern foreign-policy elite, Rostow felt betrayed and ashamed by their retreat in the face of wanton aggression.

On March 31 Johnson announced a unilateral restriction of bombing, issued a call for substantive peace negotiations, and finally added that he would not seek a second elected term in office. Rostow's hope that the president would declare an expanded war on Southeast Asian communism was shattered. The era of apparently limitless global activism, ushered in by Franklin Delano Roosevelt and Harry Truman, had approached a dead end in the form of the Vietnam War. From George Kennan in 1946 to Paul Nitze in 1950, successive American intellectuals had called for greater U.S. involvement in the world. With each passing year, American "interests" expanded until they encompassed the world from Southeast Asia to sub-Saharan Africa. Walt Rostow was the most ardent advocate of Democratic liberal internationalism, but following the fateful meeting of the Wise Men in March 1968, that age dissolved. President Richard Nixon would devote his attention to recognizing China, negotiating an end to the Vietnam War, and delegating power to regional actors such as the shah of Iran. The guiding principle that drove U.S. foreign policy had shifted from Rostow's concern for "nation-building" to the cost-cutting exercise that was the "Nixon Doctrine." A belief in the necessity of retrenchment drove American foreign policy until Ronald Reagan and the neoconservative ascendancy. For Rostow all that remained was to ensure that any peace brokered between the United States and Hanoi provided a rock-solid security guarantee to South Vietnam.

AT THE HEART of the Johnson administration, the desire for substantive negotiations replaced the usually divisive discussion of military alternatives. While Rostow's advice on escalating the war following the Tet Offensive had been rejected out of hand, LBJ continued to respect his national security adviser's judgment, patriotism, and desire to protect South Vietnam. On April 2 Rostow observed, "I still believe the critical objective is to get Thieu to make in a month's time or so, an offer to the VC to let them run as a political party under the Constitution." While this was likely to encounter resistance, South Vietnam's "behavior could be quite different if they knew that we intended that they be the central participant in the negotiation for a settlement."[53] Rostow wanted the South Vietnamese president Nguyen Van Thieu, not an American diplomat, to be the key player in any negotiation with North Vietnam. He reasoned that Thieu would more fiercely resist calls to rein in the U.S. military, and would only agree to a peace based on the most favorable terms to his bitterly divided nation. "While not surrendering our freedom of action wholly or giving Thieu a blank check," Rostow conceded, "we must convince both Thieu's government (and his military) and the South Vietnamese people that we shall be in the closest possible consultation with their government."[54] The best chance that Rostow had for saving South Vietnam, and ensuring a continued U.S. commitment to the conflict, was to push Thieu to the forefront of negotiations. Rostow's strategy for peace was directly at odds with that envisioned by Averell Harriman.

The choice of the veteran Harriman as chief negotiator was one that Rostow viewed with undisguised hostility. On April 3 Rostow joined forces with Maxwell Taylor, the former chairman of the Joint Chiefs of Staff and U.S. ambassador to Saigon, in calling for Deputy Secretary of Defense Cyrus Vance to head negotiations. "With all due respect to Governor Harriman," Rostow and Taylor wrote with very little respect, "we do not believe that he is the man to carry this negotiation—should it develop—beyond its first stage." Rostow identified two reasons to back up his objection. First, "his health is not all that good," and, second, "he lacks—and has always lacked—an understanding and sympathy with the South Vietnamese." While Rostow conceded that "Averell is 100% correct that we should not let Saigon have a veto over our position in the negotiations," he doubted whether "he is in a mood to bring them along and to give them the confidence that will be necessary if a viable solution, in the U.S. interest, is to emerge."[55] Rostow had earlier clashed with Harriman over the issue of bombing pauses and he feared that he was purely driven by personal glory and partisan politics—not by any desire to keep South Vietnam out of harm's way. The national security adviser was probably correct on both counts.

Rostow's anti-Harriman campaign failed nonetheless. Johnson opted for a man who had contributed significantly to the shaping of twentieth-century international relations. In discussions with aides, LBJ described Harriman's position within the administration in the same way as he referred to FBI Director J. Edgar Hoover: "I'd rather have him inside the tent pissing out than outside the tent pissing in."[56] In addition to being a potential nuisance on the outside, Averell Harriman possessed the kind of diplomatic credentials that the president could scarcely ignore—he had performed distinguished service as the U.S. ambassador to Moscow and had secured the "neutralization" of Laos in 1962—and he already held the job title of "Ambassador for Peace." Johnson, however, did share some of Rostow's concerns about Harriman's lack of sensitivity to the South Vietnamese and his desire to secure peace at a potentially unacceptable cost. In a handwritten note to Rostow, the president agreed that "the point about reciprocal concessions needs to be understood within the U.S. government at the earliest possible time. Otherwise, we will find that we have given away the present position of negotiating strength which Hanoi has so generously given us [sarcasm added by the president]—with nothing in return."[57]

Harriman's brief was to establish contact with North Vietnam's representatives, convince them to embark on a mutual de-escalation of violence, and agree to support free elections in South Vietnam in which the NLF would lay down its weapons and stand for election as a peaceful, legitimate political party. The president made sure that his basic negotiating instructions were wedded to some strict conditions: a unilateral American bombing pause was assuredly *not* an option, and South Vietnam was to be afforded the power of veto over any bilateral arrangement that Harriman made with Hanoi's negotiators.[58] Cyrus Vance was finally chosen to accompany Harriman to Paris, yet LBJ and Rostow still remained concerned that the team looked dovish. With the president's approval, Rostow placed a trusted hawk, the NSC staffer William J. Jorden, on the inside to keep tabs on what was happening. As Jorden recalled, Rostow sent him to Paris "to keep an eye on those bastards [Harriman and Vance] and make sure that they didn't give away the family jewels."[59] Harriman's graciousness compelled him to observe, in a studiously polite phone conversation with Rostow on April 4, "You'd be doing a tremendous favor if [Jorden] could come along."[60] Harriman was evidently unaware that Jorden's primary purpose was one of surveillance.

As preparations for Harriman's mission began in earnest, Rostow expressed concern to the president that one of his "negotiating objectives" was to wind down the American air war. "Our 'objective' is not a cessation of bombing," Rostow argued, "it is prompt and serious substantive talks looking towards peace."[61] Through a timely interjection from Clark Clifford, Harriman was permitted to retain his negotiating criteria untouched. Harriman complained that Rostow's objections to his position were "irrelevant" and that "there is no doubt that Clifford's initiative saved the [negotiating] instructions from mutilation." Ominously, Harriman wrote that "the Secretary of State did not make any contribution."[62] That the man charged with managing U.S. diplomacy seemed so little interested in Harriman's efforts did not augur well. It was becoming clear to Harriman that Rusk and Rostow were shaping up to serve as a barrier to his aim of securing a swift settlement. *The Washington Post*'s Drew Pearson had long been concerned by Rostow's significant leverage with the president and was appalled that Harriman's bona fides were being questioned so aggressively. On April 19 Pearson wrote despairingly that Rostow has "been able to make his ideas on Southeast Asia stick with Lyndon Johnson . . . No one who knows Rostow questions his integrity. But they do question his judgment."[63]

On April 28, echoing his memorandum of April 2, Rostow presented Rusk with what he described as "an off-beat idea." Since the southern settlement was the heart of the matter, Rostow wondered whether it might not be a good idea for "Thieu to take the initiative and actively seek private negotiations with 'a member' of the NLF, using a trusted man." Placing Thieu at "the center of things" would mean that the "initiative to shape destiny" would be in the correct hands. This was infinitely preferable to predicating peace on "the outcome of U.S.-Hanoi talks, etc."[64] Still concerned by Averell Harriman's "lack of sympathy for the South Vietnamese," Rostow wanted the president to take power away from his negotiating team and place it with the government of South Vietnam. That Hanoi would countenance directly negotiating with Thieu—the leader of a "puppet" state it did not recognize—was unrealistic. Yet Rostow believed that Hanoi would agree to settle with Saigon, and had the evidence to prove it. "In VC villages," Rostow reported to Johnson, "the children are being taught to chant the following: 'Blood will flow in May; there will be peace in June.' If they are stirring these kinds of hopes, it must mean, technically, that they are thinking about a quick, rather than protracted, negotiation."[65] Technically, alas, the children's chants meant nothing of the sort. The North Vietnamese government was wholly unwilling to agree to terms with Saigon in a swift, bilateral settlement.

Rostow continued to believe that the South Vietnamese president would be more amenable to lifting the restrictions imposed upon the bombing campaign than Harriman. On May 10 Rostow expressed hope that the United States would begin "bombing between the 19th and 20th parallels soon." Rostow believed that if America failed to bomb North Vietnam with sufficient vigor, Hanoi might "overrate the effectiveness of pressure on us on the whole bombing issue." This erroneous assumption on Hanoi's part "might protract the phase of negotiating reciprocal action in return for a total bombing cessation." Bombing for peace was Rostow's mantra. But of course these none-too-subtle promptings were not all about the negotiations. Rostow also felt "that we could get more trucks before they got to South Vietnam if we bombed along the road between the 19th and 20th."[66] Harriman was predictably opposed to Rostow's plan, writing that "reinstitution of the bombing between the nineteenth and twentieth parallels might retard the [negotiation]."[67] He later remarked of Rostow, "I never want to see another memo from that man."[68]

INFORMAL NEGOTIATIONS WITH the North Vietnamese delegation began at the Majestic Hotel in Paris on May 10. With characteristic eloquence Harriman declared upon his departure from Washington, "We shall leave no path unexplored for an honorable peace . . . We go in a spirit of sincerity and good faith. If that spirit is matched by the other side, progress can be made toward our goal of a peaceful settlement."[69] It took little time, however, for Rostow to detect problems and argue yet again in favor of a rapid military escalation.

Rostow clashed once more with Averell Harriman and Clark Clifford. Of the defense secretary's objections to his plans for more bombing, Rostow wrote, "What Clark's analysis does not say . . . is what policy we should follow if there is no break in the Paris talks and if they continue to 'read the telephone book' to us each time we meet. I doubt that we can sit still indefinitely under such circumstances." Were the Democratic Party to select New York senator Robert Kennedy in Chicago, and were the U.S. public to elect him in November, Rostow feared that North Vietnam would simply stall until the second President Kennedy offered a more favorable settlement. To prevent this from happening, Rostow recommended that the president mine "the North Vietnamese harbors and/or send some of our forces northwards across the DMZ."[70] Invading North Vietnam, Rostow reasoned, would render President Robert Kennedy an unlikely prospect.

Frustrated by Rostow's belligerence, Harriman wrote on June 4 that "it would be a great mistake to threaten to bomb urban areas in North Vietnam if enemy attacks against Saigon continue . . . To actually bomb Hanoi or Haiphong in present circumstances would, we believe, lead Hanoi to break off these talks and have other adverse reactions."[71] Responding to Harriman's concerns, Rostow dispatched a brutally pessimistic memorandum to the president. "I have reluctantly come to the conclusion," Rostow warned, "that if we are to preserve the talks in Paris, we shall have to take the risk of breaking them up . . . I believe they are laughing at us and playing us for suckers on the diplomatic-military front, in the short-run." Rostow advised the president that he "have Averell tell the North Vietnamese that we shall have to match every rocket in Saigon with, at least, a bomb on Hanoi." Rostow was sympathetic to Clifford's view that this "could be a mortal blow to the Vice President's political position." Nevertheless, "Clark is wrong in believing that we—or the Vice President—can continue to live with the undignified and humiliating position where . . . they refuse to negotiate seriously in Paris."[72]

Vice President Hubert Humphrey's political prospects were a crucial consideration for both Averell Harriman and Clark Clifford. Both men were keen to reach a Vietnam settlement that would push Humphrey toward victory in the November 1968 presidential election, when Humphrey was likely to face Richard Nixon, a man who Clifford and Harriman reviled. The vice president had become privately skeptical about the Vietnam War through 1967 and 1968, but LBJ had made it clear that if he vented his reservations publicly, he would oppose his nomination for the presidency. The Minnesotan had to perform a tightrope act. As public opposition to the war increased, it made sense for Humphrey to declare his independence from the Johnson administration. But if the vice president pushed LBJ too far, he would face the full force of the president's wrath. After a heated meeting with the president in the summer of 1968, Humphrey confided to his doctor, "Do you know what [LBJ] had the nerve to say to me, after all the insults I've taken from him the last four years? He said that if I didn't watch my p's and q's [on Vietnam], he'd see to it personally that I lost Texas [on election day] . . . He said he'd dry up every Democratic dollar from Maine to California—as if he hasn't already. I had trouble holding back, but I wasn't going to come down to that bastard's level."[73] Humphrey was stuck somewhere between a rock and a hard place.

Rostow was becoming concerned that the defense secretary was too interested in securing Humphrey's election and insufficiently concerned with South Vietnam's future as an independent, Western-inclined nation. Irritated by Clifford's skewed priorities, Rostow attempted to cut the Pentagon out of the information loop—he refused to forward reports from the Paris negotiations to the defense secretary. The State Department's executive secretary, Benjamin Read, was appalled by Rostow's crass discourtesy and set up a "private messenger service" to circumvent the national security adviser's information embargo.[74]

It is thus no challenge to understand why Averell Harriman took to describing Rostow as "America's Rasputin" for the unsavory influence he exerted on presidential decision making.[75] Rostow had been marginalized by Clifford following the Tet Offensive, but the national security adviser was successfully reasserting himself during the Paris peace negotiations. Once again Rostow was alone in delivering to Johnson what he deemed unpalatable truths about the dim prospects for peace. He buried CIA reports that questioned the efficacy of America's bombing campaign, sought to marginalize the defense secretary, and worked hard to ensure that Harriman held no aces in his diplomatic pack of cards. His hostility toward the Paris peace negotiations struck a chord with a president disillusioned with his liberal critics and in no hurry to secure peace for purely domestic political ends. Rostow and Johnson had forged a strong relationship during the Americanization of the conflict. In adversity, once again, the national security adviser helped persuade the president that he should not pursue peace at any cost; that South Vietnam's fate was more significant than that of his vice president.

Harriman and Clifford had a candid telephone conversation on June 21 in which they discussed the central problem facing them; namely, that they appeared to be the only two high-level Johnson administration employees interested in securing peace in Vietnam. For Clifford the main problem was that the president was under the sway of "pessimistic" advisers who were counseling an aloof response to the North Vietnamese. Clifford told Harriman that the president "is informed that it is terrible with our position with SVN, our own troops and even our posture in the world for us to permit Saigon to be shelled while Hanoi is not touched. He is beginning to get restive. Tied up with this approach is, I think, an effort on the part of some to indicate that perhaps nothing will come out of Paris." Clifford believed there was only one way to quiet the complaints of those "very militaristic gentlemen" (by which he meant Rostow) who counseled the escalation of the air war, and that was to stress the fact that the talks in Paris were producing some hopeful "straws in the wind," even if this did not tally with the facts. If the U.S. media were to report that Harriman was making some headway in Paris, then it would be harder for the president to sanction the type of bombing raids being recommended by Rostow. "What I think we must do," Clifford observed with rare cunning, "is in the most guarded manner to indicate that something is happening."[76] Clifford reasoned that expressions of exaggerated hope on the issue of negotiations would trump Rostow's undue confidence in the ability of the U.S. military to still win the war.[77] It was a remarkable way for the Johnson administration to operate. Clifford believed that prospects were so hopeless for the administration's doves that a gentle deception might convince the U.S. public to undermine the hawks.

THROUGH THE LONG, FRAUGHT SUMMER of 1968, the United States was bitterly divided over the Vietnam War. And other bloody events began to sully Americans' faith in their nation. In the first half of the year, there were over two hundred campus demonstrations against the U.S. engagement in Vietnam.[78] Columbia University housed the most violent clashes, where one thousand police officers wielding nightsticks forcibly broke up a peaceful sit-in. Martin Luther King Jr. was assassinated in Memphis in April 1968. His murder provoked a visceral response across the nation, as riots, looting, and the burning of urban areas escalated rapidly. U.S. Army units had to be deployed in Washington, D.C., to protect the nation's capital from the chaos that threatened to engulf it. In June 1968 a Palestinian political extremist, Sirhan Bishara Sirhan, assassinated the much-loved presidential candidate Robert Kennedy. And bringing all of these crises and tragedies into the sharpest possible focus, the Democratic National Convention in August—held under the unforgiving glare of saturation media coverage—displayed in microcosm a nation turned violently on itself. Delegates inside the convention debated the war with ill-concealed rancor. Outside the convention hall, antiwar protestors taunted the police, engaged in disruptive tactics, and then finally fought the police in pitched, bloody battles on Chicago's streets. Foreign conflicts are so often defined for posterity by the manner in which they are perceived at home. The difference between the Second World War and Vietnam War could not have been clearer.

In what remained of the Johnson administration, the president veered between bellicosity and restraint, mirroring the divisions among his policy advisers and across America as a whole. Clifford later lamented that Lyndon Johnson acted more "like a legislative leader, seeking consensus among people who were often irreconcilably opposed than like a decisive commander-in-chief giving his subordinates orders."[79] While Clifford described 1968 as the most difficult year of his life, Dean Rusk recalled that the negotiating period was "a blur" in which he survived only through a daily dose of scotch, aspirin, and cigarettes.[80] Recognizing that his presidency had little time left, Johnson was too exhausted and dispirited to lift himself above the ennui that had set in. *Time* reported that there existed an "unfamiliar atmosphere of tranquility" in the White House, detecting signs that Johnson "had placed himself in the past tense."[81]

Harriman and Vance wanted the president to buck up and exert far more restraint over the military, but Johnson seemed to care little either way. The president's chief negotiators wanted peace for its own sake, but also feared that protracted negotiations, with no end in sight, would leave the door ajar for a Republican election victory.[82] Johnson, however, appeared relaxed by the prospect of Democratic defeat in the November election. Hubert Humphrey's attempts to placate the liberal wing of the Democratic Party irritated the president, and he seemed unfussy as to whether the Minnesotan succeeded him. At one point Johnson argued that the Republicans had been "a lot more help to us than the Democrats in the last few months."[83] The president was not going to be rushed into making an unsustainable peace. To this end Rostow placed in front of Harriman as many impediments as possible.

As Rostow expected, Saigon's objections to being presented with anything that remotely resembled a fait accompli ensured that negotiations stalled. Unperturbed, Harriman continued to call on the president to cease all bombing in North Vietnam.[84] Vice President Hubert Humphrey— virtually assured of the Democratic nomination following Bobby Kennedy's assassination in Los Angeles and further aided by the fact that Eugene McCarthy was not a popular choice among state delegates to the national convention—wholeheartedly supported Harriman's efforts, and wanted to give him the greater latitude he desired. Rostow instead advised that the president should "stabilize the growing fever for a commitment to a unilateral bombing pause."[85] The national security adviser was opposed to any emollient gestures, instead arguing in favor of a great deal more bombing. According to Harriman, Johnson "went through the roof" when he heard that Hubert Humphrey had endorsed Harriman's bombing halt. The president dug his heels in, to Rostow's relief, and the U.S. bombing campaign continued as before.

With little happening on the negotiating front, Rostow sought to make sense to the president of the chaos that engulfed American society in 1968. To keep Johnson's spirits up, Rostow reported on such questions as "how our society [can] produce at the same time men of the quality of our young marines and other fighting men and hippies and draft-card burners." Rostow answered that "if many of the dissidents actually were in Vietnam and faced the reality of the problem, they would change."[86] There was a particularly obstinate quality to Rostow's musings as his tenure in the White House approached its end. He eschewed scholarly detachment, making no effort to conceal his outrage at those who opposed the war. Rostow provided the soothing answers that Johnson, no doubt, wanted to hear, and it impacted significantly on the course of U.S. foreign policy. A morose, isolated Johnson continued to follow Rostow's advice in not giving Harriman the negotiating inducements he desired. The president referred to Harriman's telegrams that were conciliatory to the North Vietnamese as "mush," and complained bitterly, "The enemy is using my own people as dupes."[87] On August 22 Harriman wrote, "I believe that the failure of the President to stop all bombing of North Vietnam in late July or early August (as we recommended) is an historic tragedy of possibly wide consequences."[88] If this analysis is correct, then Rostow bears significant responsibility for the failure of Harriman's pursuit of peace.

Increasingly, domestic politics, and Johnson's legacy, came to consume Rostow's energies as the negotiations stalled predictably in Paris. On September 16 Rostow wrote to the president that he had given some thought to formulating "my equivalent for 1968 of 'Let's Get This Country Moving Again' "—his eloquent contribution to Kennedy's 1960 election victory. Struggling to match his earlier concision, Rostow came up with "We're not going to let a handful of white and black punks turn this country over to Wallace, Strom Thurmond, and those who base their campaign on their support."[89] Rostow was evidently concerned that liberal opposition to the Vietnam War played into the hands of unrepentant segregationists like the former Alabama governor George Wallace—who stood for the presidency in 1968 as an independent candidate—and Strom Thurmond, the Republican senator for South Carolina who served as an important ally of Richard Nixon in his efforts to woo the American South. Rostow was surely correct that the chaotic Democratic Convention in Chicago was a godsend to Richard Nixon's electoral prospects, and his pursuit of what he later described as the "silent majority" of middle-class American patriots who were appalled by the civil disobedience practiced by the younger generation. Nevertheless, Rostow's negative rallying cry smacked of desperation, and it was not a line that Hubert Humphrey found particularly useful.

Through the late summer of 1968, the vice president made some tentative steps to detach himself from the Johnson administration's position on negotiations with North Vietnam. On a special NBC-TV *Meet the Press* program, Humphrey declared, "I believe that we could and should stop the remaining bombing of the north if we receive indication that there is restraint and reasonable response from Hanoi. I think that is a common sense provision." In a clearly worded warning to Richard Nixon to steer clear of politicizing the Paris negotiations in the forthcoming presidential campaign, Humphrey added: "I believe that the candidates who are nominated by the respective political parties owe it to the American people and owe it to the men in the field in Vietnam to make it crystal clear to Hanoi that they are not going to get a better deal [after the election]."[90] During the Democratic Convention in Chicago, Humphrey had reluctantly agreed to support the president's hard-line platform on Vietnam—a decision that had split the party and that had led to Humphrey being taunted as the president's lapdog. Stung by this criticism, Humphrey was beginning to realize that defeating Nixon would require him to adopt a position that placed him closer to his fellow Minnesotan presidential candidate, Eugene McCarthy.

On the weekend of September 14–15, Harriman and Vance reported back with some positive news from Paris. They had completed a significant private conversation with the main North Vietnamese negotiators, Le Duc Tho and Xuan Thuy, who had displayed a willingness to commence serious negotiations as soon as the bombing stopped.[91] Unimpressed by what was in reality a significant breakthrough, Rostow wrote hopefully to the president on September 16, "If you judge diplomacy has failed," how about "bombing Cambodia . . . bombing Hanoi-Haiphong, mining Haiphong . . . and [launching] ground attacks north of the DMZ."[92] Even at this late stage in the proceedings, Rostow remained hopeful that Johnson might agree to his incendiary invasion plans. In making such recommendations Rostow displayed little appreciation of the temper of the times—and the manner in which popular perceptions of the Vietnam War had changed.

Rostow continued to express concern that Harriman was exceeding his limited mandate, and wanted the president to make clear that he was not to pursue peace at any cost. During a September 17 meeting with Harriman, with Rostow in attendance, Johnson stated clearly, "I shall count on you, Averell, to lead the Party and the Government in demanding a resumption of bombing if they violate these understandings."[93] Things were looking desperate for Harriman and Hubert Humphrey, who was lagging behind Nixon in the polls. "Do not believe what you hear about Humphrey's campaign being bad," Harriman wrote to Cyrus Vance despairingly, "because it's worse than you think." During a private conversation in Washington, D.C., in September 1968, Harriman asked Clifford "bluntly whether he felt the President wished to see Humphrey defeated [in the presidential election]." After pausing for a while to measure his response, Clifford replied, "If you agree it is just between you and me, I believe you're right: the President wants to see him defeated."[94] If something significant did not happen in Paris soon, then a Nixon presidency was looking increasingly likely.

JOHNSON WAS CLEARLY shedding few tears over Humphrey's poor showing at the polls. Nevertheless, pressure was growing on LBJ to test out North Vietnam's willingness to embark on substantive negotiations. For its part Hanoi had a clear preference that Hubert Humphrey defeat Richard Nixon in November. On October 11 North Vietnam tried to boost the vice president's flagging campaign by agreeing to commence formal negotiations in Paris, with representatives from the United States, the NLF, and South Vietnam, if America ceased its bombing campaign.[95] Finally agreeing to Harriman's requests for a substantial diplomatic bargaining chip, the president responded to Hanoi's offer by setting the date for a U.S. bombing halt as October 31—just a few days before the presidential election. The decision was made a little too late to push Humphrey over the finish line, but was taken in a timely enough fashion to suggest that Johnson remained interested in securing peace before his presidency ended. LBJ had gained watertight assurances from the Joint Chiefs of Staff that the military could manage a bombing pause. The chairman of the Joint Chiefs, Earle Wheeler, explained that the U.S. could easily resume bombing if North Vietnam embarked on another offensive.[96]

This news provoked understandable panic within the Nixon campaign, which feared that Hubert Humphrey would be the main beneficiary of Johnson's latter-day conversion to peacemaking. Henry Kissinger was the insider who informed Nixon's campaign manager, John Mitchell, that the Johnson administration planned to halt the bombing campaign. As the historian Herbert Schandler writes, "Kissinger had met privately in Paris with Harriman, Vance, and other members of the delegation in mid-September, just before the first [official] Harriman-Vance meeting with the North Vietnamese, and they had shared with him their frustration and brought him up to date on the state of negotiations."[97] In setting up this meeting, Kissinger had deployed a tactic that was close to his heart—disingenuous flattery and manipulation—to build Harriman's confidence. He wrote to Harriman on August 15, "There is a chance that I may be in Paris around September 17 and I would very much like to stop in and see you then. I am through with Republican politics. The party is hopeless and unfit to govern." Kissinger lied to convince Harriman that he was sympathetic to his efforts and that any issues discussed would be held in confidence.[98]

Representing Richard Nixon—as head of the nationwide "Republican Women for Nixon"—a prominent Chinese-American businesswoman named Anna Chennault warned the South Vietnamese ambassador Bui Diem that President Johnson planned to embark upon substantive, direct negotiations.[99] Chennault advised that President Thieu should refuse to participate in these talks prior to the election, since he was certain to get better terms under the hawkish Richard Nixon than the liberal Hubert Humphrey. This underhand ploy placed partisan politics ahead of the lives of American troops in the field. Henry Kissinger and Richard Nixon share a great deal of shame for advocating a strategy that was all but treasonous. They acted in concert with a foreign leader to frustrate the declared intentions of the U.S. government.

It did not take long for the Nixon camp's machinations to reach the president's line of vision. At the end of October, Walt's brother, Undersecretary of State Eugene Rostow, discovered that Nixon wanted the Paris negotiations stymied.[100] Based on information provided by an informant in the Republican campaign, Eugene Rostow explained that "these difficulties would make it easier for Nixon to settle after January. Like Ike in 1953, he would be able to settle on terms which the president could not accept, blaming the deterioration of the situation between now and January or February on his predecessor."[101] Later, on October 29, Walt Rostow reported to the president that he possessed incendiary information "on how certain Republicans may have inflamed the South Vietnamese to behave as they have been behaving." Rather than going public with evidence that might have derailed the Nixon campaign, however, Rostow cautioned that the "materials are so explosive they could gravely damage the country whether Mr. Nixon is elected or not."[102]

Emboldened by the information provided by Chennault, President Thieu had reacted "emotionally and disjointedly" to Johnson's bombing halt and warned the U.S. ambassador to Saigon, Ellsworth Bunker, "You cannot force us to do anything against our own interests."[103] On November 1 Thieu made a pugnacious speech in which he pilloried Johnson's decision and disassociated the South Vietnamese government from Averell Harriman's efforts in Paris. Bunker reported the following day that an increasingly petulant Thieu had "closeted himself in his private apartment in independence palace" and was refusing to meet with him in person. Bunker concluded that Thieu was "convinced that Nixon will win and will follow a hawkish policy, and therefore he can afford to wait."[104] The impact of the Nixon team's meddling in the peace negotiations is thus clearly discernible. Yet it is likely that Rostow, while contemptuous of the Republican tactics deployed, was sympathetic to Chennault's aim of securing a peace more likely to preserve South Vietnam's independence. The national security adviser instinctively favored Nixon's approach, rather than a Humphrey-brokered peace.

Rather than making a public case against Nixon's meddling, Rostow suggested the president set up a private meeting with the Republican presidential candidate in which Johnson would advise Nixon that he "may wish to caution his men to be exceedingly circumspect in dealing with the inexperienced and impressionable South Vietnamese."[105] The president was amenable to Rostow's advice. On September 30 Hubert Humphrey had delivered a speech in Salt Lake City that declared his political independence from the Johnson administration's Vietnam policy and expressed his support for an unconditional bombing pause. Johnson was infuriated by Humphrey's lack of respect in voicing such defeatist sentiment. In Johnson's opinion the vice president had turned toward the dove side for purely political gain, and in doing so he had proven his own disloyalty.[106]

Johnson was initially tempted to go public with the Chennault revelation: "It would rock the world if it were said he [Thieu] were conniving with the Republicans. Can you imagine what people would say if it were to be known that Hanoi has met all these conditions and then Nixon's conniving with them kept us from getting it?" Ultimately, however, Johnson seemed little concerned by Humphrey's fading electoral prospects, or

Nixon's Machiavellian maneuver.[107] Lyndon Johnson did exactly as Rostow advised. He sent a politely worded, private rebuke to Richard Nixon. This episode was hugely significant, both with regard to the extended duration of the Vietnam War and the future of U.S. domestic politics. The Vietnam War dragged on until January 1973, while 1968 was a nadir for the Democratic Party from which it has scarcely recovered. Anna Chennault, Walt Rostow, and Lyndon Johnson shared the same aim: that a viable, capitalist South Vietnam should emerge from the ashes of war. Rostow acted in accordance with this goal, and dispensed advice that kept on track a Nixon election victory.

The president ordered that a U.S. bombing pause take effect as planned on October 31.[108] In a candid, affectionate memorandum to LBJ, Rostow confided, "The only safety I have known over these difficult eight years has been to consult my judgment and my conscience. And I know that has also been your only solace." In making this difficult decision, Rostow observed, "you can always count on me." Sympathizing with Johnson's predicament, in the sense that LBJ's decision to institute a bombing halt was receiving flak from both the left and the right in American politics, the national security adviser wrote, "You will be accused of playing politics if you let this slide—and politics against the party you lead. Harriman and the Russians will see to that."[109] Rostow was obviously relaxed at the prospect of letting the bombing pause gambit "slide," and Averell Harriman had clearly sunk very low in Rostow's estimation for him to warrant comparison with the nefarious Soviets. Nevertheless, the national security adviser believed that the U.S. Air Force could land a few more blows as the deadline for the bombing pause approached. Like a teenager being dragged from a fight, still swinging punches, Rostow added, "We cannot guarantee that every unit will get the word by the time of the bombing cessation. Therefore, they should not complain if there is some spillover for, say, 7 hours after the time they specify."[110]

While the bombing pause gave a last-minute boost to Humphrey's hitherto listless campaign, the American people elected Richard Nixon their president on November 5 by a narrow popular plurality of 510,000 votes. While popular dissent against the Vietnam War was vocal, and profoundly damaging to the unity of the Democratic Party, Nixon's "silent majority" turned out in sufficient numbers to defeat the vice president.

Campaigning on the theme of "law and order," Nixon astutely capitalized on the riots and violence that had shaken the United States through 1968—which he attributed directly to the liberal excesses of the Johnson presidency. Nixon also pursued a so-called southern strategy during the campaign, in which he appealed to white southerners who had traditionally been staunchly Democratic, but had since been driven away by the progressive civil rights agenda pursued by Johnson and Humphrey. Vietnam had critically undermined the Democratic Party, and Richard Nixon—touting his (spurious) claim that he possessed a "secret plan" to resolve the conflict—was the main beneficiary.

Predictably, the Paris negotiations henceforth foundered on Saigon's unwillingness to agree to terms under a lame-duck president, with the appealing prospect of the red-baiter Nixon just around the corner. While genuine opportunities for negotiating a peace settlement had been evident earlier in the year, Johnson's October 31 bombing pause was too little, too late. Yet even at this stage—as negotiations flatlined with little prospect of resuscitation—Rostow wanted Harriman out of Paris. He devised a devious plan to achieve this aim. Writing on November 7, Rostow informed the president that Harriman was to turn seventy-seven years of age on November 15: "It just occurred to me that if we wish to send him off in style, we could give him a big party, involving all his friends over the years—and then get him out of Paris for the next stage." Aware that this scheming advice might be frowned upon, Rostow added sheepishly, "Whether that's a good idea or not, I thought you would wish to know that his birthday is coming up."[111] Johnson ignored Rostow on this occasion and sent a warm message: "Happy Birthday to a man who does not seem to get any older. It has been obvious for years that you have found what Ponce De Leon looked for in vain. As one about to become an elder statesman myself, I offer you five acres of Blanco County for your secret."[112]

WITH NIXON ASSUMING the mantle of president-elect, Rostow felt less inclined to suppress his pent-up frustrations at Johnson's failure of military will in 1966 and 1967. Rostow was deeply disappointed that the president had failed to follow his advice and invade North Vietnam, and respectful detachment made way for some barbed comments in their still-frequent correspondence. Briefing Johnson on how to deal with the *Los Angeles Times* journalist Ted Sell's likely questions on the fraught nature of civilian-military relations, Rostow suggested that the president say that "there have been areas of disagreement. Generally speaking, the military has wanted to use more power, earlier and faster. They may have been right. But the president had other considerations to think of."[113] Subtle this was not. Yet Johnson did not explode at Rostow, as he undoubtedly would have done with anyone else who displayed the temerity to question his judgment. While Rostow and Johnson were yesterday's men, they remained close through their final lame-duck months in office. Johnson was bitter toward his political enemies and the press, Rostow detested Averell Harriman and was contemptuous of the CIA, and both were aghast that spineless antiwar protestors had sullied their great nation, betraying the brave U.S. troops fighting a just, necessary war. In adversity two curmudgeonly men griped at their respective enemies—both imagined and real.

Recognizing that the substantive part of his job had ended—and that Harriman-baiting was not as satisfying as it once had been—Rostow concluded his career as national security adviser denigrating those who questioned the Vietnam War's necessity. On November 15 Rostow forwarded an "extremely interesting—and sadly recognizable—passage on intellectuals and war" written by George Orwell. "The English intelligentsia were, on the whole, more defeatist than the mass of the people," Orwell wrote, and this disaffection was evident in "large numbers of intellectuals" who found it difficult "not to side with any country hostile to Britain."[114] Lashing out at America's intelligentsia was cathartic to Rostow, and provided some cheer to the president. As Rostow neared the end of his foreign-policy career, however, it was clear that America's intelligentsia felt the same way about Rostow. As his official life neared its end, job offers from the likes of MIT, Yale, and Harvard were noticeable in their absence. Worried that Rostow might struggle to find work, in light of his now controversial status as the world's most belligerent development theorist, Johnson asked Rostow and his wife to join him at the University of Texas at Austin to help establish the Lyndon Baines Johnson School for Public Affairs. Rostow gratefully accepted the job, relieved that he had an academic perch to which to return.

EPILOGUE

1969–2003

URING THE 1968 PRESIDENTIAL CAMPAIGN, Richard Nixon
had declared that he would secure "peace with honor" with North
Vietnam.[1] Following his defeat of Hubert Humphrey, the president's
strategy became clear: American troops would be withdrawn and
primary responsibility for waging the war transferred to South Vietnam. It
amounted to a strategy of staged retreat that was given the more positive
spin of "Vietnamization." While South Vietnam assumed greater responsibility for fighting the war, the U.S. military targeted its immediate neighbors. In 1969 Nixon ordered a bombing campaign against Cambodia to
destroy North Vietnamese sanctuaries. In 1970 American and South Vietnamese troops launched an "incursion" into Cambodia to mark and destroy the North Vietnamese bases that the bombing raids had failed to
identify. The U.S. invasion of Cambodia did not give a critical boost to
South Vietnamese morale, nor did it undermine the effectiveness of the
North Vietnamese army. Indeed, some have argued that Nixon destabi-
lized Cambodia to the point where it became susceptible to radicalization
of the most malevolent form.[2]

In May 1972 the North Vietnamese army launched a massive Easter
Offensive that was designed to replicate the Tet Offensive's psychological
impact and surpass it in terms of sustainable battlefield momentum. This
comprehensive PAVN-NLF campaign brought some early successes, yet

Nixon refused to apply the brakes on his withdrawal strategy. Instead, he launched the most intense bombing campaign of the war, code-named Linebacker, which beat back the communist offensive and safeguarded South Vietnam's integrity. Negotiations between Nixon's national security adviser, Henry Kissinger, and Le Duc Tho—who remained in place as North Vietnam's chief negotiator—continued through the summer and fall of 1972. On October 26, 1972, Kissinger famously declared that "peace is at hand."[3]

A few days prior to the November 7 presidential election—in which Nixon was expected to crush the challenge of the (all too) liberal senator from South Dakota, George McGovern—President Thieu, fearing that South Vietnam was about to be sold down the river in the most "dishonorable" way, demanded substantial changes to Kissinger's negotiating platform. He sought a watertight assurance that the United States would come to his aid in the event of a large-scale North Vietnamese invasion, and demanded that enemy troops be escorted from his nation in the event of any ceasefire. Hanoi, in turn, went public with Thieu's wrecking-ball strategy and demanded that the United States not deviate from the basic assumptions from which they had been working. (Le Duc Tho and Kissinger had privately agreed that President Thieu should be encouraged to assent to a comprehensive settlement with the NLF during a ceasefire period in which North Vietnamese troops would be permitted to remain where they stood.) Nixon had to compel North Vietnam to stay with the negotiations and convince Thieu that he had no plans to abandon his nation. He did this by first commencing a brutally destructive bombing campaign against North Vietnam over the Christmas period which targeted the centers of Hanoi and Haiphong. Second, the president warned Thieu that if he continued to obstruct peace, the United States would conclude a bilateral settlement with Hanoi and cease all aid, consigning South Vietnam to a dismal fate. Dangling a carrot as well as wielding a stick, Nixon further implored: "I repeat my personal assurance to you that the United States will react very strongly and rapidly to any violation of the agreement."[4] Nixon's two-pronged strategy of military coercion and political arm-twisting—based on nonbinding promises—created its intended results.

On January 23, 1973, Kissinger and Le Duc Tho signed a peace treaty that closely resembled what had been privately agreed upon three months previously. Indeed, George McGovern and liberal critics of the Vietnam War argued that it was strikingly similar to the agreement that Averell Harriman might have brokered in 1968 had the Nixon campaign team not torpedoed his efforts. In a bravura press conference after the signing of the treaty, Henry Kissinger sold its merits convincingly, and conveyed the impression that North Vietnam had made more significant concessions than the United States—that the peace achieved was indeed honorable. Reflecting the widespread belief that the peace treaty signified a genuine stalemate, if not victory, President Nixon's approval rating increased to its highest-ever level of 68 percent in February.[5]

America's Vietnam War had come to a negotiated conclusion, and Henry Kissinger was accorded significant plaudits for his efforts. Le Duc Tho and Kissinger were jointly awarded the 1973 Nobel Peace Prize. Tho refused to accept the award, however, and stated that peace did not exist in his country—a clear hint that peace in Vietnam was unsustainable. In March 1975 North Vietnam invaded South Vietnam and made a rapid advance toward the capital. Shorn of American military support, the South Vietnamese army was defeated quickly and decisively—the hollowness of "Vietnamization" became obvious to all. Saigon fell to the North Vietnamese army within a month, and the nation was reunified under communist rule. It was an embarrassingly swift conclusion to America's longest war: Nixon's "peace with honor" lasted just over two years. With its superpower sponsor gone, South Vietnam lacked the wherewithal to stand alone. From Austin, Texas, Walt Rostow observed these events with a sinking heart.

ROSTOW VACATED his office in the White House on January 28, 1969, and Henry Kissinger moved in the following day. The two men were strikingly similar in many respects. Both hailed from humble Jewish backgrounds and both attained success at the pinnacle of American academia. Kissinger nonetheless took U.S. foreign policy down a very different path than Rostow. While Rostow stressed the opportunities for doing good that came with international preeminence, Kissinger focused on the necessary limitations of America's vast though finite resources. While Rostow thought that the American people should pay higher taxes to finance its global mission, Kissinger believed that dishing out money to advance American values was no substitute for nuanced, realist diplomacy.[6] That Kissinger would so promptly reject his predecessor's activist legacy could hardly have consumed Rostow at the time, however, busy as he was preparing for a very new life. A few days after leaving the White House, Rostow and his family made the long journey southwest from Washington, D.C., to Austin, Texas.

Rostow recalled that the traveling party constituted his "wife, two teenage children, mother-in-law, [and] standard poodle."[7] The move to Texas was quite an adventure for a family that had spent little time away from the elite home comforts of the northeastern seaboard. An Ivy League–educated intellectual to his very core, Rostow must have found the University of Texas a very different proposition from Columbia, Oxford, Cambridge, and MIT—the four universities at which he had previously taught. While UT was wealthy and housed some impressive faculty members, it was the college football team—the Longhorns—that was the undoubted star of the campus. Its sixty-thousand-capacity stadium rose above a city in which orange-clad revelers dominated Saturdays in the fall. A city that had grown wealthy through the oil industry baked in 100-degree temperatures for much of the summer and enjoyed pleasant respite only through the winter and early spring. Rostow's move to Texas was an assault on senses and sensibilities that had been honed in a very different environment.

Yet in spite of the many differences, Rostow made Texas his home for the thirty-four years that remained of his life. His taking up permanent residency was not really that surprising. That Rostow got on famously with Lyndon Johnson had already suggested that he would take the city to his heart. Austin was a liberal town in a deeply conservative state. A youthful place, with more bookshops per head than anywhere outside of Princeton, New Haven, and Cambridge, Austin was hardly the archetypal Texan city. And Johnson's more attractive character traits were evident in so many of Austin's residents: proud, progressive, and welcoming.

While Austin offered a convivial environment in which to lay down roots, the intellectual opportunities offered by the University of Texas were also well suited to Rostow's requirements. Blessed with a light teaching load, Rostow had much time to ponder the woes that had befallen American foreign policy—and the part that he had played in bringing the United States to the cusp of victory in the Vietnam War. Aside from mulling over the recent past, Rostow also assisted his old boss in establishing the Lyndon

Baines Johnson Library and the Lyndon Baines Johnson School for Public Affairs. In his first few years away from government, Vietnam never consumed Rostow as it did so many others, but it was never far from his mind. This was hardly surprising, given that Rostow was helping Johnson write his autobiography. The task compelled Rostow to cast an eye over events that were still painfully resonant. The eventual outcome was decidedly mixed.

Lyndon Johnson's presidential memoir, *The Vantage Point*, was a disappointing affair. It failed to provide any new insights into the peculiar combination of traits—both positive and less savory—that drove Johnson to the zenith of American government. A vibrant, colorful personality managed to bequeath to the nation the driest possible autobiographical portrait. But this was probably Johnson's intention. An embittered man in his postpresidential career, Johnson felt obliged to divulge only the unvarnished facts as he saw them. The joy that Johnson took in telling colorful anecdotes escaped him on the page, and he sought to restrict personal participation in the writing of his memoir to the barest minimum. His aides Doris Kearns, Harry Middleton, and Bob Hardesty were employed to write the majority of the book, while Walt Rostow drafted the bulk of the material relating to foreign affairs. Failing to muster the enthusiasm to write even the most basic outline sketch from which his writing team could work, Johnson, as Kearns recalled, "sat down to talk in front of the tape machine [and] froze . . . His language became artificial and he insisted on having sheaves of memos on his lap before he'd say a word. The audience was too far away, too abstract, too unknown."[8] Doing most of the legwork himself, Rostow analyzed in detail the documentary record relating to the Vietnam War. In revisiting those lost bureaucratic battles so soon after their passing, Rostow could not resist venting his frustrations.

One example serves well to illustrate this ill-concealed bitterness—what Rostow would have viewed as a cathartic revisiting but others might describe as "not letting go." On March 14, 1970, Rostow wrote to Johnson, "Re-reading the Clifford Report, I was much struck by the gross overestimate of the enemy's capabilities that runs through it." Over two years had passed since Clark Clifford's appointment as defense secretary precipitated Rostow's fall from grace, but still it clearly rankled. Writing Johnson's memoir—including the dismal story of how Rostow had been thwarted in February and March 1968, and what it portended for the Vietnam War—

was like revisiting the scene of a successful robbery from the victim's perspective. Rostow concluded his memorandum by observing, "My point is not to criticize or score points but to underline the role of this kind of pessimism in the March 4 report and in the minds of the members of Clifford's staff who drafted it."[9] Rostow viewed himself as a foiled prophet of U.S. victory in the Vietnam War. That there are few warm words for Clark Clifford in *The Vantage Point* owes a great deal to Rostow's contribution.[10] As a testimony to Lyndon Johnson's momentous life, *The Vantage Point* failed through a narrowness of vision and a surfeit of self-pity.

Flawed as it was, Johnson's memoir was at least delivered to the publisher on time. The three postpresidential tasks that Johnson set himself during his final days in the Oval Office were finished quickly, and he soon grew restless. In September 1970 the LBJ School for Public Affairs took its first class of students. Thanks to the industry of his writing team, his memoir was completed just two years after his leaving office. Then in May 1971, the LBJ Library opened to a glittering array of guests, including President Richard Nixon. The vast concrete building jutted out imposingly on the UT campus, perched on a prime elevated position. Yet while the LBJ Library stood proud in Austin, Texas, its existence barely registered across the nation as a whole. In many respects the LBJ Library closely mimicked Lyndon Johnson's now localized stature. The former president possessed drive in abundance, but he now viewed very limited horizons. What remained for a man of his standing to do?

Johnson's answer was to overindulge. While he had cut out smoking, junk food binges, and serious drinking during his presidency, Johnson saw no reason to act sensibly now that Richard Nixon was encamped in the White House. One friend recalled that he "smoked like a fiend," while Congressman Wilbur Mills remembered that by the summer of 1972 Johnson "was way overweight . . . I was worried about him because he was so excessively fat."[11] Johnson had suffered from serious heart problems in the past, and his fondness for life's vices hastened his demise. On January 22, 1973, just four years after leaving office, Lyndon Baines Johnson passed away. A close intimate of the president from 1965 onward, Rostow was saddened by Johnson's death, losing not just the man who championed his career so effectively, but a close friend and ally in adversity. While the two men had their strategic differences, they were always resolved in good faith, and their rapport was uncomplicated and warm. Lyndon Johnson was a political giant and a man to mourn. In the wake of his friend's death, Rostow left the Vietnam War behind and refocused considerable energy on his academic work.

Rostow had been a prolific writer at MIT in the 1950s and at the University of Texas he continued to produce work at an astonishing rate. From 1969 to 2003, Rostow wrote twenty-one books in total, averaging one book every eighteen months. The list of his works is impressive, as it encompasses so many of Rostow's disparate intellectual concerns: *The World Economy: History and Prospect* (1978), *Why the Poor Get Richer and the Rich Slow Down* (1980), *British Trade Fluctuations, 1868–1896: A Chronicle and Commentary* (1981), *The Division of Europe After World War II* (1981), *Theorists of Economic Growth from David Hume to the Present: With a Perspective on the New Century* (1990), and *The Great Population Spike and After* (1998). That his book production continued so rapidly also suggests that Rostow did not spend much time agonizing over his controversial tenure at the White House and State Department. On those rare occasions that Rostow did turn to consider his part in escalating the Vietnam War, he viewed his role with pride.

His first memoir, *The Diffusion of Power*, devoted many pages to the Vietnam War, and none of them were repentant. Rostow revisited the lost battles of that fateful conflict and concluded that John F. Kennedy was particularly culpable with respect to America's military failings. He judged Kennedy's failure to grasp the nettle in 1962 and invade Laos and North Vietnam as "the greatest single error of U.S. foreign policy in the 1960s."[12] While Lyndon Johnson escaped such a damning verdict, he did not get off scot-free. In Rostow's opinion Johnson overestimated the likelihood that China would intervene militarily in Vietnam and was unduly concerned about the prospect of nuclear war. But the figure that attracted most of his scorn was the former secretary of defense. Robert McNamara had simply lost his nerve in 1966, Rostow concluded, and the United States had paid serious consequences for his irresolution. The only person whose record toward the Vietnam War was unimpeachable was Rostow himself. It is little surprise then that the haunted McNamara and bullish Rostow clashed through their supposed golden years on whether Vietnam was a necessary war.

As Rostow comfortably managed his transition to a new life as the Uni-

versity of Texas's most prolific resident, Robert McNamara lived and
worked in Washington, D.C., as the president of the World Bank. McNamara left the Johnson administration a tearful, broken figure, failing even
to determine for himself whether he had resigned or had been fired. Lyndon Johnson had earlier feared that McNamara was on the cusp of following the path trodden by America's first defense secretary—James
Forrestal had committed suicide in 1949 by throwing himself from the six-
teenth floor of Bethesda Hospital. Consumed by inner demons, Forrestal
and McNamara bore more than a passing resemblance. However, McNamara did not allow his residency at the Pentagon to get the better of him.
At the World Bank, McNamara took a strong lead in addressing the most
vexing issues of global poverty. Working unrelenting hours through the
1970s, McNamara avoided as best he could serious reflection on the part
he played in escalating the Vietnam War—the greatest, most tragic mistake of his career. In 1981, however, his relatively distinguished tenure at
the World Bank came to a close. At the age of sixty-five, the former defense secretary could avoid Vietnam's gaze for no longer.

Robert McNamara decided to repent for the errors of judgment he
made in recommending the Americanization of the Vietnam War. His immediate family had been split over the war in the mid-1960s, when his son
joined the ranks of antiwar activists. McNamara had personally lost faith
in the conflict somewhere between 1965 and 1966. Presenting an insin-
cere façade of support for a war he viewed with hostility had taken its toll
on McNamara through to the early 1990s. Whether it was informed by a
desire to confess his sins therapeutically, or simply to add his views to the
historical record, McNamara produced a memoir that shook not just the
publishing world but also the nation. In 1995 *In Retrospect: The Tragedy and
Lessons of Vietnam* was published. The most famous passage of the book ar-
rives early in the preface:

> We of the Kennedy and Johnson administrations who participated in
> the decisions on Vietnam acted according to what we thought were the
> principles and traditions of this nation. We made our decisions in light
> of those values. Yet we were wrong, terribly wrong. We owe it to future
> generations to explain why.

In 350 tightly written pages, McNamara laid bare the skewed reasoning that had informed U.S. policy toward the Vietnam War. Resisting what might have been a natural impulse to distribute blame liberally—it was not just "McNamara's War," but Rusk's, Bundy's, and Rostow's War too—McNamara assumed for himself the bulk of responsibility for America's tragic crusade. In the conclusion McNamara identifies eleven main causes "for our disaster in Vietnam." As they contradict Rostow on virtually every count, they are worth paraphrasing here:

1. We misjudged the geopolitical intentions of our adversaries.
2. We totally misjudged the political forces in South Vietnam by overestimating their dedication to freedom and democracy.
3. We underestimated the power of nationalism to motivate North Vietnam and the Vietcong.
4. We were profoundly ignorant of the history of Southeast Asia and did not have any genuine experts to consult.
5. We failed to recognize the limitation of U.S. technology in confronting unconventional, highly motivated people's movements.
6. We failed to draw Congress and the American people into a full and frank discussion and debate of the pros and cons of a large-scale U.S. military involvement in Southeast Asia before we initiated the action.
7. We failed to retain public support because we did not explain fully what was happening and why we were doing what we did.
8. We failed to display humility. We do not have a God-given right to shape every nation in our image or as we choose.
9. We failed to bring on board international support.
10. Not all problems can be solved perfectly. We may have to live with an imperfect, untidy world.
11. We at the top of government failed to debate the Vietnam War effectively and thoroughly.[13]

The McNamara of 1995 thus represents a very different vintage from the number-crunching rationalist hired by Jack Kennedy in 1961. While limitations exist in McNamara's mea culpa, his willingness to address his own inadequacies is laudable. To Rostow, however, McNamara had simply insulted the memories of those who had died for a noble cause. Rostow remained unmovable in his belief that America's only mistake with regard to the Vietnam War was not waging the conflict with sufficient ferocity. Outraged by McNamara's sanctimonious volte-face, he drafted a strongly worded response published by *The Times Literary Supplement* in June 1995.

In rebutting McNamara's charge that Vietnam was an unnecessary war, Rostow argued that America's taking a stand against the insurgency in South Vietnam saved the rest of the region from an emboldened communist onslaught. Pointing out that the independent, noncommunist nations of Southeast Asia "quadrupled their real GNP between 1960 and 1981," Rostow doubted that such record growth would have happened had the United States withdrawn from Vietnam in 1963. Making the obvious point that all of America's wars provoked controversy and internal dissent—citing the Revolutionary War, the War of 1812, the Mexican War, the Civil War, the Spanish-American War, the First World War— Rostow offers the familiar shibboleth that war does not please everybody, but is often necessary:

> No one has promised that American independence itself, or America's role as a bastion for those who believe deeply in democracy, could be achieved without pain or loss or controversy. The pain, loss and controversy resulting from Vietnam were accepted for ten years by the American people. That acceptance held the line so that a free Asia could survive and grow . . . Those who died or were wounded in Vietnam or are veterans in that conflict were not involved in a pointless war.[14]

While Rostow avoids personal recrimination in the article itself, it later became clear that he thought little of McNamara as a man. Rostow believed that the former defense secretary had repented for crimes he did not commit, and in doing so betrayed America's selfless sacrifice through his own weak-mindedness. In private interviews Rostow questioned McNamara's state of mind, implying that he suffered a nervous collapse that led to this unworthy work.[15] Rostow is correct to suggest that McNamara experienced emotional low points in his post-Pentagon career, but *In Retrospect* is not the work of someone lacking intellectual and emotional lucidity. Yet Rostow's angry response to McNamara's memoir does require serious attention. He was right to point out that the U.S. government "at no time in my experience, ever lacked knowledge of Asia or Asians."[16] Following the publication of *In Retrospect*, a number of respected Asia specialists pointed out that they had sent to McNamara a number of skeptical reports based on genuine expertise—and that the defense secretary ignored all of them. Is it not possible that Rostow is correct in other areas too? Central to his postbellum justification of the war is the assertion that the Pacific "Tiger Economies" would never have assumed stature were it not for America's forbearance through the Vietnam War. What are we to make of this justification?

In some respects Rostow's argument is a clever one. How does one argue against the unassailable statistics that he marshals? It is true that the nations of the Pacific Rim enjoyed rapid economic growth from 1960 through to the present. Who is to say that they would not have gone red had America washed its hands of the Vietnam conflict? Yet upon closer examination, it becomes clear that Rostow's reasoning rests on some flimsy foundations. The historian Robert McMahon has questioned Rostow's self-justificatory rationale more effectively than anyone else.[17] In examining Rostow's defense in detail, I draw unapologetically upon McMahon's impressive case for the prosecution.

While Rostow made his famous "Case for the War" (and against McNamara) in 1995, he had long thought that the United States had in some ways "won" the Vietnam War. Through American military action in Vietnam, the members of the Association of Southeast Asian Nations (ASEAN—comprising Indonesia, the Philippines, Malaysia, Thailand, Singapore, and Brunei) were untroubled by communism and hence reaped profound economic rewards. In 1986 Rostow presented this argument in *The United States and the Regional Organization of Asia and the Pacific, 1965–1985*, although he had initially laid out his thesis at earlier lectures and symposia.[18] Rostow's justification for the Vietnam War possessed significant political resonance and the conservative press latched upon it eagerly. In 1985 a front-page report in *The Wall Street Journal* swallowed Rostow's line entirely, observing, "The U.S. war effort—despite its ultimate failure—pumped billions of dollars into the region and provided what Asian leaders now call 'breathing room' for their fledgling post-colonial governments."[19] Rostow's "buying time" thesis was then taken up enthusiastically by a band of intensely nationalist scholars referred to as the "Vietnam Revisionists." Academic orthodoxy in 1980 assumed that the Vietnam War was a tragic error of judgment on America's part. These revisionists rebelled against this defeatist sentiment and sought to recast the Vietnam War in a more glorious light. Rostow finally refined this line of thinking in a 1996 article in *Diplomatic History*. While the United States had lost the "test of will" in Vietnam, it had "won the war in Southeast Asia."[20]

Rostow's rationale was potent, as it allowed American conservatives and nationalists to refashion the Vietnam War as another broadly conceived victory—not as America's one and only defeat. This argument, however, is intellectually unworthy on many different levels. His theory deftly altered the terms of the debate about the Vietnam War's necessity and disingenuously shifted the standards by which we judge success and failure. Rostow's argument has a veneer of intellectual respectability but is in reality compromised by dubious assumptions, doubtful logic, and significant leaps of faith. As Robert McMahon observes, each of Rostow's points tends to "conflate intentions with consequence. Each, moreover does grave injustice to the issue of causality."[21]

That America's intervention in the Vietnam War stabilized Southeast Asia has no respectable basis in fact. Cambodia was more stable prior to U.S. intervention in the Vietnam War than afterward. The same was of course true of Laos. In 1965 Indonesian government forces brutally suppressed an incipient Marxist insurgency and in doing so killed half a million alleged "communists." While this was a tremendous result for U.S. foreign policy, CIA Director Richard Helms could find no evidence that Johnson's military commitment to Vietnam played any part in emboldening the Indonesian generals. The CIA actually concluded that the rise of Suharto and eventual destruction of the communists "evolved purely from a complex and long-standing domestic political situation."[22] Indonesia's anticommunist assault represented the single most important political development in the region during the Vietnam War. And this development had nothing to do with United States actions. But Rostow assumes American omniscience and foresight in other troublesome respects.

Rostow's assertion that America was a central player in the creation of ASEAN needs to be taken with a liberal pinch of salt. Rostow ascribes the creation of ASEAN to Lyndon Johnson's prescience, but it owed much more to American heavy-handedness in the region. ASEAN emerged primarily as an *Asian* alternative to the two superpowers meddling in their affairs. In April 1966 the Thai foreign minister Thanat Khoman told the foreign ministers of Malaysia and the Philippines that it was imperative that "we take our destiny into our own hands instead of letting others from far away mould it at their whim."[23] Let there be no doubt that this was not a ringing endorsement of Johnson's leadership. ASEAN was created to allow Southeast Asians to gain their independence from U.S. leadership. Its creation was an unintended consequence of the Vietnam War. The United States in this respect was not a sage guide but a negative reference point.

At core Rostow made a dogged case that the United States military presence in South Vietnam made safe the entire region. His theory rests on a similar reasoning to that of an unlikely fictional bedfellow—Homer Simpson—and this comparison is more pertinent than it might first appear. A grizzly bear terrorizes Springfield and a high-tech, high-cost, twenty-four-hour "Bear Patrol" is established to ward off any further frightening incursions. To Homer's delight, the patrol "works" and there are no further bear attacks on Springfield. He observes triumphantly that the "Bear Patrol is working like a charm." "That's specious reasoning," his daughter Lisa retorts. "According to your logic this rock keeps tigers away." Intrigued, Homer asks how it works. "It doesn't," Lisa replies. "How so?" her father inquires, undeterred. "It's just a rock," Lisa replies, "but I don't see a tiger anywhere." "Lisa," concludes Homer, "I want to buy your rock."[24] Rostow believed that America's own Bear Patrol—the U.S. Army in Vietnam—had kept communists from terrorizing Southeast Asia. It is difficult to counter without delving into counterfactual history—for the communists, like the bears, did not come—but it fails to convince on many levels.

Rostow remained steadfast in his fidelity to the Vietnam War to the end. His doing so has an almost heroic quality. Loath to betray the soldiers who fought the good fight in Southeast Asia, Rostow gained a lot of respect in military and political circles for meeting McNamara's assertion that the war was "terribly wrong" with his own upbeat assessment that it was absolutely right—and that it actually represented a victory of sorts. Yet while this line was comforting to many, it was dismaying to many more. Consistency is not a laudable trait if you are consistently wrong. Robert McNamara tortured himself through the postwar period because he possessed the imagination to question his own conduct. Rostow eschewed self-examination and thus remained serene. While it enabled him to enjoy the rest of his life in the way that McNamara perhaps has not, Rostow's obstinacy was in many ways insulting to the Vietnamese and Americans who died in their tens of thousands to allegedly assist rapid economic growth in the Pacific region. Rostow spent a great deal of his retirement putting considerable effort into establishing the Austin Project—an organization that seeks to address inner-city poverty in the predominantly black neighborhoods of Austin and provide "a level playing field for all our young." This was entirely in keeping with Rostow's great qualities as a progressive advocate of assisting the less fortunate. His virulent anticommunism, however, helped set in motion a brutal series of events for the United States and Vietnam. Of the Vietnam War, Rostow later commented, "I don't spend much time worrying about that period."[25] He died on February 14, 2003, in Austin, Texas, and is buried in Woodlawn Cemetery in New York City.

MISDIRECTED BENEVOLENCE CAN GO tragically awry, and such is the story of Walt Rostow and the Vietnam War. His colleagues in the Kennedy and Johnson administrations often joked that Rostow envisioned "a TV set in every thatched hut."[26] And this idealism—so easy to caricature—is a significant part of Rostow's psychological makeup. If only those uninformed people in the developing world could understand that *The Stages of Economic Growth* provided the true path to social harmony and material success. Everyone would win by following Rostow's model, although those who did not would suffer. In this respect Graham Greene's *The Quiet American* provides a pertinent parallel. As the cynical English narrator says of the young crusader Alden Pyle, "He was impregnably armored by his good intentions and his ignorance."[27]

The key to unlocking the puzzle as to why the development-inclined Rostow became the most hawkish civilian member of the Kennedy and Johnson administrations is *The Stages of Economic Growth*. Setting himself the task of "answering" Karl Marx as a sophomore at Yale ensured that Rostow remained fixated with Marxism for a considerable period—over twenty years in total. This study imbued in Rostow an almost pathological desire to eradicate communism wherever it threatened the societal dynamic that he believed drove history. When Rostow finally presented his alternative to Marxism in 1960, it represented both the zenith of his academic career and its end. So Rostow became a U.S. foreign-policy adviser and assumed a prime position to hurry along the history he had so recently mapped out. Rostow was defending not just South Vietnam, but the viability of his thesis. Communism did not fit into any of Rostow's stages, and hence it had to be confronted.

The French existentialist writer Albert Camus was an ardent critic of communist ideology. Camus disliked the fact that communism claimed divine right to represent the world's future. From this absolute faith in historical inevitability, Camus argued that there inevitably arose "slave camps under the flag of freedom [and] massacres justified by philanthropy."[28] Isaiah Berlin similarly took to task what he termed "monism," a belief in an "all embracing system guaranteed to be eternal," whose cheerleaders became "ruthless fanatics, men embraced by an all-embracing coherent vision."[29] But what of American ideology? Can cruelty be perpetrated in the name of freedom and democracy? In 1964 the journalist William Pfaff wrote perceptively, "The West does not like to admit this fact about itself . . . but it has been capable of violence on an appalling scale, and has justified that violence as indispensable to a heroic reform of society or of mankind."[30]

Rostow played a significant role in meting out significant destruction to a nation—Vietnam—enduring a civil war that was fought in the name of postcolonial rebellion, communism, religion, regional factionalism, democracy—a bewildering array of factors that do not lend themselves to black-and-white solutions. Yet Rostow instead discerned a simple picture of one-sided aggression: South Vietnam was suffering at the hands of the NLF because of northern-directed infiltration. The crisis afflicting Diem's regime was not indigenous, but directed by Ho Chi Minh. Therefore, Rostow reasoned that America could only end this situation, and assure South Vietnam's future, by bombing North Vietnam and deploying U.S. troops in vast numbers. Rostow's role in escalating the Vietnam War is significant.

Under Kennedy, Rostow helped shape U.S. counterinsurgency strategy and became the first to formulate a plan for bombing North Vietnam into submission and the first to recommend the deployment of ground troops. During the Johnson administration, the Rostow Thesis helped guide the Rolling Thunder bombing campaign, while his appointment as national security adviser allowed Rostow to shape policy from a position that afforded genuine, immediate leverage with the president. Not only did Rostow help escalate the intensity of the conflict, but his implacable opposition to a number of peace initiatives also helped scupper any chance that a series of negotiating intermediaries—Harold Wilson, Henry Kissinger, and Averell Harriman—might have had to resolve the conflict during a Democratic administration. Walt Rostow was a key architect of the Americanization of the Vietnam War.

Rostow's story will be familiar to anyone with more than a passing interest in contemporary international relations. His apparent duality of personality (the development-minded dove and anticommunist hawk) has found parallel expression in the career of Paul Wolfowitz. Indeed, today's neoconservatives have taken up Rostow's internationalist, crusading mantle and have run with it to potent effect.[31] The former president of the World Bank, and architect of the second Iraq War, Wolfowitz is identifiably Rostovian with respect to his reading of international relations: it is beholden upon the United States, as the world's preeminent nation, to democratize and do "good"—at the bayonet's point if necessary. Both Rostow and Wolfowitz seem influenced by the Genevan Enlightenment philosopher Jean Jacques Rousseau's illiberal injunction that "freedom" does not necessarily arise from personal volition: "Whoever refuses to obey the general will shall be forced to be compelled to do so by the whole body. This means nothing else than that he will be forced to be free."[32] All ideologies can do awful things when they are pursued with unyielding determination.

Rostow and the neoconservatives have in fact been proved right on some of the great issues of the twentieth century. Marxism-Leninism was indeed a morally abhorrent system that extinguished liberty, stifled creativity, and failed to provide adequate economic incentives and benefits to its people. Liberal capitalism "won" the Cold War, its virtues have been vindicated, and "democracy" has proved itself worthier than any other form of government. Yet intervening abroad to instill these values has produced decidedly mixed results. Rostow, Wolfowitz, Richard Perle, Francis Fukuyama, and others believe in the redemptive powers of liberal capitalism in the same way as evangelical Christians believe in God—they act as if their value system is divinely authored and view deviations from the righteous path as heresy.[33] But surely it is better to allow nations to take their own path to enlightenment. Might not the heretics come around to liberal capitalism more rapidly and enthusiastically if the United States acted as an exemplar, rather than as a militarized agent for change? Tin-pot dictators and international pariahs often lose their mystique when they do not have an enemy to confront.

ON JUNE 13, 1961, during a speech at Fort Bragg, North Carolina, Rostow suggested for the first time that the United States might have to bomb North Vietnam to curtail its support for the NLF. The language that Rostow employs to describe communism provides clues as to his future pugnacity. "They are the scavengers of the modernization process," Rostow exclaimed. "Communism is best understood as a disease of the transition to modernization."[34] In his histories of social reform, sexuality, and medicine in the nineteenth century, the French philosopher Michel Foucault highlights the manner in which seemingly neutral descriptive terms, such as "unnatural" or "sick," were deployed by judges, teachers, and sexologists to legitimize force against that which was deemed "deviant."[35] In characterizing communism as parasitic—as a "disease"—Rostow, in similar fashion, was following many in America who, in demonizing communism in Manichaean terms, contributed to America's fateful, misguided venture into Southeast Asia. Correct in his estimation that liberal capitalism would win the long-run battle for hearts and minds, Rostow nonetheless viewed diversions from this path as an affront to a value system he had devised— as a mutation of history that required a prompt and unequivocal response.

In a 1967 interview with *Life*, Rostow claimed, "I have learned that men who say they have no theory are controlled by bias."[36] Rostow was an ideologue and as such was not given to self-doubt. But in the formulation of foreign policy, this can hardly be described as a positive attribute. While much of his life was dedicated to "doing good" with respect to alleviating poverty and advocating the expanded distribution of foreign aid, Rostow's contribution to the making of the Vietnam War will stand as his most fateful legacy. That Rostow never expressed remorse for his role in the conflict is impressive with respect to his intellectual consistency, but it tells a story in itself.[37] Rostow could never detect errors in the theories he created in his academic career, nor in the memoranda he prepared while in government. He believed that he was in possession of a fundamental truth that was impervious to contingency and counterargument. Rostow's lack of intellectual curiosity played a large part in making a war that was misguided in conception, and that produced uniformly bleak consequences.

Notes

ABBREVIATIONS

DDEL   Dwight D. Eisenhower Library, Abilene, Kansas

FRUS   U.S. Department of State, *Foreign Relations of the United States*, vols. 1–34 (Washington, D.C.: Government Printing Office, 1991–2005)

JFKL   John F. Kennedy Library, Boston, Massachusetts

LBJL   Lyndon Baines Johnson Library, Austin, Texas

LOC   Library of Congress, Washington, D.C.

NSF   National Security Files

Pentagon Papers   [U.S. Department of Defense], *The Pentagon Papers: The Department of Defense History of United States Decision-Making on Vietnam*, Senator Gravel edition (Boston: Beacon Hill, 1971)

POF   Papers of President Kennedy, President's Office Files

SMML   Seeley G. Mudd Manuscript Library, Princeton, New Jersey

TNA: PRO   The National Archives, London: Public Records Office

INTRODUCTION

1. See Notes of Meeting, February 27, 1968, *FRUS*: Vietnam, January–August 1968, 354, for the official record of the meeting, and Clark Clifford with Richard Holbrooke, *Counsel to the President: A Memoir* (New York: Random House, 1991), 484–85, for the unexpurgated version.

2. Townsend Hoopes, *The Limits of Intervention: An Inside Account of How the Johnson Policy of Escalation in Vietnam Was Reversed* (New York: Davis McKay, 1969), 61.

3. Quoted in Anatoly Dobrynin, *In Confidence: Moscow's Ambassador to America's Six Cold War Presidents* (New York: Times Books, 1995), 144.

4. David Kaiser, *American Tragedy: Kennedy, Johnson, and the Origins of the Vietnam War* (Cambridge, Mass.: Belknap Press of Harvard University Press, 2000), 69.

5. On McGeorge Bundy's career, see Andrew Preston, *The War Council: McGeorge Bundy, the NSC, and Vietnam* (Cambridge, Mass.: Harvard University Press, 2006), and Kai Bird, *The Color of Truth: McGeorge Bundy and William Bundy, Brothers in Arms* (New York: Simon and Schuster, 1998).

6. Cited in Robert T. Schulzinger, *A Time for War: The United States and Vietnam, 1941–1975* (New York: Oxford University Press, 1997), 220.

7. John Prados, *The Blood Road: The Ho Chi Minh Trail and the Vietnam War* (New York: John Wiley and Sons, 1998), 375.

8. Minutes of Weekly Luncheon, September 12, 1967, Tom Johnson Meeting Notes File, box 2, LBJL.

9. Christopher Hitchens, *The Trial of Henry Kissinger* (New York: Verso Books, 2002), 6–16.

10. Walt W. Rostow to Dean Rusk, February 13, 1964, *FRUS*: Vietnam, 1964, 72–74.

ONE: THE EDUCATION OF WALT WHITMAN ROSTOW

1. The laws that formed the Pale of Settlement were passed in 1795 and 1835. See Zvi Getelman, *A Century of Ambivalence: The Jews of Russia and the Soviet Union, 1881 to the Present* (Bloomington: Indiana University Press, 2001), 11, and Benjamin Nathans, *Beyond the Pale: The Jewish Encounter with Late Imperial Russia* (Berkeley: University of California Press, 2002).

2. Zvi Getelman, *A Century of Ambivalence*, 12.

3. See M. M. Posan, "Walt Rostow: A Personal Appreciation," in Charles P. Kindleberger and Guido di Tella (eds.), *Economics in the Long View: Essays in Honour of W. W. Rostow* (New York: New York University Press, 1982), 1–2.

4. For an interesting discussion of the experience of Russia's Jewish population in America, see Deborah Dash Moore, *At Home in America: Second Generation New York Jews* (New York: Columbia University Press, 1981), and Annelise Orleck, *The Soviet Jewish Americans* (Lebanon, N.H.: University Press of New England, 1999).

5. Edwin G. Burrows and Mike Wallace, *Gotham: A History of New York City to 1898* (New York: Oxford University Press, 1999), 1116. Alfred Kazin also provides an evocative description of the Brownsville neighborhood of Brooklyn in *A Walker in the City* (New York: Harcourt, 1951).

6. On Victor Rostow's early life in New York, I am indebted to David Grossman Armstrong, "The True Believer: Walt Whitman Rostow and the Path to Vietnam" (unpublished Ph.D. dissertation, University of Texas at Austin, 2000), 26–58.

7. Quoted in David Grossman Armstrong, "The True Believer," 34.

8. Walt W. Rostow, *Concept and Controversy: Sixty Years of Taking Ideas to Market* (Austin: University of Texas Press, 2003), 3.

9. Ibid., 4.

10. Ibid., 3–5.

11. Ibid., 1.

12. David Grossman Armstrong, "The True Believer," 40–41.

13. Walt W. Rostow, *Concept and Controversy*, 5.

14. David Grossman Armstrong, "The True Believer," 42–44.

15. Ibid., 50.

16. Walt W. Rostow, *Concept and Controversy*, 7.

17. For the book on the events that so roused Rostow's imagination, see Charles Lindbergh, *The Spirit of St. Louis* (1953; reprint edition, New York: Scribner, 1998).

18. Walt W. Rostow, *Concept and Controversy*, 7.

19. Ibid., 6.

20. Quoted in David Grossman Armstrong, "The True Believer," 65.

21. Ibid., 66.

22. For a comprehensive history of Yale University, see Brooks Mather Kelley, *Yale: A History* (New Haven, Conn.: Yale University Press, 1974).

23. "History of the Class of Nineteen Thirty-Six," Yale University Archives, and David Grossman Armstrong, "The True Believer," 66–67.

24. Richard Bissell with Jonathan E. Lewis and Frances T. Pudlo, *Reflections of a Cold Warrior* (New Haven, Conn.: Yale University Press, 1996), 11, and Walt W. Rostow, *Essays on a Half-Century: Ideas, Policies, and Action* (Boulder, Colo.: Westview Press, 1988), 2.

25. Walt W. Rostow, *Essays on a Half-Century*, 2.

26. David Grossman Armstrong, "The True Believer," 71.

27. Lester Tanker, *The Kennedy Circle* (Washington, D.C.: Robert B. Luce, 1961), 41.

28. Karl Marx and Friedrich Engels, *The Communist Manifesto* (1848; new edition, Oxford: Oxford World Classics, 1998).

29. Walt W. Rostow, *Concept and Controversy*, 11.

30. Ibid., 18.

31. Quoted in David Grossman Armstrong, "The True Believer," 85.

32. For those whose interest is piqued, Rostow and Heath composed music to accompany Aristophanes' lyrics for a performance of *The Frogs* by the Balliol players in 1938. See Walt W. Rostow, *Essays on a Half-Century*, 5. See also Edward Heath, *Music: A Joy for Life* (London: Sidgwick and Jackson, 1976), 50–51.

33. Walt W. Rostow, *Concept and Controversy*, 22.

34. Oliver Jensen (ed.), *Class of 1936: 50 Years Out* (New Haven, Conn.: Yale University Alumni Records Office, 1986), 28.

35. Walt W. Rostow, *Concept and Controversy*, 23.

36. For more on these articles, see M. M. Postan, "Walt Rostow: A Personal Appreciation," 8.

37. David Grossman Armstrong, "The True Believer," 103–104, and Richard Bissell, *Reflections of a Cold Warrior*, 11.

38. Quoted in David Grossman Armstrong, "The True Believer," 100.

39. Arthur D. Gayer with Walt W. Rostow and Anna Jacobson Schwartz, *The Growth and Fluctuation of the British Economy, 1790–1850*, 2 volumes (Oxford: Clarendon Press, 1953).

40. Walt W. Rostow, *Concept and Controversy*, 28.

41. Ibid., 28.

42. Godfrey Hodgson, obituary for Walt Rostow, *The Guardian*, February 17, 2003.

43. Walt W. Rostow, *Concept and Controversy*, 28.

44. Alan J. Levine, *The Strategic Bombing of Germany, 1940–1945* (Westport, Conn.: Praeger, 1992), 77.

45. Walt W. Rostow, "The London Operation: Recollections of an Economist," in George C. Chalou (ed.), *The Secret War: The Office of Strategic Services in World War II* (Washington, D.C.: National Archives and Records Administration, 1992), 55.

46. Walt W. Rostow, *Pre-Invasion Bombing Strategy: General Eisenhower's Decision of March 25, 1944* (Austin: University of Texas Press, 1981).

47. On April 5, 1944, the 15th Air Force attacked oil facilities near Ploesti in Romania. However, this attack was ordered only because small marshaling yards were located near the refineries. Oil was the secondary target, but was bombed with devastating results. See David Grossman Armstrong, "The True Believer," for a comprehensive treatment of Rostow's World War II service. Interestingly, Primo Levi alludes to the Ploesti attacks in *If This Is a Man/The Truce* (London: Penguin, 1989), 363.

48. Walt W. Rostow, *Pre-Invasion Bombing Strategy*, 82.

49. Rostow also argued that had America not taken a military stand in Vietnam, Southeast Asia's "economic miracle" would be all but a pipe dream. See Walt W. Rostow, "The Case for the War," *Times Literary Supplement*, June 9, 1995.

50. George W. Ball, *The Past Has Another Pattern* (New York: W. W. Norton, 1982), 411.

51. David MacIsaac (ed.), *The United States Strategic Bombing Survey*, vol. 4 (New York: Garland Publishing, 1976), 1–2.

52. Kimber Charles Pearce, *Rostow, Kennedy, and the Rhetoric of Foreign Aid* (East Lansing: Michigan State University Press, 2001), 3.

53. Quoted in Terence Bell, "The Politics of Social Science in Post-War America," in Larry May (ed.), *Recasting America: Culture and Politics in the Age of Cold War* (Chicago: Chicago University Press, 1989), 76.

54. Walt W. Rostow, *Concept and Controversy*, 60.

55. Quoted in Frances S. Saunders, *Who Paid the Piper? The CIA and the Cultural Cold War* (London: Granta, 1999), 7–8. See Saunders for an evocative depiction of postwar Europe.

56. Walt W. Rostow, interview with the author, August 7, 2002.

57. Walt W. Rostow, *The Division of Europe After World War II* (Austin: University of Texas Press, 1981), 52.

58. Quoted in Walt W. Rostow, *Concept and Controversy*, 80.

59. Michael J. Hogan, *The Marshall Plan* (New York: Cambridge University Press, 1987), 35.

60. Walt W. Rostow, *The Division of Europe After World War II*, 4–7 and 54–57.

61. Walt W. Rostow, *The Diffusion of Power: An Essay in Recent History* (New York: Macmillan, 1972), 8–9.

62. Quoted in Frank L. Kluckhohn, *Lyndon's Legacy: A Candid Look at the President's Policymakers* (New York: Devin-Adair Co., 1964), 190.

63. John Kenneth Galbraith, *A Life in Our Times* (Boston: Houghton Mifflin, 1981), 241.

64. Quoted in David Halberstam, *The Best and the Brightest*, twentieth-anniversary edition (New York: Ballantine Books, 1992), 161.

65. Quoted in David Grossman Armstrong, "The True Believer," 186.

TWO: THE MAKING OF AN ANTICOMMUNIST ZEALOT

1. David Holloway, *Stalin and the Bomb: The Soviet Union and Atomic Energy, 1939–1956* (New Haven: Yale University Press, 1995).

2. Quoted in David Grossman Armstrong, "The True Believer," 203.

3. Nils Gilman, *Mandarins of the Future: Modernization Theory in Cold War America* (Baltimore: Johns Hopkins University Press, 2003), 158.

4. James R. Killian Jr., *The Education of a College President: A Memoir* (Cambridge, Mass.: MIT Press, 1985), 67.

5. Walt W. Rostow, *Eisenhower, Kennedy, and Foreign Aid* (Austin: University of Texas Press, 1985), 202–203.

6. For a recent discussion of the efficacy of wielding soft power, see Joseph S. Nye, *The Paradox of American Power: Why the World's Only Superpower Can't Go It Alone* (New York: Oxford University Press, 2002).

7. Walt W. Rostow, "On Ending the Cold War," *Foreign Affairs* 65 (1987), 836.

8. John Kenneth Galbraith, "For Foreign Aid in a New Packaging," review of Walt W. Rostow and Max F. Millikan, *A Proposal: Key to an Effective Foreign Policy, New York Times Book Review*, January 18, 1957, 22.

9. Quoted in Frances FitzGerald, *Fire in the Lake: The Vietnamese and the Americans in Vietnam* (Boston: Little, Brown, 1972), 16.

10. Quoted in Chester Cooper, *The Lost Crusade: America in Vietnam* (New York: Dodd, Mead and Company, 1970), 79. For a recent narrative account of the battle of Dien Bien Phu, see Martin Windrow, *The Last Valley: Dien Bien Phu and the French Defeat in Vietnam* (London: Weidenfeld and Nicolson, 2005).

11. Walt W. Rostow, with Richard Hatch, Frank Kierman Jr., and Alexander Eckstein, *The Prospects for Communist China* (New York: John Wiley and Sons, 1954), 96.

12. See Christian G. Appy, *Patriots: The Vietnam War Remembered from All Sides* (New York: Viking, 2003), 44–45.

13. Quoted in George C. Herring, *America's Longest War: The United States and Vietnam, 1950–1975*, 2nd ed. (New York: Knopf, 1979), 41.

14. Cited in Gordon H. Chang, *Friends and Enemies: The United States, China, and the Soviet Union, 1948–1972* (Stanford, Calif.: Stanford University Press, 1990), 25.

15. Speech by Walt W. Rostow, "The Challenge Facing the United States," delivered at the Naval War College, Newport, R.I., August 25, 1954, MC 188, box 10, folder 288, Institute Archives and Special Collections, MIT Libraries, Cambridge, Mass.

16. Walt W. Rostow, *The United States in the World Arena* (New York: Harper and Row, 1960), 244.

17. For a discussion of these factors, see George C. Herring, *America's Longest War*, 14–15.

18. Quoted in Jean Lacoutre, *Ho Chi Minh: A Political Biography* (New York: Penguin, 1968), 119.

19. Robert Buzzanco, "The United States and Vietnam, 1950–1968: Capitalism, Communism and Containment," in Peter L. Hahn and Mary Ann Heiss, *Empire and Revolution: The United States and the Third World Since 1945* (Columbus: Ohio State University Press, 2001), 96.

20. David Grossman Armstrong, "The True Believer," 222.

21. www.sourcewatch.org/index.php?title=C.D._Jackson.

22. Dwight D. Eisenhower, "Special Message on Foreign Economic Policy, March 30, 1954," in *Public Papers of the Presidents of the United States: Dwight D. Eisenhower* (Washington, D.C.: Government Printing Office, 1954), 352.

23. See Walt W. Rostow, *Eisenhower, Kennedy, and Foreign Aid*, 76.

24. Max F. Millikan and Walt W. Rostow, *A Proposal: Key to an Effective Foreign Policy* (New York: Harper and Brothers, 1957), 1.

25. Walt W. Rostow, *The United States in the World Arena*, 330.

26. G. Thomas Goodnight, "Hans J. Morgenthau in Defense of the National Interest: On Rhetoric, Realism and the Public Sphere," in Francis A. Beer and Robert Harriman (eds.), *Post-Realism: The Rhetorical Turn in International Relations* (East Lansing: Michigan State University Press, 1996), 154.

27. Walt W. Rostow, *The Diffusion of Power*, 61.

28. Max F. Millikan and Walt W. Rostow, *A Proposal*, 5.

29. Ibid., 4.

30. Ibid., 151. Rostow later used this quote in a speech titled "The Great Transition: Tasks of the First and Second Postwar Generations," *Department of State Bulletin*, March 27, 1967.

31. Chester Bowles to Walt W. Rostow, August 3, 1956, Bowles Papers, box 154, folder 574, Yale University Archives.

32. Walt W. Rostow to Chester Bowles, August 20, 1956, Bowles Papers, box 154, folder 574, Yale University Archives.

33. Cited in David Halberstam, *The Best and the Brightest*, 155.

34. John F. Kennedy to Eugene Rostow, October 16, 1956, Papers of President Kennedy, Pre-Presidential Papers, box 550, JFKL.

35. Walt W. Rostow, *The Diffusion of Power*, 125.

36. Ibid.

37. Ibid.

38. David Halberstam, *The Best and the Brightest*, 157.

39. Walt W. Rostow, oral history, JFKL, 3.

40. Walt W. Rostow, *The Diffusion of Power*, 106.

41. Walt W. Rostow, statement before the Senate Committee on Foreign Relations, 84th Congress, Second Session, 1958, 284–86.

42. For a concise discussion of the rationale that informed Kennedy's India policy, see Kimber Charles Pearce, *Rostow, Kennedy, and the Rhetoric of Foreign Aid*, 16–18.

43. The Rostow-penned speeches were John F. Kennedy, "The Choice in Asia—Democratic Development in India, March 25, 1958," and "The Economic Gap, February 19, 1959," both in John F. Kennedy, *A Compilation of Statements and Speeches Made During His Service in the United States Senate and the House of Representatives* (Washington, D.C.: Government Printing Office, 1964), 591–608 and 789–98, respectively.

44. Cited in David Engerman, Nils Gilman, et al. (eds.), *Staging Growth: Modernization, Development, and the Global Cold War* (Amherst: University of Massachusetts Press, 2003), 212.

45. See Walt W. Rostow, oral history, LBJL, 3–8.

46. John F. Kennedy to Walt W. Rostow, September 10, 1958, Papers of President Kennedy, Pre-Presidential File, box 454, JFKL.

47. C.D. Jackson to Walt W. Rostow, August 22, 1958, C.D. Jackson Papers, Time Inc. File: Rostow, Walt W., box 75, DDEL.

48. Walt W. Rostow to Adlai Stevenson, December 10, 1958, Adlai Stevenson Papers, box 69, SMML.

49. Walt W. Rostow to C.D. Jackson, December 8, 1958, C.D. Jackson Papers, Time Inc. File: Rostow, Walt W., box 75, DDEL.

50. Walt W. Rostow, "The American National Style," *Daedalus* 87:2 (1958).

51. Walt W. Rostow, *The Stages of Economic Growth: A Non-Communist Manifesto* (Cambridge: Cambridge University Press, 1960), 2.

52. Quoted ibid., 149.

53. Ibid., 149.

54. Ibid., 151.

55. Ibid., 161.

56. Ibid., 160.

57. Ibid., 134.

58. Max F. Millikan and Walt W. Rostow, *A Proposal*, 149–50.

59. Quoted in David Halberstam, *The Best and the Brightest*, 62.

60. Ibid., 160.

61. Gilbert Rist, *The History of Development: From Western Origins to Global Faith* (New York: Zed Books, 1997), 98.

62. D. Michael Shafer, *Deadly Paradigms: The Failure of U.S. Counter-Insurgency Policy* (Princeton, N.J.: Princeton University Press, 1988), 95.

63. Walt W. Rostow to Dean Rusk, February 13, 1964, *FRUS*: Vietnam, 1964, 72–74.

64. Émile Durkheim, *The Rules of Sociological Method* (New York: Free Press, 1965), 15.

65. Harry Schwartz, "Nations Have Their Phases," *New York Times Book Review*, May 8, 1960, 6.

66. Review of *The Stages of Economic Growth, Christian Science Monitor*, April 9, 1960, 23.

67. Adlai Stevenson to Walt W. Rostow, January 16, 1959, Adlai Stevenson Papers, box 69, SMML.

68. Kenneth Boulding, "The Intellectual Framework of Bad Advice," *Virginia Quarterly Review*, Autumn 1971, 602–607.

69. Barry Supple, "Revisiting Rostow," *Economic History Review*, February 1984, 107–14.

70. Kimber Charles Pearce, *Rostow, Kennedy and the Rhetoric of Foreign Aid*, 66.

71. Robert Johnson, oral history, JFKL, 17–18.

72. Nils Gilman, *Mandarins of the Future*, 209–14.

73. Walt W. Rostow to C.D. Jackson, March 5, 1959, C.D. Jackson Papers, Time Inc. File: Rostow, Walt W., box 75, DDEL.

74. Walt W. Rostow, oral history, JFKL, 10.

75. Walt W. Rostow, *Eisenhower, Kennedy, and Foreign Aid*, 157.

76. Walt W. Rostow, oral history, JFKL, 17–18.

77. See David Grossman Armstrong, "The True Believer," 451.

78. Walt W. Rostow to President Kennedy, February 13, 1961, POF, box 64A, JFKL.

79. Walt W. Rostow, oral history, JFKL, 21–23.

80. See Walt W. Rostow, *The Stages of Economic Growth*, 134.

81. David Wise, "New Frontier Born at Boston Party," *Boston Globe*, March 7, 1961.

82. "Kennedy Diplomacy," *Economist*, November 17, 1960.

83. Walt W. Rostow, oral history, JFKL, 31–32.

84. Ibid., 32.

85. A massive (if circumspect) figure in the history of 1960s U.S. foreign policy, Dean Rusk has been subject to significant scholarly attention. See Warren I. Cohen, *Dean Rusk* (New York: Cooper Square, 1980), and Thomas J. Schoenbaum, *Waging Peace and War: Dean Rusk in the Truman, Kennedy, and Johnson Years* (New York: Simon and Schuster, 1988). For Rusk's own account, see Dean Rusk, as told to Richard Rusk, *As I Saw It* (New York: W. W. Norton, 1990).

86. Walt W. Rostow to Dean Rusk, January 6, 1961, POF, box 64A, JFKL.

87. Ibid.

88. Walt W. Rostow, oral history, JFKL, 33.

89. Dean Rusk, *As I Saw It*, 534–35.

90. Walt W. Rostow, oral history, JFKL, 34–35.

91. Ibid., 23.

92. Ibid., 37.

93. Quoted in David Halberstam, *The Best and the Brightest*, 159.

THREE: RATTLING SABERS

1. Orrin Schwab, *Defending the Free World: John F. Kennedy, Lyndon Johnson, and the Vietnam War, 1961–1965* (Westport, Conn.: Praeger, 1998), 2.

2. Diane B. Kunz, *Butter and Guns: America's Cold War Economic Diplomacy* (New York: Free Press, 1997), 94. In 1963 the historian Richard Hofstadter observed, "The Sputnik shock was more than a shock to American national vanity: it brought an immense amount of attention to bear on the consequences of anti-intellectualism in the school system and in American life at large. Suddenly the national distaste for intellect appeared to be not just a disgrace but a hazard to survival." Richard Hofstadter, *Anti-Intellectualism in American Life* (New York: Knopf, 1963), 4–5.

3. Cited in Walt W. Rostow, *The Diffusion of Power*, 182.

4. Figure cited in Thomas G. Paterson, *Kennedy's Quest for Victory* (New York: Oxford University Press, 1989), 9.

5. George W. Ball, *The Past Has Another Pattern*, 175.

6. Quoted in Arthur Schlesinger Jr., *A Thousand Days: John F. Kennedy in the White House* (Boston: Houghton Mifflin, 1965), 275.

7. Ibid., 275.

8. Quoted in Robert S. McNamara, *In Retrospect: The Tragedy and Lessons of Vietnam* (New York: Vintage Books, 1995), 30.

9. Vladimir Zubok and Constantine Pleshakov, *Inside the Kremlin's Cold War: From Stalin to Khrushchev* (Cambridge, Mass.: Harvard University Press, 1996), 253.

10. Robert S. McNamara, *In Retrospect*, 30.

11. Quoted in Michael Latham, *Modernization as Ideology: American Social Science and Nation Building in the Kennedy Era* (Chapel Hill: University of North Carolina Press, 2001), 3.

12. Roger Hilsman, *To Move a Nation: The Politics of Foreign Policy in the Administration of John F. Kennedy* (Garden City, N.Y.: Doubleday, 1967), 414.

13. Quoted in James N. Giglio, *The Presidency of John F. Kennedy* (Lawrence: University of Kansas Press, 1991), 17.

14. Quoted in Thomas G. Paterson, *Kennedy's Quest for Victory*, 16. In a section of the inaugural address that would have pleased Rostow, Kennedy vowed, "To those people in the huts and villages of half the globe struggling to break the bonds of mass misery, we pledge our best efforts to help them help themselves, for whatever period is required—not because the communists are doing it, not because we seek their votes—but because it is right. If the free society cannot help the many who are poor, it can never save the few that are rich." Kennedy Inaugural Address, January 20, 1961, W. Averell Harriman Papers, box 479, Manuscript Division, LOC.

15. Quoted in Allen J. Matusow, *The Unraveling of America* (New York: HarperCollins, 1994), 31.

16. Walt W. Rostow, *The Diffusion of Power*, 126.

17. Quoted in John B. Martin, *Adlai Stevenson and the World* (New York: Doubleday, 1977), 634.

18. Walt W. Rostow to President Kennedy, August 7, 1961, NSF, box 231, JFKL.

19. For an insightful account of the Alliance for Progress, see Stephen G. Rabe, *The Most Dangerous Area in the World* (Chapel Hill: University of North Carolina Press, 1999).

20. Robert Packenham, *Liberal America and the Third World: Political Development Ideas in Foreign Aid and Social Science* (Princeton, N.J.: Princeton University Press, 1973), 59.

21. Kennedy's Special Message on Foreign Aid, March 22, 1961, NSF, box 325, JFKL.

22. Walt W. Rostow to President Kennedy, March 13, 1961, NSF, box 325, JFKL.

23. Speech by President Kennedy, April 20, 1961, in *Public Papers of the Presidents: John F. Kennedy, 1961* (Washington, D.C.: Government Printing Office, 1962), 306.

24. Walt W. Rostow, *The Stages of Economic Growth*, 162.

25. Walt W. Rostow, *The Diffusion of Power*, 168.

26. For an outstanding recently published examination of Bundy's National Security Council—the "Little State Department"—see Andrew Preston, *The War Council*.

27. Kai Bird, *The Color of Truth*, 31.

28. Walt W. Rostow, oral history, JFKL, 43–44.

29. Quoted in Robert Dallek, *An Unfinished Life: John F. Kennedy, 1917–1963* (New York: Little, Brown, 2003), 167.

30. See Seth Jacobs, *America's Miracle Man in Vietnam: Ngo Dinh Diem, Religion, Race, and U.S. Intervention in Southeast Asia* (Durham, N.C.: Duke University Press, 2005), for a fascinating examination of the factors that led the United States to back Diem in South Vietnam.

31. Quoted in George C. Herring, *America's Longest War*, 50–51.

32. Robert T. Schulzinger, *A Time for War*, 78.

33. George C. Herring, *America's Longest War*, 57.

34. Quoted ibid., 43.

35. Quoted in George McT. Kahin, *Intervention: How America Became Involved in Vietnam* (Garden City, N.Y.: Doubleday, 1987), 187.

36. Walt W. Rostow, oral history, JFKL, 44.

37. Ibid., 44.

38. Quoted in Robert Dallek, *An Unfinished Life*, 160.

39. Walt W. Rostow, *The Diffusion of Power*, 265.

40. Walt W. Rostow, oral history, JFKL, 44–45.

41. Comments by Professor Ernest R. May made at the John F. Kennedy School of Government, Harvard University, April 25, 1995. Appendix to Robert S. McNamara, *In Retrospect*, 422.

42. Clark Clifford, memorandum of conversation, January 19, 1961, *Pentagon Papers*, vol. 2, 635–37. For more on the Eisenhower-Kennedy meeting, see Fred I. Greenstein and Richard H. Immerman, "What Did Eisenhower Tell Kennedy About Indochina? The Politics of Misperception," *Journal of American History* 79 (September 1992), 568–87.

43. Robert Komer to McGeorge Bundy, January 9, 1961, NSF, box 321, JFKL.

44. For a discussion of Rostow's views on the Laos crisis, see Noam Kochavi, "Limited Accommodation, Perpetual Conflict: Kennedy, China and the Laos Crisis, 1961–1963," *Diplomatic History* 26:1 (Winter 2002), 95–135.

45. Walt W. Rostow to Dean Rusk, January 6, 1961, POF, box 64A, JFKL.

46. Walt W. Rostow to President Kennedy, March 29, 1961, NSF, box 193, JFKL.

47. Walt W. Rostow, oral history, JFKL, 45.

48. *Newsweek* clipping, March 6, 1961, located in NSF, box 325, JFKL.

49. Walt W. Rostow, oral history, JFKL, 82.

50. Walt W. Rostow to President Kennedy, March 10, 1961, POF, box 64A, JFKL.

51. Walt W. Rostow to President Kennedy, March 23, 1961, NSF, box 193, JFKL.

52. Walt W. Rostow, oral history, JFKL, 49.

53. Walt W. Rostow to President Kennedy, April 21, 1961, POF, box 64A, JFKL.

54. John Kenneth Galbraith to President Kennedy, May 10, 1961, POF, box 29, JFKL.

55. See Rudy Abramson, *Spanning the Century: The Life of W. Averell Harriman, 1891–1986* (New York: William Morrow and Co., 1992) for a comprehensive account of Harriman's life.

56. Walt W. Rostow, "Guerrilla Warfare in the Underdeveloped Areas," *Department of State Bulletin* 45 (August 7, 1961), 231.

57. Walt W. Rostow, oral history, JFKL, 82.

58. Cited in Mark Clodfelter, *The Limits of Air Power: The American Bombing of North Vietnam* (New York: Free Press, 1989), 130.

59. Walt W. Rostow, *The Diffusion of Power*, 286.

60. Walt W. Rostow to President Kennedy, June 26, 1961, NSF, box 130A, JFKL.

61. Ibid.

62. Walt W. Rostow to President Kennedy, June 30, 1961, NSF, box 231, JFKL.

63. Quoted in Robert Dallek, *An Unfinished Life*, 343.

64. Walt W. Rostow to Dean Rusk, July 13, 1961, *FRUS*: Vietnam, 1961, 206.

65. David Halberstam, *The Best and the Brightest*, 200.

66. Walt W. Rostow to President Kennedy, August 17, 1961, NSF, box 231, JFKL.

67. Maxwell D. Taylor, *Swords and Plowshares* (New York: W. W. Norton, 1972), 227. On Taylor's Vietnam-era career, see Douglas Kinnard, *The Certain Trumpet: Maxwell Taylor and the American Experience in Vietnam* (Washington, D.C.: Brassey's, 1991).

68. See Robert Buzzanco, *Masters of War: Military Dissent and Politics in the Vietnam Era* (Cambridge: Cambridge University Press, 1996), 100, and Joint Chiefs of Staff Memorandum 716–61, October 9, 1961, "Concept of Use of SEATO Forces in Southeast Asia," *Pentagon Papers*, vol. 2, 73–79.

69. John Prados, *The Blood Road: The Ho Chi Minh Trail and the Vietnam War* (New York: John Wiley and Sons, 1998), 38.

70. Walt W. Rostow, *The Diffusion of Power*, 273–74.

71. Maxwell Taylor to the State Department, October 25, 1961, *FRUS*: Vietnam, 1961, 430.

72. "Evaluations and Conclusions," tab C, n.d., NSF, Countries: Vietnam, Taylor Report, November 3, 1961, JFKL.

73. *Pentagon Papers*, vol. 2, 92.

74. "Evaluations and Conclusions," tab C, n.d., NSF, Countries: Vietnam, Taylor Report, November 3, 1961, JFKL.

75. Walt W. Rostow to President Kennedy, November 12, 1961, *FRUS*: Vietnam, 1961, 578–79.

76. Arthur Schlesinger Jr., *A Thousand Days*, 547.

77. Chester Bowles, oral history, LBJL, 99.

78. George W. Ball, *The Past Has Another Pattern*, 366.

79. Walt W. Rostow, *The Diffusion of Power*, 278.

80. Quoted in Townsend Hoopes, *The Limits of Intervention*, 21.

81. Quoted in David Halberstam, *The Best and the Brightest*, 158. In a moving eulogy to John F. Kennedy, John Kenneth Galbraith later wrote, "Mr. Kennedy hated verbosity. Though he rejoiced in politics he hated the wordiness of the political craft. He never, at least in his adult life, opened his mouth without having something to say." "A Communication," reprinted by the Houghton Mifflin Company and delivered to Averell Harriman on December 26, 1963, box 463, W. Averell Harriman Papers, Manuscript Division, LOC.

82. Quoted in Thomas G. Paterson, *Kennedy's Quest for Victory*, 18.

83. Lincoln P. Bloomfield, "Planning Foreign Policy: Can It Be Done?" *Political Science Quarterly* 93:3 (Autumn 1978).

84. George F. Kennan, *Memoirs 1925–1950* (Boston: Little, Brown, 1967), 313.

85. Cited in Arthur Schlesinger Jr., *A Thousand Days*, 445.

86. Walt W. Rostow to President Kennedy, November 29, 1961, POF, box 65, JFKL.

87. James Reston, "Shake-Up at State," *New York Times*, November 27, 1961, 24.

88. Walt W. Rostow, oral history, JFKL, 15.

89. Ibid.

90. Robert Komer to Walt W. Rostow, December 6, 1961, NSF, box 322, JFKL.

91. Walt W. Rostow to President Kennedy, December 6, 1961, POF, box 65, JFKL.

92. Lionel McGarr to Lyman Lemnitzer, December 27, 1961, *FRUS*: Vietnam, 1961, 765.

93. Bruce Palmer Jr., *The 25-Year War: America's Military Role in Vietnam* (New York: Da Capo Press, 1984).

FOUR: A DISTANT VOICE

1. See George C. Herring, *America's Longest War*, 86.

2. As Rostow wrote Kennedy late in 1961—with an apologetic tone lest he be wasting the president's time—the president's specific authorization was required to sanction combat use of this "weed killer" because "it is a kind of chemical warfare." Walt W. Rostow to President Kennedy, November 21, 1961, NSF, box 195, JFKL. The distinction between chemical and conventional warfare was not one that bothered Joint Chiefs of Staff Chairman Lyman Lemnitzer, who once remarked that "it is strange that we can bomb, kill and burn people but are not permitted to starve them." Quoted in David Kaiser, *American Tragedy*, 165.

3. The reality was a little different. The veracity of the military reporting was being seriously questioned by the journalists Neil Sheehan and David Halberstam.

4. Roger Hilsman, *To Move a Nation*, 444.

5. Walt W. Rostow, *The Diffusion of Power*, 290.

6. Walt W. Rostow, interview with the author, August 7, 2002.

7. Figure cited in Orrin Schwab, *Defending the Free World*, 52.

8. Douglas Blaufarb, *The Counterinsurgency Era: U.S. Doctrine and Performance* (New York: Free Press, 1977), 60.

9. Draft paper by Robert Thompson, undated, *FRUS*: Vietnam, 1962, 104. Robert Thompson was the architect of Great Britain's defeat of the communist insurgency in Malaya.

10. See Philip E. Catton, "Counter-Insurgency and Nation Building: The Strategic Hamlet Program in South Vietnam, 1961–1963," *International History Review* 21:4 (December 1999), 918–40.

11. Ibid., 935.

12. Officer in Charge of Vietnam Affairs (Theodore Heavner) to Ambassador Nolting, April 27, 1962, *FRUS*: Vietnam, 1962, 359.

13. David Halberstam, *The Making of a Quagmire* (New York: Random House, 1965), 187.

14. *Pentagon Papers*, vol. 2, 131.

15. Cited in Thomas G. Paterson, *Kennedy's Quest for Victory*, 242.

16. Roger Hilsman, *To Move a Nation*, 220.

17. Neil Sheehan, *A Bright Shining Lie: John Paul Vann and America in Vietnam* (London: Jonathan Cape, 1989), 309–12.

18. Robert Johnson to Walt W. Rostow, October 16, 1962, *FRUS*: Vietnam, 1962, 736–38. Andrew Krepinevich in *The Army and Vietnam* (Baltimore: Johns Hopkins University Press, 1986) argues that counterinsurgency was the right strategy in theory, but the U.S. Army's dismissal of the strategic hamlet program as "a fad" helped contribute to its demise. Securing the countryside would have been less costly in human and financial terms, Krepinevich argues, and might have also conceivably created a more durable South Vietnam.

19. James C. Scott, *Seeing Like a State: How Certain Schemes to Improve the Human Condition Have Failed* (New Haven, Conn.: Yale University Press, 1998), 343.

20. Memorandum from Kenneth Young to Walt W. Rostow, February 17, 1961, NSF, box 325, JFKL.

21. Cited in Michael Latham, *Modernization as Ideology*, 112.

22. Walt W. Rostow, *The Diffusion of Power*, 286.

23. The historian Larry E. Cable argues that U.S. policymakers and the military consistently overestimated North Vietnam's contribution to the southern insurgency, while neglecting its more significant indigenous roots. Thus, "in an attempt to solve a problem that did not exist [the United States] created a problem that could not be solved." See Larry E. Cable, *Conflict of Myths: The Development of Counterinsurgency Doctrine and the Vietnam War* (New York: New York University Press, 1988), 225, and *Unholy Grail: The U.S. and the Wars in Vietnam, 1965–1968* (London: Routledge, 1991).

24. Bernard Fall, "Master of the Red Jab," *Saturday Evening Post*, November 24, 1962, reprinted in *Reporting Vietnam: American Journalism, 1959–1975* (New York: Library of America, 1998), 21, 27.

25. Ibid., 28.

26. Bernard B. Fall, *Viet-Nam Witness: 1953–1966* (New York: Praeger, 1966), 114.

27. Robert Brigham, *Guerrilla Diplomacy: The NLF's Foreign Relations and the Vietnam War* (Ithaca, N.Y.: Cornell University Press, 1999).

28. John Lewis Gaddis, *Strategies of Containment: A Critical Appraisal of Postwar American National Security Policy* (New York: Oxford University Press, 1982), 200.

29. Walt W. Rostow to Dean Rusk, February 14, 1962, NSF, box 294, JFKL.

30. Final draft of Basic National Security Policy, June 22, 1962, NSF, box 294, JFKL, 5, 11.

31. Ibid., 3, 4, 25.

32. Ibid., 28, 182.

33. McGeorge Bundy to Walt W. Rostow, April 13, 1962, NSF, box 294, JFKL.

34. Carl Kaysen, oral history, JFKL, 99–102. Quoted in Bruce Kuklick, *Blind Oracles: Intellectuals and War from Kennan to Kissinger* (Princeton, N.J.: Princeton University Press, 2006).

35. Carl Kaysen to Walt W. Rostow, April 16, 1962, NSF, box 294, JFKL.

36. Maxwell Taylor to Walt W. Rostow, April 23, 1962, NSF, box 294, JFKL.

37. Letter from George Kennan to Walt W. Rostow, May 15, 1962, *FRUS*: National Security Policy, Vietnam, 1962, 8, 286–87.

38. Ibid., 288–89.

39. Ibid., 299.

40. Ibid., 290.

41. Walt W. Rostow, oral history, JFKL, 64–65.

42. Robert S. McNamara with James Blight, *Wilson's Ghost: Reducing the Risk of Conflict, Killing, and Catastrophe in the 21st Century* (New York: Public Affairs, 2001).

43. Robert Komer to McGeorge Bundy, October 24, 1962, NSF, box 322, JFKL.

44. Robert Komer to Walt W. Rostow, October 26, 1962, box 322, JFKL.

45. Walt W. Rostow, oral history, JFKL, 105–107.

46. Ibid., 107.

47. Kai Bird, *The Color of Truth*, 16.

48. Ernest R. May and Philip Zelikow, *The Kennedy Tapes: Inside the White House During the Cuban Missile Crisis* (Cambridge, Mass.: Harvard University Press, 1998), 436.

49. Ibid., 437.

50. Walt W. Rostow to Dean Rusk, November 28, 1962, NSF, Papers of Walt W. Rostow, box 13, LBJL.

51. Walt W. Rostow to Averell Harriman, February 2, 1963, NSF, Papers of Walt W. Rostow, box 13, LBJL.

52. Walt W. Rostow to Dean Rusk, July 4, 1963.

53. Walt W. Rostow to McGeorge Bundy, January 2, 1963, NSF, box 303, JFKL.

54. Walt W. Rostow to Dean Rusk, January 4, 1963, NSF, box 303, JFKL.

55. McGeorge Bundy to Bromley Smith, July 30, 1963, NSF, box 314, JFKL.

56. Robert Komer to McGeorge Bundy, January 12, 1963, NSF, box 303, JFKL.

57. Robert Komer to McGeorge Bundy, January 12, 1963, NSF, box 303, JFKL.

58. Quoted in Fredrik Logevall, *Choosing War: The Lost Chance for Peace and the Escalation of the War in Vietnam* (Berkeley: University of California Press, 1999), 377.

59. Walt W. Rostow, *The Diffusion of Power*, 288.

60. Walt W. Rostow to Dean Rusk, June 7, 1963, NSF, Papers of Walt W. Rostow, box 13, LBJL.

61. Quoted in George C. Herring, *America's Longest War*, 96.

62. Henry Cabot Lodge to Dean Rusk, August 29, 1963, *Pentagon Papers*, vol. 2, 240.

63. Walt W. Rostow, oral history, JFKL, 85.

64. Roger Hilsman, *To Move a Nation*, 482.

65. Quoted in George C. Herring, *America's Longest War*, 104.

66. Quoted in Robert Schulzinger, *A Time for War*, 122.

67. Quoted in George C. Herring, *America's Longest War*, 106. On November 4, 1963, a jubilant John Kenneth Galbraith wrote to Averell Harriman, "The South Viet Nam coup is a great feather in your cap. Do get me a list of all the people who told us there was no alternative to Diem." John Kenneth Galbraith to Averell Harriman, November 4, 1963, W. Averell Harriman Papers, box 463, Manuscript Division, LOC.

68. Arthur Schlesinger Jr., *A Thousand Days*, 997–98.

69. Numerous commentators and historians take Diem's assassination to be a dark moment in U.S. foreign-policy history. They argue that Diem provided a stability

that was never replicated by his successors—that Diem represented South Vietnam's last, best hope. See Ellen Hammer, *A Death in November: America in Vietnam, 1963* (New York: Dutton, 1987); Patrick L. Hatcher, *The Suicide of an Elite: American Internationalists and Vietnam* (Stanford, Calif.: Stanford University Press, 1990); and Cecil B. Currey, *Edward Lansdale: The Unquiet American* (Boston: Houghton Mifflin, 1988). For a corrective to this view, see David Anderson, *Trapped by Success: The Eisenhower Administration and Vietnam, 1953–1961* (New York: Columbia University Press, 1991).

70. Walt W. Rostow, oral history, JFKL, 84

71. Walt W. Rostow, interview with the author, August 7, 2002.

72. Walt W. Rostow to Dean Rusk, November 1, 1963, NSF, Papers of Walt W. Rostow, box 13, LBJL.

73. Roger Hilsman, oral history, Columbia University Archives, 23.

74. David Kaiser, *American Tragedy*, 8.

75. Walt W. Rostow, oral history, LBJL, 23.

76. Walt W. Rostow, oral history, JFKL, 87.

77. Walt W. Rostow to President Johnson, September 15, 1967, NSF, Memos to the President: Walt W. Rostow, box 22, LBJL.

78. Quoted in *Washington Post*, July 14, 1971.

79. Quoted in Andrew Rotter (ed.), *Light at the End of the Tunnel: A Vietnam War Anthology* (Washington D.C.: SR Books, 1999), 68.

80. *Public Papers of the President: John F. Kennedy, 1963* (Washington, D.C.: Government Printing Office, 1964), 894–98.

81. Lyndon B. Johnson, *The Vantage Point: Perspectives of the Presidency, 1963–1969* (New York: Holt, Rinehart and Winston, 1971), 153.

82. Walt W. Rostow, oral history, JFKL, 143. Here Rostow's list of usual suspects is a peculiar one. Joseph Alsop was a hawk, Scotty Reston was a moderate, and Phil Graham later supported the war.

83. Memorandum for the Record, November 25, 1963, Meeting Notes File, box 1, LBJL.

84. Quoted in Robert Schulzinger, *A Time For War*, 127.

FIVE: THE ROSTOW THESIS

Epigraph. Walt W. Rostow to William Bundy, Papers of Walt W. Rostow, box 13, LBJL.

1. Quoted in Warren Cohen and Nancy Tucker (eds.), *Lyndon Johnson Confronts the World: American Foreign Policy, 1963–1968* (Cambridge: Cambridge University Press, 1994), 147.

2. Quoted in Walter Isaacson and Evan Thomas, *The Wise Men* (New York: Simon and Schuster, 1986), 643.

3. See Robert Caro, *The Master of the Senate: The Years of Lyndon Johnson, Volume III* (New York: Knopf, 2002), for an artful account of Johnson's Senate career.

4. Quoted in Thomas Schwartz, *Lyndon Johnson and Europe: In the Shadow of Vietnam* (Cambridge, Mass.: Harvard University Press, 2003), 29. Schwartz provides an important corrective to LBJ's reputation as a ham-fisted manager of American foreign

policy by concentrating on his deft handling of the central Cold War theater: Western Europe.

5. Quoted in Robert Packenham, *Liberal America and the Third World*, 91.

6. On LBJ's lack of interest in African affairs, see Terence Lyons, "Keeping Africa off the Agenda," in Warren Cohen and Nancy Tucker (eds.), *Lyndon Johnson Confronts the World*. As Lyons writes, "From Johnson's perspective, Africa was best kept on the back burner, handled by the State Department bureaucracy or ignored altogether. Africa was the furthest corner of the world to Johnson, the place to threaten to send indiscreet officials who drew his ire" (245).

7. David Ekbladh, "Mr. TVA: Grass Roots Development, David Lilienthal, and the Rise of the Tennessee Valley Authority as a Symbol for U.S. Overseas Development, 1933–1973," *Diplomatic History* 26:3 (Summer 2002), 335–74.

8. Quoted in Richard E. Neustadt and Ernest R. May, *Thinking in Time: The Uses of History for Decision-Makers* (New York: Free Press, 1986), 86.

9. Quoted in Warren Cohen and Nancy Tucker (eds.), *Lyndon Johnson Confronts the World*, 50.

10. Quoted in Robert Schulzinger, *A Time for War*, 126.

11. *Pentagon Papers*, vol. 3, 200.

12. Walt W. Rostow, *The Diffusion of Power*, 505, and *Public Papers of the President: Lyndon B. Johnson, 1963–1964* (Washington, D.C.: Government Printing Office, 1964), 116.

13. Robert Komer to McGeorge Bundy, NSF, Agency File, box 51, LBJL.

14. Walt W. Rostow to Dean Rusk, February 7, 1964, NSF, Papers of Walt W. Rostow, box 13, LBJL.

15. "The Reminiscences of Roger Hilsman," 1982, Columbia University Rare Books and Manuscripts Library, 42–43.

16. Joseph Alsop, "Viet Blockade Possible," *Washington Post*, February 24, 1964.

17. *Pentagon Papers*, vol. 3, 201–202.

18. Walt W. Rostow to Dean Rusk, February 14, 1964, NSF, Papers of Walt W. Rostow, box 13, LBJL.

19. Walt W. Rostow to Dean Rusk, February 15, 1964, *FRUS*: Vietnam, 1964, 81–82.

20. Walt W. Rostow, interview with the author, August 7, 2002.

21. *Pentagon Papers*, vol. 3, 234.

22. Mark Clodfelter, *The Limits of Air Power*, 76.

23. Curtis LeMay with MacKinlay Kantor, *Mission with LeMay* (Garden City, N.Y.: Doubleday, 1965), 565.

24. Quoted in Mark Perry, *Four Stars* (Boston: Houghton Mifflin, 1989), 76.

25. Walt W. Rostow to Robert S. McNamara, September 19, 1964, *FRUS*: Vietnam, 1964, 782–85.

26. Carl von Clausewitz, *On War*, edited and translated by Michael Howard and Peter Paret (Princeton, N.J.: Princeton University Press, 1976), 585. For a Clausewitzian critique of U.S. military strategy see Harry Summers, *On Strategy: A Critical Analysis of the Vietnam War* (Novato, Calif.: Presidio Press, 1982), and Bruce Palmer Jr., *The 25-Year War*.

27. Quoted in Wallace J. Thies, *When Governments Collide: Coercion and Diplomacy in the Vietnam Conflict, 1964–1968* (Berkeley: University of California Press, 1980), 402.

28. Robert H. Johnson, "Escalation Then and Now," *Foreign Policy* 60 (Fall 1985), 139.

29. See David Halberstam, *The Best and the Brightest*, 356–58, for an in-depth analysis of the Johnson report and its repercussions.

30. Roger Hilsman to Dean Rusk, March 14, 1966. Quoted in Roger Hilsman, *To Move a Nation*, 536.

31. Seymour Martin Lipset, *Political Man: The Social Bases of Politics* (New York: Anchor Books, 1963), 442–43.

32. William H. Sullivan to Dean Rusk, February 25, 1964, NSF, Papers of Walt W. Rostow, box 13, LBJL.

33. Walt W. Rostow to William H. Sullivan, February 26, 1964, NSF, Papers of Walt W. Rostow, box 13, LBJL.

34. Walt W. Rostow to Dean Rusk, May 6, 1964, NSF, Papers of Walt W. Rostow, box 13, LBJL.

35. Quoted in H. R. McMaster, *Dereliction of Duty: Lyndon Johnson, Robert McNamara, the Joint Chiefs of Staff and the Lies That Led to Vietnam* (New York: HarperCollins, 1997), 163.

36. Summary Record of NSC Executive Committee Meeting, May 24, 1964, *FRUS: Vietnam, 1964*, 370.

37. On Goldwater's career, see Robert Alan Goldberg, *Barry Goldwater* (New Haven, Conn.: Yale University Press, 1995), and for a sympathetic account of his performance in the 1964 election, see William Middendorf, *Glorious Defeat: Barry Goldwater's Presidential Campaign and the Origins of the Conservative Movement* (New York: Basic Books, 2006.)

38. See NSAM 288, March 17, 1964, *FRUS: Vietnam, 1964*, 156.

39. The best single-volume account of Johnson's decision to escalate the Vietnam War in 1964/65 is Fredrik Logevall's *Choosing War*. Logevall argues that U.S. policymakers opted to escalate the war to protect their personal credibility as much as anything else. Logevall also makes the compelling case that LBJ's decision to escalate was far from inevitable. He criticizes the British government and Democratic leaders in the Senate for not offering a frank appraisal of the unfolding conflict and argues that real choices were available to the president. A multiarchival analysis of the highest order, Logevall's analysis nevertheless overestimates the clout that international actors might have exerted at the time. Brian VanDeMark's *Into the Quagmire: Lyndon Johnson and the Escalation of the Vietnam War* (New York: Oxford University Press, 1991) spends more time on Johnson's advisers, but is too restrained in his reluctance to criticize LBJ's fateful decision making.

40. Telephone conversation between Lyndon Johnson and Robert S. McNamara, March 2, 1964, quoted in Michael Beschloss (ed.), *Taking Charge: The Johnson White House Tapes, 1963–1964* (New York: Simon and Schuster, 1997), 258.

41. Telephone conversation between President Johnson and Walt W. Rostow, March 4, 1964, 6:05 p.m., WH Series, 3/64, WH6403.3, PNO 4, 2346, box 3, LBJL.

42. Walt W. Rostow to President Johnson, NSF, Files of Walt W. Rostow, box 6, LBJL.

43. Quoted in "Scholar Who's Number 2," *Business Week*, March 25, 1967, 12.

44. Summary Record of Meetings, Honolulu, June 2, 1964, *FRUS: Vietnam, 1964,* 430. Italics in original.

45. Department of Defense Summary, August 3, 1964, Papers of Walt W. Rostow, box 13, LBJL.

46. Ibid.

47. *Pentagon Papers,* vol. 3, 201–202.

48. Quoted in Robert D. Schulzinger, *A Time for War,* 151.

49. James Thomson Jr., quoted in Jonathan Mirsky, "Wartime Lies," *New York Review of Books,* October 9, 2003.

50. Quoted in David Halberstam, *The Best and the Brightest,* 81.

51. Quoted in Edwin E. Moïse, *Tonkin Gulf and the Escalation of the Vietnam War* (Chapel Hill: University of North Carolina Press, 1996), 243.

52. Walt W. Rostow to Dean Rusk, August 5, 1964, Papers of Walt W. Rostow, box 13, LBJL.

53. Quoted in John Prados, *The Blood Road,* 68.

54. Walt W. Rostow, *The Diffusion of Power,* 507.

55. *Department of State Bulletin,* August 24, 1964.

56. H. R. McMaster, *Dereliction of Duty,* 156.

57. SIGMA II-64, Final Report, NSF, Agency File, box 30, LBJL.

58. Ibid. For a wide-ranging analysis of SIGMA II, consult H. R. McMaster, *Dereliction of Duty,* 156–63.

59. H. R. McMaster, *Dereliction of Duty,* 158.

60. Quoted in Deborah Shapley, *Promise and Power: The Life and Times of Robert McNamara* (Boston: Little, Brown, 1993), 314.

61. William C. Westmoreland, *A Soldier Reports,* 63.

62. McGeorge Bundy, Memorandum for the Record, September 14, 1964, Meeting Notes File, box 1, LBJL.

63. Walt W. Rostow to Dean Rusk, September 19, 1964, *FRUS: Vietnam, 1964,* 784.

64. Ibid.

65. Fredrik Logevall, *Choosing War,* 269–74, and Mark Clodfelter, *The Limits of Air Power,* 52–56.

66. For an original examination of Johnson's rationale for escalation, see Yuen Foong Khong, *Korea, Munich, Dien Bien Phu, and the Vietnam Decisions of 1965* (Princeton, N.J.: Princeton University Press, 1992). Khong argues that the historical analogies touted at the time help us understand why certain decisions were made. Khong concludes that the lessons of the Korean War (a well-executed limited conflict in which the only mistake was to rile China) defined Johnson's terms of intervention in Vietnam.

67. Walt W. Rostow, *The Diffusion of Power,* 508.

68. Ibid., 508.

69. For Rostow's criticism of Johnson's military timidity with regard to waging the Vietnam War, see Walt W. Rostow, foreword to C. Dale Walton, *The Myth of Inevitable U.S. Defeat in Vietnam* (London: Frank Cass, 2002), ix–x, and Walt W. Rostow, *Concept and Controversy,* 300–304.

70. Telegram from President Johnson to the ambassador in Vietnam (Maxwell Taylor), December 30, 1965, *FRUS: Vietnam, 1964*, 1059.

71. Telephone conversation between President Johnson and Robert S. McNamara, January 22, 1965, in Michael Beschloss, *Reaching for Glory: Lyndon Johnson's Secret White House Tapes, 1964–1965* (New York: Simon and Schuster, 2001), 166.

72. H. R. McMaster, *Dereliction of Duty*, 215, and William Westmoreland, *A Soldier Reports*, 115.

73. McGeorge Bundy to President Johnson, February 7, 1965, *FRUS: Vietnam, 1964*, 185.

74. H. R. McMaster, *Dereliction of Duty*, 215, and William Westmoreland, *A Soldier Reports*, 115.

75. Walt W. Rostow to Dean Rusk, February 13, 1964, *FRUS: Vietnam, 1964*, 73.

76. "Vietnam Air Strikes Get 67% US Approval," *Washington Post*, February 16, 1965. Of the respondents, 31 percent agreed that the bombing campaign should continue at the risk of nuclear war. This was music to Rostow's ears, if not to Johnson's.

77. Walt W. Rostow to Dean Rusk, February 17, 1965, NSF, Country File: Vietnam, box 13, LBJL.

78. *Public Papers of the President: Lyndon B. Johnson, 1965* (Washington, D.C.: Government Printing Office, 1966), 394–99. Kathleen Turner argues that Johnson's desire to appease both hawks and doves is epitomized by his Johns Hopkins address. Turner examines in detail the futile public effort to convey an image of the war as an altruistic struggle. See Kathleen Turner, *Lyndon Johnson's Dual War: Vietnam and the Press* (Chicago: University of Chicago Press, 1985). Averell Harriman later wondered whether the TVA analogy was not somewhat detached from reality: "I don't want to depreciate the long-term value of Mekong development, but frankly I have found they are so far in the future that the Asian people and their leaders want action from which they can see results now." Averell Harriman to Walt W. Rostow, October 11, 1966, W. Averell Harriman Papers, box 520, Manuscript Division, LOC.

79. McGeorge Bundy, handwritten notes on agenda for luncheon meeting, April 6, 1965, Files of McGeorge Bundy, box 19, LBJL.

80. Memorandum from the director of the USIA (Carl T. Rowan) to President Johnson, February 27, 1965, *FRUS: Vietnam, January–June 1965*, 383.

81. Ibid.

82. Walt W. Rostow to Robert McNamara, April 1, 1965, Papers of Walt W. Rostow, box 13, LBJL.

83. Walt W. Rostow to Dean Rusk, July 26, 1965, Papers of Walt W. Rostow, box 13, LBJL.

84. Walt W. Rostow to Dean Rusk, September 8, 1965, *FRUS: Vietnam, June–December 1965*, 378.

85. Walt W. Rostow to President Johnson, July 31, 1967, *FRUS: Vietnam, 1967*, 652.

86. Quoted in Michael Beschloss, *Reaching for Glory*, 379.

87. Walt W. Rostow to Dean Rusk, May 17, 1965, NSF, Files of McGeorge Bundy, box 18, LBJL.

88. Telephone conversation between Lyndon Johnson and Dean Rusk, November 29, 1965, Presidential Tape Recordings Series, Tape WH6511.09, LBJL.

89. Telephone conversation between Lyndon Johnson and Robert S. McNamara, December 8, 1965, Presidential Tape Recording Series, Tape WH6512.02, LBJL.

90. Walt W. Rostow to President Johnson, December 23, 1965, *FRUS*: Vietnam, July–December 1965, 692–98.

91. Robert S. McNamara to President Johnson, July 20, 1965, NSF, Memos to the President: McGeorge Bundy, box 4, LBJL.

92. Walt W. Rostow, *The Diffusion of Power*, 448.

93. Ibid., 449.

94. Quoted in James Cameron, *Here Is Your Enemy* (New York: Holt, Rinehart and Winston, 1966), 115.

95. George Ball, quoted in Notes of Meeting, December 17, 1965, *FRUS*: Vietnam, July–December 1965, 645–46.

96. Special Intelligence Supplement, "An Appraisal of the Bombing of North Vietnam," December 21, 1965, *FRUS*: Vietnam, July–December 1965, 684.

SIX: THE PROPHET RETURNS

1. See Rudy Abramson, *Spanning the Century*, 637.

2. Letter from Walt W. Rostow to Averell Harriman, January 28, 1966, Papers of Walt W. Rostow, box 13, LBJL.

3. Ibid. The air war in Vietnam has received substantial attention in the historiography, although Rostow's role in shaping it has gone relatively unnoticed. In addition to Mark Clodfelter, *The Limits of Air Power*, see James Clay Thompson, *Rolling Thunder: Understanding Policy and Program Failure* (Chapel Hill: University of North Carolina Press, 1980); John Schlight, *The United States Air Force in Southeast Asia: The War in Vietnam; The Years of the Offensive, 1965–1968* (Washington, D.C.: Office of Air Force History, 1988); and Donald J. Mrozek, *Air Power and the Ground War in Vietnam: Ideas and Actions* (Maxwell, Ala.: Air University Press, 1989).

4. Notes of Meeting, January 22, 1966, *FRUS*: Vietnam, 1966, 105.

5. Notes of Meeting, January 24, 1966, *FRUS*: Vietnam, 1966, 127–28.

6. Notes of Meeting, January 28, 1966, *FRUS*: Vietnam, 1966, 177.

7. Ibid.

8. Robert Komer, oral history, LBJL, 27–28.

9. Memorandum from Jack Valenti to President Johnson, January 31, 1966, *FRUS*: Vietnam, 1966, 193.

10. Walt W. Rostow, oral history, LBJL, 21–22.

11. Walt W. Rostow, *The Diffusion of Power*, 454–55.

12. Kai Bird, *The Color of Truth*, 351.

13. Telephone conversation between Robert S. McNamara and Lyndon Johnson, February 27, 1966, Presidential Tape Recording Series, Tape WH6602.10, LBJL.

14. Telephone conversation between Robert S. McNamara and Lyndon Johnson, February 28, 1966, Presidential Tape Recording Series, Tape WH6602.10, LBJL.

15. Jack Valenti, oral history, Interview 4, LBJL, 26–27.

16. Dean Rusk, oral history, LBJL, 20.

17. "The Rostow Appointment," *New York Times*, April 2, 1966, A1.

18. M. Destler, "National Security Management: What Presidents Have Wrought," *Political Science Quarterly* 95:4 (Winter 1980–1981), 579.

19. Walt W. Rostow, oral history, LBJL, 26.

20. Ibid., 27.

21. Arthur Schlesinger Jr., oral history, LBJL, 30.

22. Robert S. McNamara, *In Retrospect*, and Robert S. McNamara with James Blight et al., *Argument Without End: In Search of Answers to the Vietnam Tragedy* (Washington, D.C.: Public Affairs Press, 2000). McNamara also made the allegation during "A Colloquium with Robert S. McNamara," held in Sidney Sussex College, Cambridge, on May 8, 2002.

23. Richard Helms, oral history, LBJL, 30.

24. John Prados, *Keeper of the Keys: A History of the National Security Council from Truman to Bush* (Scranton, Penn.: William Morrow and Sons, 1991), 241.

25. Quoted ibid., 240.

26. Figures cited in Maurice Isserman and Michael Kazin, *America Divided: The Civil War of the 1960s* (New York: Oxford University Press, 2000), 190.

27. Ibid., 187.

28. Quoted in David Halberstam, *The Best and the Brightest*, 627. Halberstam does not name the "Kennedy intimate."

29. Walt W. Rostow, oral history, LBJL, 21.

30. See Robert Caro, *The Master of the Senate*, and Robert Dallek, *Flawed Giant: Lyndon Johnson and His Times* (New York: Oxford University Press, 1998).

31. Robert Dallek, *Flawed Giant*, 297.

32. Joseph Califano, oral history, LBJL, 8.

33. Walt W. Rostow, oral history, LBJL, 21–22.

34. Ibid., 14.

35. Quoted in George C. Herring, *LBJ and Vietnam: A Different Kind of War* (Austin: University of Texas Press, 1995), 11.

36. Townsend Hoopes, *The Limits of Intervention*, 20.

37. Walt W. Rostow to President Johnson, April 5, 1966, *FRUS*: Vietnam, 1966, 331.

38. Walt W. Rostow to President Johnson, Dean Rusk, and Robert S. McNamara, May 6, 1966, NSF, Memos to the President: Walt W. Rostow, box 7, LBJL.

39. Walt W. Rostow to President Johnson, May 10, 1966, NSF, Memos to the President: Walt W. Rostow, box 7, LBJL.

40. Walt W. Rostow to President Johnson, April 21, 1966, NSF, Memos to the President: Walt W. Rostow, box 4, LBJL, 42.

41. Summary Notes of 550th NSC Meeting, June 17, 1966, *FRUS*: Vietnam, 1966, 439.

42. Ibid., 438.

43. Robert Komer, oral history, LBJL, 42.

44. Walt W. Rostow to President Johnson, June 25, 1966, NSF, Memos to the President: Walt W. Rostow, box 8, LBJL.

45. Quoted in Robert Schulzinger, *A Time for War*, 209.

46. Walt W. Rostow to President Johnson, July 7, 1966, *FRUS*: Vietnam, 1966, 492.

47. Gallup poll, July 24, 1966, cited in Robert Dallek, *Flawed Giant*, 376.

48. Telegram from Prime Minister Wilson to President Johnson, June 3, 1966, Prime Minister's Office, 13/1808, TNA: PRO.

49. Joint CIA-DIA Intelligence Report, August 1966, *FRUS*: Vietnam, 1966, 615.

50. SNIE Report, *Pentagon Papers*, vol. 4, 5–6.

51. Figures cited in Guenter Lewy, *America in Vietnam* (New York: Oxford University Press, 1987), 395.

52. Walt W. Rostow to President Johnson, August 2, 1966, *FRUS*: Vietnam, 1966, 551.

53. Quoted in Anatoly Dobrynin, *In Confidence*, 142.

54. Averell Harriman, memorandum of conversation with Walt W. Rostow and President Johnson, May 30, 1966, W. Averell Harriman Papers, box 52, Manuscript Division, LOC.

55. See Jason Sumner Study, "The Effects of U.S. Bombing in North Vietnam," *Pentagon Papers*, vol. 4, 111–20, and Mark Clodfelter, *The Limits of Air Power*, 99–100.

56. Robert S. McNamara to President Johnson, October 14, 1966, NSF, NSC Meetings, box 2, LBJL.

57. Walt W. Rostow to President Johnson, September 15, 1966, *FRUS*: Vietnam, 1966, 633–34.

58. See George C. Herring, *America's Longest War*, 147.

59. Robert S. McNamara to President Johnson, October 14, 1966, *FRUS*: Vietnam, 1966, 728.

60. Walt W. Rostow to President Johnson, October 24, 1966, ibid., 777.

61. CIA Intelligence Memorandum, November 1966, ibid., 802–803.

62. See George C. Herring, *LBJ and Vietnam*, 20.

63. Walt W. Rostow to President Johnson, December 5, 1966, NSF, Memos to the President: Walt W. Rostow, box 11, LBJL.

64. CIA Report, "The View from Hanoi," November 30, 1966, attached to Walt W. Rostow to President Johnson, December 5, 1966, NSF, Memos to the President: Walt W. Rostow, box 11, LBJL.

65. Walt W. Rostow to President Johnson, November 9, 1966, *FRUS*: Vietnam, 1966, 812.

66. See Editorial Note, ibid., 816.

67. President Johnson to Robert S. McNamara, transcript of telephone conversation, *FRUS*: Vietnam, 1966, 817.

68. Walt W. Rostow to President Johnson, November 28, 1966, NSF, Memos to the President: Walt W. Rostow, box 11, LBJL.

69. Cable from Walt W. Rostow to Henry Cabot Lodge, December 9, 1966, NSF, Memos to the President: Walt W. Rostow, box 11, LBJL. Symington visited South Vietnam again in September 1967 and his doubts were yet more pronounced. Yet again Rostow asked the U.S. ambassador in Saigon—Ellsworth Bunker at this stage—to help allay those reservations. "As you know, Senator Symington is in a most difficult mood about Vietnam: vacillating between all-out bombing and get out at almost any price . . . Anything you can do to stabilize his view of the problem

and give him some soundly based evidence that there is light at the end of the tunnel would be greatly appreciated." Walt W. Rostow to Ellsworth Bunker, September 24, NSF, Memos to the President: Walt W. Rostow, box 22, LBJL.

70. Quoted in John T. Rourke, *Congress and the Presidency in American Foreign Policy-Making* (Boulder, Colo.: Westview Press, 1983), 148.

71. Walt W. Rostow to President Johnson, November 30, 1966, NSF, Files of Walt W. Rostow, box 4, LBJL.

72. Ibid.

73. George C. Herring, *America's Longest War*, 153–55.

SEVEN: POSTPONING THE INEVITABLE

1. Quiang Zhai, *China and the Vietnam Wars, 1950–1975* (Chapel Hill: University of North Carolina Press, 2000), 132–35.

2. Ibid., 115.

3. Walt W. Rostow to President Johnson, July 25, 1966, *FRUS*: China, 1998, 360.

4. Walt W. Rostow to President Johnson, September 20, 1966, *FRUS*: China, 1998, 396.

5. Walt W. Rostow to President Johnson, January 9, 1967, *FRUS*: China, 1998, 499.

6. Walt W. Rostow to President Johnson, January 13, 1967, *FRUS*: China, 1998, 502.

7. Walt W. Rostow to President Johnson, May 8, 1967, *FRUS*: China, 1998, 555.

8. Walt W. Rostow to President Johnson, November 30, 1966, NSF, Files of Walt W. Rostow, box 4, LBJL.

9. After the NSC staffer James Thomson departed for Harvard, he satirized Johnson's NSC meetings in *The Atlantic Monthly*. Thomson disguises Walt W. Rostow with the name Herman Breslau and Robert Komer with the pseudonym Charles Homer. To quote Thomson, "If we could dump rice and airlift pigs at Hué and Danang, Breslau was pretty sure the other side would cave. He cautioned, however, that this was merely a hunch. 'It is not the kind of smell you can hang your hat on.' In reply, Mr. Homer said that Mr. Breslau was full of crap; Mr. Breslau had never understood Vietnam and should stop trying. Things were very, very bad but they would get infinitely worse if we dumped rice and pigs." This faux-exchange failed to amuse Johnson's national security adviser. Rostow sent Thomson's article to the president with the accompanying comment: "There is nothing really effective to be done about all this . . . We will limit our response to pointing out that people have differing ideas about what is funny." Walt W. Rostow to President Johnson, NSF, May 1, 1967, Memos to the President: Walt W. Rostow, box 15, LBJL.

10. Chairman of the Joint Chiefs (Wheeler) to Robert S. McNamara, November 8, 1966, NSF, Country File: Vietnam, box 74, LBJL.

11. James G. Hershberg, "Who Murdered 'Marigold'? New Evidence on the Mysterious Failure of Poland's Secret Initiative to Start U.S.–North Vietnamese Peace Talks, 1966," *Cold War International History Project Working Paper* (April 2000).

12. John Dumbrell and Sylvia Ellis, "British Involvement in Vietnam Peace Initiatives, 1966–1967: Marigolds, Sunflowers, and 'Kosygin Week.'" *Diplomatic History* 27:1, (January 2003), 113–49.

13. Walt W. Rostow to President Johnson, January 17, 1967, NSF, Country File: Vietnam, box 256, LBJL.

14. In July 1966 Rostow had told George Ball that contacts with Moscow "should be direct and with no intermediary." See teleconference, Rostow-Ball, July 1, 1966, Papers of George Ball, box 7, LBJL.

15. Walt W. Rostow to President Johnson, January 3 1967, *FRUS*: Vietnam, 1967, 14.

16. George C. Herring, *LBJ and Vietnam*, 102–111.

17. For firsthand accounts of Britain's negotiating initiative, see Harold Wilson, *The Labour Government 1964–1970: A Personal Record* (London: Weidenfeld and Nicolson, 1971); George Brown, *In My Way* (London: Penguin, 1972); and Chester Cooper, *The Lost Crusade* (New York: Dodd, Mead and Company, 1970).

18. In July 1966 Lyndon Johnson told Harold Wilson that to support his Vietnam policy, "a platoon of bagpipers would be sufficient, it was the British flag that was needed." See Harold Wilson, *The Labour Government*, 264.

19. For an in-depth analysis of the Wilson peace initiative, see John Dumbrell and Sylvia Ellis, "British Involvement in Vietnam Peace Initiatives, 1966–1967." For more on Phase A–Phase B and the Wilson initiative, see also George C. Herring, *LBJ and Vietnam*; Lloyd C. Gardner, *Pay Any Price: Lyndon Johnson and the Wars for Vietnam* (Chicago: Ivan R. Dee, 1995), 345–50; and T. J. Schoenbaum, *Waging Peace and War: Dean Rusk in the Truman, Kennedy, and Johnson Years* (New York: Simon and Schuster, 1988), 455–58.

20. George C. Herring, *A Different Kind of War*, 109.

21. George C. Herring, *The Secret Diplomacy of the Vietnam War: The Negotiating Volumes of the Pentagon Papers* (Austin: University of Texas Press, 1983), 437–38.

22. Michael Palliser to Harold Wilson, February 7, 1967, "Vietnam," PREM 13/1917, TNA: PRO.

23. "Visit of Mr. Kosygin to London: Record of 10 Downing Street meeting," February 7, 1967, Foreign and Commonwealth Office (FCO), 16/633, TNA: PRO.

24. Walt W. Rostow, "For the President's Diary," undated, Country File: Vietnam, box 256, NSF, LBJL.

25. See Chester Cooper, oral history, LBJL, 19.

26. Chester Cooper, *The Lost Crusade*, 362.

27. Robert S. McNamara et al., *Argument Without End*, 308.

28. Joseph Sisco, oral history, LBJL, 23.

29. Harold Wilson to George Brown, "Personal Minute," March 1967, and Brown addition, March 14, 1967, FCO 15/633, TNA: PRO.

30. Walt W. Rostow to President Johnson, January 23, 1967, *FRUS*: Vietnam, 1967, 59.

31. Telephone conversation between President Johnson and Walt W. Rostow, February 15, 1967, *FRUS*: Vietnam, 1967, 174–81.

32. Walt W. Rostow to President Johnson, February 20, 1967, NSF, Memos to the President: Walt W. Rostow, box 13, LBJL.

33. Walt W. Rostow to President Johnson, March 10, 1967, *FRUS*: Vietnam, 1967, 242.

34. Summary Notes of the 568th NSC Meeting, February 8, 1967, NSF, NSC Meetings, box 2, LBJL.

35. White House Report of President Johnson's Trip to Guam, Declassified Documents Reference Service (DDRS), 85, Document No. 002248.

36. Robert Buzzanco, *Masters of War*, 285–86.

37. Walt W. Rostow to President Johnson, April 27, 1967, Memos to the President: Walt W. Rostow, box 15, LBJL.

38. Walt W. Rostow, *The Diffusion of Power*, 513.

39. Walt W. Rostow, *Concept and Controversy*, 302.

40. Quoted in John Prados, *The Blood Road*, 209. See Prados for a colorful description of the April 27 meeting.

41. Walt W. Rostow, *Concept and Controversy*, 302.

42. Quoted in Ted Gittinger (ed.), *A Vietnam Round Table* (Austin: Lyndon B. Johnson School for Public Affairs, 1993), 76.

43. Mark Clodfelter, *The Limits of Air Power*, 106–107.

44. Memorandum dated April 27, 1967, attached to Earle Wheeler to Robert S. McNamara, May 29, 1967, Country File: Vietnam, NSF, box 81, LBJL.

45. Robert S. McNamara, *In Retrospect*, 106.

46. Robert S. McNamara et al., *Argument Without End*, 45.

47. Townsend Hoopes, *The Limits of Intervention*, 21.

48. Walt W. Rostow to President Johnson, May 19, 1967, *FRUS*: Vietnam, 1967, 420.

49. Maxwell Taylor to President Johnson, May 11, 1967, *FRUS*: Vietnam, 1967, 411.

50. Walt W. Rostow to President Johnson, May 15, 1967, Memos to the President: Walt W. Rostow, box 15, NSF, LBJL.

51. Quoted in Harry Trewitt, *McNamara* (New York: Harper and Row, 1971), 235.

52. Walt W. Rostow to President Johnson, May 19, 1967, *FRUS*: Vietnam, 1967, 420–22.

53. Mark Clodfelter, *The Limits of Air Power*, 108–109.

54. Robert S. McNamara to President Johnson, May 19, 1967, NSF, Country File: Vietnam, box 75, LBJL.

55. Walt W. Rostow to President Johnson, June 11, 1967, Files of Walt W. Rostow, NSF, box 7, LBJL.

56. Walt W. Rostow to President Johnson, July 9, 1967, *FRUS*: Vietnam, 1967, 584.

57. Quoted in Lawrence J. Korb, *The Joint Chiefs of Staff: The First Twenty-Five Years* (Bloomington: Indiana University Press, 1976), 181.

58. On the issue of Rostow's advice on South Vietnamese politics, see James McAllister, "'A Fiasco of Noble Proportions': The Johnson Administration and the South Vietnamese Elections of 1967," *Pacific Historical Review* 73:4, 619–51.

59. Owing to the increased costs of the Vietnam War, and faced with a budget deficit of $30 billion, Johnson was forced to cut spending on a raft of Great Society programs. The Teacher Corps, one of Johnson's favorite programs (perhaps owing to his early experience as a teacher in Texas), suffered a two-thirds cut in funding. See Robert Dallek, *Flawed Giant*, 399–405.

60. For a discussion of this speech, see Maurice Isserman and Michael Kazin, *America Divided*, 192.

61. Quoted in Stephen B. Oates, *Let the Trumpet Sound: The Life of Martin Luther King, Jr.* (New York: New American Library, 1982), 433–34.

62. See Kenneth O'Reilly, "The FBI and the Politics of the Riots, 1964–1968," *Journal of American History* 75:1 (June 1988), 104–105.

63. "A New Sophistication," *Newsweek*, July 10, 1967, 20–21.

64. Walt W. Rostow to President Johnson, July 8, 1967, quoted in Robert Dallek, *Flawed Giant*, 472.

65. Walt W. Rostow to President Johnson, July 11, 1967, Memos to the President: Walt W. Rostow, box 19, LBJL.

66. Quoted in David M. Barrett, *Uncertain Warriors: Lyndon Johnson and His Vietnam Advisers* (Lawrence: University Press of Kansas, 1993), 15.

67. Walt W. Rostow to President Johnson, August 9, 1967, Memos to the President: Walt W. Rostow, box 20, LBJL.

68. Mark Clodfelter, *The Limits of Air Power*, 109.

69. Notes of Meeting, August 16, 1967, Tom Johnson Meeting Notes File, box 2, LBJL.

70. Quoted in George C. Herring, *LBJ and Vietnam*, 56.

71. Quoted in Guenter Lewy, *America in Vietnam*, 384–85.

72. Walt W. Rostow to President Johnson, August 9, 1967, NSF, Files of Walt W. Rostow, box 9, LBJL.

73. Minutes of Weekly Luncheon, September 12, 1967, Tom Johnson Meeting Notes File, box 2, LBJL.

74. See George C. Herring, *LBJ and Vietnam*, 111–19, for an excellent discussion of the travails of the Pennsylvania channel.

75. Averell Harriman recorded on September 19, 1967, that McNamara "strongly supports carrying through on the Kissinger-A, M channel. He said he thought Kissinger handled it superbly. He confirmed he would oppose any bombing in the environs of Hanoi as long as these discussions were going on with [North Vietnam negotiator Mai Van] Bo." When Harriman asked him about the president's mood, McNamara replied that "he was surrounded by Rostow, Clark Clifford and others who seemed to think that victory was around the corner, to which he did not agree." Memorandum of conversation with Averell Harriman, September 19, 1967, box 486, W. Averell Harriman Papers, Manuscript Division, LOC.

76. Robert S. McNamara to President Johnson, Notes of Meeting, September 26, 1967, *FRUS*: Vietnam, 1967, 824.

77. President Johnson to Robert S. McNamara, ibid., 824.

78. George C. Herring, *A Different Kind of War*, 116–17.

79. Richard Helms to Walt W. Rostow, undated, NSF, Files of Walt W. Rostow, box 6, LBJL.

80. See Notes of Meetings, October 4, 5, 16, 17, 18, 23, Tom Johnson Meeting Notes File, box 1, LBJL.

81. Quoted in Robert K. Brigham and George C. Herring, "The PENNSYLVANIA Peace Initiative" in Lloyd C. Gardner and Ted Gittinger (eds.), *The Search for Peace in Vietnam, 1964–1968* (College Station: Texas A&M University Press, 2004), 68.

82. Walt W. Rostow to President Johnson, October 17, 1967, NSF, Files of Walt W. Rostow, box 3, LBJL.

83. See Daniel Ellsberg, *Secrets: A Memoir of Vietnam and the Pentagon Papers* (New York: Viking, 2002), 348, and Bruce Kuklick, *Blind Oracles*, 149.

84. Robert S. McNamara et al., *Argument Without End*, 341.

85. Robert S. McNamara, oral history, special interview with Robert Dallek, LBJL, 32–33. This interview is particularly interesting as it was carried out two years before the publication of *In Retrospect.*

86. Notes of Meeting, October 4, Tom Johnson Meeting Notes File, box 1, LBJL.

87. Townsend Hoopes, *The Limits of Intervention*, 84.

88. Walt W. Rostow to President Johnson, October 7, 1967, Memos to the President: Walt W. Rostow, box 23, LBJL.

89. Walt W. Rostow to President Johnson, October 18, 1967, NSF, Files of Walt W. Rostow, box 6, LBJL.

90. Walt W. Rostow to President Johnson, October 20, 1967, Memos to the President: Walt W. Rostow, box 24, LBJL.

91. Robert S. McNamara to President Johnson, November 1, 1967, NSF, Files of Walt W. Rostow, box 3, LBJL.

92. On his personal copy of McNamara's memo, Rostow wrote a number of incredulous comments, such as "How do we get this conclusion?" and "Why believe this?" Ibid.

93. Walt W. Rostow to President Johnson, November 2, 1967, NSF, Files of Walt W. Rostow, box 3, LBJL.

94. Quoted in Larry Berman, *Lyndon Johnson's War: The Road to Stalemate in Vietnam* (New York: W. W. Norton, 1989), 105.

95. Katharine Graham, oral history, LBJL, 38.

96. Dean Rusk to President Johnson, November 20, 1967, *FRUS*: Vietnam, 1967, 642.

97. Walt W. Rostow to President Johnson, December 13, 1967, NSF, Memos to the President: Walt W. Rostow, box 26, LBJL.

98. This amusing episode is recounted in Neil Sheehan, *A Bright Shining Lie*, 700–701.

99. Quoted in Robert Divine, "Perpetual War for Perpetual Peace," in Lloyd C. Gardner and Ted Gittinger (eds.), *The Search for Peace in Vietnam, 1964–1968*, 18.

100. Figures cited in George C. Herring, *America's Longest War*, 145.

101. Lady Bird Johnson, quoted in Robert Divine, "Perpetual War for Perpetual Peace," 19.

EIGHT: A WORLD CRASHES DOWN

1. Eisenhower had famously announced, "I shall go to Korea" during the 1952 campaign against Adlai Stevenson. Eugene McCarthy is quoted in David Halberstam, *The Best and the Brightest*, 650.

2. On the air war over Korea, see Mark Clodfelter, *The Limits of Air Power*, 12–26.

3. Tom Wolfe, "The Truest Sport: Jousting with Sam and Charlie." Quoted in *Reporting Vietnam*, 278.

4. Truong Nhu Tang, *A Vietcong Memoir* (New York: Vintage Books, 1986), 167.

5. Quoted in David Chantoff and Doan Van Toai, *'Vietnam': A Portrait of Its People at War* (London: I. B. Tauris, 1996), 105.

6. Ibid., 109.

7. Quoted in Mark Clodfelter, *The Limits of Air Power*, 138.

8. Walt W. Rostow to President Johnson, January 22, 1968, NSF, Memos to the President: Walt W. Rostow, box 27, LBJL.

9. Quoted in W. Scott Thompson and Donald D. Frizzell (eds.), *The Lessons of Vietnam* (New York: Crane Russak, 1977), 127.

10. Quoted from the Arlington Cemetery website: www.arlingtoncemetery.net/ridgway.htm.

11. For an excellent study of Gavin's career, see T. Michael Booth and Duncan Spencer, *Paratrooper: The Life and Times of General James M. Gavin* (New York: Simon and Schuster, 1994).

12. See Robert Buzzanco, *Masters of War*, 342–45.

13. Walt W. Rostow to President Johnson, December 28, 1967, NSF, Memos to the President: Walt W. Rostow, box 27, LBJL.

14. Walt W. Rostow to President Johnson, December 16, 1967, NSF, Memos to the President: Walt W. Rostow, box 28, LBJL.

15. For evocative descriptions of the Tet Offensive from the Vietnamese and the U.S. government perspective, see Frances FitzGerald, *Fire in the Lake*, 486–501, and George C. Herring, *America's Longest War*, 153–61, respectively. The fullest account of the Tet Offensive is provided by Don Oberdorfer, *Tet!* (Garden City, N.Y.: Doubleday, 1971). Walter Cronkite is quoted in Robert Schulzinger, *A Time for War*, 263.

16. Walt W. Rostow, *The Diffusion of Power*, 516.

17. Larry Berman is critical of Johnson's wishful thinking in the run-up to the Tet Offensive. With a presidential campaign looming, Johnson lost track of reality and thus conveyed the sunny impression (given sustenance by Rostow) that the war was being won. The president thus was complicit in the "big sell" of progress in Vietnam and contributed to the public disillusionment that followed Tet. See Larry Berman, *Lyndon Johnson's War*, 114–39.

18. Quoted in Robert Buzzanco, *Masters of War*, 311.

19. Clark Clifford with Richard Holbrooke, *Counsel to the President*, 474.

20. This memorandum, doodle and all, is reproduced in Walt W. Rostow, *The Diffusion of Power*, 517–18.

21. Walt W. Rostow to President Johnson, February 8, 1968, NSF, Memos to the President: Walt W. Rostow, box 28, LBJL.

22. Ibid.

23. Walt W. Rostow to President Johnson, February 11, 1968, NSF, Memos to the President: Walt W. Rostow, box 29, LBJL.

24. Statement of John Kenneth Galbraith, September 9, 1968, W. Averell Harriman Papers, box 463, Manuscript Division, LOC.

25. Walt W. Rostow, Memorandum for the Record, February 29, 1968, *FRUS*: Vietnam, January–August 1968, 281.

26. Walt W. Rostow to President Johnson, February 12, 1968, NSF, Memos to the President: Walt W. Rostow, box 29, LBJL.

27. Clark Clifford, oral history, LBJL, 3.

28. See Notes of Meeting, February 27, 1968, *FRUS*: Vietnam, January–August 1968, 354, for the official record of the meeting, and Clark Clifford with Richard Holbrooke, *Counsel to the President*, 484–85 for the unexpurgated version. Attending this

remarkably emotional meeting were Dean Rusk, Robert S. McNamara, Clark Clifford, Nicholas Katzenbach, William Bundy, Harry McPherson, Joseph Califano, and Walt W. Rostow.

29. Walt W. Rostow to President Johnson, February 27, 1968, NSF, Files of Walt W. Rostow, box 6, LBJL.

30. Clark Clifford with Richard Holbrooke, *Counsel to the President*, 484–85.

31. Walt W. Rostow, Memorandum for the Record, February 29, 1968, NSF, Files of Walt W. Rostow, box 6, LBJL.

32. Walt W. Rostow to President Johnson, March 6, 1968, NSF, Files of Walt W. Rostow, box 6, LBJL.

33. "White House-CIA Split on Vietnam Prospects," *Denver Post*, February 25, 1968. The story was later taken up by Frederick Collins of the London-based *Sunday Times*. An uncomfortable exchange of letters between Richard Helms and Walt W. Rostow again followed. See Richard Helms to Walt W. Rostow, March 10, 1968, NSF, Files of Walt W. Rostow, box 6, LBJL.

34. Walt W. Rostow to President Johnson, February 13, 1968, NSF, Memos to the President: Walt W. Rostow, box 29, LBJL.

35. Richard Helms to President Johnson, February 28, 1968, NSF, Memos to the President: Walt W. Rostow, box 30, LBJL.

36. Clark Clifford with Richard Holbrooke, *Counsel to the President*, 494–96.

37. Notes of Meeting, March 4, 1968, Tom Johnson Meeting Notes File, box 2, LBJL.

38. For a discussion of Clifford's report, see Robert Schulzinger, *A Time For War*, 264–67.

39. Drew Pearson to President Johnson, March 11, 1968, NSF, Country File: Vietnam, box 127, LBJL.

40. Quoted in Robert Dallek, *Flawed Giant*, 506.

41. For an incisive account of Eugene McCarthy's political career, see Dominic Sandbrook, *Eugene McCarthy: The Rise and Fall of Postwar American Liberalism* (New York: Knopf, 2004).

42. Walt W. Rostow to President Johnson, March 29, 1968, NSF, Files of Walt W. Rostow, box 16, LBJL.

43. Memorandum of conversation with Anatoly Dobrynin, April 24, 1968, W. Averell Harriman Papers, box 571, Manuscript Division, LOC.

44. Walter Isaacson and Evan Thomas, *The Wise Men*, 679–81.

45. Quoted ibid., 687.

46. Robert Ginsburgh to Walt W. Rostow, March 11, 1968, NSF, Country File: Vietnam, box 83, LBJL.

47. Quoted in Walter Isaacson and Evan Thomas, *The Wise Men*, 694.

48. Ibid., 698.

49. Walt W. Rostow to President Johnson, April 30, 1968, NSF, Memos to the President: Walt W. Rostow, box 33, LBJL. By playing the racist card against his Vietnam critics, Rostow was often not far from the mark. David L. DiLeo shows that George Ball's opposition to the Vietnam conflict arose from disdain for "Asians" and a tincture of racism. See David L. DiLeo, *George Ball, Vietnam and the Rethinking of Containment* (Chapel Hill: University of North Carolina Press, 1991). Averell Harriman also found Ball's narrow Atlanticism disconcerting. In a letter to Dean Francis Wilcox of Johns Hopkins

University, Harriman wrote: "I have been appalled by the first half of George Ball's chapter 12 in his book, *The Discipline of Power*. He shows such a complete indifference to the problems of the developing nations that I wish somebody would go to work on him. He is such an extremely capable and wise fellow that it seems strange that he has this one blind spot." Averell Harriman to Francis O. Wilcox, August 12, 1968, W. Averell Harriman Papers, box 434, Manuscript Division, LOC. Harriman had earlier written to Ball directly, "I have always thought that we saw things in much the same way, except perhaps on black Africa—I never took your views on that too seriously." May 29, 1968, W. Averell Harriman Papers, box 434, Manuscript Division, LOC.

50. Quoted in Clark Clifford with Richard Holbrooke, *Counsel to the President*, 500.

51. CIA–Department of Defense Briefing by General De Puy and George Carver, March 28, 1968, Tom Johnson Meeting File Notes, box 1, LBJL.

52. Quoted in Walter Isaacson and Evan Thomas, *The Wise Men*, 700.

53. Walt W. Rostow to President Johnson, April 2, 1968, NSF, Files of Walt W. Rostow, box 16, LBJL.

54. Walt W. Rostow to President Johnson, April 3, 1968, NSF, Files of Walt W. Rostow, box 6, LBJL.

55. Walt W. Rostow to President Johnson, April 3, 1968, NSF, Memos to the President: Walt W. Rostow, box 32, LBJL.

56. Quoted in Walter Isaacson and Evan Thomas, *The Wise Men*, 663.

57. Handwritten note from President Johnson to Walt W. Rostow, undated [approximately April 1968], NSF, Files of Walt W. Rostow, box 1, LBJL.

58. Walt W. Rostow to President Johnson, April 3, 1968, NSF, Memos to the President: Walt W. Rostow, box 32, LBJL.

59. William J. Jorden, oral history, LBJL, 4.

60. Memorandum of telephone conversation between Averell Harriman and Walt W. Rostow, April 4, 1968, W. Averell Harriman Papers, box 499, Manuscript Division, LOC.

61. Walt W. Rostow to President Johnson, April 8, 1968, NSF, Memos to the President: Walt W. Rostow, box 32, LBJL.

62. Averell Harriman, Memorandum for Personal Files, April 9, 1968, W. Averell Harriman Papers, box 571, Manuscript Division, LOC.

63. *Washington Post*, April 19, 1968, B15.

64. Walt W. Rostow to Dean Rusk, April 29, 1968, NSF, Memos to the President: Walt W. Rostow, box 33, LBJL.

65. Walt W. Rostow to President Johnson, May 6, 1968, NSF, Memos to the President: Walt W. Rostow, box 33, LBJL.

66. Walt W. Rostow to President Johnson, May 10, 1968, NSF, Memos to the President: Walt W. Rostow, box 34, LBJL.

67. Averell Harriman to Richard Helms, attached to Walt W. Rostow to President Johnson, May 16, 1968, NSF, Memos to the President: Walt W. Rostow, box 34, LBJL.

68. Quoted in Walter Isaacson and Evan Thomas, *The Wise Men*, 641.

69. Departure statement by Averell Harriman, May 9, 1968, W. Averell Harriman Papers, box 557, Manuscript Division, LOC.

70. Walt W. Rostow to President Johnson, May 22, 1968, NSF, Memos to the President: Walt W. Rostow, box 34, LBJL.

71. Averell Harriman to President Johnson, June 4, 1968, attached to Walt W. Rostow to President Johnson, June 4, 1968, NSF, Memos to the President: Walt W. Rostow, box 35, LBJL.

72. Walt W. Rostow to President Johnson, June 11, 1968, NSF, Memos to the President: Walt W. Rostow, box 35, LBJL.

73. Quoted in Walter LaFeber, *The Deadly Bet: LBJ, Vietnam and the 1968 Election* (Lanham, Mass.: Rowman and Littlefeld, 2006), 157–58.

74. See Herbert Y. Schandler, "The Pentagon and Peace Negotiations After March 31, 1968," in Lloyd C. Gardener and Ted Gittinger (eds.), *The Search for Peace in Vietnam, 1964–1968*, 329.

75. Quoted in Anatoly Dobrynin, *In Confidence*, 144.

76. Notes on telephone conversation between Averell Harriman and Clark Clifford, June 21, 1968, W. Averell Harriman Papers, box 571, Manuscript Division, LOC.

77. The North Vietnamese negotiators Xuan Thuy and Ha Van Lau were perplexed that Clifford had used the phrase "straws in the wind" with reference to their inconsequential negotiations. In a frosty meeting with Harriman, they argued, "You are attempting to soothe public opinion on your failure to act." Little could they know that Clifford's words were part of a concerted effort by doves to undermine Walt W. Rostow. Telegram from Averell Harriman and Cyrus Vance to Dean Rusk, July 10, 1968, W. Averell Harriman Papers, box 561, Manuscript Division, LOC.

78. Figure cited in George C. Herring, *America's Longest War*, 216.

79. Clark Clifford with Richard Holbrooke, *Counsel to the President*, 527.

80. Quoted in George C. Herring, *A Different Kind of War*, 164.

81. *Time*, May 3, 1968. For a compelling critique of Johnson's inability to impose any form of cohesion on war making *and* negotiations, see Wallace J. Thies, *When Governments Collide*. Thies concludes that Johnson's consistent search for consensus within his administration "provides an almost perfect example of how not to engage in coercion" (373–74).

82. See Averell Harriman, "General Review of the Last Six Months," December 14, 1968, W. Averell Harriman Papers, box 562, Manuscript Division, LOC, and Robert Schulzinger, *A Time For War*, 268.

83. Notes of President's Meeting with Foreign Policy Advisers, July 24, 1968, Tom Johnson Meeting Notes File, box 4, LBJL.

84. See Robert Schulzinger, *A Time for War*, 268–73, and George C. Herring, *A Different Kind of War*, for in-depth discussions of post–March 31 negotiations.

85. Walt W. Rostow to President Johnson, July 26, 1968, NSF, Memos to the President: Walt W. Rostow, box 38, LBJL.

86. Walt W. Rostow to President Johnson, July 13, 1968, NSF, Memos to the President: Walt W. Rostow, box 37, LBJL.

87. Quoted in Herbert Y. Schandler, "The Pentagon and Peace Negotiations After March 31, 1968," 334.

88. Averell Harriman, Memorandum for Personal Files, *FRUS*: Vietnam, August 1968–January 1969, 678.

89. Walt W. Rostow to President Johnson, September 15, NSF, Files of Walt W. Rostow, box 14, LBJL.

90. Telegram from Dean Rusk to Averell Harriman, "Excerpts of Vice President Humphrey's statements today on Vietnam on special NBC-TV 'Meet the Press' program," August 26, 1968, W. Averell Harriman Papers, box 470, Manuscript Division, LOC.

91. See Herbert Y. Schandler, "The Pentagon and Peace Negotiations After March 31, 1968," 335.

92. Walt W. Rostow to President Johnson, September 16, NSF, Files of Walt W. Rostow, box 10, LBJL.

93. Walt W. Rostow, Memorandum for the Record, September 17, 1968, NSF, Files of Walt W. Rostow, box 6, LBJL.

94. Averell Harriman, Absolutely Personal, General Review of Last Six Months, December 14, 1968, W. Averell Harriman Papers, box 521, Manuscript Division, LOC.

95. Walter Isaacson and Evan Thomas, *The Wise Men*, 711–13.

96. See Notes of Meeting with Foreign Policy Advisory Group, October 14, 1968, Tom Johnson Meeting Notes File, box 5, LBJL.

97. Herbert Y. Schandler, "The Pentagon and Peace Negotiations after March 31, 1968," 336.

98. Henry Kissinger to Averell Harriman, August 15, 1968, W. Averell Harriman Papers, box 481, Manuscript Division, LOC. For an unrestrained attack on Kissinger's actions then, and through the Nixon administration, see Christopher Hitchens, *The Trial of Henry Kissinger*.

99. For some insider perspectives, see Anna Chennault, *The Education of Anna* (New York: Times Books, 1980), 174, and Bui Diem with David Chernoff, *In the Jaws of History* (Boston: Houghton Mifflin, 1987), 234–45. For further discussion of the Chennault affair, see William Bundy, *A Tangled Web: The Making of Foreign Policy in the Nixon Presidency* (New York: Hill and Wang, 1998), 35–56.

100. Eugene Rostow's bombshell had already been corroborated by evidence gathered by the FBI, the CIA, and the National Security Agency. See Herbert Y. Schandler, "The Pentagon and Peace Negotiations After March 31, 1968," 342.

101. Notes of Meeting, October 29, Tom Johnson Meeting Notes File, box 1, LBJL.

102. Walt W. Rostow to President Johnson, October 29, 1968, NSF, Files of Walt W. Rostow, box 6, LBJL.

103. Ambassador Bunker to Dean Rusk, October 30, 1968, W. Averell Harriman Papers, box 560, Manuscript Division, LOC.

104. Ambassador Bunker to Dean Rusk, November 2, 1968, W. Averell Harriman Papers, box 560, Manuscript Division, LOC.

105. Walt W. Rostow to President Johnson, October 29, 1968, NSF, Files of Walt W. Rostow, box 6, LBJL.

106. Notes of the President's Weekly Luncheon Meeting, September 15, 1968, Tom Johnson Meeting Notes File, box 5, LBJL.

107. Quoted in Robert Schulzinger, *A Time for War*, 272.

108. On October 14 Earle Wheeler had rather presumptuously announced that the "military war has been won." It is possible that this wildly positive reading of the conflict convinced Johnson that he had little to lose in stopping the bombing. One

wonders why negotiations were necessary, however, if the NLF insurgency had already been defeated. See Notes of Meeting, October 14, 1968, Tom Johnson Meeting Notes File, box 4, LBJL.

109. Walt W. Rostow to President Johnson, October 28, 1968, NSF, Files of Walt W. Rostow, box 6, LBJL.

110. Walt W. Rostow to President Johnson, October 28, 1968, NSF, Files of Walt W. Rostow, box 6, LBJL.

111. Walt W. Rostow to President Johnson, November 7, 1968, NSF, Memos to the President: Walt W. Rostow, box 42, LBJL.

112. Lyndon Johnson to Averell Harriman, November 15, 1968, W. Averell Harriman Papers, box 558, Manuscript Division, LOC.

113. Walt W. Rostow to President Johnson, November 12, 1968, NSF, Memos to the President: Walt W. Rostow, box 42, LBJL.

114. Walt W. Rostow to President Johnson, November 15, 1968, NSF, Memos to the President: Walt W. Rostow, box 42, LBJL.

EPILOGUE

1. For a compelling argument that "peace with honor" was not achieved, see Larry Berman, *No Peace, No Honor: Nixon, Kissinger, and Betrayal in Vietnam* (New York: Free Press, 2001).

2. The journalist William Shawcross has argued that the rise of the Khmer Rouge and the murderous regime of Pol Pot can partly be attributed to the decisions made by the Nixon administration in 1969 and 1970. See *Sideshow: Kissinger, Nixon, and the Destruction of Cambodia* (New York: Simon and Schuster, 1979).

3. Quoted in William Bundy, *A Tangled Web*, 358.

4. Ibid., 361.

5. Ibid., 372–73.

6. On Kissinger's controversial career, see Jussi Hanhimaki, *Flawed Architect: Henry Kissinger and American Foreign Policy* (New York: Oxford University Press, 2005), and Walter Isaacson, *Kissinger: A Biography* (New York: Simon and Schuster, 1992).

7. Walt W. Rostow, *Concept and Controversy*, 317.

8. Quoted in Robert Dallek, *Flawed Giant*, 608.

9. Walt W. Rostow to Lyndon Johnson, March 14, 1970, NSF, Country File: Vietnam, box 75.

10. Lyndon Baines Johnson, *The Vantage Point*.

11. Quoted in Robert Dallek, *Flawed Giant*, 602–603.

12. Walt W. Rostow, *The Diffusion of Power*, 290.

13. Robert S. McNamara with Brian VanDeMark, *In Retrospect*, 321–23.

14. Walt W. Rostow, "The Case for the War," *Times Literary Supplement*, June 9, 1995.

15. Walt W. Rostow, interview with the author, August 7, 2002.

16. Walt W. Rostow, *Concept and Controversy*, 304.

17. Robert McMahon, "What Difference Did It Make? Assessing the Vietnam War's Impact in Southeast Asia." In Lloyd C. Gardner and Ted Gittinger (eds.), *Interna-*

tional Perspectives on Vietnam (College Station: Texas A&M University Press, 2000), 189–204.

18. Walt W. Rostow, *The United States and the Regional Organization of Asia and the Pacific, 1965–1985* (Austin: University of Texas Press, 1986).

19. *Wall Street Journal,* March 14, 1985, 1.

20. Walt W. Rostow, "Vietnam and Asia," *Diplomatic History* 20 (Summer 1996), 467–71.

21. Robert McMahon, "What Difference Did It Make?," 193.

22. CIA appraisal quoted in ibid., 195.

23. Robert McMahon, "What Difference Did It Make?," 197.

24. *The Simpsons,* "Much Apu About Nothing." First broadcast on May 5, 1996.

25. "Walt Rostow, Adviser to Kennedy and Johnson, Dies at 86," *New York Times,* February 15, 2003, A23.

26. Quoted in Walter Isaacson and Evan Thomas, *The Wise Men,* 619.

27. Graham Greene, *The Quiet American* (New York: Penguin, 1956), 163.

28. Albert Camus, *The Rebel* (London: Penguin, 1971), 11.

29. Isaiah Berlin, *Four Essays on Liberty* (Oxford: Oxford University Press, 1979), 170.

30. William Pfaff and Edmund Stillman, *The Politics of Hysteria: The Sources of Twentieth-Century Conflict* (New York: Harper and Row, 1964), 46.

31. It is interesting to note that Walt W. Rostow's brother, Eugene Victor Rostow, was a prominent player in the neoconservative backlash against Kissinger and Carter in the 1970s. Eugene was, ostensibly, the family neoconservative, but Walt's ideas were more significant in the manner in which they were used. What was Francis Fukuyama's *The End of History and the Last Man* (New York: Free Press, 1992), if not a postscript to Rostow's *The Stages of Economic Growth*?

32. Jean Jacques Rousseau, *The Social Contract* (Oxford: Oxford University Press, 1994), 58.

33. For a critique of the "neoconservative" influence on U.S. foreign policy, see Stefan Halper and Jonathan Clarke, *America Alone: The Neo-Conservatives and the Global Order* (New York: Cambridge University Press, 2004). For a defense of the movement's virtues, see Richard Perle and David Frum, *An End to Evil: How to Win the War on Terror* (New York: Random House, 2003). Francis Fukuyama has recently disassociated himself from his former ideological allies. See Francis Fukuyama, *America at the Crossroads: Democracy, Power, and the Neoconservative Legacy* (New Haven, Conn.: Yale University Press, 2006).

34. Cited in Frank M. Osanka, *Modern Guerrilla Warfare* (New York: Free Press of Glencoe, 1962), 466.

35. Paul Rabinow (ed.), *The Foucault Reader* (London: Penguin Books, 1991), ii–vi.

36. Thomas B. Morgan, "The Most Happy Fella in the White House," *Life,* December 1, 1967.

37. Walt W. Rostow, interview with the author, August 7, 2002.

Bibliography

PRIVATE PAPERS

Acheson, Dean. Oral history. John F. Kennedy Library, Boston, Massachusetts.

Alsop, Joseph. Oral history [interviewed by Elspeth Rostow]. John F. Kennedy Library, Boston, Massachusetts.

———. Papers. Manuscript Division, Library of Congress, Washington, D.C.

Ball, George. Oral history. Lyndon Baines Johnson Library, Austin, Texas.

Bowles, Chester. Oral history. Columbia University Rare Books and Manuscript Library, New York, New York.

———. Oral history. John F. Kennedy Library, Boston, Massachusetts.

———. Papers. Yale University Archives, New Haven, Connecticut.

Bundy, McGeorge. Oral history. John F. Kennedy Library, Boston, Massachusetts.

Califano, Joseph. Oral history. Lyndon Baines Johnson Library, Austin, Texas.

Clifford, Clark. Oral history. Lyndon Baines Johnson Library, Austin, Texas.

Gordon, Lincoln. Oral history. John F. Kennedy Library, Boston, Massachusetts.

Graham, Katharine. Oral history. Lyndon Baines Johnson Library, Austin, Texas.

Harper and Row. Special Manuscript Collection. Columbia University Rare Books and Manuscript Library, New York, New York.

Harriman, W. Averell. Oral history. Columbia University Rare Books and Manuscript Library, New York, New York.

———. Oral history. Lyndon Baines Johnson Library, Austin, Texas.

———. Papers. Manuscript Division, Library of Congress, Washington, D.C.

Helms, Richard. Oral history. Lyndon Baines Johnson Library, Austin, Texas.

Hilsman, Roger. Oral history. John F. Kennedy Library, Boston, Massachusetts.

———. Oral history. Lyndon Baines Johnson Library, Austin, Texas.

———. Reminiscences. Columbia University Rare Books and Manuscript Library, New York, New York.

Jackson, C.D. Papers. Dwight D. Eisenhower Library, Abilene, Kansas.

Johnson, Robert H. Oral history. John F. Kennedy Library, Boston, Massachusetts.

Jorden, William J. Oral history. Lyndon Baines Johnson Library, Austin, Texas.

Katzenbach, Nicholas D. Oral history. Lyndon Baines Johnson Library, Austin, Texas.

Kaysen, Carl. Oral history. John F. Kennedy Library, Boston, Massachusetts.

Kennedy, John F. Pre-Presidential File. John F. Kennedy Library, Boston, Massachusetts.

Komer, Robert. Oral history. Lyndon Baines Johnson Library, Austin, Texas.

Lippmann, Walter. Papers. Yale University Archives, New Haven, Connecticut.

Mann, Thomas. Oral history. John F. Kennedy Library, Boston, Massachusetts.

McNamara, Robert S. Oral history. Lyndon Baines Johnson Library, Austin, Texas.

Millikan, Max. Papers. Massachusetts Institute of Technology Archives, Boston, Massachusetts.

Moscoso, Teodoro. Papers. John F. Kennedy Library, Boston, Massachusetts.

Nitze, Paul. Papers. Manuscript Division, Library of Congress, Washington, D.C.

Rostow, Walt W. Files. Lyndon Baines Johnson Library, Austin, Texas.

———. Oral history. John F. Kennedy Library, Boston, Massachusetts.

———. Oral history. Lyndon Baines Johnson Library, Austin, Texas.

———. Papers. Lyndon Baines Johnson Library, Austin, Texas.

Rusk, Dean. Oral history. John F. Kennedy Library, Boston, Massachusetts.

———. Oral history. Lyndon Baines Johnson Library, Austin, Texas.

Schlesinger, Arthur M., Jr. Oral history. John F. Kennedy Library, Boston, Massachusetts.

———. Oral history. Lyndon Baines Johnson Library, Austin, Texas.

———. Papers. John F. Kennedy Library, Boston, Massachusetts.

Sisco, Joseph. Oral history. Lyndon Baines Johnson Library, Austin, Texas.

Sorensen, Theodore C. Oral history. John F. Kennedy Library, Boston, Massachusetts.

———. Papers. John F. Kennedy Library, Boston, Massachusetts.

Stevenson, Adlai. Papers. Seeley G. Mudd Manuscript Library, Princeton, New Jersey.

Taylor, Maxwell. Oral history. John F. Kennedy Library, Boston, Massachusetts.

———. Oral history. Lyndon Baines Johnson Library, Austin, Texas.

Valenti, Jack. Oral history. Lyndon Baines Johnson Library, Austin, Texas.

W. W. Norton. Special Manuscript Collection. Columbia University Rare Books and Manuscript Library, New York, New York.

GOVERNMENT DOCUMENTS AND RECORDS

National Security File. John F. Kennedy Library, Boston, Massachusetts.

President's Office File. John F. Kennedy Library, Boston, Massachusetts.

National Security File. Lyndon Baines Johnson Library, Austin, Texas.

Presidential Tape Recording Series, Lyndon Baines Johnson Library, Austin, Texas.

Tom Johnson Meeting Notes File, Lyndon Baines Johnson Library, Austin, Texas.

PUBLISHED PRIMARY DOCUMENTS

Public Papers of the President: John F. Kennedy. Washington, D.C.: Government Printing Office, 1962–1964.

Public Papers of the President: Lyndon B. Johnson. Washington, D.C.: Government Printing Office, 1964–1969.

Public Papers of the Presidents of the United States: Dwight D. Eisenhower. Washington D.C.: Government Printing Office, 1954.

[U.S. Department of Defense]. *The Pentagon Papers: The Department of Defense History of United States Decision-Making on Vietnam.* Senator Gravel edition. Boston: Beacon Hill, 1971.

U.S. Department of State. *Department of State Bulletin, 1961–1964.* Washington, D.C.: Government Printing Office, 1961–1964.

———. *Foreign Relations of the United States, 1961–1968.* Vols. 1–34. Washington, D.C.: Government Printing Office, 1991–2005.

MEMOIRS

Ball, George W. *The Past Has Another Pattern: Memoirs.* New York: W. W. Norton, 1982.

Bissell, Richard, with Jonathan E. Lewis and Frances T. Pudlo. *Reflections of a Cold Warrior.* New Haven: Yale University Press, 1996.

Bowles, Chester. *Promises to Keep: My Years in Public Life.* New York: Harper and Row, 1971.

Brown, George. *In My Way.* London: Penguin, 1971.

Bui Diem, with David Chernoff. *In the Jaws of History.* Boston, Houghton Mifflin, 1987.

Chennault, Anna. *The Education of Anna.* New York: Times Books, 1980.

Clifford, Clark, with Richard Holbrooke. *Counsel to the President: A Memoir.* New York: Random House, 1991.

Cooper, Chester. *The Lost Crusade: America in Vietnam.* New York: Dodd, Mead and Company, 1970.

Dobrynin, Anatoly. *In Confidence: Moscow's Ambassador to America's Six Cold War Presidents.* New York: Times Books, 1995.

Ellsberg, Daniel. *Secrets: A Memoir of Vietnam and the Pentagon Papers.* New York: Viking, 2002.

Fall, Bernard B. *Viet-Nam Witness: 1953–1966.* New York: Praeger, 1966.

Galbraith, John Kenneth. *A Life in Our Times.* Boston: Houghton Mifflin, 1981.

———. *Letters to Kennedy.* Cambridge, Mass.: Harvard University Press, 1988.

Galland, Adolf. *The First and the Last.* New York: Holt, 1954.

Heath, Edward. *Music: A Joy for Life.* London: Sidgwick and Jackson, 1976.

Hilsman, Roger. *To Move a Nation: The Politics of Foreign Policy in the Administration of John F. Kennedy.* Garden City, N.Y.: Doubleday, 1967.

Hoopes, Townsend. *The Limits of Intervention: An Inside Account of How the Johnson Policy of Escalation in Vietnam Was Reversed.* New York: Davis McKay, 1969.

Johnson, Lyndon Baines. *The Vantage Point: Perspectives of the Presidency, 1963–1969.* New York: Holt, Rinehart and Winston, 1971.

Kennan, George F. *Memoirs 1925–1950.* Boston: Little, Brown, 1967.

Killian, James R., Jr. *The Education of a College President: A Memoir.* Cambridge, Mass.: MIT Press, 1985.

Komer, Robert. *Bureaucracy at War: U.S. Performance in the Vietnam Conflict.* Boulder, Colo.: Westview Press, 1986.

LeMay, Curtis, with MacKinlay Kantor. *Mission with LeMay.* Garden City, N.Y.: Doubleday, 1965.

Luce, Don, and John Sommer. *Viet Nam: The Unheard Voices.* Ithaca, N.Y.: Cornell University Press, 1969.

Palmer, Bruce, Jr. *The 25-Year War: America's Military Role in Vietnam.* New York: Da Capo Press, 1984.

Rusk, Dean, as told to Richard Rusk. *As I Saw It.* New York: W. W. Norton, 1990.

Speer, Albert. *Inside the Third Reich.* New York: Macmillan, 1970.

Tang, Truong Nhu. *A Vietcong Memoir.* New York: Vintage Books, 1986.

Taylor, Maxwell D. *Swords and Plowshares.* New York: Norton, 1972.

Thompson, Robert. *Defeating Communist Insurgency: Experiences from Malaya and Vietnam.* London: Chatto and Windus, 1966.

Westmoreland, William. *A Soldier Reports.* New York: Dell, 1976.

Wilson, Harold. *The Labour Government 1964–1970: A Personal Record.* London: Weidenfeld and Nicolson, 1971.

INTERVIEWS

Interview with Walt W. Rostow, August 7, 2002, Austin, Texas.

SECONDARY SOURCES: BOOKS

Abramson, Rudy. *Spanning the Century: The Life of W. Averell Harriman, 1891–1986.* New York: William Morrow and Co., 1992.

Almond, Gabriel A., and James S. Coleman (eds.). *The Politics of the Developing Areas.* Princeton, N.J.: Princeton University Press, 1960.

Anderson, David. *Trapped by Success: The Eisenhower Administration and Vietnam, 1953–1961.* New York: Columbia University Press, 1991.

——— (ed.). *Shadows on the White House: Presidents and the Vietnam War.* Lawrence: University of Kansas Press, 1993.

Appy, Christian G. *Patriots: The Vietnam War Remembered from All Sides.* New York: Viking, 2003.

Barrett, David M. *Uncertain Warriors: Lyndon Johnson and His Vietnam Advisers.* Lawrence: University Press of Kansas, 1993.

Beer, Francis A., and Robert Harriman (eds.). *Post-Realism: The Rhetorical Turn in International Relations.* East Lansing: Michigan State University Press, 1996.

Berlin, Isaiah. *Four Essays on Liberty.* Oxford: Oxford University Press, 1979.

Berman, Larry. *Planning a Tragedy: The Americanization of the War in Vietnam.* New York: W. W. Norton, 1982.

———. *Lyndon Johnson's War: The Road to Stalemate in Vietnam.* New York: W. W. Norton, 1989.

Beschloss, Michael R. (ed.). *Taking Charge: The Johnson White House Tapes, 1963–1964.* New York: Simon and Schuster, 1997.

———. *Reaching for Glory: Lyndon Johnson's Secret White House Tapes, 1964–1965.* New York: Simon and Schuster, 2001.

Bird, Kai. *The Color of Truth: McGeorge Bundy and William Bundy, Brothers in Arms.* New York: Simon and Schuster, 1998.

Blaufarb, Douglas. J. *The Counterinsurgency Era: U.S. Doctrine and Performance, 1950 to the Present.* New York: Free Press, 1977.

Booth, T. Michael, and Duncan Spencer. *Paratrooper: The Life and Times of General James M. Gavin.* New York: Simon and Schuster, 1994.

Brands, H. W. (ed.). *What America Owes the World: The Struggle for the Soul of Foreign Policy.* Cambridge: Cambridge University Press, 1998.

———. *Beyond Vietnam: The Foreign Policies of Lyndon Johnson.* College Station: Texas A&M University Press, 1999.

Brigham, Robert. *Guerrilla Diplomacy: The NLF's Foreign Relations and the Vietnam War.* Ithaca, N.Y.: Cornell University Press, 1999.

Bundy, William. *A Tangled Web: The Making of Foreign Policy in the Nixon Presidency.* New York: Hill and Wang, 1998.

Burrows, Edwin G., and Mike Wallace. *Gotham: A History of New York City to 1898.* New York: Oxford University Press, 1999.

Buzzanco, Robert. *Masters of War: Military Dissent and Politics in the Vietnam Era.* Cambridge: Cambridge University Press, 1996.

Cable, Larry E. *Conflict of Myths: The Development of Counterinsurgency Doctrine and the Vietnam War.* New York: New York University Press, 1986.

———. *Unholy Grail: The US and the Wars in Vietnam, 1965–1968.* London: Routledge, 1991.

Cameron, James. *Here Is Your Enemy.* New York: Holt, Rinehart and Winston, 1966.

Camus, Albert. *The Rebel.* London: Penguin, 1971.

Caro, Robert. *The Master of the Senate: The Years of Lyndon Johnson, Volume III.* New York: Knopf, 2002.

Chalou, George C. *The Secret War: The Office of Strategic Services in World War II.* Washington, D.C.: National Archives and Records Administration, 1992.

Chang, Gordon H. *Friends and Enemies: The United States, China, and the Soviet Union, 1949–1972.* Stanford, Calif.: Stanford University Press, 1990.

Chantoff, David, and Doan Van Toai. *'Vietnam': A Portrait of Its People at War.* London: I. B. Tauris, 1996.

Clausewitz, Carl von. *On War.* Edited and translated by Michael Howard and Peter Paret. Princeton, N.J.: Princeton University Press, 1976.

Clodfelter, Mark. *The Limits of Air Power: The American Bombing of North Vietnam*. New York: Free Press, 1989.

Cohen, Warren I. *Dean Rusk*. New York: Cooper Square, 1980.

Cohen, Warren I., and Nancy B. Tucker (eds.). *Lyndon Johnson Confronts the World: American Foreign Policy 1963–1968*. Cambridge: Cambridge University Press, 1994.

Currey, Cecil B. *Edward Lansdale: The Unquiet American*. Boston: Houghton Mifflin, 1988.

Dallek, Robert. *Flawed Giant: Lyndon Johnson and His Times, 1961–1973*. New York: Oxford University Press, 1998.

———. *An Unfinished Life: John F. Kennedy, 1917–1963*. New York: Little, Brown, 2003.

Davis, David Brion (ed.). *The Fear of Conspiracy: Images of Un-American Subversion from the Revolution to the Present*. Ithaca, N.Y.: Cornell University Press, 1971.

DiLeo, David L. *George Ball, Vietnam and the Rethinking of Containment*. Chapel Hill: University of North Carolina Press, 1991.

Durkheim, Émile. *The Rules of Sociological Method*. New York: Free Press, 1965.

Engerman, David, Nils Gilman, et al. (eds.). *Staging Growth: Modernization, Development and the Global Cold War*. Amherst: University of Massachusetts Press, 2003.

FitzGerald, Frances. *Fire in the Lake: The Vietnamese and the Americans in Vietnam*. Boston: Little, Brown, 1972.

Freedman, Lawrence. *Kennedy's Wars: Berlin, Cuba, Laos and Vietnam*. New York: Oxford University Press, 2000.

Fukuyama, Francis. *The End of History and the Last Man*. New York: Free Press, 1992.

———. *America at the Crossroads: Democracy, Power, and the Neoconservative Legacy*. New Haven, Conn.: Yale University Press, 2006.

Gaddis, John Lewis. *Strategies of Containment: A Critical Appraisal of Postwar American Security Policy*. New York: Oxford University Press, 1982.

Gardner, Lloyd C. *Pay Any Price: Lyndon Johnson and the Wars for Vietnam*. Chicago: Ivan R. Dee, 1995.

Gardner, Lloyd C., and Ted Gittinger (eds.). *International Perspectives on Vietnam*. College Station: Texas A&M University Press, 2000.

Gayer, Arthur D., with Walt W. Rostow and Anna Jacobson Schwartz. *The Growth and Fluctuation of the British Economy, 1790–1850*. 2 volumes. Oxford: Clarendon Press, 1953.

Gelb, Leslie, and Richard Betts. *The Irony of Vietnam: The System Worked*. Washington, D.C.: Brookings Institution, 1979.

Getelman, Zvi. *A Century of Ambivalence: The Jews of Russia and the Soviet Union, 1881 to the Present*. Bloomington: Indiana University Press, 2001.

Giglio, James N. *The Presidency of John F. Kennedy*. Lawrence: University of Kansas Press, 1991.

Gilman, Nils. *Mandarins of the Future: Modernization Theory in Cold War America*. Baltimore: Johns Hopkins University Press, 2003.

Gittinger, Ted (ed.). *A Vietnam Round Table*. Austin: Lyndon B. Johnson School of Public Affairs, 1993.

Glover, Jonathan. *Humanity: A Moral History of the Twentieth Century*. New Haven, Conn.: Yale University Press, 2000.

Goldberg, Robert Alan. *Barry Goldwater*. New Haven, Conn.: Yale University Press, 1995.

Greene, Graham. *The Quiet American.* New York: Penguin, 1956.

Greenspan, Ezra (ed.). *The Cambridge Companion to Walt Whitman.* Cambridge: Cambridge University Press, 1995.

Hahn, Peter L., and Mary Ann Heiss. *Empire and Revolution: The United States and the Third World Since 1945.* Columbus: Ohio State University Press, 2001.

Halberstam, David. *The Making of a Quagmire.* New York: Random House, 1965.

———. *The Best and the Brightest.* Twentieth-anniversary edition. New York: Ballantine Books, 1992.

Hammer, Ellen J. *A Death in November: America in Vietnam, 1963.* New York: Dutton, 1987.

Hatcher, Patrick L. *The Suicide of an Elite: American Internationalists and Vietnam.* Stanford, Calif.: Stanford University Press, 1990.

Hendrickson, Paul. *The Living and the Dead: Robert McNamara and Five Lives of a Lost War.* New York: Knopf, 1996.

Herring, George C. *America's Longest War: The United States and Vietnam, 1950–1975.* 2nd ed. New York: Knopf, 1979.

———. *The Secret Diplomacy of the Vietnam War: The Negotiating Volumes of the Pentagon Papers.* Austin: University of Texas Press, 1983.

———. *LBJ and Vietnam: A Different Kind of War.* Austin: University of Texas Press, 1995.

Hill, Polly. *Development Economics on Trial: The Anthropological Case for the Prosecution.* Cambridge: Cambridge University Press, 1986.

Hilsman, Roger. *To Move a Nation: The Politics of Foreign Policy in the Administration of John F. Kennedy.* New York: Doubleday, 1967.

Hitchens, Christopher. *The Trial of Henry Kissinger.* New York: Verso Books, 2002.

Hofstadter, Richard. *Anti-Intellectualism in American Life.* New York: Knopf, 1963.

Hogan, Michael J. *The Marshall Plan.* New York: Cambridge University Press, 1987.

——— (ed.). *America in the World: The Historiography of American Foreign Relations Since 1941.* Cambridge: Cambridge University Press, 1995.

Holloway, David. *Stalin and the Bomb: The Soviet Union and Atomic Energy, 1939–1956.* New Haven: Yale University Press, 1995.

Hunt, Michael H. *Ideology and U.S. Foreign Policy.* New Haven, Conn.: Yale University Press, 1987.

Hunt, Richard A. *Pacification: The American Struggle for Vietnam's Hearts and Minds.* Boulder, Colo.: Westview Press, 1995.

Isaacson, Walter, and Evan Thomas. *The Wise Men.* New York: Simon and Schuster, 1986.

Isserman, Maurice, and Michael Kazin. *America Divided: The Civil War of the 1960s.* New York: Oxford University Press, 2000.

Jacobs, Seth. *America's Miracle Man in Vietnam: Ngo Dinh Diem, Religion, Race and U.S. Intervention in Southeast Asia, 1950–1957.* Durham, N.C.: Duke University Press, 2005.

Joes, Anthony J. *The War for South Viet Nam, 1954–1975.* New York: Praeger, 1989.

Kahin, George McT. *Intervention: How America Became Involved in Vietnam.* Garden City, N.Y.: Doubleday, 1987.

Kaiser, David. *American Tragedy: Kennedy, Johnson, and the Origins of the Vietnam War.* Cambridge, Mass.: Belknap Press of Harvard University Press, 2000.

Kazin, Alfred. *A Walker in the City*. New York: Harcourt, 1951.

Khong, Yuen Foong. *Korea, Munich, Dien Bien Phu, and the Vietnam Decisions of 1965*. Princeton, N.J.: Princeton University Press, 1992.

Kindleberger, Charles P., and Guido di Tella (eds.). *Economics in the Long View: Essays in Honour of W. W. Rostow*. New York: New York University Press, 1982.

Kinnard, Douglas. *The War Managers*. Hanover, N.H.: University Press of New England, 1977.

———. *The Certain Trumpet: Maxwell Taylor and the American Experience in Vietnam*. Washington, D.C.: Brassey's, 1991.

Klein, Christina. *Cold War Orientalism: Asia in the Middlebrow Imagination, 1945–1961*. Berkeley: University of California Press, 2003.

Kluckhohn, Frank L. *Lyndon's Legacy: A Candid Look at the President's Policymakers*. New York: Devlin-Adair Co., 1964.

Kolko, Gabriel. *Anatomy of a War: Vietnam, the United States and the Modern Historical Experience*. New York: Random House, 1985.

Korb, Lawrence J. *The Joint Chiefs of Staff: The First Twenty-Five Years*. Bloomington: Indiana University Press, 1976.

Krepinevich, Andrew. *The Army and Vietnam*. Baltimore: Johns Hopkins University Press, 1986.

Kuklick, Bruce. *Blind Oracles: Intellectuals and War from Kennan to Kissinger*. Princeton, N.J.: Princeton University Press, 2006.

Kunz, Diane. *Butter and Guns: America's Cold War Economic Diplomacy*. New York: Free Press, 1997.

Lacoutre, Jean. *Ho Chi Minh: A Political Biography*. New York: Penguin, 1968.

Latham, Michael. *Modernization as Ideology: American Social Science and Nation Building in the Kennedy Era*. Chapel Hill: University of North Carolina Press, 2001.

Levi, Primo. *If This Is a Man / The Truce*. Translated by S. J. Woolf. London: Penguin, 1989.

Levine, Alan J. *The Strategic Bombing of Germany, 1940–1945*. Westport, Conn.: Praeger, 1992.

Lewy, Guenter. *America in Vietnam*. New York: Oxford University Press, 1987.

Lindblom, Charles E., and David Cohen. *Usable Knowledge: Social Science and Social Problem Solving*. New Haven, Conn.: Yale University Press, 1979.

Lipset, Seymour M. *Political Man: The Social Bases of Politics*. New York: Anchor Books, 1963.

Littauer, Ralph, and Norman Uphoff. *The Air War in Indochina*. Boston: Beacon Press, 1971.

Logevall, Fredrik. *Choosing War: The Lost Chance for Peace and the Escalation of the War in Vietnam*. Berkeley: University of California Press, 1999.

Luce, Don, and John Sommer. *Viet Nam: The Unheard Voices*. Ithaca, N.Y.: Cornell University Press, 1969.

MacIsaac, David (ed.). *The United States Strategic Bombing Survey*. Vol. 4. New York: Garland Publishing, 1976.

Martin, John B. *Adlai Stevenson and the World*. New York: Doubleday, 1977.

Martz, John D. *United States Policy in Latin America: A Decade of Crisis and Challenge*. Lincoln: University of Nebraska Press, 1988.

Marx, Karl, and Friedrich Engels. *The Communist Manifesto.* 1848. New edition. Oxford: Oxford World Classics, 1998.

Matusow, Allen J. *The Unraveling of America.* New York: HarperCollins, 1994.

May, Ernest R., and Philip Zelikow. *The Kennedy Tapes: Inside the White House During the Cuban Missile Crisis.* Cambridge, Mass.: Harvard University Press, 1998.

May, Larry (ed.). *Recasting America: Culture and Politics in the Age of Cold War.* Chicago: University of Chicago Press, 1989.

McMaster, H. R. *Dereliction of Duty: Lyndon Johnson, Robert McNamara, the Joint Chiefs of Staff and the Lies That Led to Vietnam.* New York: HarperCollins, 1997.

McNamara, Robert S., with Brian VanDeMark. *In Retrospect: The Tragedy and Lessons of Vietnam.* New York: Vintage Books, 1995.

McNamara, Robert S., with James Blight. *Wilson's Ghost: Reducing the Risk of Conflict, Killing, and Catastrophe in the 21st Century.* New York: Public Affairs, 2001.

McNamara, Robert S., with James Blight et al. *Argument Without End: In Search of Answers to the Vietnam Tragedy.* Washington, D.C.: Public Affairs Press, 2000.

Middendorf, William. *Glorious Defeat: Barry Goldwater's Presidential Campaign and the Origins of the Conservative Movement.* New York: Basic Books, 2006.

Millikan, Max, and Donald Blackmer. *The Emerging Nations.* Boston: Asia Publishing House, 1961.

Millikan, Max, and Walt W. Rostow. *A Proposal: Key to an Effective Foreign Policy.* New York: Harper and Brothers, 1957.

Moïse, Edwin E. *Tonkin Gulf and the Escalation of the Vietnam War.* Chapel Hill: University of North Carolina Press, 1996.

Moore, Deborah Dash. *At Home in America: Second Generation New York Jews.* New York: Columbia University Press, 1981.

Mrozek, Donald J. *Air Power and the Ground War in Vietnam: Ideas and Actions.* Maxwell, Ala.: Air University Press, 1989.

Nash, Manning. *Unfinished Agenda: The Dynamic of Modernization in Developing Nations.* Boulder, Colo.: Westview Press, 1984.

Nathans, Benjamin. *Beyond the Pale: The Jewish Encounter with Late Imperial Russia.* Berkeley: University of California Press, 2002.

Neustadt, Richard E., and Ernest R. May. *Thinking in Time: The Uses of History for Decision-Makers.* New York: Free Press, 1986.

Nye, Joseph S. *The Paradox of American Power: Why the World's Only Superpower Can't Go It Alone.* New York: Oxford University Press, 2002.

Oates, Stephen B. *Let the Trumpet Sound: The Life of Martin Luther King, Jr.* New York: New American Library, 1982.

Oberdorfer, Don. *Tet!* Garden City, N.Y.: Doubleday, 1971.

Orleck, Annelise. *The Soviet Jewish Americans.* Lebanon, N.H.: University Press of New England, 1999.

Osanka, Frank M. *Modern Guerrilla Warfare.* New York: Free Press of Glencoe, 1962.

Packenham, Robert A. *Liberal America and the Third World: Political Development Ideas in Foreign Aid and Social Science.* Princeton, N.J.: Princeton University Press, 1973.

Pape, Robert A. *Bombing to Win: Air Power and Coercion in War.* Ithaca, N.Y.: Cornell University Press, 1996.

Parmet, Herbert S. *JFK: The Presidency of John F. Kennedy.* New York: Penguin, 1983.

Paterson, Thomas G. *Kennedy's Quest for Victory.* New York: Oxford University Press, 1989.

Pearce, Kimber Charles. *Rostow, Kennedy and the Rhetoric of Foreign Aid.* East Lansing: Michigan State University Press, 2001.

Perry, Mark. *Four Stars.* Boston: Houghton Mifflin, 1989.

Pfaff, William, and Edmund Stillman. *The Politics of Hysteria: The Sources of Twentieth-Century Conflict.* New York: Harper and Row, 1964.

Prados, John. *Keeper of the Keys: A History of the National Security Council from Truman to Bush.* Scranton, Penn.: William Morrow and Sons, 1991.

———. *The Blood Road: The Ho Chi Minh Trail and the Vietnam War.* New York: John Wiley and Sons, 1998.

Preston, Andrew. *The War Council: McGeorge Bundy, the NSC, and Vietnam.* Cambridge, Mass.: Harvard University Press, 2006.

Rabe, Stephen G. *The Most Dangerous Area in the World.* Chapel Hill: University of North Carolina Press, 1999.

Rabinow, Paul (ed.). *The Foucault Reader.* London: Penguin Books, 1991.

Rist, Gilbert. *The History of Development: From Western Origins to Global Faith.* New York: Zed Books, 1997.

Rostow, Walt W. *The United States in the World Arena.* New York: Harper and Row, 1960.

———. *The Stages of Economic Growth: A Non-Communist Manifesto.* Cambridge: Cambridge University Press, 1960.

———. *View from the Seventh Floor.* New York: Harper and Row, 1964.

———. *The Diffusion of Power: An Essay in Recent History.* New York: Macmillan, 1972.

———. *The Division of Europe After World War II.* Austin: University of Texas Press, 1981.

———. *Pre-Invasion Bombing Strategy: General Eisenhower's Decision of March 25, 1944.* Austin: University of Texas Press, 1981.

———. *Eisenhower, Kennedy, and Foreign Aid.* Austin: University of Texas Press, 1985.

———. *Essays on a Half-Century: Ideas, Policies, and Action.* Boulder, Colo.: Westview Press, 1988.

———. *Concept and Controversy: Sixty Years of Taking Ideas to Market.* Austin: University of Texas Press, 2003.

Rostow, Walt W., with Richard Hatch, Frank Kierman Jr., and Alexander Eckstein. *The Prospects for Communist China.* New York: John Wiley and Sons, 1954.

Rotter, Andrew J. (ed.). *Light at the End of the Tunnel: A Vietnam War Anthology.* Washington, D.C.: SR Books, 1999.

Rousseau, Jean-Jacques. *The Social Contract.* Oxford: Oxford University Press, 1994.

Rust, William J. *Kennedy in Vietnam: American Foreign Policy, 1960–1963.* New York: Scribner and Sons, 1985.

Saunders, Frances S. *Who Paid the Piper? The CIA and the Cultural Cold War.* London: Granta, 1999.

Schlesinger, Arthur, Jr. *A Thousand Days: John F. Kennedy in the White House.* Boston: Houghton Mifflin, 1965.

———. *A Life in the Twentieth Century: Innocent Beginnings, 1917–1950.* New York: Houghton Mifflin, 2000.

Schlight, John. *The United States Air Force in Southeast Asia: The War in Vietnam; The Years of the Offensive, 1965–1968.* Washington, D.C.: Office of Air Force History, 1988.

Schoenbaum, Thomas J. *Waging Peace and War: Dean Rusk in the Truman, Kennedy, and Johnson Years.* New York: Simon and Schuster, 1988.

Schulzinger, Robert T. *A Time for War: The United States and Vietnam, 1941–1975.* New York: Oxford University Press, 1997.

Schwab, Orrin. *Defending the Free World: John F. Kennedy, Lyndon Johnson, and the Vietnam War, 1961–1965.* Westport, Conn.: Praeger, 1998.

Schwartz, Thomas. *Lyndon Johnson and Europe: In the Shadow of Vietnam.* Cambridge, Mass.: Harvard University Press, 2003.

Scott, James C. *Seeing Like a State: How Certain Schemes to Improve the Human Condition Have Failed.* New Haven, Conn.: Yale University Press, 1998.

Shafer, D. Michael. *Deadly Paradigms: The Failure of U.S. Counter-Insurgency Policy.* Princeton, N.J.: Princeton University Press, 1988.

Shapley, Deborah. *Promise and Power: The Life and Times of Robert McNamara.* Toronto: Little, Brown, 1993.

Shawcross, William. *Sideshow: Kissinger, Nixon, and the Destruction of Cambodia.* New York: Simon and Schuster, 1979.

Sheehan, Neil. *A Bright Shining Lie: John Paul Vann and America in Vietnam.* London: Jonathan Cape, 1989.

Shesol, Jeff. *Mutual Contempt: Lyndon Johnson, Robert Kennedy, and the Feud That Defined a Decade.* New York: W. W. Norton, 1997.

Simpson, Christopher. *Universities and Empire: Money and Politics in the Social Sciences During the Cold War.* New York: New Press, 1998.

Smith, R. B. *An International History of the Vietnam War.* London: Macmillan, 1985.

Smith, Tony. *The United States and the Worldwide Struggle for Democracy in the Twentieth Century.* Princeton, N.J.: Princeton University Press, 1994.

Strober, Gerald S., and Deborah H. Strober. *Let Us Begin Anew.* New York: HarperCollins, 1993.

Summers, Harry. *On Strategy: A Critical Analysis of the Vietnam War.* Novato, Calif.: Presidio Press, 1982.

Tanker, Lester. *The Kennedy Circle.* Washington, D.C.: Robert B. Luce, 1961.

Thies, Wallace J. *When Governments Collide: Coercion and Diplomacy in the Vietnam Conflict, 1964–1968.* Berkeley: University of California Press, 1980.

Thompson, James Clay. *Rolling Thunder: Understanding Policy and Program Failure.* Chapel Hill: University of North Carolina Press, 1980.

Thompson, Kenneth W. *The Johnson Presidency: Twenty Intimate Perspectives of Lyndon B. Johnson.* New York: University Press of America, 1986.

Thompson, W. Scott, and Donald D. Frizzell (eds.). *The Lessons of Vietnam.* New York: Crane Russak, 1977.

Trewitt, Harry. *McNamara.* New York: Harper and Row, 1971.

Turner, Kathleen. *Lyndon Johnson's Dual War: Vietnam and the Press.* Chicago: University of Chicago Press, 1985.

VanDeMark, Brian. *Into the Quagmire: Lyndon Johnson and the Escalation of the Vietnam War.* New York: Oxford University Press, 1991.

Walton, C. Dale. *The Myth of Inevitable U.S. Defeat in Vietnam.* London: Frank Cass, 2002.

Westad, Odd Arne (ed.). *Reviewing the Cold War.* London: Frank Cass, 1999.

Wiegersma, N. *Vietnam: Peasant Land, Peasant Revolution.* London: Macmillan, 1988.

Windrow, Martin. *The Last Valley: Dien Bien Phu and the French Defeat in Vietnam.* London: Weidenfeld and Nicolson, 2005.

Woods, Randall B. J. *William Fulbright, Vietnam, and the Search for a Cold War Foreign Policy.* Cambridge: Cambridge University Press, 1998.

―――. (ed.). *Vietnam and the American Political Tradition: The Politics of Dissent.* Cambridge: Cambridge University Press, 2003.

Zhai, Quiang. *China and the Vietnam Wars, 1950–1975.* Chapel Hill: University of North Carolina Press, 2000.

Zubok, Vladimir, and Constantine Pleshakov. *Inside the Kremlin's Cold War: From Stalin to Khrushchev.* Cambridge, Mass.: Harvard University Press, 1996.

SECONDARY SOURCES: ARTICLES

Baber, Zaheer. "Modernization Theory and the Cold War." *Journal of Contemporary Asia* 31, no. 1 (May 2003).

Bloomfield, Lincoln P. "Planning Foreign Policy: Can It Be Done?" *Political Science Quarterly* 93, no. 3 (Autumn 1978).

Boulding, Kenneth. "The Intellectual Framework of Bad Advice." *Virginia Quarterly Review* 47, no. 4 (Autumn 1971).

Catton, Philip E. "Counter-Insurgency and Nation Building: The Strategic Hamlet Program in South Vietnam, 1961–1963." *The International History Review* 21, no. 4 (December 1999).

Destler, I. M. "National Security Advice to US Presidents: Some Lessons from Thirty Years." *World Politics* 29, no. 2 (January 1977).

―――. "National Security Management: What Presidents Have Wrought." *Political Science Quarterly* 95, no. 4 (Winter 1980–81).

Dumbrell, John, and Sylvia Ellis. "British Involvement in Vietnam Peace Initiatives, 1966–1967: Marigolds, Sunflowers, and 'Kosygin Week.' " *Diplomatic History* 27, no. 1 (January 2003).

Ekbladh, David. "Mr. TVA: Grass Roots Development, David Lilienthal, and the Rise of the Tennessee Valley Authority as a Symbol for U.S. Overseas Development, 1933–1973." *Diplomatic History* 26, no. 3 (Summer 2002).

Engerman, David. "Modernization from the Other Shore: American Observers and the Costs of Soviet Economic Development." *The American Historical Review* 105, no. 2 (April 2000).

Greenstein, Fred I., and Richard H. Immerman. "What Did Eisenhower Tell Kennedy About Indochina? The Politics of Misperception." *Journal of American History* 79, no. 2 (September 1992).

Hafaele, Mark. "John F. Kennedy, USIA and World Public Opinion." *Diplomatic History* 25, no. 1 (Winter 2001).

Hershberg, James G. "Who Murdered 'Marigold'? New Evidence on the Mysterious Failure of Poland's Secret Initiative to Start US–North Vietnamese Peace Talks, 1966." *Cold War International History Project Working Paper*, no. 27 (April 2000).

Johnson, Robert H. "Escalation Then and Now." *Foreign Policy*, no. 60 (Fall 1985).

Jones, Matthew. "The United States, Laos and Cambodia in the Johnson Years." *Diplomacy and Statecraft* 13, no. 1 (March 2002).

Kochavi, Noam. "Limited Accommodation, Perpetual Conflict: Kennedy, China and the Laos Crisis, 1961–1963." *Diplomatic History* 26, no. 1 (Winter 2002).

McAllister, James. " 'A Fiasco of Noble Proportions': The Johnson Administration and the South Vietnamese Elections of 1967." *Pacific Historical Review* 73, no. 4 (November 2004).

McMahon, Robert J. "Contested Memory: The Vietnam War and American Society, 1975–2001." *Diplomatic History* 26, no. 2 (Spring 2002).

Mirsky, Jonathan. "Wartime Lies." *New York Review of Books*, October 9, 2003.

O'Reilly, Kenneth. "The FBI and the Politics of the Riots, 1964–1968." *Journal of American History* 75, no. 1 (June 1988).

Preston, Andrew. "Balancing War and Peace: Canadian Foreign Policy and the Vietnam War, 1961–1965." *Diplomatic History* 27, no. 1 (January 2003).

Pye, Lucian. "Armies in the Process of Political Modernization." In J. Johnson (ed.), *The Role of the Military in Underdeveloped Countries*. Princeton, N.J.: Princeton University Press, 1962.

Rostow, Walt W. "The American National Style." *Daedalus* 87, no. 2 (1958).

———. "Guerrilla Warfare in the Underdeveloped Areas." In Marcus G. Rankin and Bernard Fall (eds.), *The Vietnam Reader*. New York: Vintage, 1967.

———. "The Strategic Role of Theory: A Commentary." *Journal of Economic History* 31, no. 1 (March 1971).

———. "On Ending the Cold War." *Foreign Affairs* 65, no. 4 (Spring 1987).

———. "The Case for the War." *Times Literary Supplement*, June 9, 1995.

———. "Vietnam and Asia." *Diplomatic History* 20, no. 3 (Summer 1996).

"A Roundtable Review: McNamara's *In Retrospect*." *Diplomatic History* 20, no. 3 (Summer 1996).

Shafer, D. Michael. "The Unlearned Lessons of Counterinsurgency." *Political Science Quarterly* 103, no. 1 (Spring 1988).

Supple, Barry. "Revisiting Rostow." *Economic History Review* 33, no. 1 (February 1984).

UNPUBLISHED PH.D. DISSERTATION

Armstrong, David Grossman. "The True Believer: Walt Whitman Rostow and the Path to Vietnam." Unpublished Ph.D. dissertation, University of Texas at Austin, 2000.

Index

Johnson, Lyndon Baines (*continued*)
secretary of defense by, 218–20; death
of, 246–47; Great Society programs of,
132, 133, 141, 194, 206, 207, 283*n59*;
and ground force escalation, 155–56,
189, 190; Johns Hopkins University
address by, 132, 151, 277*n78*; and
McNamara's disillusionment with war,
4, 175, 178, 188–89, 193, 201, 203,
217, 248; nature of Rostow's
relationship with, 10–12, 21–22,
167–69, 180, 239–40, 244; and 1968
election, 206–207, 220–21, 223,
228–29, 231–39, 286*n17*; 1964
reelection campaign of, 141, 159; and
peace initiatives, 184–86, 197–200,
223–26, 282*n18*, 284*n75*; presidential
library of, *see* Lyndon Baines Johnson
Library; presidential memoir of,
245–46; and racial violence, 194–95;
and retired generals' opposition to war,
210–12, 221; Rostow appointed
national security adviser by, 161–70,
172; and Rostow Thesis, 141–43, 147,
256; speeches of, 39; and Tet
Offensive, 3, 213–15, 221; and Tonkin
Gulf incident, 143–45; "Wise Men"
and, 192, 193, 217, 221–23
Johnson, Robert, 67, 107, 138–39
Johnson, U. Alexis, 154
Joint Chiefs of Staff, 11, 177, 197, 224,
270*n2*; bombing strategy of, 137,
149–51, 160, 170, 184, 191, 196, 200,
204, 235; ground force escalation
advocated by, 11, 189, 192, 193; and
Laos, 91, 96; SIGMA II war-game
simulation of, 145
Jorden, William J., 225
Joyce, James, 22

Kaiser, David, 9, 127–28
Kaiser, Philip, 27
Kapital, Das (Marx), 80
Katzenbach, Nicholas, 94, 198, 287*n28*
Kaysen, Carl, 113, 184
Kazin, Alfred, 260*n5*
Kearns, Doris, 245
Kennan, George, 38, 75, 89, 100, 112,
114–16, 132, 146, 216, 222, 223
Kennedy, John F., 5–6, 8–9, 29, 38, 60,
108, 131, 181, 210, 247–48, 254, 255,

269*n81*; Agency for International
Development established by, 7, 79,
135; American University speech by,
123; assassination of, 10, 127–30;
Basic National Security Policy
prepared by Rostow for, 110, 112–14;
and Bay of Pigs invasion, 89–91; and
Berlin, 68–69, 92–94; bombing
strategy rejected by, 139; breakdown of
relationship between Rostow and,
9–10, 99–101, 103, 104; cabinet and
staff appointments of, 70–72, 76–77,
217, 249; chemical defoliant use
authorized by, 103, 270*n2*; during
Cuban Missile Crisis, 117, 119, 120,
174; and Diem regime, 83–86,
124–27; and domino theory, 80;
election of, 70; first meeting of Rostow
and, 56–57; foreign-aid policy of,
78–79, 95; inauguration, 6, 72, 76,
267*n14*; Johnson's relationship to
foreign-policy advisers of, 134,
167–69; and Khrushchev's saber-
rattling, 75; and Laos, 86–88, 92, 191;
"no enemies on the right" strategy of,
133; nuclear war as "greatest
nightmare" of, 94; presidential
campaign of, 56, 58–59, 69–70, 75,
233; Rostow-Taylor report to, 95–96,
98–99, 103; in Senate, 9, 50, 57–58,
68; and Stevenson's 1956 presidential
campaign, 55–56; strategic hamlet
program of, 105; Third World
susceptibility to Marxism-Leninism
feared by, 79; on tour of Middle East,
Asia, and Indochina, 82
Kennedy, Joseph, 29, 31
Kennedy, Robert F., 71, 82, 95, 117–18,
169, 220–21, 228, 231, 232
Kennedy-Cooper Resolution, 58
Keynes, John Maynard, 24–25, 29, 30
Khan, Nguyen, *see* Nguyen Khan
Khe San, Battle of, 220
Khmer Rouge, 291*n2*
Khong, Yuen Foong, 276*n66*
Khrushchev, Nikita, 5, 62, 74–78, 92–93;
during Cuban Missile Crisis, 118–20,
174
Killian, James R., Jr., 45
Kim Il-Sung, 42, 43
Kindleberger, Charles, 36–37, 40
King, Martin Luther, Jr., 194, 231